THE PEARL OF DARI

PUBLIC CULTURES OF THE
MIDDLE EAST AND NORTH AFRICA

Paul A. Silverstein, Susan Slyomovics, and Ted Swedenburg, *editors*

THE PEARL OF DARI
Poetry and Personhood among Young Afghans in Iran

Zuzanna Olszewska

Indiana University Press
Bloomington & Indianapolis

This book is a publication of

Indiana University Press
Office of Scholarly Publishing
Herman B Wells Library 350
1320 East 10th Street
Bloomington, Indiana 47405 USA

iupress.indiana.edu

© 2015 by Zuzanna Olszewska

All rights reserved

No part of this book may be reproduced or utilized in any form or by any means, electronic or mechanical, including photocopying and recording, or by any information storage and retrieval system, without permission in writing from the publisher. The Association of American University Presses' Resolution on Permissions constitutes the only exception to this prohibition.

The paper used in this publication meets the minimum requirements of the American National Standard for Information Sciences—Permanence of Paper for Printed Library Materials, ANSI Z39.48–1992.

Manufactured in the United States of America

Cataloging information is available from the Library of Congress

ISBN 978-0-253-01752-9 (cloth)
ISBN 978-0-253-01760-4 (paperback)
ISBN 978-0-253-01763-5 (ebook)

1 2 3 4 5   20 19 18 17 16 15

For my parents.

I was possessed by
a contradictory nostalgia
for things I had never known,
for emptiness: the recesses of Bamiyan.
          John Ash, from "Recess" in *The Parthian Stations*

Never durst poet touch a pen to write
until his ink were temper'd with Love's sighs
          William Shakespeare, *Love's Labour's Lost*

Contents

	Preface	xi
	Acknowledgments	xiii
	A Note on the Translations, Transliteration, and Dates	xvii
	Introduction	1
1	Border Crossings and Fractured Selves: A History of the Afghan Presence in Iran	34
2	The Melancholy Modern: The Rise of a Refugee Intelligentsia	63
3	Afghan Literary Organizations in Postrevolutionary Iran	93
4	The Social Lives of Poets and Poetry	123
5	Modern Love: Poetry, Companionate Marriage, and Recrafting the Self	155
6	"When Your *Darun* Speaks to You": Ethics of Revelation and Concealment in Lyric Poetry	185
	Conclusion	210
	Epilogue	215
	Notes	217
	References	237
	Index	259

Preface

THE TITULAR PEARL of Dari encompasses a variety of meanings that are central to the themes of this book. First, it refers directly to the name of one of the Afghan refugee cultural organizations with which I worked in Iran, the *Mo'asseseh-ye Farhangi-ye Dorr-e Dari* or Pearl of Dari Cultural Institute. Dari here is a direct reference to the dialect of Persian that is spoken in contemporary Afghanistan and that is one of the official languages of that country, while the pearl is its literature, often portrayed as a valuable gem.

The poetic couplet from which this figure derives, however, is much older than Afghanistan and suggests a different meaning of the word Dari: *Man ān-am ke dar pā-ye khukān narizam / mar in qeymati dorr-e lafz-e dari rā* (I am he who will not throw at the feet of swine / this precious pearl of the Dari language). This is a couplet by Naser Khosrow Qobadiyani, an eleventh-century Persian poet and scholar who traveled widely but was born and died in what is today Afghanistan. In historical usage, the term Dari refers to the Middle Persian language spoken at the court of the pre-Islamic Sassanids and is thought to be a contraction of *darbāri* (of the court). Rather than merely being a token of difference, then, it is actually a reminder of the common linguistic origins of Persian dialects that predate the formation of both modern Iran and Afghanistan. Naser Khosrow himself is claimed as a literary ancestor by both Iranians and Afghans.

The couplet represents Naser Khosrow's retort when asked why he did not compose eulogistic poems for rulers, whom he sees as unworthy of the beauty of words. On yet another level, then, someone familiar with the poem might relate it to the politically neutral stance of Dorr-e Dari's founders and their insistence that, following decades of violence in Afghanistan, the road to national unity, development, and progress lies in cultural work that should not be sullied by ideological partisanship. (This stance is complicated by the fact that Dari is not the mother tongue of all the people of Afghanistan, and its status as lingua franca of the country has long been challenged by politicized efforts to promote Pashto, topics that this book can touch on only briefly.)

Finally, to me, the phrase echoes one of the major themes of this book, that of a constant navigation between outside appearances and inner truths in the construction of the self: the pearl in the oyster shell.

Acknowledgments

THE FACT THAT my work engaged with both the very public and the more intimate aspects of my informants' lives was not without challenges for me in the writing of this ethnography. On the one hand, it did not make sense to pseudonymize the poets whose referenced published work, for which they deserved full credit, was being discussed. As public figures they expected to be named and were used to their work being critiqued and interpreted. On the other, many of the details of their life stories, including some that affected their poetic output, were sensitive, and so following extensive discussions with them, I have either separated these aspects from named poets in the text, sought explicit permission to write about them, or been obliged to exclude them altogether. Any resulting loss of ethnographic richness was disappointing but I considered it unavoidable within the framework of this book. I hope there will be opportunities to write other kinds of stories in the future.

This book and the research leading to it would not have been possible without the assistance and input of a great many people and organizations, to whom I am deeply indebted. My initial research was funded by the Scatcherd European Scholarship, the Vice-Chancellor's Fund Award, and research funds from Wolfson College and the Institute of Social and Cultural Anthropology at the University of Oxford, while my travel to Iran was funded by the British Institute of Persian Studies. I am grateful to Dominic Brookshaw and John Gurney for first introducing me to the sweetness of Persian and facilitating my language study in Iran. In Iran, I was introduced to the Afghan community by Fatemeh Ashrafi of Hami, the Association for the Protection of Refugee Women and Children; and by Homa Hoodfar, Sarah Kamal, Marzieh Sharifi, and Maryam Golduzian. Fariba Adelkhah, Roxanne Varzi, Sayed Askar Mousavi, and Alessandro Monsutti gave me valuable advice and support. Massoumeh Farman-Farmaian and Safak Pavey of UNHCR Tehran provided me with information and Johannes van der Klaauw and Jadwiga Pietrzak offered friendship and support in Mashhad. I am particularly grateful to Professor Mohammad Yahaghi, Head of the Persian Literature Department of the Faculty of Letters and Humanities at Ferdowsi University of Mashhad, for kindly arranging an affiliation with the department that enabled me to use its library and facilities.

I am profoundly grateful to Seyyed Abu Taleb Mozaffari and Mohammad Kazem Kazemi, my Ostāds, and all the members of the Dorr-e Dari Cultural Institute for so readily welcoming me into their fold and sharing their love of poetry, their extensive knowledge, and their friendship with me. Not only this ethnography, but also my life would have been far poorer had I not met them.

I would like to express my heartfelt gratitude for the warm and generous hospitality of Maryam and Nader, Farzaneh and Mohammad, Farnaz and her family, Maryam and her family, Seyyed Asadollah and his family, and Nahid and her family, who hosted me for considerable lengths of time during my stays in Iran. Elyas, Belgheis, and all their brothers and sisters played the role of guides, friends, siblings, interpreters (linguistic and cultural), accomplices, and confidantes; each of them is extraordinary in his or her own way, and my research would not have been possible without them. Latifah Jafari and Asef Hossaini provided formal and informal research assistance, introductions to refugee organizations, fact-checking, and cultural observations, while Najieh Gholami helped with translations and was always willing to hear out my ideas; I thank them all for their support and friendship.

I am deeply indebted to Paul Dresch, for his intellectual guidance, his spirited approach to ethnography, his insistence on scholarly rigour, and his precise and thorough editing. My work was initially coaxed in the right direction by Wendy James. Walter Armbrust and Setrag Manoukian offered productive critiques and invaluable advice in the preparation of the book. Drafts of several chapters were read by Dawn Chatty, Roxanne Varzi, Edmund Herzig, David Pratten, Orkideh Behrouzan, Darryl Li, and Huma Yusuf, and benefited enormously from their painstaking comments and encouragement. Margaret Mills, William Beeman, and Setrag Manoukian reviewed earlier versions of this book and gave valuable advice. My poetry translations were considerably enriched and made more accurate thanks to the careful eyes of Belgheis Jafari, Asef Hossaini, Fatemeh Shams, Orkideh Behrouzan, and Dominic Brookshaw. I am grateful to my editor Rebecca Tolen for her patient guidance and faith in the project, to Deborah Oliver for exceptional copyediting, and to Nancy Lightfoot for seeing the book through to completion. I would also like to thank Michael Athanson, the Bodleian Library's deputy map librarian, for his assistance in creating the map of western Asia, as well as the authors of all the poems in this book for their kind permission to reproduce the transliterated originals.

This book took its final shape at St. John's College, Oxford, and the Anthropology Department at the London School of Economics and Political Science, and I am most grateful to these institutions for their inspiring environments and for the fruitful discussions I had with many colleagues, but particularly Martin Stokes, Craig Jeffrey, Mohamad-Salah Omri, Anna Stirr, Robert Young, Maurice Bloch, Charles Stafford, Mukulika Banerjee, Laura Bear, and Ana Gutierrez Garza. An early version of the book was presented in the form of the Evans-Pritchard Lectures at All Souls College, Oxford, in May 2013. I am grateful to the Warden and Fellows of the college for this wonderful opportunity and to David Gellner for his hospitality and guidance. I also thank the audiences of that series and numerous other seminars for helpful feedback. I am lucky to count a number of brilliant anthropologists as dear friends and I am grateful for all their inspiration and support, both intellectual and practical, over the years, especially Nicolette Makovicky, Mekhala Krishnamurthy, Darryl Li, Orkideh Behrouzan, and Alicia Blum-Ross. All errors, of course, remain my own.

Finally, I would like to thank my parents, Piotr and Barbara, and my brother, Marek, for instilling in me a love of both travel and scholarship and for their lifelong support, and my partner, Adham, for his love, patience, and unwavering faith in my work, and for reminding me of the wide world beyond my desk.

A Note on the Translations, Transliteration, and Dates

THIS BOOK IS concerned with an art form that harnesses the intricacies of language, itself a cultural system, to achieve a particular effect. Burton Raffel's work *The Art of Translating Poetry* (1988) illuminates the many difficulties of attempting to translate poetry into other languages. The translator must balance different claims, linguistic and aesthetic, the latter of which Raffel considers the more challenging: "How is the translator to reproduce in the new language the peculiar force and strength, the inner meanings as well as the merely outer ones, of what the original writer created solely and exclusively for and in a different language and a different culture?" (1988: 156). He believes that the scholar who translates must herself be a poet, while the translator must also be a scholar.

Given that poetry in its cultural contexts is the subject of this book, I have tried to keep my translations literal and to take as few aesthetic liberties as possible. Instead, I explain the poetry's "inner" and "outer" meanings through close readings of several works, adding clarifications and explanations in parentheses or endnotes where necessary. Particularly in translations from blank verse, some of the lines will be lexically and syntactically similar enough to English to replicate for the reader something of the aesthetic experience of the original. However, much of the sensory pleasure of rhymed, metric verse—particularly the rhythmic patterning of alternating long and short syllables used in Persian prosody, different to the metric feet of stressed and unstressed syllables used in English—will not be accessible to the reader; and indeed is difficult for any non-native speaker of Persian to grasp. Raffel emphasizes that "no two languages having the same prosody, it is impossible to re-create the prosody of a literary work composed in one language in another language" (1988: 83). Translations of a high literary merit from as many aspects as possible are therefore a separate undertaking and must be left for another work. All translations from original material in Persian are mine unless otherwise specified.

I use a modified form of the International Journal of Middle Eastern Studies' (IJMES) transliteration system for Persian. Consonants are consistent with this system, but diacritics are not used to distinguish letters that have the same pronunciation in Persian. The only long vowel I mark with a diacritic is the aleph (*ā*, similar to English *a* in *all*) as contrasted with *a*, the short vowel (which is very close to the English *a* in *at*). The other short vowels are rendered with the closest English equivalent to the way they are spoken in standard contemporary Iranian

xvii

xviii | *A Note on the Translations*

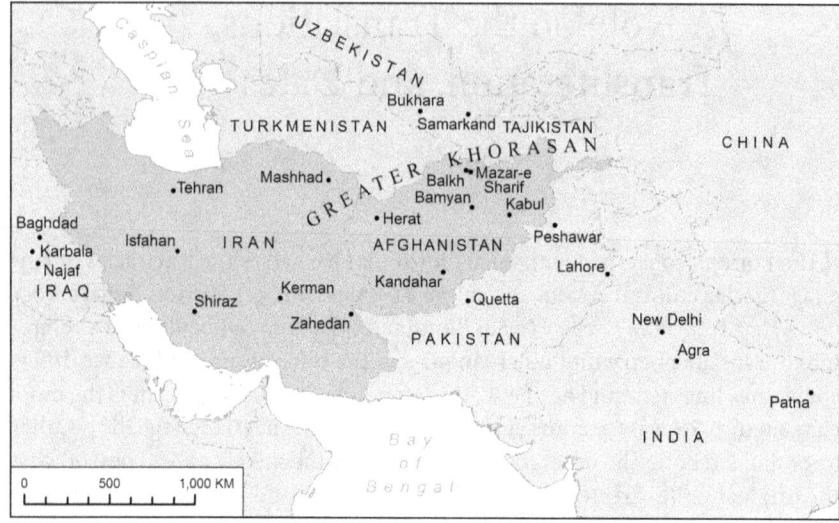

Map of western Asia showing present-day borders of Iran and Afghanistan, major cities, and key sites associated with Persian literature and Shi'a Islam that appear in this book. Produced with the Natural Earth program.

Persian, so I use *e* and *o* rather than *i* and *u*. Long ی is rendered *i* and rhymes with English *me*; و is rendered *u* and sounds like the *oo* in English *moon*. Long vowels read as diphthongs are rendered as follows: *ei* for medial ی and *ey* when it is in the final position (both rhyme with English *may*); a doubled medial ی is *-yy-*. و as a diphthong is rendered *ow*, rhyming with English *mow*. Final ه is indicated by *eh* except in the case of common monosyllabic words, in which case it is rendered simply as *e* (e.g., *panjareh*, but *se, che, ke, be*), all rhyming with English *eh*. The plural suffix *hā* is preceded by a dash. Ayn is indicated by ' and hamza is indicated by '.

In the case of quotations from colloquial speech, I transcribe rather than transliterate the words, representing vowel sounds as above. In a very few cases, I change the vowel system to indicate standard Afghan Persian pronunciation, in which case the short vowels revert to *i* and *u* and final ه is written *ah*. The shift is indicated in the text and should be clear to the reader. In quotes, I keep the transliteration used by other authors as is; in the discussion this may lead to various spellings of the same word.

Certain Arabic words used in a general rather than local sense (such as *hijrah*) are transliterated according to Arabic rather than Persian conventions. Others, such as *hijab, jihad, chador,* and *hadith*, are common enough in English usage that they are not italicized in the text.

Names of people and organizations appear with ayn (‘) and hamza (’) as relevant but with no other diacritics. However, an initial ayn in names is omitted, for clarity and because it does not affect the pronunciation.

All dates are A.D. (anno Domini) except those in Persian-language references (at the end of the bibliography), which follow the format "anno Persico/anno Domini." "Anno Persico" refers to the Iranian Solar Hejri calendar.

THE PEARL OF DARI

Introduction

THE TAXI DRIVER is not sure he has heard me correctly. "*Sākhtemān?*" he repeats, to make sure. "Yes." He shakes his head slightly, evidently wondering what business I have in what is considered the rough part of town, and starts the car. We drive through the uptown part of Mashhad, the white marble facades and intricate stuccowork of the houses of the wealthy glistening behind their high outer walls. We maneuver our way through heavy traffic onto the ring road and pick up speed, the hazy mountains to our right, the crowded city to our left, with the gilded shrine of Imam Reza at its heart. We circle around the city and the shrine. By the time we turn off the ring road at the other end toward a suburb built outside it, the houses are small, meager, one- or two-story structures of unplastered dun-colored brick, the streets dustier and bustling with old cars, buses, and people, the walls hand-painted with colorful advertisements for various products and shops. This is the *pā'in-e shahr*, the "downtown" or lower-income neighborhoods, whose inhabitants are mostly Afghan refugees and Iranian migrants from rural areas. I direct the driver through ever-narrower lanes into the heart of the quarter known as Dahmetri-ye Sakhteman, after the main road that bisects it.

We pull up outside the house of an Afghan cleric from the Hazarajat, in a tiny lane with a water channel running down the middle. I get out and the taxi backs out slowly from the lane. Most of the other houses are hidden behind anonymous gates in brick walls, but this one has a decorative cement cornice above the gate, in a free interpretation of European neoclassical style. The words sculpted in the cement form a calligraphic frieze in Persian: *Donyā joz hich dar hich, hich nist* (The world is nothing but nothing-within-nothing), a nihilistic statement attributed to King Solomon in a major Shi'a collection of hadith.[1] The hand that sculpted this belongs to the cleric's son, and it is the same hand that has fashioned the decorative cement and plasterwork on the gleaming facades of dozens of uptown Iranian houses, most of whose builders were Afghans. This decoration on a much more modest house is a humble reminder of the skilled labor of Afghan craftsmen and builders, which has contributed a great deal to Iran's rapid postrevolutionary urban expansion. But the fact that it is the only such fanciful ornament in this neighborhood, along with the despondency of the quotation itself, are emblems of the social and economic distance between Afghans and many Iranians. On another level, it hints at the importance of a tradition of literate scholarship and textual authority within this population.

Some time later, I am in another rickety taxi with the cleric's other son, Elyas, a poet who has gained some renown in both Iranian and Afghan literary circles, and two of his sisters. They are taking me on my first visit to the Dorr-e-Dari (Pearl of the Dari Language) Cultural Institute (hereafter Dorr-e Dari). It is a Friday in August 2005, and as always, there will be a poetry reading and criticism session, followed by a short-story-writing class, attended exclusively by young Afghan refugees. I am heading there because of Elyas's sister, Belgheis, whom I met by chance on my first trip to Mashhad several years earlier and whose family's warm hospitality convinced me to consider returning to do fieldwork among Afghans in Iran. I kept in touch with her while we both studied in Tehran—I on a Persian language course, she for her master's in French literature—and during one of our periodic meetings in the capital's Laleh Park, she tipped me off to some of the interesting work her brother and other Afghan poets were doing.

We drive a little farther along the ring road to its easternmost point, passing agricultural land and some ancient freestanding brick minarets, then turn toward the city center, into a maze of small streets at Pich-e Telgerd. Despite the presence of a large new government hospital, mosque, and neatly laid-out public park named after the Basij (the volunteer militia that helped consolidate the revolution), this is an area dominated by small concrete houses and tiny shops, greengrocers whose colorful mounds of fruit are stacked on the pavements, a sandwich shop run by an Iraqi refugee, a bakery with a perpetual queue, and, in the quiet back alleys, workshops where men make brooms out of stiff, twiggy sorghum stems.

We enter a doorway in a lane of broom makers. Leaning against the wall at the bottom of the staircase is a hand-painted sign bearing the name Dorr-e Dari Cultural Institute, as if someone feared it would attract too much attention if hung outside. Upstairs at the entrance to what was once a residential flat is an array of shoes, and everyone pauses to remove their own before entering. It is an unassuming place, and difficult to imagine as the headquarters of one of the most ambitious intellectual enterprises among Afghan refugees anywhere in the world—quite appropriately, a pearl in a rough outer shell.

Inside, a crowd of people is waiting for Elyas to begin the poetry session as master of ceremonies. He opens with a fragment of a poem by Federico García Lorca, translated by the Iranian modernist poet Ahmad Shamlu, to set the tone for the session. One by one, he invites young poets to take a seat beside him at the table at the front of the room and read their work. I am particularly struck by one young woman, dressed all in black and wrapped in a black chador (I learn

Figure 0.1. The environs of the Dorr-e Dari Cultural Institute in Mashhad.

4 | *The Pearl of Dari*

Figure 0.2. The poets of Dorr-e Dari, 2007. In the back row, Amanollah Mirza'i is third from the left, Gholamreza Ebrahimi is fourth, and Ali Ja'fari is seventh. In the front row, Ma'sumeh Ahmadi is first from the left, Seyyed Abu Taleb Mozaffari is fourth, Rahimeh Mirza'i is fifth, and Hossein Heidarbeigi is sixth.

later that she is twenty-five-year-old Rahimeh Mirza'i). As she reads she is very still and her eyes are fixed shyly on the table, but she is wearing a hint of mascara. From what little I can catch of the poetic language, I understand, to my surprise, that the poem is about the *Mona Lisa*:

Labkhand bezan
Jahān be kām-e to-st
Na parishāni-ye gisu'i ke borq'eh'i bepushānad-ash
na sormeh-ye anduhi ke māh-at rā betārānad
va na ghorbati
    dar joghrāfiā-ye sineh-ye mardi majhul
To āfarideh shodi
jāvedāneh
dar dast-hā-ye bozorg-e 'eshqi
tabdār va moltaheb
    bi gham-e farāmushi
Labkhand-e to
amvāj-e mowzun-e kodām tarāneh ast

ke az oqiānus-hā ham gozar kardeh ast
                bedun-e daqiqeh'i taghyir
Monā Lizā
labkhand ke mizani
mehi az farāmushi jahān rā farā migirad.

Smile;
the world is to your liking.
Neither the anguish of tresses covered by a burka,
nor the kohl of sorrow darkening your moon,
nor exile
    inside the territory of an unknown man's chest.
You were created
to be eternal
by the great hands of a
    feverish and impassioned love,
        free from the sorrow of forgetting.
Your smile
is the rhythmic waves of which song
that has crossed even the oceans,
        without a minute of change?
Mona Lisa,
when you smile,
the world is overcome with a mist of forgetting.

                (Original published in Mirza'i 1386/2008: 39–41)

    The audience applauds, and then Elyas invites the next poet to read. As Mirza'i returns to her seat, I am struck by the fact that she has been mounting a critique of gender relations in her society, but even more so that she was using a masterpiece of European art as a reference point. Her words also seemed bolder than the figure she cuts in person. Later, after I have spoken to some of the young women and scribbled down their home phone numbers, I record an interview with Seyyed Abu Taleb Mozaffari, the director of the center. I ask what the figure of the poet represents in Persian culture. In the past, he tells me, a poet was someone who was a great person from many points of view—faith, manners, education, thought, and artistic expression. Now, on the other hand, it is usually people who are sensitive, unusual, and "romantic" (he uses the word that entered Persian from French, complete with the French pronunciation); who find themselves outside society in some way. Elyas has been listening to the interview and chips in to say he agrees.

    Absorbing this information later, I wanted to know more about this change. It seemed to me that I had correctly imagined Afghan refugees' poetic activities to be a useful lens to explore broader questions of identity and social change in exile, but also of changes in subjectivity and conceptions of the person in Iranian society at large. I was struck by the earnestness and dedication with which they pursued artistic, intellectual, and educational activities despite their apparently humble surroundings, and although their family members had been landless peasants in Afghanistan and were presently manual laborers in Iran. I wanted to know: Who were these young poets and what accounted for these fervent aspirations? What motivated them to compose the poems that they read to each other every week and then discussed and critiqued? Who supported their endeavors? What styles and techniques were they using, and why did they consider themselves unusual people? What were they trying to communicate, to whom, and why were they using poetry to communicate it? During several visits to Iran over the following three years, I attempted to answer these questions.

This book, the result of that work, is an ethnography of poetry and its place in a particular society, particularly of how it is used to formulate, express, and consolidate certain kinds of persons and ideas of personhood in a migrant population. I carry out this analysis on three levels. First, I present an ethnographic portrait of urban-based Afghan refugees in the Islamic Republic of Iran and their subject formation through biopolitical and bureaucratic management by the state (among other things, through contact with educational and health care institutions and a restricted labor market on the one hand, and legal marginalization and social ostracism on the other), and their own cultural and political organizing. Second, I examine the cultural politics of this population in these circumstances, focusing on the history of organizations such as Dorr-e Dari and literary production in the context of political and social change. I also look at the relations between poets, their individual biographies, their patrons and audiences; and the historical trajectories of poetic genres in a regional context. To my knowledge, this the first time that a sociological or ethnographic study of poetic texts and their production and circulation has been attempted in a modern Persian-language setting.

Finally, I move from these macro analyses to a more fine-grained description of how young Afghan refugees use the composition, performance, and circulation of a verbal art form pragmatically, both to make collective claims about identity and to pursue personal ends. Like Rahimeh Mirza'i with her poem about the Mona Lisa, they appeal to certain ideas about cosmopolitanism, ideals of gender equality, and the need for social criticism through literature to fashion themselves as cultivated and enlightened individuals. These personas are self-consciously modern and carry a certain prestige. They are thus among the few forms of cultural capital available through which young Afghans, who can legally work only in menial professions in Iran, might improve their lives. My analysis thus traces the extent to which the formation of modern forms of subjectivity and ideas about personhood extend beyond the upper and middle classes to impoverished and marginalized populations in Iran both through top-down management and through aspiration, a problem that is too rarely considered in the ethnography of the contemporary Islamic Republic.

While literature may be a resource for such personal projects, literature's meaning and purpose themselves are contested and vary with context: works that push too many boundaries of form and content may be praised by some, but dismissed as ugly, immoral, or irresponsible by critics. They may also fail to be perceived as poetry at all by bemused members of the generation of their authors' parents, and finding an appropriate audience is a challenge. Meanwhile, it is also possible to remain politically safe, if morally suspect to some, by working within the bounds of the "Committed" (*mota'ahhed*) literature favored by the revolutionary state. Faced with such examples of what Bourdieu (1993) has called "position-taking," I came to perceive a close link between moral and aesthetic claims in young poets' work. Indeed, they often faced difficulties in balancing competing ethics of self-expression and self-restraint. These difficulties appeared to me to extend to a tension between exposition and concealment that lay at the very heart of Persian lyric poetry.

Given that the young Afghans in Iran who engaged in literary or other cultural activities numbered in the hundreds or at most thousands, however, we might ask the question, why study a marginal activity in an already marginal population? Leaving aside arguments about the inherent anthropological interest of any human endeavor, it is precisely these "obscure aspirants to elite status," as Barber describes newly literate people in colonial Africa (2006b: 1), who are often the greatest cultural innovators, having to bridge an abundance of life contradictions engendered by their intermediate statuses. Indeed, many of the people described by the contributors to Barber's edited collection, *Africa's Hidden Histories* (2006a), were involved in literary circles and other practices of reading and writing similar to those of the Afghans in Iran, for broadly similar aspirational reasons. Even when their practices are ephemeral and destined to be forgotten (which is not necessarily the case for all of my interlocutors, some of whom are well-known in Iran), they are nonetheless developments in the history and spread of literary forms that are worth remarking. The global literary historical work of Franco Moretti (2005) shows that the rise, fall, and spread of genres and devices, rather than specific canonical texts, ought to be the true object of knowledge in literary history, and literary historians ought to pay attention to these "populations" of texts and genres, including those that "deviate, innovate, branch out, flourish for a while, fail and are eclipsed" (Barber 2007: 40–41).[2] Anthropologists can also assist in this project through deeper engagements with some of the more obscure branches of these populations and the people who create them, creating a perspective on literature that takes us well beyond the limited writers and texts that are written into official canons.

My project is aligned with those of the "anthropology of international borders" (Donnan and Wilson 1999) and "anthropology on the margins of the state" (Das and Poole 2004) that posit that "much can be learnt about the centers of power by focusing on their peripheries" (Donnan and Wilson 1999: xiii), whether physical or metaphorical, and that "margins are a necessary entailment of the state, much as the exception is a necessary component of the rule" (Das and Poole 2004: 4). Thus, the difficult and contradictory situation of Afghans who are legally marginalized in Iran helps to reveal certain paradoxes inherent in the Islamic Republic. For example, although the state frequently employs the rhetoric of religious solidarity in pursuit of its aims and Ayatollah Khomeini once famously declared that "Islam has no borders," the reality is that the Islamic Republic has managed to establish an "Islam *with* borders" and a regime of national preference with regard to social and economic rights. In the realm of immigration policy, at the very least, the Islamic Republic is very much a modern nation-state pursuing a rather ad hoc realpolitik, not too different from those of liberal Western democracies.

Approaches to the Anthropological Study of Migrant Literature

In the title essay in his collection *Reflections on Exile,* Edward Said discusses the paradox that exile, while compelling and romantic as an idea, is "terrible to experience" (2002: 173). Nonetheless, through their suffering, exiled writers and poets manage to "lend dignity to a condition legislated to deny dignity—to deny an identity to people" (175). But Said is curiously despondent about the potential for this kind of literary redemption in some parts of the world:

> As you move further from the Atlantic world, the awful forlorn waste increases: the hopelessly large numbers, the compounded misery of "undocumented" people suddenly lost, without a tellable history. To reflect on exiled Muslims from India, or Haitians in America, or Bikinians in Oceania, or Palestinians throughout the Arab world means that you must leave the modest refuge provided by subjectivity and resort instead to the abstractions of mass politics. Negotiations, wars of national liberation, people bundled out of their homes and prodded, bussed or walked to enclaves in other regions: what do these experiences add up to? Are they not manifestly and almost by design irrecoverable? (Said 2002 [1984]: 176)

One cannot help but detect a note of rising panic at the thought that millions of people are being consigned to an irretrievable void of fruitless lives, without a "tellable history" and with "irrecoverable experiences," simply by virtue of being non-Western and not having the good fortune to be exiled in the West. In reality, however, if we believe that refugees beyond the Euro-American world have no consciousness of their predicaments, that they are not reflecting on or telling and recording their histories, and that they are not engaging politically and intellectually with those experiences, it is simply because we are not listening. Too often they are treated as "matter out of place" and constructed as victims without history and politics by the very humanitarian institutions that seek to help them (Malkki 1995b, 1996). Some of the genres in which experiences of exile are memorialized and debated are not even recognized by outsiders as expressive genres at all (Powles 2004, 2005). The world's peripheral "backwaters," much less the people uprooted from them, are rarely considered to have such a thing as an intellectual history. I hope to turn the focus back from the "mass politics" of forced migration to subjectivity and individual creativity.[3]

Academic trends and political circumstances draw scholarly attention to some kinds of cultural production at the expense of others. In the case of contemporary Iran, anthropologists and other scholars have flocked to describe and explain phenomena that have captured the world's attention, such as postrevolutionary cinema;[4] a middle-class youth culture perceived as defiant and its rebellious fashions, flirtations, and underground music;[5] or the growing popularity of blogs and the internet in Iran and its diaspora.[6] Perhaps because it is more difficult to translate, less tailored to international audiences, and more embedded within a long and highly self-referential tradition than the richly visual Iranian cinema (cf. Fischer 2004: 258), or because it is perceived as less obviously subversive and current than blogs or less "modern" than prose genres such as the novel, contemporary Persian poetry has been given little to no attention outside of Iran and Afghanistan.

This does not appear to be a new problem: the great historian of Persian literature Edward Granville Browne lamented a century ago that Western scholars "constantly assert that there is no modern Persian poetry worth reading" (1914: xvi). He attributed this "pernicious error" to a combination of political malice and sheer ignorance and emphatically asserted that poetry was alive and well in Persia (ibid.). He observed that Iranians had shown great poetic vitality in the years of the Constitutional Revolution (1905–1911), taking up its political and cultural concerns and developing new ways to express them poetically. From the late nineteenth century onward, poetry has been extensively used to introduce, inculcate, praise, question, reject, and reconfigure the modern condition in the Persian-speaking world. It continues to enjoy widespread popularity today as a tradition descended from the great Persian classical tradition, yet positioning itself as distinct from it. Afghan refugees in Iran, whether literate or nonliterate, have since the 1980s continued to compose and enjoy poetry more than any other art form, and literary activities have been their preeminent form of cultural organizing. In postrevolutionary Iran itself, poetry has been the art form most strongly promoted and considered least morally problematic by the state (Shams 2015a), but it has also been used extensively by those opposed to the state.

Poetry has long held extraordinary significance throughout the Persian-speaking world. Poets traditionally possessed an aura of wisdom and authority: "People use the prefix 'Sha'er mega' ('The poet says') to substantiate argument"

(Azoy 2004: 11). In a largely nonliterate society, oral literature in local vernaculars was in the past a medium of mass communication, a popular pastime and social activity, and a portable repository of cultural, historical, and philosophical knowledge. Written literature in the Persian language, meanwhile, was for centuries an integral part of culture and polite learning in the courts of kings and, together with Islam, a unifying force in multiethnic kingdoms and empires from Iran to Central Asia and India. As Dorr-e Dari's director Mozaffari told me in that first interview, the poet was the epitome of the great man, the learned philosopher-scholar for whose thoughts verse was the most appropriate vehicle, and poets were often admired boon companions and advisors to kings. But literature has also been "a domain as well as an instrument of cultural and political contention" in Persian-speaking lands (Ghani 1988: 428) and, as such, its study benefits from a sociological perspective. Throughout the history of Persian literature, poets have been supported by powerful patrons and enlisted to praise them, but they have also subjected religious and political elites to merciless, if often veiled, scrutiny. By adopting the persona of "the Poet" or by quoting poets, one is given a certain degree of license for social criticism, precisely because of poetry's allusive, allegorical, and ambiguous qualities. But this is not without its limits, and poets have been imprisoned, exiled, or assassinated for their critical political opinions.[7]

In contemporary Iran, the Persian poetic heritage has, through an ongoing nationalist project that has foregrounded "culture," become identified as a quintessentially "Iranian" art form. Manoukian has explored this process in his ethnographic work on the city of Shiraz: "Poetry is sometimes language, sometimes articulation of common sense, and sometimes just the names of a few poets, or a visit to their tombs. . . . Poetry, even when used as an empty signifier, is an articulation of the self" (Manoukian 2004: 41). It is a form of discourse both so hegemonic that each new regime (including the Islamic Republic) seeks to appropriate the great poetry of the classical canon into its fold and is open-ended enough to allow it to do so: "poetic heritage becomes the public and shared ground of the Iranian nation, rather than the instrumental tool of this or that political constituency" (Manoukian 2011: 74).

It is particularly appropriate among any group of Persian speakers in exile to pay attention to their poetry because it comes with a ready-made vocabulary and emotional scripts for thinking and writing about this condition: "it is poetry, especially sufi (mystic) poetry, that provides the paradigmatic worldview and language of exile, embodying a variety of journeys, returns, and unifications" (Naficy 1991: 286). In this particular case, the unusual circumstance of a shared—but contested—language and literary heritage between refugees and their host population means that poetry has become a forum for dialogue and debate between Afghan and Iranian intellectuals—a forum for presenting claims both to difference and to unity. Rather than the "hybridized" "third space" that Bhabha (1990) describes as emerging, for example, in the writing of exiles in the West, who navigate between their own culture and that of their adopted home, the literary activities of Afghans in Iran represent their claim to inclusion in what they believe is their birthright, too: the singular "public and shared ground" of the Persian poetic heritage.

I was inspired to take poetry as an object of inquiry seriously by a number of compelling ethnographies of tribal oral poetry (Caton 1990, Abu-Lughod 1986, Edwards 1986b, Boesen 1983). They showed how the rhetoric, imagery, convention, and contexts of poetry and its performance relate both performers and listeners to their community by reminding them how they are implicated in its ethical codes and past and future events and by reaffirming the community's image of itself. Caton, for example, focuses on the socially constitutive power of poetry, showing how "more obviously than in the West, poetry in tribal Yemen is both the creation of art and the production of social and political reality in the same act of composition. To compose a poem is to construct oneself as a peacemaker, as a warrior, as a Muslim" (1990: 21–22). He describes how this is done in particular through tribal performance genres of poetry, the *balah* and the *zamil,* rooted in the speech genres of social intercourse such as greetings and challenge-and-retort routines. Edwards, meanwhile, argues that the Pashto verses composed at the time of the Soviet invasion of Afghanistan made armed resistance appear as the only honorable course of action for Pashtun men by making specific references to their honor code: "The poet's role is to make present and explicit the individual's relationship to his past and his future and thereby direct him to see that his self-realization comes in relation to the social and temporal universe of which he is part" (1986b: 506).

Oral poetry also frequently gives the poet license to say what is unacceptable in other forms of discourse, or to creatively express apparent contradictions in social ideology. Boesen (1983) documented an oral form of poetry that is almost exclusively the preserve of Pashtun women, the *landay*. Anticipating Abu-Lughod's similar finding for Egyptian Bedouin women (1986), she wrote that although Pashtun women basically shared the ideology of an honor-bound society founded upon the premise of control of women by men, they expressed their divergent views in the form of oral poetry. In some respects the "alternative conscience" they reveal reflects the "general dilemma inherent in the relation between ideology and individual practice," but in this case, there is also a specific dilemma: "that of being both Pakhtun and women" (Boesen 1983: 107). Women's poetry is thus able to take up themes contrary to the honor code, such as romantic love, but with certain limitations. Abu-Lughod's work stresses the importance of performative context: abstract verses about love and loss may only acquire meaning when interpreted in the context of an individual's life, usually known to other members of the community (1986: 171–177).⁸ Poems describing the sentiments of weakness and romantic love that violate the codes of honor and modesty are usually only recited in front of intimates, such as close friends, social peers and lovers (1986: 233–234). Thus poetry, writes Abu-Lughod, "is the discourse of intimacy . . . [and] indexes social distinctions by following the lines of social cleavage" (234). The sharing of poetry in Iran, too, typically took place among intimates (Beeman 2001: 46–47), but with new forms of poetic sociability and new ideas about the purposes of poetry, this conception has changed.

In my research, I soon encountered a problem that these meticulously detailed but largely synchronic works on oral poetry did not help me address. I was repeatedly told by Afghan poets that there had been a fundamental shift between the refugee poetry of the 1980s–1990s and that of the 2000s through to the time of my research, and this was indeed apparent in the published work from each of these periods. This shift no doubt reflected an experiential and discursive gap between first-generation refugees who had lived many years in Afghanistan before migrating, and those born or raised and educated mostly in Iran, who were in their late teens and twenties when I met them. But it also reflected changes in the Islamic Republic's cultural policy and broader political events: from the favoring of largely propagandistic works supporting the revolution and the war against Iraq (or Afghanistan's war against Soviet Russia) in the 1980s, to a greater liberalization under more pragmatic governments from the mid-1990s onward. Thus, the martial and religiously inflected refugee poetry of the 1980s had given way to more subjective lyric poetry; a proliferation of forms, genres, and styles; and a greater spirit of experimentation, social criticism, and ambivalence about identity, in keeping with the general diversity of Iranian poetry at this time (Anushiravani and Hassanli 2007). The young poets of the day fitted Mozaffari's second archetype: their work was personal and intensely inward looking, but also reflected a keen observation of society by those sensing they are slightly apart from it.

To understand such changes, I sought more diachronic studies of poetics and poetic change that took into account transformations in modes of authority and technologies of transmission. Bowen, in a historical ethnography of the poetics of the Gayo people of Sumatra, provides an example of the first. He critiques a trend in the ethnography of the time to explain social phenomena, particularly the past, by holding cultural forms constant and interpreting them as authoritative "texts" (Bowen 1991: 4–5; he gives Geertz's work on the Balinese theater state as an example [1980]). Drawing on more dynamic studies of the history of literary forms (e.g., Bakhtin 1981, 1986; Williams 1977; Jakobson 1960), he emphasizes that poetics and sociopolitical developments should be seen "not as a set of static correspondences but as a dialectic between forms of discourse and forms of authority" (Bowen 1991: 143). Such a dialectical perspective provides the context for understanding changes in the Gayo poetic forms of ritual speaking, sung poetry and historical narratives through twentieth-century transitions from Dutch colonialism, through the rise of nationalism and Islamic modernism to the advent of an Indonesian nation-state (3–6). Miller's work on poets in Yemen (2005, 2007) explores another kind of transformation: the link of "modes of social subjectivity to historical shifts in media practice" (2007: 454). Focusing on poets and singers who disseminate their work on audiocassettes in southern Yemen, he offers a nuanced reading of such shifts by exploring how Yemenis understand the ethical valences of different kinds of media, particularly the visual and the sonic, the graphic and the oral, and their various recombinations, and how they deploy them for rhetorical purposes. Thus he dramatizes Yemeni poets' "struggle . . . to craft moral authority [and] to promote and preserve their relevance for contemporary audiences" (ibid.: 2).

During my research, I came to understand that not only technological changes in the transmission of poetry, but also the effects of politics on cultural institutions, state policies and audiences played an essential role in the transformations that had occurred in poetry in the Islamic Republic of Iran. A complex perspective on cultural production in an urban society was thus required, one that dialectically linked the poet to institutions for disseminating poetry, and both of these to audiences and their tastes. Bourdieu's writings (1993, 1996) on the modern field of cultural production help to relate the literary output of particular writers to their location in a complex culture industry, market forces, and both material and symbolic rewards and honors. While Bourdieu expresses many of these forces in a schema built on the dualism between autonomous and commercial art in practice, there are many possible forms of cultural production in the spectrum between the perfectly autonomous and the perfectly market-driven, and they are all subject to contentions by actors located in various positions in the hierarchies of symbolic and economic value. This is "a struggle often expressed in the conflict between the orthodoxy of established traditions and the heretical challenge of new modes of cultural practice, manifested as *prises de position* or position-takings" (Johnson 1993: 16–17). Literary critics (who, in the case of Iran, are usually also poets or writers) are those with the authority to determine the criteria by which a literary work may be judged and whether or not it constitutes literature, so their position takings matter.

I consider the utility and limitations of Bourdieu's theory for understanding the shift that occurred in Afghan refugee poetry, particularly its difficulties in accounting for political poetry, an anomalous category for Bourdieu, as Zimbler (2009) has argued. I suggest that it might be explained in terms of a move away from poetry as a medium for the transmission of a political message to a large, defined audience (Shi'a Afghan refugees in Iran interested in the outcome of the war in Afghanistan and with stakes in various political and armed groups and ideologies). There occurred a rupture with that audience and a reorientation toward a new, more restricted audience—Iranians and Iran-educated Afghans with intellectual leanings—enabling greater autonomy and access to a different kind of symbolic capital, one with greater value for the current generation: cultivation of a critical and sensitive artistic persona. The shift to a more restricted kind of production largely for an audience of other writers enables a greater degree of formal, generic, and stylistic experimentation in a milieu in which this constitutes the primary literary value. However, a variety of ethical and aesthetic position takings, both praise and condemnation of poetic ability *and* individual morality, accompany the activities of the young generation of poets and have made this transition anything but smooth.

Barber's groundbreaking work (2007) helpfully brings together many diverse strands of literary and sociological theories to articulate a framework for the anthropological study of texts, regardless of whether they are oral or written. A text, she writes, is a "tissue of words," woven together and given form (2007: 1); texts are "the hot spots of language: concentrations of linguistic productivity, forms of language that have been marked out to command heightened attention—and sometimes to stimulate intense excitement, provoke admiration and desire, or be the mainstay of memory" (3). She pays particular attention, as I do, to the idea of texts as constitutive of persons or ideas of personhood, to audiences' role in the construction and interpretation of texts, and to the role of genre in priming an audience to respond to a particular convention in a particular way. Drawing on examples from various African oral genres (2007: 103–136) and Alfred Gell's notion that an art object can be seen as a projection of its creator, an "extended mind" (Gell 1998: 104), Barber shows how the composition of texts about oneself allows both self-proclamation and a kind of detachment that allows them to become public. She emphasizes that "the literary text does not *depict* or *disclose* existing social relations and subjectivities; rather it is part of the 'technology' by which they are produced"; it "holds up models of what a person should be" (Barber 2007: 106, 109).[9] Modes of address, the use of pronouns and the vocative case, claims about recognition and reputation, allusions, analogies and metaphors, all "precipitate the conception of the self" (2007: 136).

Winegar's study of modern artists in Egypt and their "reckoning" with ideas about modernity, tradition, and the role of artists in a postcolonial nation (2006) provides an elegant model for an ethnography that combines multiple layers of analysis, from the politics of a field of cultural production to the individual search for an authentic personhood through artistic practice. Following Bourdieu (1984) and Eagleton (1990), she attempts to displace the naturalness of taste and aesthetic values, showing how they are strictly tied to power, ideology and a range of interests even when they masquerade behind a "fantasy of [artistic] autonomy" (Winegar 2006: 4). It is Egyptian artists' training and relationship with various state and international institutions and audiences, Winegar argues, that shape the form and content of their work, as well as their ideas about how to be true to themselves and about what counts as good art. I take up this idea of contested ideas of an authentic voice as a measure of poetic value in this book.

These ethnographic studies have emphasized the importance of attention to the social efficacy of poetry and its socially constitutive aspects; to poetry's ability to express dominant or counterdiscourses of morality or power; to contexts of poetic reception; to the dialectic of social, political, and literary trends in history; to the shifting and mingling of oral and textual modes of authority in literature; and to the importance of plotting the relations among poets, audiences, and institutions in a field of cultural production in order to understand poetic change. All these themes have guided my research and analysis.

The Anthropology of Subjects and Persons

Throughout this book I refer to subjectivity and personhood, two closely related but distinct concepts, as well as the interplay between them. Like the many other anthropologists who have adopted it as an analytical category, I understand subjectivity as a kind of self-awareness that is both internally and externally shaped, formed at the locus of (or out of the tension between) individual reflection and participation in society. It is a way of linking inner processes and affective states with the external imposition of norms through the workings of power and political economies.[10] Foucault puts it as follows: "There are two meanings of the word *subject:* subject to someone else by control and dependence, and tied to his own identity by a conscience or self-knowledge" (1982: 212). Similarly, Ortner sees subjectivity as both "the ensemble of modes of perception, affect, thought, desire, fear, and so forth that animate acting subjects," *and* "the cultural and social formations that shape, organize and provoke" them (2005: 31). This dynamic analytical synthesis of inner and outer forces is significant, for it shows that, on the whole, anthropologists have moved beyond the antihumanist tendencies of late twentieth-century poststructuralist thinkers who sought to dissolve the notion of the bounded, autonomous, coherent and universal self and focused solely on the power relations that created the illusion of its existence.[11] Rather, anthropologists have accepted the idea of the cultural and historical contingency of subjectivity while also recognizing that the subject is "at once a product and agent of history" and that "subjectivity is not just the outcome of social control or the unconscious; it also provides the ground for subjects to think through their circumstances and to feel through their contradictions" (Biehl, Good, and Kleinman 2007: 14). It is this creative and reflective dimension of subjectivity that is of particular interest to us here, and I explore how creative subjectivity is also mediated by artistic genres, conventions, institutions, and cultural politics.

If subjectivity, then, is an etic analytical category that helps social scientists relate the inner states of individuals to wider social, political and economic forces, I take personhood to represent emic models of what it is to be a person, how to be a good one, and the nature of that person's relationship with others. Subjectivity is *our* model *of* how individuals are shaped by and respond to society, whereas personhood is an indigenous model *of* and *for* the individual's place in social reality, to borrow Geertz's typology of symbolic systems (1973b: 93). Conceptions of personhood are tightly bound up with ideas about the self, kinship, gender, the body, and politics, and they also constitute juridical categories. Mauss (1985 [1938]) was the first to remark on the historical uniqueness of the individualized, self-contained, autonomous conception of the person in the modern 'West'; Geertz later chimed in that this was "a rather peculiar idea in the context of the world cultures" (1984 [1974]: 126). In an effort to avoid ethnocentrism, anthropologists subsequently uncovered other ways of being in other parts of the world that they claimed were more relational and in which persons ought really be seen as "dividuals" (Marriott 1976, Strathern 1988); with "permeable" or "partible" bodies (Busby 1997); or subsumed within collectivities and hierarchies that prescribe their social roles and identities in their entirety, as Dumont famously argued of India (1970).

But emphasis on such differences is a matter of normative ideology and of changes in anthropological theories and fashions over time (LiPuma 1998), as well as of imprecision in the way notions like "self" and "person" are defined (Spiro 1993). In reality, as LiPuma contends, it may be possible to discern both individual and relational modalities and facets of personhood in all societies (1998: 56). Ideologies of individualism often ignore the true interdependence of all persons, and there is a great diversity of cultural conceptions of personhood worldwide for whose representation a 'West vs. the Rest' dichotomy is simply inadequate (Spiro 1993: 143–144). Mines (1988, 1994), too, has taken the proponents of the Indian dividual and the Dumontian *Homo hierarchicus* to task by showing that individualism *is* understood and valued in India, although it is a different kind of individualism to that associated with the West: it is contextually dependent, unequally distributed, and increases with a person's age. Echoes of this approach work very well in Iran.

Subjectivity in Postrevolutionary Iran

A number of recent ethnographies have taken steps toward the study of subjectivity and personhood in postrevolutionary Iran, but for the most part these aspects of them have been tacit, under-theorized, and problematic in their assumptions.[12] The most prominent recent monographs by a younger generation of Iranian émigré social scientists (Varzi 2006, Khosravi 2008, Mahdavi 2009) have tended to focus on the experiences of one particular milieu—that is, mostly secular, middle- or upper-middle-class youth in Tehran—while paying little attention to other classes, the provinces and rural areas, non-Persian ethnic groups, migrants and refugees, or individuals and groups who align themselves with the moral and political ideologies of the state. These and other accounts published in the first decade of the 2000s seem to have in common a strong tendency to focus on social phenomena that are interpreted as acts of resistance to and rebellion against the political establishment and the moral order it espouses.[13]

I have explored some of the discursive reasons for this trend elsewhere (Olszewska 2013; see also Adelkhah 2009), but here we are more interested in the assumptions they reveal about processes of subject formation. Secular, middle-class subjects seem to arise autonomously, and must then busy themselves with resisting an alien subjectivity that a pernicious government attempts to force on them. Khosravi is explicit about this: he is concerned with "the pervasive struggle by the young people [of Tehran] to resist a subject position imposed on them from above" (2008: 1) through everyday practices and creative projects that add up to a "culture of defiance" (2008: 3). Mahdavi writes of a new climate of sexual and social licentiousness among Tehran's youth that is seen as "embodying resistance and rebellion" against the state by an attack on its norms of sexual modesty and gender segregation, amounting to a "sociocultural revolution" (2009: 3). Varzi explores the overbearing media tools employed by the state to create pious Islamic subjects, and what she sees as their ultimate failure as a large group of secular youth learn to reject the images they are bombarded with and discover that they must "be creative in order to find freedom" (2006: 130). These authors thus espouse a model of human agency located in "the political and moral autonomy of the subject," like the feminist scholars critiqued by Mahmood (2005: 7).

Yet, as many poststructuralist scholars and those inspired by them have argued, the individual subject is in fact discursively constructed by power structures and becomes self-aware even as she is subordinated by them (Foucault 1980, 1982; Butler 1990; Mahmood 2005: 17). The Marxist literary theorist Eagleton puts it rather eloquently: there is no "pre-given space of interior subjectivity, which is then, in a secondary move, colonised, disfigured, brain-washed, manipulated by certain sinister external powers" (1985: 101). Rather, all forms of subjectivity arise in a dynamic field, never innocent of the power that acts on them through a variety of modalities both visible and diffuse, whether through coercion or persuasion. Even subjectivities that purport to have an interest in creative and autonomous self-expression, to be protected from the inroads of oppressive politics at all costs, are themselves always already constituted by political forces (Eagleton 1985; Bourdieu 1993, 1996). Rhetorics of resistance, then, may in fact obscure their own origins as *cultural dispositions* crucial for the distinction and reproduction of social classes and other groups, and we must ask what forces contribute to the socialization of rebellious middle-class youth in Iran: class or generational awareness? Prerevolutionary memories or cosmopolitan desires transmitted through global mass media and the internet? Or perhaps even the unintended effects of state policies themselves?

While I cannot answer that question fully here, several commentators have noted that the growth of the Iranian middle class has been a result of the "developmental push" and the "modernizing efforts" of the Islamic Republic itself, and that the disaffections expressed by this class are typical of countries where "upwardly mobile middle classes perceive themselves blocked by the state from the pathways to social power" (K. Harris 2012: 436, 451). Abrahamian (2009) has underlined the oft-overlooked facts that the Islamic Republic is at heart a welfare state, and that its strength lies in its economic and social populism and its successful development policies that have enormously benefited the poor. But while some upwardly mobile groups have felt thwarted as the emergence of newly educated youth outpaced the economy's ability to create jobs, others have benefited more directly. The state has created a loyal "rentier class" through the disbursement of financial incentives and other privileges to those who readily embraced its ideology, notably less-privileged rural and urban residents, veterans and martyrs of the revolution and the war with Iraq, and the traditional middle classes who had remained religiously conservative, and who had not benefited from the economic policies of the prerevolutionary Pahlavi state (Bayat 2010: 116–117). But even these incentives had the paradoxical effect of empowering certain constituencies and creating or legitimating modernist aspirations and new, more autonomous conceptions of personhood and agency in, for example, pious working-class women—albeit within an Islamic framework (e.g., Afary 2009: 295, Hoodfar 2009, Sadeghi 2009).

Adelkhah's work represents a rare critique of the perception of "a supposedly absolute rift between despotism and freedom" (2009: 209) in many social scientific studies of Iran, resulting in a more nuanced understanding of subject formation. In her ethnography of Iranian ways of being modern (1999), she stresses the need to consider the interpenetration of state and society and recognize the continuities with the trends of the prerevolutionary era, showing how the revolutionary state has gradually become bureaucratized, professionalized, and technocratically oriented. It promotes the use of reason in public life (including in religion) and biopolitics in the management of the population, and enforces policies that contribute both to state centralization and to the production of the kind of individualized, self-reflexive subjects that Giddens (1991) sees as the hallmark of the late modern age. New subjectivities are thus reflected in new ideals of personhood, to which consumerism and a culture of competition both contribute; both have been woven into the fabric of religious practice (e.g., with prizes for Qur'an recitation competitions and lavish attention to fashion and makeup at all-women religious gatherings [Adelkhah 1999: 147, 169]). The extended patriarchal family has also been challenged by the rise, both in fact and in cultural representations, of the nuclear family and the autonomy of the conjugal couple; while an interest in care for and development of the self is reflected in a boom in self-help manuals (ibid.: 149–152, 153).

Adelkhah illustrates these transformations by tracing changes and continuities in a model of ethical personhood, that of the *javānmard* (man of integrity), an ethic of "gentlemanly" behavior rooted in the Iranian past that takes on a new meaning in the Islamic Republic. Focusing on this ethic allows Adelkhah to show how individuals exercise personal choice and agency in cultivating lifestyles across both the private and public spheres, and indeed shows how these are intrinsic to the idea of "being modern" (1999: 162). A *javānmard* has traditionally meant one who subscribes to a social ethic (*javānmardi*) of selflessness, and has all the qualities of a man, in particular generosity and courage, but also honor, humility, and rectitude (Adelkhah 1999: 31, 33). Rather than building up a reputation and a following of clients through generosity, hospitality, and sometimes judicious use of violence as in the past, the ethic now emphasizes respect for the rule of law and good citizenship, suggesting the expansion of state sovereignty into once-private realms. Indeed, the ethic is closely linked in moral terms to the concept of the social being (*ādam-e ejtemā'i*) propagated by the ideologues of the revolution: the person who is active and committed to others in the public arena while maintaining piety and respectability in private life (Adelkhah 1999: 5). While previously a strictly masculine ethic, as reflected in its very name, it now also applies to women as they, too, increasingly become social beings who are active (*fa'āl*) outside the home.[14]

Not all social changes in contemporary Iran have been the result of government policies. It is important to take into account the effects of population movements following the war with Iraq, rapid urbanization, a dramatic demographic transition from high population growth in the 1980s to a fall in birthrates since then, an increasingly youthful and educated population, increasing female literacy and labor-market participation, the flourishing of the informal economy and problems in the formal economy (Keddie 2006: 285, Adelkhah 1999: x), as well as the arrival of new technologies such as satellite television and the internet. Observers of intellectual trends in Iran speak of a "revolution of ideas, a mostly silent contest over the very meaning and essence of Iranian identity, and, more importantly, where Iran and Iranians ought to go from here," as well as the emergence of multiple new political discourses (Kamrava 2008: 1). All of these have led to the development of complex and diverse subjectivities that are some combination of Iranian, Islamic, *and* inexorably modern, and thanks to the Islamic Republic's development work and populist outlook, these may be observed among the inhabitants of the *pā'in-e shahr* (lower-income areas) as much as among the elites.[15]

The case of Afghan refugees in Iran helps us to see how the state has succeeded in creating subjectivities that are some combination of Islamic and "modern" even in the most marginal of its residents, through a heavy investment in education and public health care. For Afghans and millions of poor Iranians, they coincided with their aspirations for a better life, as the state-promoted ideologies and lifestyles were seen as a path to upward mobility. Thus, in Gramsci's formulation, because Iran's stance toward the refugees was at least initially one of persuasion and opportunity rather than coercion, including a prominent educational mission (1971: 258), its relation to the refugees may be seen as hegemonic, or more accurately a strained kind of 'hegemony at arm's length' that, given the precariousness of documented Afghan refugees' legal situation, has shaded at times into coercion and domination. But their proximity to or interchangeability with a large number of "illegal," undocumented Afghan migrants who were subjected to periodic crackdowns, roundups, and deportations, meant that the vast majority of Afghans were one arbitrary decision away from illegality and all the vulnerability it entailed. The resulting alternation of persuasion and coercion created subjectivities that are "strangely composite" (Gramsci 1985: 189), including both a strong feeling of entitlement to inclusion, and a profound sense of exclusion in Iran, akin to what Bosniak (2006) has called "alien citizenship."

Afghanistan, too, saw often turbulent changes wrought by years of war and new forms of political allegiance and contestation that emerged in the 1980s and 1990s. The once-oppressed Hazaras, for example, used the years of instability to their advantage to emerge politically stronger and more united than ever, adopting social changes that were nothing short of a "social revolution" (Mousavi 1998: 179). A history of intense cross-border ties between Iran and Afghanistan meant that political, intellectual, and social developments in the two countries affected each other profoundly. The experiences and subjectivities of Afghan refugees in Iran—and, inevitably, their poetic output—have thus been shaped both by war and politics in Afghanistan, and by the revolutionary modernity of the Islamic Republic.

Amid all this turmoil, is it possible to identify a model of personhood that holds true in Iran? Given great social diversity and the cultural transformations of recent history, it would necessarily be something of a moving target, because many groups are in the process of contesting various aspects of personhood. Restricting myself to Afghans in Iran, Mines's "mixed" model of personhood in South India (1994) resonates most closely with my experience of this group. It is true that many of them are members of large, patriarchal families that play an important role in defining and securing their interests, and whose honor and reputation all seek to uphold. Until very recently, most people did not marry outside their ethnolinguistic or kin group. Thus, the self remains to an extent relational and dependent on these collectivities. However, as in South India, individual talents, educational and career achievements, and virtues—such as generosity, hospitality, and humility—are recognized and praised, and it is possible to become a person of prominence and high esteem (*ādam-e barjasteh*) who is known by many for these qualities. Individuality has a public and private face very similar to what Mines found. On the one hand, one accrues a public reputation and biography; but on the other, people have individual ambitions, dreams, tastes, personalities, loves, and interests, and many are prepared to go to great lengths and even face conflict with their families to realize them, though reconciling the two is preferable if at all possible. Where there is a contradiction, these personal interests may remain secret, known only to a few confidantes; but in most other cases, as Mines also found, one's public and private lives are closely intertwined (1994: 13).

As in South India, for Afghans in Iran individuality is also hierarchical and contextual, in the senses that more powerful people have more scope for individual action and their individuality is more pronounced and more widely known. This is particularly important to remember in relation to gender: traditionally, a woman's individuality was a matter for the privacy of the home and her closest family and was hidden from the public eye (excepting a handful of powerful, usually aristocratic, historical female figures). Over the past century or so, however, democratic and women's movements in Iran have gained for women the right to an education, to vote, and to work and participate in public life in nearly all the same arenas as men, and many Afghans are also increasingly embracing these ideals.

Thus we see that, as LiPuma contends for Melanesia (1998), the coming of modernity, the nation-state and associated legal and economic structures to Iran has encouraged the foregrounding of ideologies that envision and celebrate more individualist conceptions of personhood. The coming of republicanism has given mainstream legitimacy to the idea of individual rights (*hoquq*), including women's rights, in postrevolutionary Iran (Osanloo 2009); and even the religious ideologues of the revolution emphasized the idea of individual subjectivity and agency, albeit mediated by God's subjectivity (Vahdat 2002: 134–181). I focus on the ensuing debates and processes as they unfold—on the cultural claims that people make about personhood—and present personhood as a dynamic system of symbolism and practice. I explore literary activity as a method for achieving individual esteem and admiration by both men and women, but also the possibility for introspective self-awareness and creative expression.

Afghans in Iran: A Brief Overview

Following the Marxist coup d'état in Kabul on 17 April 1978 and the Soviet invasion in December 1979, some 4 million Afghans fled to neighboring countries and an additional 3 million were internally displaced. Subsequent political events—resistance, civil war, and repressive theocratic government—since the 1980s led to further population movements on an unprecedented scale.[16] At its peak, the number of Afghans in the Islamic Republic of Iran was close to 3 million. Yet their presence there was and remains something of a paradox. They have been welcomed as oppressed co-believers and yet excluded as noncitizens; appreciated for their cheap, diligent labor and yet blamed for stealing jobs; lauded as fellow Persian speakers and yet mocked as primitive country cousins; allowed to settle in cities and integrate into Iranian society and yet discriminated against in most aspects of public life. As a result, they are an absent presence: living alongside Iranians, yet strangely invisible.[17]

Afghans' experiences in Iran, along with the constantly shifting bureaucratic management of them by the Iranian state, have inevitably affected their subjectivities and self-definition. Even as they gradually integrated into their host society, settling into lower-income neighborhoods, finding jobs, pursuing education, benefiting from ration cards and subsidies, moving (with certain restrictions) around the country, and to some extent being able to pursue their own cultural and political activities, they remained juridically apart, with an uncertain status. Through the media, secular and religious education and everyday life, they also came into contact with both the revolutionary Shi'ism and the modernity of the Islamic Republic, which many wholeheartedly supported and that came to play a crucial role in the self-definition of many Iran-educated Afghan youth, as we shall see.

The poets I worked with at Dorr-e Dari were all Shi'as and native speakers of Persian in one of its regional variations. Most were Hazaras, like the majority of the Afghan inhabitants of Mashhad.[18] There were also a smaller number of people originally from the city of Herat in western Afghanistan—a group who refer to themselves simply as Heratis rather than their ethnic label of Tajiks—who were either poets or involved in other aspects of cultural production. There were also the Seyyeds (Persian plural *Sādāt*), a Shi'a group claiming descent from the Prophet Mohammad, some of whom came from urban areas such as Mazar-e Sharif or Kabul, but most of whom came from rural areas in central Afghanistan where they lived alongside the Hazaras.[19] Among poets and intellectuals, the Seyyeds seemed to be overrepresented, for reasons that are discussed.

In Mashhad, the Heratis mostly inhabit lower-middle-class residential areas southwest of the Shrine of Imam Reza, such as Adl-e Khomeini and the areas around Falakeh-ye Zedd. The Heratis' main community and religious assembly venue, their *hosseiniyyeh*, is located near these areas. Meanwhile, the Hazaras and Sadat have mostly settled in the areas east of the Shrine, particularly Kuy-e Tollab (the Seminarians' Quarter). They also, together with Iranian migrants from rural areas, gradually built up the agricultural areas outside Mashhad's ring road to the east, especially Golshahr, Dahmetri-e Sakhteman, Panjtan, Al-Teymur, and Jaddeh-ye Siman, with small brick houses clustered around narrow, twisting lanes. Various services and utilities (e.g., gas supply, electricity and sewers, waste collection, paved roads, public schools, clinics, and parks) were gradually provided to these areas by the municipality in the 1990s. It should be noted that the willingness and ability of municipalities to extend such services were part of the Islamic Republic's social and economic populism, which has dramatically improved the lives of the poor (Abrahamian 2009: 14). Collectively, these areas are known as the *pā'in-e shahr,* or downtown, both geographically and symbolically opposed to the *bālā-ye shahr,* the uptown or wealthy neighborhoods at the opposite end of the ring road, stretching on either side of Vakilabad Boulevard. Golshahr is particularly well-known as an Afghan neighborhood. It has many Afghan-owned small businesses, while one of its marketplaces—known simply as the *Sholugh Bāzār* (crowded/busy market)—is filled with street hawkers of a variety of consumer goods and handcart vendors of fruit and vegetables, and is often said to be reminiscent of Kabul.

These areas are unique among Afghan communities in Iran for their levels of political, cultural, and educational activities. In the 1980s, the dominant organizations among the refugees were armed political parties, most of which were set up with Iranian assistance to fight the Soviets, but that ended up fighting a civil war against each other in the Hazarajat in the early 1980s. Although they are now less obviously partisan or political than they were in the 1980s and '90s, dozens of grassroots Afghan organizations, mostly educational initiatives, religious centers, and cultural groups, continue to be very active, creating an environment of Afghan mobilization and self-help on a much larger, more visible, and more cohesive scale than in other cities in Iran. Such activity, however, is very much in keeping with the climate of civic engagement that has been created among the Iranian inhabitants of low-income areas of large cities since the early 1990s (Hoodfar 2009, Sadeghi 2009).

A Cultural History of Mashhad

Mashhad is Iran's second-largest city, located between two mountain chains in the northeast of the country near the borders with Turkmenistan and Afghanistan. It is home to around 2.5 million people, but the actual population is approximately double that at any given moment due to the presence of pilgrims, 20 million of whom visit the city every year (Zabeth 1999: 9, 12). It is the capital of Iran's Khorasan-e Razavi province, a whittled-down part of the once vast region of Greater Khorasan, stretching across the border into Afghanistan. Approximately a hundred thousand Afghan refugees live in Mashhad.

The city grew on the site of a village called Sanabad near the ancient town of Tus. The eighth Imam of the Shi'a faith, Reza, was martyred there in 818 AD and was buried next to the Abbasid caliph Harun al-Rashid, who had died there ten years earlier. The village began to be called Mashhad al-Reza (the place of martyrdom of Reza), a domed shrine was built over the tomb by the end of the century, and its bazaars began to grow as it increasingly attracted Shi'a pilgrims. The shrine was frequently damaged in invasions and rebuilt by successive rulers, who saw the patronage of sacred architecture as an important means of asserting their own authority. In 1009, Sultan Mahmud of Ghazni built a burial chamber over the tomb and fortifications around it. The Mongol raids of 1220 largely spared the city, and survivors migrating from other devastated cities in Greater Khorasan further increased its population (Zabeth 1999: 12–14).

During the reign of the Timurid Dynasty, Mashhad became one of the major cities of Khorasan, and in 1418 the Emperor Shahrokh's wife Gowharshad endowed the shrine complex with a grand mosque, which remains largely intact. After the decline of the Timurids, the first Safavid Shah Esma'il conquered the city, and it was retaken from Uzbek invaders by the Safavid Shah Abbas in 1597. Shah Abbas, who did much to strengthen Shi'ism as the state religion of Iran, encouraged the growth of Mashhad as a place of pilgrimage (*ziyārat*), and is reported to have made the pilgrimage himself—on foot—from his capital, Isfahan, a distance of almost a thousand kilometers. Mashhad thrived under the Safavids, and several religious schools and minarets were added to the shrine complex during this period, as well as golden tiles for the dome. Nader Shah Afshar, ruler of Iran for a brief period in the mid-eighteenth century, made the city his capital and was a generous benefactor of the shrine. It was then taken by the first Qajar ruler Aqa Mohammad Khan in 1796 (Zabeth 1999: 14–15).

The Pahlavi Shahs of the twentieth century did not endear themselves to the people of Mashhad. In 1935, in response to Reza Shah's heavy-handed modernization programs, including the unveiling of women, many people took refuge (*bast*) in the shrine. The local police refused to violate the shrine's sanctity, but after four days troops arrived from Azerbaijan and broke the standoff. Dozens were killed and hundreds injured during the attack, seriously damaging relations between the monarchy and the *'olamā*, or clergy. In the mid-1970s, Mohammad Reza Shah's urban redevelopment plan for Mashhad included the razing of the dense bazaar immediately surrounding the shrine, creating instead a park and a traffic rotary that encircled the shrine. The plan was "so unpopular that bulldozers and construction equipment were often bombed or sabotaged, but it created something more attractive to 'modern' taste" (Keddie 2006: 223). A corollary of this plan was the dispersal of the bazaar merchants who formed a unified political bloc with the *'olamā* and a potential source of opposition; the plan was successful in this respect but further stoked their resentment in the period leading up to the revolution (ibid.). It also tore the shrine out of the urban fabric and isolated it from daily life, turning it into a monument for tourists and people practicing their faith in private (Zarkar, Baghoolizadeh, and Shams 2013).

The intellectual milieu of Mashhad has been simultaneously more religious than many other Iranian cities—due to the presence of the Shrine of Imam Reza, known simply as the *Haram*, and the powerful *howzeh-ye 'elmiyeh* (theological seminary, usually referred to simply as the *Howzeh*)—and highly literary.[20] Khorasan has, in cultural terms, been Iran's "most fertile intellectual territory, a place where philosophy, arts, and literature have historically flourished" and where "literature and religion became an integral way of life" (Boroujerdi 1996: 100). Mashhad was home, between 1944 and 1963, to the Kanun-e Nashr-e Haqa-yeq-e Eslami (Center for the Propagation of Islamic Truths), founded by the religiously trained high school teacher Mohammad-Taqi Shari'ati; the center nurtured a generation of lay religious intellectuals who propagated "an Islam that was militant, modern, and dynamic" and at odds with both "the government and the leftist forces it was trying to unseat but also with the city's conservative seminarians" (ibid.: 102).[21] Many of the center's alumni were later key activists of the 1979 Islamic Revolution, while the man widely acknowledged to be the chief lay ideologue of the revolution was none other than Shari'ati's son, Ali.

Mashhad's civic activity and intellectual ferment were not restricted to modernizers, however, with a number of conservative associations and charitable endowments offering free religious lecture halls, medical clinics, and Qur'anic schools (Boroujerdi 1996: 103), as well as the *Howzeh* itself. Secular, state-sponsored education, meanwhile, received a boost with the founding of an institute in 1939 that became a fully fledged university by 1963, renamed Ferdowsi University in 1973 after the great eleventh-century poet. The university's Faculty of Literature, whose most famous graduate and professor was Ali Shari'ati, became an important center for the politicized literature popular from the 1950s to the 1970s (Boroujerdi 1996: 104–105). Nearby Tus, renowned as the birthplace of Ferdowsi, became a tourist destination with the completion of a monumental mausoleum (*ārāmgāh*) for the poet in 1934. A famous Mashhad-born modernist poet, Mehdi Akhavan-Sales, was buried beside it in 1990. This combination of literature, religion, and modernist developments continued after the revolution and left a deep imprint on Afghan intellectual life in Mashhad, as we shall see.

At the time of my research, Mashhad seemed to be dominated by sacred rather than secular definitions and institutions of culture. This large city boasted no more than a handful of cinemas, and, unlike other major cities, no art galleries or officially approved pop concerts each year (Manoukian 2011 on Shiraz). It had only a few of the Western-style cafés that were becoming so popular as meeting places for young people in Tehran. In fact, it was said that the only public venue for the performance of live music in the whole city was a traditional teahouse called Hezardastan, which offered evenings of classical art music, but that program was suspended during the mourning month of Moharram in 2006 and later called off indefinitely. But access to satellite television and the internet, as well as rampant bootlegging of films and music, were giving residents access to a widening range of media and arts that were previously limited in Mashhad. Taxi drivers in Mashhad, as in other Iranian cities, almost invariably played pop music on their cassette players, from which the voices of the famous prerevolutionary female singers were heard nearly as frequently as those of men.[22] Although my Afghan friends and I did not learn about them until later, several musicians who would become well-known in Iran and abroad as stars of an underground rock music scene, including Mohsen Namjoo and Abdi Behravanfar, hailed from Mashhad or nearby towns and drew inspiration from Western genres as well as from classical poetry and the folk music of Khorasan.

At the officially sanctioned level, however, poetry seemed to be the most flourishing art form in Mashhad. Poets based there claimed that Khorasan was the poetic center of Iran, due both to long-standing tradition and recent institutional and popular efforts. Poetry evenings (singular *shab-e she'r*) or festivals (singular *jashnvāreh*) were organized in honor of the Shi'a Imams on the anniversaries of their martyrdom—or, in the case of the occulted Twelfth Imam who did not die, on his birthday. Even the conservative *Howzeh* began to hold poetic congresses in the 1990s, to which seminarians from all over the country travelled. As the Islamic Republic's cultural policy loosened in the late 1990s, particularly under the presidency of Mohammad Khatami (1997–2005; Balaghi 2009), more and more informal initiatives and a self-described current of "postmodern" poetry emerged in the city. Afghan refugees living in the city were quick to become involved in these activities, particularly since some Iranian organizations were keen to cultivate contacts with them in the ideological atmosphere of the 1980s.

Methodology

My entry into the Afghan community in Mashhad was facilitated by Hami, an Iranian nongovernmental organization (NGO) that works with refugee women and children. It was at one of their workshops in 2003 that I met Belgheis. Subsequently I was introduced to Dorr-e Dari by her brother Elyas, one of its active members. I became particularly close to the family of Belgheis and Elyas, and I lived in their house in Sakhteman during my last stay in Mashhad. For the rest of my time in Iran, though I made daily visits to the Afghan areas, I lived with Iranian families, from whom I learned much about Iranian perceptions of Afghans.

Focusing on poetry proved to be a sound choice both in practical and in ethical terms. As someone interested in an esteemed art form of which this refugee community was extremely proud, I was warmly welcomed to the institute's sessions and to countless other cultural and educational organizations among the refugees. I would probably not have encountered such openness had I been researching more overtly political issues, although the intense curiosity and hospitality almost invariably accorded to visitors from the West in Iran would probably have aided me in any case. My active participation in such meetings also included faltering attempts to translate my own poetry or—later—even compose it in Persian, which earned me some indulgence or perhaps points for effort if not achievement. However, I believe that my ability to recite a few poems from memory in English and Polish in meetings very early on added to my credibility among people who still hold such a skill in high esteem.

In the twelve months that I spent in Iran in total, I was predominantly based in Mashhad and my methodology focused above all on participant observation of the activities of Dorr-e Dari. Every Friday, Dorr-e Dari hosted a poetry reading and criticism session, followed by a similar session for short story writers. I also participated in a wide range of events Dorr-e Dari organized on an ad hoc basis: launches of books published by members, talks given on various topics or commemorating various occasions, classes in copyediting, classical music, and English; and informal gatherings based around shared meals or daytrips to the mountains (known as *ordu,* or camp), to which only Dorr-e Dari "regulars" were invited. I also attended Qand-e Parsi (the Sweetness of Persian), an annual festival of Afghan youth literature in Tehran in September 2005, and visited individual poets at their homes in Mashhad as well as Tehran, Varamin, and Qom.

Another major component of my methodology consisted of in-depth, recorded interviews in which I collected the life histories and traced the poetic careers of my informants, as well as asking them to define a kind of meta-poetics of Persian poetry: what is poetry? Who is a poet? What does poetry do in society? All in all, I recorded fifty-seven in-depth interviews with educated Afghans engaged in a variety of activities, and had dozens of other informal conversations. Thirty-two of these interlocutors were poets—exactly half of them men and half women.

I soon realized that in many ways my fieldwork was an example of "studying up," and that despite my having taken some courses in Tehran and Oxford, there was an enormous body of Persian literature that bore upon the work of my informants and of which I was more ignorant than many children. In 2007, I took an intensive course of private tutorials with two of the best-known Afghan poets, Mohammad Kazem Kazemi and Seyyed Abu Taleb Mozaffari, on the history of Persian literature, complete with close reading of classical texts. This gave me an unusual perspective on Persian literary history, which was not the narrative prevalent in the mainstream Iranian academy. Their narrative included non-Iranian writers in the Persian language, such as the seventeenth-century Indian poet Bidel, on whom Kazemi is an authority. They emphasized that today's Afghanistan is considered to be the cradle of the post-Arab invasion Persian language and literature and that the Ghaznavid dynasty (975–1187), which ruled from Ghazni in today's Afghanistan, was among the greatest patrons ever known of Persian literature. They also drew special attention to the work of poets born in today's Afghanistan, such as Mowlana (Rumi), or to scenes from famous works such as Ferdowsi's *Shāhnāmeh* (*Book of Kings*) considered to be the national epic of Iran, which take place in Afghanistan, the historic kingdoms of Zabol and Kabol (Kabul).

Other aspects of fieldwork proved to be challenging at more fundamental levels. As a human encounter that relies on familiarity and trust, fieldwork should, I believe, involve some form of reciprocal exchange. This may be particularly trying in a situation involving drastically different access to resources. For many of my friends, who were impoverished refugees without a stable legal status in their host country but nonetheless with fervent aspirations of furthering their educations, learning English, and improving their lives by moving to a Western country whether through refugee resettlement or by winning a scholarship, I was clearly also a resource and a source of information about the outside world, and this probably explained the many competing offers of hospitality that I regularly received. As Winegar reflected of her research among modern artists in Egypt (2006: 29), I sometimes felt that I was an honored guest simply by virtue of being a European and a student at Oxford University, and it seemed that this fact alone often conferred prestige on friends who introduced me as such to others. Although it made me deeply uncomfortable at first, I did not deny this aspect of our friendships because, after all, I was also there to further my own career. Instead, I tried to base our rapport on my own willingness to reciprocate my friends' help in any way that I reasonably could, acknowledging that our relationships were based on mutual assistance and common interests that frequently led to deep affection.

Such a commitment meant that I gave advice on resettlement and university applications, wrote reference letters for my research assistants and language students, brought gifts from abroad, and lent money for educational purposes. I volunteered as an English teacher in an informal Afghan secondary school in South Tehran for a few months when I was a language student in the capital, and later held English classes on the Dorr-e Dari premises for the young poets. I took my poet friends out to dinner, cooked, or ordered food for large groups, in return for the many occasions on which they offered me their hospitality. I brought gifts back for my closest friends every time I returned from abroad. I even did a *nazr*, organizing a big meal in fulfillment of a vow (I vowed to do it if successfully granted a visa), in which I, with a small army of women and girls, spent the night cooking a giant vat of *āsh*, a thick soup of herbs, pulses, and noodles, for fifty people. Reciprocity also meant agreeing to be interviewed in turn by the many technically and journalistically savvy young Afghans, whether for the radio or their publications, much to my embarrassment when the complexity of the concepts I wished to discuss far exceeded my language ability early on in my fieldwork.

Trust and intimacy were a minefield that I learned to navigate slowly, by trial and many errors. Many facts that I learned about my friends' lives concerned things that may seem innocuous in the West but were secret, perhaps even a matter of life and death for my friends: forbidden love affairs, secret rendezvous, interethnic relationships, even secret marriages. I realized that sometimes even an individual's closest family members did not know his or her secrets. Although I had such privileged information about the lives of a number of people, in the end there were many people that I spent a good deal of time with who never confided in me. I also realized to my chagrin that being too open about certain aspects of my own life could be costly, as gossip was rife and operated as a mechanism of social control. I had to train myself to live a compartmentalized life, learning what information to keep from which people, with whom I had to behave more modestly and guardedly, with whom I could relax, and in whom I myself could confide. In this way I gained a better, but still imperfect, understanding of how public and private behavior is structured in this community, a topic that I explore at length.[23]

But even as I learned to operate in this way, I faced dilemmas as an anthropologist. Sometimes the information I was party to was fascinating ethnographic material—such as the extent of clandestine premarital relationships between young people in a conservative area of an Iranian city, and the active steps young women often took to initiate such relationships. At other times, the coded metaphorical meanings of poems were apparent to me but not to others, but because they would be immediately recognizable to anyone who knew the poets in question and happened to read my work, I have not felt able to write about some of them at all—indeed, I was specifically requested not to publish the secrets of individuals by the senior members of Dorr-e Dari when I spoke to them candidly about "red lines" that they did not wish me to cross in my published work.

Although I lived continuously with an Afghan family for just two months, this stay taught me a great deal about various aspects of everyday life in the lower-income neighborhoods, comparatively socially conservative by Iranian standards, which had remained intangible until then: particularly interpersonal relations, everyday sociability, gossip, and codes of morality and proper behavior. As I walked through the back lanes of Sakhteman and Golshahr with my friends or accompanied them to other parts of the city, I learned about the tactical adjustments they made, as young, unmarried women, to present themselves in various ways in different contexts. They would spend many minutes in front of the mirror before leaving the house, applying sunscreen to keep their skins fair and almost-invisible amounts of makeup. When going to the city, wishing to be seen as educated individuals but not stand out, they would wear the standard and officially promoted dress of students and employees, the *maqna'eh* (tailored, unpatterned head covering resembling a hood) and *mānto* (overcoat, typically knee length), in dark, solid colors, but not the optional black chador (loose veil) that signals the religiously conservative or deeply pious and is a common sight in Mashhad. However, following the gentle chiding of an uncle, the older sisters agreed to wear chadors when walking around their own neighborhood, as befitted the daughters of a cleric and a Seyyed (descendant of the Prophet). One said that if she did not have a chador she liked to visibly carry a book in her hand, to mark her as a respectable student and thus avoid gossip. This careful management of external appearances, in apparent contrast to—but not ultimately dissimilar from—the personal revelation involved in lyric poetry, is discussed further in chapter 6.

As for myself, for a long time I avoided making adjustments, abiding by the state dress code in public but wearing clothing acceptable to myself—comfortable, season-appropriate and colorful—which, while not out of place in more affluent parts of Mashhad, and barely even fashionable by Tehran standards, attracted a little too much attention in the downtown areas. As a guest, I was indulged and protected from the consequences of such behavior for a long time. I was also helped by my generally reserved demeanor, particularly when I was not yet comfortable with the language, which unexpectedly fitted well with cultural ideals of proper comportment, particularly for women, as *sangin* (solemn and serious, lit. heavy) rather than *sabok* (light, foolish, uninhibited) (see Milani 1992: 2–3, Fischer 2004: 215–216). However, when I was harassed on a number of occasions by adolescent boys or taxi drivers in the lower-income neighborhoods, my feelings of anger and humiliation gave me pause about prioritizing my own standards when it came to dress.

On one occasion, I performed a dance routine (copied from a music video) to an Arabic song with Belgheis's youngest sister for a small all-female audience at their cousin's engagement party. This was, as far as I know, well-received; we prepared another dance for the much larger wedding party when I visited again the following year. But at that time, I was living with this family, and the neighbors had begun to gossip about my relationship with them. On Belgheis's advice, we canceled the dance at the last minute, because she was afraid the neighbors would "make up a thousand stories" (*hezār tā harf o hadis dar biārand*). I still attended the wedding but kept a low profile, stung by this realization and the feeling of having been judged as a potential liability to the family's honor. After that, I was much more sensitive to the unintended consequences of acting in a manner that had previously seemed innocuous to me. Ironically, the longer I spent among Afghan families, the more I learned about codes of modesty and internalized feelings of shame, and the less comfortable I felt about taking off my headscarf in front of men in the privacy of the home—even though this had been normal for me when staying with more secular Iranian families.[24] These mistakes and small moments of embarrassment—about which many young Afghan women had their own stories[25]—in fact helped me to better understand the boundaries of appropriate behavior and the tensions between self-control and self-expression.

My fieldwork continued in many ways even after I returned from Iran, thanks to new communication technologies. I stayed in touch with many of the poets on a regular basis through email and instant messaging, which had become extremely popular among them, and regularly read the blogs that many of them launched between my first and last visits. This online fieldwork benefited me because the discussions of poems in the comments section of people's blogs, being written, were easier for me to understand, return to, and analyze than the verbal discussions in poetry criticism sessions, not all of which I was able to record. However, they remained a more ephemeral and spontaneous form of expression than formal written reviews of poetry, an intermediary form between written and spoken genres (Doostdar 2004), and involved many participants, thus recalling the back-and-forth debate of poetry criticism sessions. Internet-based contact over several years also helped me to develop closer friendships with many poets, since it obviated many rules of formality in face-to-face interactions. I have since met up with my interlocutors and their families in places as diverse as Afghanistan, the United States, England, Germany, France, and Australia; and I count many of them now simply as friends.

Outline of the Book

I begin my discussion in chapter 1 with a transnational perspective on the cultural and literary history and ethnography of Afghans in Iran that rubs against the grain of dominant nationalist historical narratives. I trace the history of migration in the region, dating back to a time before the consolidation of the nation-states of Iran and Afghanistan. I contrast this with more recent Afghan migrations to Iran and the evolution of new legal statuses and terminologies (such as the loaded term *refugee,* often claimed—or denied—strategically). Aggressive attempts at introducing birth control, public health measures, and restricted mobility among this group represent a will to biopolitical management; while frequent campaigns of roundups, expulsions, and exclusion from basic services reinforce Afghans' sense of a continually precarious existence in Iran. I look at popular Iranian perceptions of Afghans and how they are bound up with discursive constructions of Iranian identity, particularly through the media and arts of the Islamic Republic. But just as Afghans became a problematic category in Iran after the rise of nationalism, I examine similarly problematic areas in literary historiography, such as the exclusion of those parts of the Persianate world that do not fall within the borders of modern Iran from so-called Persian literary history (or the suppression of biographical details that would mark certain poets out as non-Iranian). I introduce a number of Afghan writers who are quietly working to change this narrative of exclusion in nationalist and literary historiography.

Chapter 2 explores the formation of Afghan refugee *rowshanfekrān,* or intellectuals, in Iran, particularly in the context of the Islamic Republic's revolutionary Shi'i, populist ideology. I describe the effects on the refugee population of various government policies, particularly in the domains of education, religious practice, and women's rights. These effects have been contradictory, given Afghans' status as noncitizens who have both benefited and suffered from Iran's populism. I then consider how these practices have resulted in an ambivalent refugee "structure of feeling," liminal in several different ways, and a melancholy disposition that sets the tone for much refugee poetry. I look at the life and work of one master poet, Seyyed Abu Taleb Mozaffari, to illustrate the process of the gradual 'de-ideologization' of intellectuals in Iran, as well as the many contradictions that refugee intellectuals continue to face.

Chapter 3 traces the history of Afghan literary and cultural organizations in Iran from the 1980s to the present, situating them in a field of literary production, in the context of Iranian cultural policies and changing political circumstances in both Iran and Afghanistan. I then examine structural reasons for the shift between the political poetry of Mozaffari's generation and the more restricted, subjective production of second-generation refugees. In addition to providing an outlet for mistreatment and humiliation, due to its historical prestige, being a poet is also one of the few forms of cultural capital with which refugees can improve their situation in Iran. As such, many of the younger poets are now orienting their outputs to more restricted Iranian audiences at literary festivals and competitions, and prefer to publish with Iranian rather than Afghan publishers (though few achieve this distinction).

In chapter 4 I explore the social trajectories of poems among Afghan refugees. I look at the typical background and training of poets, the processes of inspiration and creation of poetry, and the means of dissemination and reception of poetry. I focus in particular on the poetry criticism sessions of the Dorr-e Dari Cultural Institute in Mashhad, showing how they combine an older pedagogical model centered on the eminent personage of the master poet with a more flexible and dialogic mode based on criticism and discussion circles. I then look at how poetry is used in social life, whether through claims to authority or ritual efficacy produced by quoting appropriate couplets in speech or writing, or by engaging in social dialogue through one's own poetry. I look at the practice of divination using the poetry of Hafez, suggesting the poetic tradition's deep and ambiguous reserves of meaning and poetic hermeneutics as a social practice.

Chapter 5 focuses on love and love poetry, a category of contemporary Afghan poetry no less important now than it has always been in the history of Persian poetry. Although love (*'eshq*) and the lover (*'āsheq*) are major tropes in Persian poetry and Iranian/Afghan culture, they used to be "extra-structural" phenomena with little role in marriage and social reproduction. Now, an increasingly well-educated and cosmopolitan young generation of Afghans is advocating for companionate marriages based on romantic love and an appreciation of individuals' unique qualities, reflecting and contributing to a major change in conceptions of personhood in this population. Poetry becomes a way to express such feelings and to attract a mate, but also functions as a "technology of the self" through which poets interfere in their own *habitus* to fashion romantic new selves.

Chapter 6 explores the shifting boundaries of public and private with respect to self-expression in lyric poetry. For many refugee poets, being a *rowshanfekr* is the most desirable form of cultural capital they can aspire to in the context of a highly discriminatory Iranian society. But they then face the problem of a tension between self-expression and self-restraint that is bound up with a major structuring dichotomy in Persian culture: that between inside and outside, the true inner self versus the guarded, potentially duplicitous external self. Throughout the history of Persian literature, the stakes of balancing the two judiciously have been particularly dramatic for women, who are popularly associated with the inner, hidden, vulnerable, and protected domain. Yet, there are other competing values and sources of symbolic capital at stake for young Afghan poets and intellectuals, and they must tactically balance the need to project themselves as enlightened (and therefore, open-minded, critical, and honest) social observers with the need to behave appropriately in the conservative neighborhoods in which they live. Aesthetic norms and claims to authenticity of expression are therefore closely bound up with a questioning of personal morality.

In the conclusion, I reflect on the light shed by Afghan refugee poetry on questions of modern personhood and subjectivity in the contemporary Islamic Republic. I argue that the tone of much refugee poetry is the result of—and in turn, helps to cultivate—a melancholic, liminal, and ambivalent disposition; a feeling of being incomplete, and neither fully Afghan nor Iranian. The shared literary heritage of Afghans and Iranians is perhaps the sole refuge that allows such split selves to feel whole again, as well as providing a modicum of prestige and material comfort. In some ways, the feeling of internal exile that many Iranian intellectuals feel in their own country is not so distant from that of the refugees, and together many choose to celebrate liminality, incompleteness, and contradiction by embracing avant-garde, self-proclaimed postmodern poetry.

Finally, an epilogue describes the subsequent fates of the book's main actors, the continued economic deterioration of Afghans' situation in Iran, and hopeful new policies under the government of President Rowhani.

1 Border Crossings and Fractured Selves
A History of the Afghan Presence in Iran

GOLSHAHR

It doesn't matter
on which side the sun came up,
on which side the moon went down.
In your alleys, sorrow.
In your alleys, beauty.
In your alleys, the sound of the handcart men
who cry out the freshness of their wares;
the footsteps that startle
    the always-mute walls out of sleep;
the eyes that turn my dark midnights
    into delirious muttering.
In your alleys
is a fluttering of wings that comes from distant mountains.

I begin from your farthest walls,
a place where even my friends don't come anymore,
with my old briefcase in my hand,
like a shepherd whose sheep have all been torn apart by wolves,
like a commander to whom no letter is posted.

Longing for the wild winds of the Pamirs,
the song of a *dobeiti* in the mountains;
longing for the fresh fish of Helmand,
and soldiers invalided by war,
I pass through your streets.
Old men on the edge of the dark shadows
relive the memories of their horses' manes
and the water channels that ran to the white poplars and apple trees.

The dusty children smile
at the marbles they play with in the dust,

not caring about all this exile,
not caring about the melody from afar,
not the green orchards of Baghchar,
nor the wheat fields of Sangtakht
whose mornings are drunkenness and wine and drink.
You are an empty water jar on my shoulder
that I must carry
to the bright waters of Bamyan and the speed and intoxication of the Jeyhun
and the forgotten wine taverns of Ghazni
as if you were a bullet
shot toward my unforgotten wounds.

I bring your longings home with me.
I share them with Ali,
I share them with Masih,
like an apple that I got from the handcart men
or herbs from the women in the fields.
You are an avalanche that suddenly overcomes me.

    Hossein Heidarbeigi

This poem vividly describes the streets and lanes of Golshahr, an Afghan-dominated neighborhood on the outskirts of Mashhad, with their noisy handcart vendors, old men watching the world go by from the shadows, children playing marbles, and the nearby agricultural fields in which farmers cultivate herbs (see fig. 1.1). But it also describes something that Golshahr's older inhabitants still carry in their memories: nostalgia for rural, mountainous regions of Afghanistan with fields and orchards, horses and clear water, and inescapable reminders of war. The expansive geographical scope of that homeland, from the Jeyhun (Amu Darya or Oxus) River in the north to Helmand in the south, clearly evokes Afghanistan as a whole, but there is a special emphasis on Baghchar and Sangtakht, small villages in the central Hazarajat region from which the poet himself hails. In Golshahr, the figures in the poem are all exiles, whether former shepherds or commanders of the anti-Soviet jihad. Memories of another place preoccupy both the old men sitting in the shade and the poet himself, and are apt to arrive suddenly like an avalanche, an alighting bird, a melody from afar, or footsteps that awaken one at night. In this way, the landscape of Golshahr is intertwined with another place, a place without which its own existence is incomplete (Olszewska 2013b). The poem was written in 2007 by Hossein Heidarbeigi, a Hazara student of the Mashhad *Howzeh*, at the request of his friend and fellow poet Seyyed Zia' Qasemi, to accompany a film Qasemi was making about Golshahr for his filmmaking degree in Tehran. It is a testament to the transnational lives of many of Golshahr's residents.

Figure 1.1. A Hazara handcart vegetable vendor, a common sight on the streets of Golshahr.

This chapter situates those lives in a broader historical and geographical context: one that recognizes the necessity of a regional approach to the study of the politics, economy, culture, and certainly the literature, of this population. Recent Afghan migration is situated within a longer history of frequent population movements in the region, and the political division of Iran and Afghanistan into separate states is a relatively new development. More recently, continued Iranian cultural and political influence in Afghanistan has had dramatic consequences, particularly during the Hazara civil war of the 1980s, in which refugee communities supported competing armed groups that were fighting amongst themselves rather than against the Soviet army in Afghanistan. Given this intertwined history, the degree of social and legal discrimination Afghans face in Iran is particularly ironic. I examine representations of Afghans in Iranian discourse and the extent to which Afghan refugees internalize or reject such visions.

Running through these themes is a paradox emblematic of the transformations underway in this region. On the one hand, it continues to be the reality that Afghans are transnationally mobile, adaptable, and flexible enough to exploit an existence within their own weak state or on the margins of other states (Monsutti 2010). On the other, their very mobility causes them to confront and be persuaded by a discourse that negates the idea of transnational mobility: a "national order of things" that fixes people as rooted in certain places and excludes them from citizenship in others, casting refugees as "matter out of place" (Malkki 1995b). The power of Iranian nationalism has resulted in just such a situation: feeling excluded in Iran, Afghans long to participate as full citizens in their own homeland. While their forefathers may have identified primarily with their home cities or villages, or indeed simply with their patrilineal descent groups, Heidarbeigi's poem shows that for many of those in Iran, at least, the extent of their imagined community now stretches from the Amu Darya to Helmand. The conflicting emotions and frustrated senses of belonging that result from this situation are frequently played out in refugee poetry, and form the backdrop to most of the poetic output explored in this book.

Afghan Mobility in Historical Perspective

The majority of the Afghan intellectuals with whom I worked were Shi'a and Persian-speaking (ethnic Hazaras, Hazara Seyyeds, and Tajiks from the city of Herat). All of these groups had a long-standing historical connection with the territory that is now Iran. Indeed, until the mid-eighteenth century, much of today's Afghanistan formed part of the Greater Khorasan region of the Iranian empires, and the city of Herat was known as the Pearl of Khorasan, but Iranian influence and the intermingling of peoples continued long after the territories broke away. Iran had irredentist claims on Herat and other parts of Afghanistan up to the mid-nineteenth century, when it unsuccessfully fought several battles with the British, who were seeking to expand into the west of the country (Kashani-Sabet

1999: 30–33). As recently as the 1970s, Herat was seen by other citizens of Afghanistan as a place apart, almost an extension of Iran (Doubleday 1988: 15). Iran's influence—cultural, political, religious, economic, and infrastructural—continues in Afghanistan to this day, particularly in the west and among Afghan Shi'as.

But even when the Afghan state's borders began to be demarcated in the late nineteenth century, its people continued to embrace mobility throughout the region as a cultural, political, and economic strategy.[1] Such migrations were induced by economic or political necessity—though the distinction between these causes is often blurred—and were often given a religious resonance. Forced resettlement was frequently employed as a tool of political subjugation by rulers, but flight across borders was just as frequently used as a gesture of political defiance and autonomy, often cast in terms of the preservation of the true religion, Islam.

Both pastoral nomadism and migration for trade or employment have supplemented agriculture, whose resources, such as land or water, are often fiercely contested, and whose fruits are unpredictable in Afghanistan's mountainous and drought-prone terrain. Both types of movement took on a seasonal pattern, and transhumant nomads and labor migrants were not deterred by international borders (Pedersen 1990). Labor migration was and continues to be connected to seasonal agricultural cycles: thus, for example, farmers from the southern Hazarajat region would find work in the coal mines of Pakistani Baluchistan after the almond harvest in September, returning home to work in their fields in the spring. During the Soviet invasion, meanwhile, Hazara *mojāhedin* (resistance fighters) would work in the coal mines in winter but spend the summer fighting with one of the resistance groups. Thus, spring and autumn have typically been times of transition and intensified mobility (Monsutti 2005b: 101, 149).

The case of the Hazaras illustrates both the difficulty in distinguishing between economic and political motives for migration, and the way it has become embedded in cultural values and practices. The situation in the Hazarajat, one of the poorest regions of Afghanistan, has been compounded by the destruction of war in recent times and by active discrimination in infrastructure provision and development by successive Kabul governments: "War and poverty have been mutually reinforcing factors propelling hundreds of thousands of Hazaras abroad" (Monsutti 2005b: 123). Since the 1960s, Hazaras have been regularly migrating to Iran and to the Gulf states to engage in a variety of low-wage occupations. Indeed, migration may be seen as a rite of passage to full adulthood for young Hazara men, a means of securing independence and acquiring the assets necessary to marry and support a family (Monsutti 2005a). Established transnational migration channels exist between Afghanistan and Iran and cross-border movements are multidirectional and recurrent (Stigter 2005a, 2005b). A complex system of migration, trade, and remittances between Afghanistan, Iran, and Pakistan is sustained through trust based on kinship ties among Hazara men (Monsutti 2004).

Expressly political motives have also been responsible for migrations both into and out of Afghanistan in recent centuries. The Durrani Amirs used forced relocations to quell opposition to their state-building campaigns, particularly Abdur Rahman at the end of the nineteenth century, while whole populations chose to evade the Amirs' control by crossing the borders to British India or Qajar Iran. The Kabul government's conquest of the mountainous Hazarajat in 1891–1893 was particularly brutal, and after this campaign successive waves of Hazara migrants departed for Quetta in Baluchistan (which had been incorporated into the British Raj in 1887) or Khorasan province in Iran.[2] In the south and east, meanwhile, the Pashtun tribes have found themselves straddling the Durand Line, demarcating the border between Afghanistan and Pakistan, and have used this situation to their political and economic advantage while retaining cultural and political autonomy from both states (Edwards 1986a: 316).

In all these regions, then, borders were porous and were exploited by the local populations for their own interests. This constant and often strategic movement, which has remained bidirectional even in times of conflict, leads Monsutti to argue that migration and *raft o āmad* (coming and going) is for many citizens of Afghanistan a way of life. Thus, he argues, "we are a long way from the figure of the refugee compelled to leave his or her homeland in the face of a towering threat, with the vague hope of one day being able to return" (2005b: 146). When one adopts a transnational, actor-centered analytical perspective, the image presented by NGOs and the media of the helpless, vulnerable refugee, stripped bare of politics and history, is certainly misleading (Monsutti 2010, Malkki 1996).

Within this complex history of regional migration, inhabitants of Afghanistan were visiting Iran as migrant workers, pilgrims, or merchants long before the period of conflict that began in 1978. Afghan Shi'as have been making pilgrimages for hundreds of years to the pilgrimage sites of Iran or via Iran to the holy cities of Najaf and Karbala in Iraq (Mousavi 1998: 148). The Hazaras who had settled and integrated into Iranian society in the nineteenth and early twentieth centuries eventually became Iranian citizens and came to be classified as an ethnic group known as Khāvari or Barbari. Large numbers of Afghan citizens had sought employment in Iran from the 1960s onward, particularly during the terrible famine that struck the northwest of the country in 1971–1972, so several hundred thousand were already living in Iran as migrant workers by 1978 (Centlivres and Centlivres-Demont 2000: 151).

Afghan Refugees in Iran:
From Oppressed Co-Believers to Deportable Aliens

Following the coup of 1978 and the Soviet invasion of December 1979, the number of Afghans in Iran climbed steadily throughout the 1980s until it peaked in 1991 at 3 million people, according to Iranian government estimates (UNHCR 2001).[3] At the time of my research, the number of registered refugees in Iran was just over 900,000 people, with a further 1 million estimated to be in the country illegally and without documentation (IRIN 2008). In the 1980s, Ayatollah Khomeini had welcomed Afghans to Iran for ideological reasons: the Islamic Republic embraced its co-believers who were suffering at the hands of the atheist Soviets, and it also wished to export its own revolution to Afghanistan. In all probability, Afghans were also needed for their labor in a country whose young men were being sent to the front to fight Iraqi forces and dying in large numbers, and the Iranian economy benefited from their labor during the 1980s and the period of postwar reconstruction that followed. But this warm welcome soon wore thin, and in the 1990s the focus shifted to repatriation and prevention of new arrivals, now classed as illegal.

In the 1980s, Afghans were accepted as refugees prima facie and issued residence permits in Iran, granting them a number of rights that were very generous given the large numbers the country was hosting—one of the largest refugee populations in the world. Holders of these permits were granted indefinite permission to stay in Iran and were entitled to subsidized health care, food, and fuel, and to free primary and secondary education and adult literacy training. The vast majority—over 90 percent—were able to settle freely on the outskirts of cities rather than in refugee camps, and although they were not legally allowed to own property, in cities such as Mashhad many enjoyed de facto ownership of their homes through customary contracts of sale or lease (*rahn*) (Abbasi-Shavazi et al. 2005: 19). The small percentage of Afghans living in camps is significant, for it has meant that the vast majority have established social ties with their Iranian neighbors and come into contact with local Iranian institutions.

The label *refugee* is politicized, used by both displaced people and host governments in ways that suit their own ends. The documents issued to Afghans arriving in the 1980s bore the label of *mohājerin,* a term of Arabic origin for emigrants, invoking the *hijrah* or flight of the Prophet Mohammad from Mecca to Medina in 622 A D.[4] The word conveys the Islamic duty of hosting those choosing to leave their homes due to religious oppression. After Khomeini's death in 1989 and the fall of the Communist government in Afghanistan in 1992, Iran's bureaucracy quietly redesignated Afghans as *āvāregān,* a word that also means forced migrants but without the religious overtones. Later still, documents issued to them used the terms *atbā'-e khāreji* or *atbā'-e bigāneh,* simply "foreign nationals," deftly absolving the state of any humanitarian obligations toward them.[5] Although Iran is a party to international refugee law and has its own domestic laws relating to refugees, even the early documents issued to Afghans conveyed only the legal status of foreign nationals with residence permits based on a law dating back to 1931 (Ebadi 2008: 28).[6] The United Nations High Commissioner for Refugees (UNHCR), which has run a small and underfunded operation in Iran from 1983, regularly refers to the Afghans in Iran as refugees but, as in many countries, has had difficulty persuading the Iranian government to override its domestic concerns and maintain internationally mandated standards of refugee recognition and rights provision.[7] Iranian policy toward them has thus been subject to vagaries and reversals depending on prevailing domestic and foreign policy interests, becoming more restrictive over time, such that the majority of Afghans have lived for decades in conditions of poverty and precariousness (Ruiz 1992: 3, ICRI 1998).

The reasons for Afghan migration to Iran from 1978 onward were complex and combined political, religious, economic, and other motives.[8] After the events of 1978 and 1979, both Sunni and Shi'a clergy in Afghanistan declared a jihad, or struggle against religious oppression, against Soviet troops and encouraged emigration, or *hijrah*, in response to an invasion by a power with colonialist intentions and an atheist ideology. Young men left to avoid conscription into the army, then seen as a certain death sentence. Clerical families left to avoid persecution for their religious activities; others, to avoid reprisals for their political opposition (Abbasi-Shavazi et al. 2005: 14–15).[9] Still others fled relentless bombardment by Soviet forces and the loss of their livelihoods. Many were happy to be going to Iran, a country that had just declared itself an Islamic Republic, and sought to protect the honor of their wives and daughters (*nāmus*) from violation by soldiers (Abbasi-Shavazi et al. 2005: 14–15). One ethnographic study goes further, claiming that people migrated in protest at the interference with traditional Afghan society's gendered moral order that the Communist government aggressively pursued in 1978, for example through instituting a new family law and compulsory education for girls (Hoodfar 2004).

In the early 1990s, particularly after the fall of the Communist government of Najibullah in Afghanistan in 1992 and changing domestic economic and social concerns such as unemployment in Iran, refugee policy began to emphasize repatriation and prevention of illegal entry. Refugees' identity cards began to be confiscated by law enforcement authorities and replaced with temporary permits of limited validity (Foyouzat 1996). Various other entitlements, such as the right to free education for children, have been gradually curtailed over the ensuing years. Afghans, particularly men and those without documents, began to live in fear of periodic roundups and deportation operations (*Afghāni begir*—Get the Afghans, as they are colloquially known among Afghans), living in a state of vulnerability produced by their deportability (see IRIN 2005).

Even so, the civil war in Afghanistan (1992–1996) and the subsequent conquest of most of the country by Taliban forces, as well as the U.S.-led bombing campaign at the end of 2001, generated new flows of Afghan refugees to Iran. New registration exercises (*amāyesh*), largely intended to facilitate repatriation and refugee management by standardizing refugee statuses, were carried out by the Ministry of the Interior's Bureau for Aliens and Foreign Immigrants' Affairs

(BAFIA) in 2001 and again in June 2003, but the cards issued in the latter exercise had to be renewed every three months for individuals and every six months for families (UNHCR 2004b). Afghanistan's fragile economy and poor security situation still compel many Afghan men to seek employment in Iran, even if it involves entering the country illegally or overstaying visas.

Following the U.S.-led occupation of Afghanistan in 2001, most of the Iranian government's and UNHCR's joint efforts continued to focus on repatriation. Under a series of formal repatriation agreements between Iran, Afghanistan, and the UNHCR from 2002 onward, a million Afghans had returned with UNHCR assistance by September 2004 (IRIN 2004), in addition to almost 568,000 "spontaneous returnees" who returned on their own (UNHCR 2004b).[10] The carrot-and-stick tactics of UNHCR and the Iranian government, along with moderate improvements in security in Afghanistan, compelled many Afghans to return, but repatriation rates declined sharply after 2006 (IRIN 2007a). Most reports on the subject of refugees' attitudes to repatriation noted that, fearing continued fighting or ethnic tensions (in the case of Shi'a Hazaras, who had been singled out for attack by the Taliban), a shattered economy and lack of security, work, education, and medical facilities, most were extremely ambivalent about returning (Ruiz 1992, Turton and Marsden 2002, Abbasi-Shavazi et al. 2005, IRIN 2007a), particularly those who had been in Iran for a long time and had become well-integrated into Iranian life. As the legal situation of refugees in Iran deteriorated, the UNHCR began submitting requests for resettlement to third countries in 1999.[11] A UNHCR official privately told me that the organization had little clout in improving refugees' lives as long as the Iranian government had this simple trump card in any negotiations: "There are simply too many of them." In such a situation, repatriation and resettlement to third countries seemed to be the only durable solutions available—a fact confirmed by the emphasis of the most recent UNHCR policy documents on Afghans in Iran (UNHCR 2013).

Yet there is evidence that "illegality" is a convenient category that has been actively produced by the state for its own purposes, just as it has in many other countries around the world, where continually evolving immigration lawmaking and enforcement have subjected ever greater numbers of migrants to arrest, detention, and deportation (De Genova and Peutz 2010: 1). The line between "legal" and "illegal" immigrants is often fragile, as evidenced by a massive deportation campaign launched in 2007 by Iran's hard-line Interior Minister Mostafa Pur-Mohammadi. In theory, it targeted undocumented, so-called illegal immigrants, but in practice many vulnerable people—including unaccompanied women and children, or simply those who were not carrying their documents when stopped by the police—were also detained and deported. By June 2008, approximately 490,000 had been arrested, kept in deportation camps for days, and then expelled from the country. In the process, families were reportedly separated, people were beaten, abused, or told to pack their belongings on an hour's notice, and in some cases women and unaccompanied children were deported without their families. On the Afghan side of the border many had nowhere to go and lived in tent camps set up by international organizations (Hashemi 2011). The campaign continued through the region's worst winter in decades; many died of cold. The resulting humanitarian crisis in Afghanistan led to the sacking of two ministers, yet the whole episode was generally unnoticed in the wider world (IRIN 2007b, 2007c, 2007d, 2007e, 2008).

Even for documented Afghans, "legality" is a difficult status to maintain or prove and is itself not a guarantor of many freedoms. Residence permits are usually valid for a short time, and the process of extending them is often onerous and expensive, requiring gathering a good deal of paperwork, facing long queues, and paying taxes and other fees. Mobility restrictions are placed on documented Afghans, who must apply for a travel permit (*nāmeh-ye taraddod*) when going to another province on even a brief trip; they may be detained if unable to produce one even if they are legally resident in the country. Afghan poets from Mashhad traveling to Tehran for a literature festival, for example, always had to obtain such a permit, which could take weeks to process. In recent years, many cities and provinces have also been declared "Afghan-free zones" where even Afghans with valid documents have been expelled. For example, all Afghans, whether legal or illegal, had been banned from ten coastal towns in Mazandaran in 2008; but in 2012 they were banned from the entire province, their identity cards and residence permits declared invalid, and any form of assistance to them decreed a crime (A. Ahmadi 2012). As the province attracts large numbers of domestic tourists, including upper-class Iranians who own seaside villas on the Caspian coast, "public safety" was given as a justification for this eviction. Over the years, the provinces of Gilan, Lorestan, Hamedan, and Kermanshah have also either banned or restricted Afghan residents (Karami and Mortazavi 2012).

This situation cannot be separated from the paradoxical position Afghans occupy on the Iranian labor market. Afghans form an essential part of the labor force in Iran, well-known for their work in low-waged, low-status, or dangerous jobs, with a reputation for efficiency and reliability.[12] They have not been able to work legally without valid residence permits since 1993, and both employers and employees found to be violating this rule are heavily fined. During periods of increased government vigilance, people are stopped in the streets and asked to show their identification cards, failing which they are arrested and deported. At such times, men without documentation must stay at home, and their households rely on the income raised by women and children, often in ill-paying jobs (ICRI 1998: 1). Yet, despite such restrictions, in practice undocumented Afghans still have access to jobs most of the time, and some sectors are heavily dependent on their labor. The Iranian chief of police, Brigadier-General Esmail Ahmadi-

Moqaddam, for example, in 2013 opposed the deportation of Afghans, saying: "A few years ago, when we ejected Afghans from the country, we saw that a large number of dairy farms and brickworks ground to a halt. Iranians are looking for work but they won't do these jobs and won't climb a tree to pick fruit. Our youth, being educated, want a desk and a mobile phone to do business deals" (BBC Farsi 1392/2013). Afghans also continue to fill an important niche in Iran's flourishing informal economy and many have even found opportunities for upward mobility over time (Abbasi-Shavazi et al. 2005: 1). Monsutti has described the situation of alternating toleration and harassment or expulsions as a game of cat and mouse, intended to allow the Iranian economy to benefit as much as possible from Afghans' labor in low-wage, poorly regarded occupations, without letting them feel too comfortable in the country and thus settling there permanently (2005b: 129). But in a politically volatile context of high unemployment among Iranians themselves, the informal basis of most Afghans' employment keeps their wages low and makes them ultimately disposable.

A growing body of work by anthropologists demonstrates that this problem is by no means unique to Iran. Indeed, the worldwide pervasiveness of such "deportation regimes" reveals that they are considered indispensable tools of statecraft that affirm state sovereignty through the defense of international borders (De Genova and Peutz 2010, De Genova 2010). Reflecting on the situation of Mexican migrants in the United States, De Genova has argued that the "production of illegality" serves paradoxically as a tool for *incorporating* a disempowered workforce into the state: it is a frequently radicalized "apparatus for sustaining . . . migrants' vulnerability and tractability" (De Genova 2004: 161). Illegality is a convenient political tool: one day immigrants can do dirty work for low wages while being blamed for high unemployment and crime; the next, frustrated constituencies can be mollified with swift deportation actions. Living in fear of deportation produces palpable effects on immigrant subjectivity—a sense of having a "fractured self," torn between a feeling of belonging to the community and being an excluded other (Coutin 2011: 5; see also De Genova 2002).

The exclusion of Afghans in Iran, then, has a criminalized and a racialized dimension, but it is also medicalized. Refugees' bodies, and those of women in particular, have been a site of biopolitical intervention by Iranian public health officials. Tober writes that when she questioned Iranian health professionals on Iran's biggest health problem, many of them replied, without a hint of irony, that it was "Too many Afghanis!" (2007: 265), due to their higher rates of infectious diseases, including tuberculosis and cholera. Their high fertility rates were seen to strain the public health care system. Tober describes the work of public health programs in the Isfahan region aiming to inculcate "health-promoting behavior," which included "basic sanitation, including the importance of boiling of water, the importance of separating animal and human living spaces, and other ways to prevent dysentery and eye diseases in children. They also promoted family planning as part of a package aimed at improving overall family health" (ibid: 272). One doctor's presentation, evidently patronizing in tone, stressed the importance of basic hygiene and tidiness, and urged Afghans not to think of themselves as inferior to Iranians. Tober's observations of an urban clinic revealed that although many Afghan women were grateful for having the option of birth control, they were suspicious of the motives of what they saw as a much more aggressive and coercive promotion of contraception for refugees as compared to Iranian women: "All Afghan women were told that they 'must' use some form of family planning, and the choices that were offered were methods that the nurse, rather than the patient, had control over" (2007: 276).[13]

But these interventions are not merely top-down impositions. They are also a good example of what Rejali calls the "tutelary" techniques of exercising power that emerged in twentieth-century Iran, which rely on guidance, dialogue, and a collaborative shaping of self-understanding to render people governable (1994: 84). Educated Afghans in particular have readily accepted modern teachings on hygiene and family planning, and the degree to which Afghans in Iran have internalized a medicalized fear of Afghanistan itself is reflected in the number of women who request permanent sterilization in the event of repatriation or deportation to Afghanistan, rather than risking death in childbirth (Tober 2007: 276–277).

Taken together, the multiple levels of exclusion experienced by all Afghans in Iran, whether documented or "illegal," have profound "spiritual and psychological consequences" (*ta'sirāt-e ruhi o ravāni*), in the words that I frequently heard. I met many people who were depressed, fearful, and unable to make plans for the future because of the uncertainty of their situations. I was told about a notorious Afghan collaborator, whose job was to identify his compatriots on the street in Iranian police roundups. He apparently never failed to be accurate, and when asked for his secret, he said it was simply that Afghans always walked in a particular way: with hunched shoulders and with their heads down.[14] Stories of families separated by roundups and deportations would be circulated in hushed tones. One of these told of an Afghan man who visited his wife in hospital, leaving two young children locked at home to keep them safe. However, he was arrested by Iranian authorities and summarily deported. By the time he was able to make his way illegally back into Iran, the neighbors had found the bodies of his children, who had starved to death in the house. Other apocryphal stories tell of atrocities at several infamous detention or deportation camps, including Askar Abad near Varamin, Tall-e Siah near Zahedan, and Sefid Sang near Mashhad. The most tragic of these occurred in 1998 at Sefid Sang, when 630 detained Afghan men and women protesting poor conditions in the camp were allegedly massacred by the guards and by machine gun fire from helicopters (Fisk 2008).[15]

These days, Afghan bloggers and filmmakers are beginning to document such tragedies (Sarem 1390/2012, Fisk 2008). Only a few years earlier, however, they only found their way into refugee poetry as cryptic references. Elyas Alavi, for example—one of a large number of young poets who make despair and despondency their poetic hallmarks—alludes to some of the phantom horrors that stalk the Afghan-Iranian borderlands, such as the kidnapping or selling of Afghan girls in the border region near Zabol, and the Tall-e Siah detention camp:

> Pā-hā-yat bu-ye min midahad
> dahān-at bu-ye gorosnegi
> shāneh-hā-yat āvār āvār
> āvāregi
> 'Araq-at rā pāk kon
> Mardān-e Zāboli barā-ye dokhtar-at talā mikharand
> Pesar-at dar chāh-hā-ye Tall-e Siāh sirāb ast
> tā abad.

> Your legs smell of landmines,
> your mouth of hunger,
> your shoulders of homeless homeless
> homelessness.
> Wipe away your sweat;
> the men of Zabol are buying gold to take away your daughter.
> In the well-shafts of Tall-e Siah your son's thirst has been quenched
> for all eternity.

> (Fragment of "Āvāz-e gharib" ["A Desolate Voice"]; original in Alavi 1386/2008: 24–25)

When the poem appeared in the book he published with an Iranian press, Elyas anticipated that Iranian readers were unlikely to recognize the significance of the name Tall-e Siah (Black Hill), despite its black reputation among Afghans, as he added a footnote in which he explained, perhaps no less obliquely, that this was "a camp for refugees."

A friend of Elyas's, Gholamreza Ebrahimi, composed a colloquial *dobeiti* (folk quatrain) more recently in praise of the identity card at a time of mass arrests and deportations:

> To rā miguyam ey nur-e do dideh
> ke mardom harche dideh az to dideh
> Mabādā lahzeh'i dur az to bāsham
> vagarna khāneh-am Sang-e Sefid-e!

> I speak of you, O light of my two eyes!
> For whatever people have experienced [good or bad], it's thanks to you.
> May I not be parted from you for a second,
> otherwise my home will be Sefid Sang!

> (Gholamreza Ebrahimi, "Kart-e Shenāsā'i" ["Identity Card"], unpublished poem shared by the author)

The Figure of "the Afghan" in Iranian Discourse

Afghan refugees continue to cite the pan-Islamic slogan of Ayatollah Khomeini that "Islam has no borders" in order to assert the legitimacy of their presence in Iran (Adelkhah and Olszewska 2007: 151), but the slogan rings increasingly hollow. For Afghans not only face a variety of legal exclusions in Iran, they also encounter prejudice and discrimination from ordinary Iranians—what Hoodfar has called "cultural chauvinism" (2010). During my stint as a volunteer English teacher in an informal Afghan school in South Tehran, I once witnessed young Iranian schoolchildren passing by on the street and shouting through the small window into our bare basement classroom: *"Afghāni kesāfat!"* (filthy Afghans). My pupils barely reacted, telling me that this was a regular occurrence for them (see Kamal 2010). I would hear Iranian mothers telling their children that, if they did not behave, the "Afghāni" would take them away. Afghans seem also to be used as a convenient scapegoat for all manner of ills by populist politicians, including unemployment, the spread of infectious diseases, drug trafficking, and serious crimes such as kidnapping, rape, and murder.[16] Afghanistan and Afghans play an important role in the Iranian imagination, central to reflections about identity and citizenship (Adelkhah and Olszewska 2007). Nonetheless, the Afghan remains a spectral figure, one used to frighten children in the same way as the Taliban were used to instill fear in adults. What accounts for this situation?

Despite its relatively recent loss of Herat and parts of western Afghanistan in the mid-nineteenth century (Kashani-Sabet 1999: 30–33), Iran is now seen as a "territorially satisfied" state with no irredentist claims (Farhi 2005: 10). Although it retains extensive economic, political, and security interests in its neighbor, it appears that the forces of Iranian nationalism and the rationalizing order of the nation-state have won the contest with pan-Islamism and other cross-border ties. Indeed, some have argued that the ideal of pan-Islamism never existed beyond the level of official rhetoric even in the early days of the Revolution (Buchta 2002, Farhi 2005). That Afghans should occupy an inferior position is also due to the fact that they serve as a means of self-definition for Iranians: an Other from whom they may distance themselves in order to raise their own status. Indeed, given their shared linguistic, cultural and religious heritage, Iranians' disdain seems to be a classic case of Freud's narcissism of small differences.

In the past few decades, the phenomenon of the rise and evolution of Iranian nationalism has been sensitively studied in a number of historical works (Kashani-Sabet 1999, 2002; Boroujerdi 1996; Tavakoli-Targhi 2001). Beginning around the mid-nineteenth century, a variety of forces came together to promote a growing discourse and sentiment of nationalism in the empire ruled by the Qajar dynasty, including a failure to resist encroachments by foreign powers (Kashani-Sabet 2002: 164–165). Kashani-Sabet has argued that while nationalism has subsequently been a powerful influence, "a prevailing philosophy in the culture and politics of Iran," its content has shifted over time (164). However, defining the "authentic Iranian Self" has always involved implicit or explicit comparisons to, or a distancing from, a number of other cultural reference points that do not always work as simple binary pairs. Thus, writes Tavakoli-Targhi, "identification with European culture provided an important component for the long process of historical dissociation from the Arab-Islamic culture that occurred in the nineteenth century" (2001: 103). This was partly done by drawing on racialist ideas of European Orientalists who propagated the idea of the Aryan—as distinct from the Semitic—race and included Iranians in it (Kashani-Sabet 2002: 165–166).

In the twentieth century, the process of asserting a so-called authentic, native Iranian identity by Iranian intellectuals in the face of Western cultural, political, and economic domination was a kind of "Orientalism in reverse" (Boroujerdi 1996: 10–14). That is, it revalued the aspects of Iranian culture portrayed as retrogressive by Western Orientalists, such as mysticism and pre-Islamic statecraft and philosophy, but it did not abolish the idea of "a fundamental ontological difference separating the natures, peoples, and cultures of the Orient and the Occident" (12). In conversations with Iranians (and Afghans), I was often surprised and frustrated by their earnest talk of the differences between "us Orientals" (*mā sharqi-hā*) and "you Occidentals" (*shomā gharbi-hā*); the exact boundaries of the regions or peoples classified by these terms were slippery. The "West," when people were in a mood to generalize, was still spoken of as the abode of rationality (*'aql*) and order (*nazm*), whereas the East was the home of *ehsās* (emotion), of mysticism, spirituality, and religious feeling, and of poetry.[17]

Afghans, too, used such rhetoric. When I asked why poetry had played such an important historical role in Afghanistan, the well-known poet and literary critic, Seyyed Abu Taleb Mozaffari, replied: "One of the reasons is that usually people from the east, Orientals, are more emotional. That is, they give more weight to the spiritual, the emotional, than to rationality. And Afghanistan is part of Oriental society." This statement seemed to be complicated by his next words: "In the past, most religious, scientific, and cultural knowledge was in the form of poetry. When [people] learned philosophy or mysticism, they would become familiar with poetry—even the sciences of logic and mathematics, they would learn through poetry." This deep-rooted dichotomy affected my personal interactions, too, as a representative of "the West." A close friend even offered this analysis of my behavior: "When you are in Iran or Afghanistan, you are more emotional; but when you go back to the West, you become more rational and logical."

Despite the fact that the 1979 revolution could be considered an effective political victory for anti-Western nativism (although Boroujerdi qualifies this as a "tortured triumph"), the older admiration for and sense of inadequacy vis-à-vis the West persist as an uncomfortable and guilty indulgence of many Iranians. I heard them expressed with surprising regularity, and they are a recurring theme in much scholarship on prerevolutionary and postrevolutionary Iran. Jahanbegloo writes that "This complex sentiment of inferiority mixed with that of the loss of the Iranian self through the global domination of the West has been the foundation for theoretical elaborations on the two concepts of tradition and modernity among four generations of Iranian intellectuals"; how to resolve this remains an "agonizing question" (2004: xii). There are many indications that this sentiment has persisted, despite the Islamic Republic's vigorous anti-Western propaganda and its nonaligned slogan of "Neither East nor West." Pointing out an irony in Iranian state primary school textbooks' presentation of role models, Mehran notes that all of the contemporary scientists and inventors introduced in them are Euro-American, while all the contemporary Iranian role models are religious leaders. She concludes that a deep-rooted sense of inferiority vis-à-vis the West persists in Iran (Mehran 2002: 246).

For all their stated Third Worldist sympathies, postrevolutionary Iranian intellectuals have engaged little with de-essentializing or hybridizing developments in postcolonial theory or literature produced by expatriates from former European colonies in South Asia, Africa, or the Middle East.[18] They have so long been oriented toward the West as their principal interlocutor, whether loved or hated, that they have failed to notice that the essential West as they perceive it no longer has much ideological currency, overtaken by more globalizing forces, both economic and cultural, as Dabashi (2004) argues rather stridently in an article on the "blindness" of the philosopher Abdolkarim Sorush. Perhaps more dangerous is the lack of knowledge about their immediate neighbors and their own history beyond stereotypes and limiting grand narratives.

In a classic case of projections of the Other really being a story about the Self's preoccupations, their ideas about Afghans enable Iranians to reflect on the distances they have already traveled. In fact, rather than being a simple dyad, there exists a triad of points of reference through which the self is reflected upon, which might be termed West, East, and Farther East.[19] Seeing Afghanistan, the Farther East, as *more* "backward" (*aqab-māndeh*, lit. remaining-behind) than Iran, is perhaps helpful for Iranians to mark off the "progress" (*pishraft*, lit. going-forward) they have already made in becoming more modernized, and an admonition not to slip backward: the temporal and spatial metaphors implied by these common terms are revealing. Many Iranians seemed to imagine Afghanistan as a barren wasteland. When, after a trip to Afghanistan in 2007, I showed photographs of splendid fifteenth-century Timurid architecture in Herat to some Iranian friends in Tehran, one young university-educated woman exclaimed in genuine surprise, "Did Iranians go there to build those mosques for them?" She was also surprised by neatly tended flowerbeds in a photo of a pleasure spot outside Kabul. Her sister paused thoughtfully, reflecting on how little they knew about Afghanistan. Mindful of most Iranians' indignation at being misrepresented in the West, she remarked, "That's probably what people in the West say about us when you show them pictures of Iran!"

Afghanistan is thus cast as the lurking, darker side of the Self, particularly so during the time of Taliban rule, which was seen as the victory of obscurantist religious fanaticism that was uncomfortably familiar.[20] According to Tohidi, "many Iranian Muslim reformers have identified conservative Islamists of Iran with the Afghan Taliban" (2002: 219). She cites one leading Iranian feminist who, polemicizing against a proposed law for sex segregation of hospitals, wrote in a 1998 editorial, "The path you have taken ends in Afghanistan!" (219). Another example is the response of Samira Makhmalbaf, filmmaker and precocious daughter of Mohsen Makhmalbaf, to a question about why she had made a film in Afghanistan (*Panj-e 'asr/At Five in the Afternoon*, 2003). She replied: "This film is not only about Afghanistan but it could very well have taken place in Iran. *The Taliban are our backwardness*" (Makhmalbaf Film House 2003, emphasis added). One comedy series screened on Iranian public television, *Chahār Khuneh/Four Homes* (Sorush Sehat 2007), had a character called Shanbeh (Saturday), played by popular actor Javad Razavian. Shanbeh is a supposedly Afghan charlatan, complete with a funny name, a quaint (though inaccurately Afghan) accent and "traditional" dress. He insinuates himself into the life of an Iranian family, wreaking much slapstick havoc. Yet the audience learns in an early episode that he is in fact from a remote desert village in Iran, merely posing as an Afghan to gain sympathy. Still later, they learn that the son-in-law of the family comes from the same village and deceitfully changed his name before marrying their daughter. In a subtle way, Shanbeh's deceit, avarice, laziness, and other vices reflect poorly on and satirize Iranians rather than Afghans, dramatizing class prejudice and anxiety about the unstable relationship between social status and external appearance in contemporary Iran.

Yet Afghans in Iran are greeted not only with taunts and xenophobia. The mother of the family in *Four Homes* sympathizes with Shanbeh, and similarly, in real life there has been a great deal of sympathy for the plight of Afghans, with fund-raising campaigns, donations, and sincere friendships. The welcome Afghans received from the state in the 1980s was more generous than what many Western countries provided to refugees. This was underlined in a blog post by Afghan poet Mohammad Sarvar Raja'i (Raja'i 1386/2008) in which he recalls a well-known Iranian artist, Ezzatollah Entezami, almost weeping while announcing his fund-raising campaign for hungry Afghan refugee children on national television in November 2001. Raja'i considers this an unforgettable moment of Iranian-Afghan solidarity. However, he uses this and other acts of kindness as an ironic preface to what is actually a critical piece about the distortions and stereotypes of *Four Homes*. The timing of Entezami's campaign was not without political significance: Raja'i subtly notes that this gesture, coming soon after the U.S. invasion of Afghanistan, was probably an attempt at "winning the hearts" (*fath-e del-hā*) of Afghan refugees who might otherwise have been won over by the Americans' defeat of the Taliban.

This anecdote illustrates how the figure of the Afghan is politicized in Iran. It is a topic of internal political contention among conservatives and those reformists who hope for a more open civil society in Iran. Certain Iranian activists for refugee rights had close ties to the Khatami presidency, and two of the few articles to publicly denounce the mass deportations of 2007 were published in the opposition *Ham-mihan* daily just weeks before it was banned for the second time by President Ahmadinejad's conservative government (Abazari 1386/2007, Ahmadi-Aryan 1386/2007). When Afghans were banned in 2012 from entering a popular park in Isfahan on the grounds of "safety and security," hundreds of young Iranians joined Facebook groups declaring "I too am Afghan" and "No to racism" (A. Ahmadi 2012). Sympathetic comments are often made by Iranian readers in the blogs of young Afghans. However, such sympathy notwithstanding, Afghans for the most part remain politically mute and invisible in Iran, except as a problem to be managed.

Their muteness, or perhaps Iranians' unwillingness to hear what they say, is elegantly illustrated by two films generally hailed as sympathetic portrayals of Afghan refugees and Afghanistan. They are Majid Majidi's *Bārān* (lit. Rain)/*Baran* (2001) and the aforementioned *At Five in the Afternoon* by Samira Makhmalbaf.[21] In *Baran*, the eponymous heroine, a young Afghan girl who dresses as a boy in order to take her father's place on a construction site when he is injured, does not speak a single word in the whole film. When she cries out in pain in one scene, she is not even given the dignity of her voice ringing out—instead, her voice is muffled by sound effects that make it sound otherworldly. That is perhaps the point. The film is not really *about* Afghans, but, as in most of Majidi's films, the plot is a vehicle for a mystical allegory. The mysterious Afghan girl functions unwittingly as a spiritual guide for the self-realization of an Iranian boy who falls in love with her and gives up everything, including his national identity card, to help her. In so doing, he learns how to be selfless. The heroine of *At Five in the Afternoon* has a voice and dreams of becoming president of Afghanistan, but she speaks remarkably little for a young girl who presumably has a lot to say. Instead, the film is filled with languid scenes of her walking up and down the corridors of the ruined Dar al-Aman palace in Kabul with her burka pulled away from her face, her footsteps echoing to draw attention to the high-heeled shoes she can now freely wear. She retreats to this place to rehearse her political speeches, but because she does so silently, the viewer can only guess at their content. The mute image replaces any real understanding of her predicament that might have been achieved. The figure of the Afghan in public discourse is thus a mirror turned toward the Iranian subject's own fears and fantasies.

Persian Literary Historiography and the Distortions of Nationalism

As a corollary to the exclusion of Afghans from citizenship in Iran, Afghan literary history has been written out of the classical Persian canon; or rather, Persian literary history has been appropriated as belonging to Iran alone. Persian literature as a scholarly discipline, a selective canon, and the historical narrative that we know today arose contemporaneously in Iran and Afghanistan with their consolidation as nation-states (W. Ahmadi 2004b, 2008; Clinton 1372/1994), polities very different in shape and nature to the geographical area in which that literary tradition was once practiced. As such, discussions of Persian literary history are replete with assumptions and lacunae that often tell us more about the politics of the time they were written than about the texts under consideration. An account of these debates provides us with a useful background to the literary discourses in which Afghan poets in Iran are currently immersed and in which they actively participate.

An attempt to survey the history of the Persian-language literature of Iran and Afghanistan must first of all confront the problem of a discrepancy between literary tradition and contemporary geographical space. As W. Ahmadi has put it in an article drawing much-needed attention to this problem, "the present extent of Persian cultural space does *not* correspond to any one modern national polity and the Persian language is *not* the repository of any one 'national soul.' Persian literature has historically transcended well-defined territoriality and has never been exclusively 'Iranian literature' or 'Afghan literature' or 'Tajik literature' (or, for that matter, 'North Indian literature')" (2004a: 408, original emphasis). Yet much Persian literary history by contemporary Iranians and others is discursively bound up with nationalism and historiographical efforts to legitimize the nation-state.[22] "Viewed as solely Iranian language, historians of Iran . . . consider [as] unworthy Persian texts produced outside of the country. The conventional Persian literary histories, moreover, regard poetry as a characteristically *Iranian* mode of self-expression" (Tavakoli-Targhi 2001: 16, emphasis added). This has led to a situation in which many "homeless texts" remain unknown or ignored because they fall between the cracks of different nationalisms following "the emergence of *history with borders,* a convention that [has] confined historical writing to the borders of modern nation states" (9, original emphasis).[23]

It bears remembering that many of the most revered classical Persian poets were in fact born in what is today Afghanistan: the thirteenth-century mystic known in the West as Jalal al-Din Rumi was born in Balkh, and the fifteenth-century Abd al-Rahman Jami lived and died in Herat. The legendary eleventh-century King Mahmud of Ghazni, also a poet, is given the honor of being considered the greatest patron ever known in Persian literary history (Rypka 1968: 173) and his Ghaznavid dynasty played a crucial role in the revival of Persian literature after the Arab conquest of the region four centuries earlier. Moreover, there was never a single, fixed center of Persian culture, but rather an intensive circulation of learned people and literati throughout the region; in fact, "the center(s) of Persian literary and cultural activity has been continuously shifting due to larger socio-economic and political developments" (W. Ahmadi 2004a: 408). Before the eighteenth century, as the crossroads between the Persian-speaking and Muslim-dominated lands of India, Iran, and Transoxiana, Afghanistan lay at the hub of the multiple networks of connections between literati in these regions who shared a common culture (Ghani 1988: 434). Despite the incursions of the Russian and British Empires into Transoxiana and India, respectively, Persian remained an international language until the nineteenth century, with Persian-language publications printed in India outnumbering not only those published in other languages there, but also Persian-language publications in Iran (Tavakoli-Targhi 2001: 9).

Thus, it is more accurate to speak of a *Persianate* literary milieu and culture dating back to the tenth century, which transcended the shifting borders of empires, princedoms, and nation-states across a broad geographical expanse. It was held together by a common language, a literary canon (even if the shape of that canon changed over time), and a repertoire of poetic forms and genres with strict rules of prosody, but it was by no means monolithic.[24] Among its practitioners were poets who were highly mobile and subject to influences from diverse regions, philosophies, religions, and other languages. Many poets and writers in Persian were bilingual or multilingual, particularly in languages such as Arabic, Turkish, Urdu, and Pashtu, in whose literatures they often also left an important mark. New styles arose in the outer reaches of this cultural milieu, notable among which is the Indian style (*sabk-e hendi*) that developed in the Mughal Empire among poets of Persian and Central Asian origin in the sixteenth century, and later traveled back to influence the poetry and prose of older Persian-speaking areas (Bečka 1968: 497). Such movements were a response to the politics of the day: the centers of Persian poetic production were pushed to India and the Ottoman Empire from the sixteenth century onward because the Safavid dynasty, which established Shi'ism as the state religion of Iran, did not patronize nonreligious poetry (Karimi-Hakkak 1995: 28). Known for its complex forms and expressions, the Indian style became particularly popular in the region encompassing today's Tajikistan and Afghanistan, enduring well into the nineteenth century and beyond (ibid., Ghani 1988: 435).[25]

This circulation between centers of Persianate cultural influence is illustrated by the biographies of several poets of different eras.[26] Mowlana Jalal al-Din

Mohammad Balkhi, or Rumi (1207–1273), was born to a well-known family of scholars in Balkh in present-day Afghanistan.[27] In the midst of the catastrophic Mongol invasion, his father, a preacher, moved the family in 1221–1222 via the Islamic pilgrimage sites and Damascus to Konya in Anatolia (modern-day Turkey), where Rumi lived until his death. Rumi is often mentioned by both contemporary Afghans and Iranians as the most significant and beloved mystical poet, and careful study and discussion is still devoted to his work, particularly his *ghazals* and the *Masnavi-ye ma'navi* (*The Spiritual "Masnavi"*), comprising 27,000 couplets. Zein al-Din Mahmud Vasefi (1485–ca. 1566), born in Herat, was an important literary figure and a scribe and tutor at the court of Timurid Sultan Hossein Bayqara in Herat, and later at the court of the Uzbek ruler of Tashkent. He also visited Samarkand and Bukhara and traveled extensively throughout northern Iran and Central Asia (Bečka 1968: 501, Subtelny 1984). Mirza Mohammad Ali Sa'eb Tabrizi (1601/2–1677/8) was born in a village near Isfahan to a merchant from Tabriz, studied in Isfahan, completed the hajj, lived for a time in Kabul and Kashmir, and worked in the courts both of Mughal emperor Shah Jahan in Agra and the Safavid Shah Abbas II in Isfahan (Rypka 1968: 302). He composed poetry in both Persian and Turkish and is known as one of the great exponents of the Indian style.[28]

While Sa'eb Tabrizi's name is still well-known in Iran thanks to his connection with the Safavid court, a major casualty of the emergence of "history with borders" has been Bidel, considered by Persian speakers *outside Iran* to be the pinnacle of the Indian style (Bečka 1968: 497). Abu al-Ma'ani Abd al-Qader Bidel Dehlavi (1644–1721) was born in Azimabad (present-day Patna, India), during the reign of Shah Jahan, and his life was concurrent with the period of the decline and disintegration of Mughal rule. His family was of Central Asian Uzbek descent, though his mother tongue is reported to have been Bengali, and he also learned Urdu, Sanskrit, and Persian. His most important works, many of which exhibit a religiously tolerant spirit, include *masnavi*s comprising philosophical, religious, and mystical meditations, as well as notes from his travels across the Indian subcontinent and Indian folktales (Bečka 1968: 519).

Every year on the anniversary of Bidel's death, his followers would gather around his tomb in a meeting known as *'ors-e Bidel* (Bidel festival) to read his works (Kazemi 1385/2006; see also Bečka 1968: 516–17). This tradition gradually evolved into regular gatherings of *Bidel-shenāsān* (Bidel scholars), complete with lectures and musical performances, including annual gatherings for *Bidel-khāni* (reading and interpretation of Bidel), which were adopted as far away as Kabul and present-day Tajikistan. While Bidel's works and renown spread throughout Mughal India, Afghanistan, and Central Asia by the middle of the eighteenth century and remained influential until the twentieth, he is all but unknown inside Iran, although a study of his work was eventually published in 1988 by the renowned Iranian poet and literary critic Mohammad Reza Shafi'i Kadkani

(1366/1988). The reasons for this neglect include the nationalist tendencies that wrote out of the literary canon Persian-speaking poets and writers who did not live within Iran's current borders. This was not the case in Afghanistan because of weaker nationalist tendencies (Kazemi 1384/2005a); though certainly the ability of Afghan poets to claim Bidel and the Indian style as part of their own lineage was facilitated by the postcolonial Indian and Pakistani states' disowning of their Persian-language heritage (Green 2013: 13). Afghan intellectuals resident in Iran have spearheaded efforts to arouse interest in Bidel. Only since 2005 has an annual congress of Bidel scholars in the tradition of *'ors-e Bidel* been organized in Tehran, with the presence of many Afghan speakers and singers (Kazemi 1385/2006). An Afghan poet living in Iran whose work is discussed below, Kazemi has studied Bidel for over two decades and published a critical edition of Bidel's *ghazals* (1386/2007).

As Afghanistan, too, coalesced into a modern nation-state in the twentieth century, governments faced a dilemma that persists to this day: one of shoehorning the literary output of an ethnically diverse and mobile people, whose literati were embedded in a variety of transnational networks and influenced by myriad imported political ideologies, into an immobile and unified state (Green 2013). For example, there was much debate as to whether the national language ought to be Persian or Pashtu—the former being the lingua franca, administrative language, and mother tongue of a large proportion of the population, the latter being the language of the large and powerful ethnic group from which the royal family and ruling classes derived. But despite vigorous attempts in the 1930s and 1940s to promote Pashtu and make it the dominant language of literary production in Afghanistan, this experiment largely failed. By 1964, when a new constitution formally enshrined both languages as the official languages of the state, attempts to establish Pashtu as the single official language had been abandoned (W. Ahmadi 2008: 48).[29] Mahmud Tarzi, the influential founder of literary modernism in Afghanistan in the early twentieth century, first advocated Pashtu but later conceded that due to the illustrious history of Persian literature, and the number and stature of its practitioners in Afghanistan, it was indeed worthy of being called "'our' national literature" (quoted in ibid.: 47).[30] Tarzi did, however, promote the idea that the Persian spoken in Afghanistan was a distinct language called Dari (Green 2013: 12–13). Ironically, both historical and contemporary efforts to create a national literature and cultural identity for Afghanistan have had a strong transnational dimension, as both the present work and others (e.g., Green and Arbabzadah 2013) make clear.

The Afghan Response

How have Iran-educated Afghan intellectuals responded to the multiple levels of exclusion they experience in Iran? They are caught in a double bind—they feel marginalized in Iran, not simply legally but also existentially. And yet, being

Figure 1.2. Mohammad Kazem Kazemi speaking at an Iranian poetry reading on the occasion of the birthday of the Twelfth Imam, Mashhad, 2005.

educated people who have been exposed to the state's ideology of "Islamic modernity," like Iranians, they have internalized the idea that Iran is civilizationally superior to Afghanistan. This comes complete with the temporal disjunction typical of modern "allochronic" thinking about the Other (Fabian 2002). An Afghan friend studying at Tehran University described to me in an email how depressed she was at her likely imminent return to Afghanistan in 2004: "Can you believe that in the twenty-first century there is a country whose cities resemble poor, small and isolated villages?" It is indeed difficult to believe that these worlds exist contemporaneously; Afghanistan has been left behind. If Iranians are caught in a limbo between East and West, educated Afghans in Iran are in a more complicated state, somewhere between West, East, and Farther East.

Yet some intellectuals, poets foremost among them, see the need to intervene in this situation. The Bidel scholar, well-known poet, critic, and literary historian Mohammad Kazem Kazemi, born in Herat in Afghanistan but educated in Iran and a resident of Mashhad for thirty years, has devoted much of his career to promoting the cultural activities of his compatriots. He also seeks to remind Iranians of their shared literary, linguistic and cultural heritage with Persian-speaking Afghans, rather than of their differences. In a book titled *Hamzabani va bizabani/On Sharing a Tongue and Being without a Tongue*, Kazemi 1382/2003), he cites a survey he conducted among educated people in Mashhad that revealed that most respondents did not know that people in Iran, Tajikistan and Afghanistan speak the same language, and most could name few or no contemporary Persian writers from outside Iran. The book arose from his indignation at this state of affairs, but it is telling that he adopts an apologetic tone and emphasizes that he does not mean to offend anyone: "I am aware that raising such discussions is like walking on the blade of a sword. Expressing certain realities may lead the speaker to be accused of Afghan nationalism by Iranian friends, while raising other matters may make him appear to be a sell-out and identity-less in the eyes of Persian speakers from Afghanistan; and I have kept both these probabilities in mind" (Kazemi 1382/2003: 8).

This book was published by a small Afghan publisher in Tehran and it is not clear how many Iranians it reached. But Kazemi is more famous for "Bāzgasht" ("Return"), a long poem in a *masnavi* form that he published in an Iranian newspaper in the early 1990s, of which many Iranians still remember the opening lines. It was ironically addressed to "the Muslim nation of Iran." In it, he variously accuses Iranians of indifference and of scapegoating Afghans and blaming them for all social ills. Yet he reminds them that in the 1980s they suffered together, each nation fighting a war of invasion, each suffering heavy losses. Ultimately, he defiantly says that he will return to Afghanistan, because he is organically connected to his homeland, to its mosques, the tombs of its martyrs, and its struggle for freedom. It is the place where the exile is made whole again.[31]

> *Ghorub dar nafas-e garm-e jāddeh khāham raft*
> *piādeh āmadeh budam, piādeh khāham raft*
> *Telesm-e ghorbat-am emshab shekasteh khāhad shod*
> *va sofreh'i ke tohi bud, basteh khāhad shod*
> *va dar havāli-ye shab-hā-ye 'eid, hamsāyeh!*
> *sedā-ye geryeh nakhāhi shenid, hamsāyeh!*
> *Hamān gharibi ke qollak nadāsht, khāhad raft*
> *va kudaki ke 'arusak nadāsht, khāhad raft*
>
> *Cheguneh bāz nagardam? Ke sangar-am ānjā-st*
> *Cheguneh? Āh, mazār-e barādar-am ānjā-st*
> *Cheguneh bāz nagardam? Ke masjed o mehrāb*
> *va tigh, montazer-e buseh bar sar-am ānjā-st*
> *Eqāmeh bud o azān bud, ānche injā bud*
> *Qiyām bastan o Allāhu-akbar-am ānjā-st*
> *(...)*

At sunset, in the hot breath of the road I will go,
on foot just as I once arrived, on foot I will go.
The lingering spell of exile will be broken on this night;

the tablecloth that I could never fill, be folded up.
And in the air on eves of happy feast days, neighbor!
No longer shall you hear the sound of weeping, neighbor!
The stranger with no penny to his name shall be gone.
The child that had no doll or cradle, too, shall be gone.

How could I not return, when my battle trench is there?
How? Oh, the memory of my brother's grave is there.
How could I not return, when the mosque and the mihrab,
the sword which waits to kiss my head, all of these are there?
A time to build, a time to pray, were all that I had here;
my fight for freedom and my cries of 'God is great!' are there.
(...)

(Fragments; original reprinted in Kazemi 2005b: 40)[32]

In this poem, like many critical intellectuals in the past, Kazemi was able to say in elegant and memorable verse what few others had been given the right to say in a public forum, and to engage in a critical dialogue with his Iranian counterparts and Iranian society in general, highlighting the role of poetry as ethical discourse and public intervention (Caron 2013).

More recently, in "Shamshir o Joghrāfiyā" ("The Sword and Geography"), a long poem consisting of two linked *ghazals* written in 2011, Kazemi highlighted the arbitrariness and absurdity of the creation of militarized borders in the middle of a region once joined by trade and a common culture, language and religion. This transformation is neatly encapsulated by the metonymic image of a piece of rubble from the arch of a ruined old building being turned into a stone for a slingshot:

Bādi vazid o dasht-e setarvan dorost shod
Tāqi shekast o sang-e falākhan dorost shod
Shamshir ru-ye naqsheh-ye joghrāfiyā david
In sān barā-ye mā o to mihan dorost shod
Ya'ni ke az masāleh-e divār-e digarān
yek khākriz bein-e to vo man dorost shod
Bein-e tamām-e mardom-e donyā gol o chaman
Bein-e man o to, ātash o āhan dorost shod.

A wind blew and a barren plain was formed;
an arch crumbled and a slingshot stone was formed.
A sword raced across the map of geography:
in this way, for you and us, homelands were formed.
That is to say, from the materials of other people's wall,
between you and me a bulwark was formed.
Between all the peoples of the world, flowers and meadows;
between you and me, fire and iron were formed.

The othering process of nationalism is given additional emphasis by the repetition and mirroring of the following lines:

> *Yek su man istādam o guyi khodā shodam*
> *Yek su to istādi o doshman dorost shod*
> *Yek su to istādi o guyi khoda shodi*
> *Yek su man istādam o doshman dorost shod*

> I stood on one side and it's as if I became a god;
> you stood on the other side and an enemy was formed.
> You stood on one side and it's as if you became a god;
> I stood on the other side and an enemy was formed.

Each nation has become a god unto itself and, as if by magic, turned those that happened to live on the other side of the line into enemies.

Kazemi then expresses the hope that solidarity and cooperation based on the shared Persian language may flourish once again:

> *Mā shākheh-hā-ye to'am-e sib-im o dir nist*
> *bāri degar shokufeh biārim to'amān*
> *bā ham rahā konim do tā sib-e sorkh rā*
> *dar howz-hā-ye kāshi-ye goldār-e bāstān*
> *Bar naqsheh-hā-ye kohneh khatti tāzeh mikeshim*
> *az kucheh-hā-ye Qunieh tā Dasht-e Khāvarān*
> *Tir o kamān be dast-e man o to-st, hamvatan*
> *Lafz-e Dari biāvar o bogzār dar kamān.*

> We are twinned apple branches and it's not too late
> for us to blossom together once again;
> to release together two red apples
> into the pools of ancient flowered tiles.
> On the old, weathered map we trace a new line
> from the lanes of Konya to the plains of Khavaran.
> The bow and arrow are in your and my hands, compatriot:
> bring a Dari word and fit it to your bow.

> (Fragments; original in Kazemi 1390/2011)

"The Sword and Geography" is rich with literary and topographical allusions that function as metonyms for the shared heritage of the past and its geographical expanse. There is a mention of Rostam, hero of the *Shāhnāmeh;* and the nostalgic scent of the Mulian River made famous by the tenth-century poet Rudaki, who was born in what is today Tajikistan and is considered the father of Persian poetry. Konya, although now in Turkey, is the location of Rumi's tomb; while the plains of Khavaran near Balkh in what is today Afghanistan are associated with other poets (being the birthplace, for example, of the twelfth-century Anvari). Another classical reference is in the hopeful couplet: "Perhaps once again someone from Balkh and Bamyan / will come with a caravan of silks to Sistan." This recalls the well-known opening of a poem by Farrokhi Sistani, an eleventh-century panegyric poet to the Saffarid and Ghaznavid courts: "With a caravan of silks I left Sistan / with garments spun from the heart, woven from the soul."

Kazemi also plumbs modernist poetry for images of unity in diversity. He presents an image of the Simorgh, which calls to mind Attar's twelfth-century mystical epic *Manteq al-Teir/The Conference of the Birds*, in which a group of birds sets out to find the fabled phoenixlike creature, only to find that they, the thirty birds (*si morgh*), are themselves the Simorgh. But Kazemi borrows one whole *mesra'* (individual line of a poem) about the Simorgh from a poem by Nima Yushij (acknowledging this in a footnote), thus clasping together the Iranian modernist poetry of the twentieth century and the mystical tradition of the past. There is also a reference to the Iranian revolutionary song of the 1970s, "Yār-e Dabestāni-ye Man" ("My Schoolmate"), in which the experience of common suffering under the teacher's cane binds the schoolmates together and galvanizes them to political action.

Kazemi writes in his blog that the poem went through a long process of refinement, with several versions read and critiqued at poetry sessions, until finally in 2013 he recited it at a poetry event sponsored by the supreme leader of Iran, Ali Khamene'i. While this move was welcomed by some Afghans as a rare opportunity to present criticism of Iranian attitudes to refugees in a public forum, others criticized it as kowtowing to an oppressive government for personal gain. The appearance of Kazemi and other poets at this event sparked a heated debate in Afghan refugee circles, both online and offline, but ambivalence about trading poetry for pay or favors—the tension between poetry as commodity and poetry as ethical discourse—has a history almost as long as Persian literature itself (Sharlet 2011: 7, 14), and I take it up again in later chapters.

Today, the presence of Afghan writers and poets in Iran, Pakistan, and farther afield may be seen as a continuation of the history of intellectual circulation, much like the networks of exiled Iranian writers and political activists whose dissident journals in Istanbul, Cairo, Calcutta, Paris, and London in the late nineteenth century played such an important role in the subsequent unfolding of Iranian history (Parsinezhad 1380/2001: 15). Only their itineraries have changed: the intellectual and cultural centers of emigrant Persian speakers today are more likely to be in Melbourne, Toronto, London, or California than in Central Asia or India, and their favored media are more likely to be self-published blogs or online magazines. In fact, we might add "the Poet" to the "transnational figures of the Pilgrim, the Merchant, the *Havaledar* [money-transfer agent], and the Migrant, which frequently overlap and traverse the same routes" in this region (Adelkhah and Olszewska 2007: 157). As we have seen, however, a crucial change is that these transnational figures must increasingly submit to the growing strength and bureaucratization of the region's states and to confront the rise of xenophobic nationalism. Thus, their attempt to counter such tendencies by engaging in poetic activities may be seen as a struggle for visibility, perhaps for their very survival.

Afghan poets place themselves within and celebrate this continuum of movement and circulation, while at the same time acknowledging the rise of normative nationalism. Seyyed Zia' Qasemi, director of the documentary film about Golshahr, recalls Rumi's travels in a lyrical reflection on his own life: *"Ey ruh-e sargardān-e sargardān-e sargardān! / Az Balkh tā Qunieh, az Behsud tā Tehrān"*—"O wandering, wandering, wandering spirit! / From Balkh to Konya, from Behsud [Qasemi's birthplace] to Tehran" (Qasemi 1386/2007: 10–11). But a poem by Mahbubeh Ebrahimi, Qasemi's wife and a prominent cultural activist in her own right, reveals the extent to which Afghans have internalized the idea that they cannot be whole as long as they are not in their own country, and the almost mystical power they attribute to the homeland to heal the wounds of exile, a sentiment commonly expressed by young refugees (Kantor and Saito 2010, Kamal 2010). She describes her trip to an area near the border with Afghanistan, and her hopefulness at the coming of political change and the rebirth of her country:

Bar tāblo neshasteh shodeh marz, chand bār
Ya'ni cheqadr māndeh be to? Chand entezār?
Bar tāblo gharib neshasteh ast nām-e to
Dar sineh showq-e radd shodan az sim-e khārdār
In su shekasteh talkh ghazal dar galu-ye man
Ān su shekofteh she'r be lab-hā-ye Qandehār
Ey bād! Buseh-hā-ye marā tā lab-ash bebar
Beneshān be guneh-hā-ye zemestān gol-e anār
Hālā ke sabzeh sar zadeh az jā-ye zakhm-hā-sh
Ey abr! Geryeh-hā-ye marā bar tan-ash bebār
In su kenār-e marz neshasteh ast entezār
Ān su shekofteh ast lab-e rud nowbahār

On the sign sits [the word] Border, time and again,
so how much is left until [I reach] you? How much longer to wait?
On the sign desolately sits your name;
in my breast, a longing to cross the barbed wire.
On this side, broken and bitter, a ghazal in my throat;
on that side, poetry blossoms on the lips of Kandahar.
O Wind! Convey my kisses to its lips,
place a pomegranate flower on the cheeks of winter.
Now that green shoots have sprung from its wounds,
O Cloud! Rain my tears down on its body.
On this side, expectation sits beside the border;
on that side, the river bank blossoms in the new spring.

(Original in M. Ebrahimi 1386/2008: 17)

This poem contains an opposition that has become a recurring trope in Afghan refugee poetry in Iran, that between the fractured exilic self "here" versus the potential for wholeness and healing "there." On "this side" of the border the poet is "broken and bitter" and unable to express herself, whereas "on that side, poetry blossoms." As many other poets have done, Ebrahimi is recapitulating Kazemi's earlier use of this trope in his poem "Return":

> *Shekasteh bāli-am injā, shekast-e tāghat nist*
> *Karāneh'i ke dar ān khub miparam ānjā-st*
> *Magir khordeh ke yek pā vo yek 'asā dāram*
> *Magir khordeh ke ān pā-ye digar-am ānjā-st.*

> My wings are broken here, perhaps, but not my fortitude;
> the shores from which I long to fly with joyful ease are there.
> Do not find fault that I have only one leg and one crutch;
> do not find fault: my other leg is firmly planted there.

(Fragment of "Return"; original in Kazemi 1384/2005b: 40–43)

Such rhetoric notwithstanding, Afghans have been able to engage with many of the institutions of the modern, postrevolutionary Iranian state—such as education, health care, and public broadcasting—and consume their cultural products, on more or less the same footing as Iranian citizens. Many of these practices and ideas were new to Afghans originating in poor, rural areas of Afghanistan, remote from the centers of state power, and occasioned profound social transformations, particularly among the most educated groups. Although Afghans remain aliens, then, it is perhaps more accurate to refer to a kind of "alien citizenship," a kind of partial membership in the body politic that describes the de facto state of affairs in many countries and recognizes that borders are porous (Bosniak 2006). The apparent contradiction between these two sets of forces is at the heart of young, Iranian-educated Afghans' self-perception as incomplete, fractured, and a "burnt generation" (*nasl-e sukhteh*; Kamal 2010), belonging neither to Iran nor to Afghanistan.

2 The Melancholy Modern
The Rise of a Refugee Intelligentsia

> A few years ago, I happened to sit next to a lady on a bus who introduced herself as a master's student in law. That day, our words about the limited number of bus seats reserved for women compared to men[1] led to a discussion of women's rights, and we spoke a lot about the difference between women's and men's blood money (*diyeh*) and inheritance, custody rights, the equality of men's and women's rights, and so on. We had a lively exchange. As she was getting off, she said something that has bothered me all these years. She said, "I hadn't thought an Afghan woman would even understand what rights are, let alone look at her rights from a religious point of view while being an intellectual (*rowshanfekr*) at the same time." That Iranian woman's words struck me as strange, but they forced me to think a little about what she had said, especially because in these years I have witnessed many changes in the thought and behavior of my compatriot women in exile.
>
> Zahra Hosseinzadeh

THESE WORDS BY Zahra Hosseinzadeh, one of the leading female poets of Dorr-e Dari, appeared in an issue of its journal the *Third Script* devoted to the topic of Afghan intellectuals. In this issue, members of Dorr-e Dari and Afghan intellectuals in other countries betray their preoccupation with this topic in nearly forty articles and interviews exploring the rise and predicaments of intellectuals in Afghanistan and the Islamic world. Hosseinzadeh, like many of the other authors, traces a historical pedigree for herself by describing the emergence of scholarly, political, and artistic women in twentieth-century Afghanistan. But we may inquire, along with her Iranian interlocutor, how it is that a group of educated Afghan intellectuals, writers, and cultural activists—both men and women—has arisen in Iran. What social conditions have allowed the flourishing of educational and cultural initiatives in Afghan refugee communities in Iran? How have Afghan refugee poets embraced and reinvented the idea of the *rowshanfekr*?

The word *rowshanfekr* literally translates as "enlightened thinker" and signifies not merely an educated and cultured person but one who is sensitive to the ills of her society and strives to transform it. The idea of social and political commitment in literature was seen throughout the twentieth century as explicitly modern and opposed to the alleged detachment of those who persisted in writing "outmoded" *gol-o-bolbol* (rose-and-nightingale) poetry. The committed writer in Iran and Afghanistan has been expected to identify with the poor and downtrodden, to give a voice to their struggles, and to be an agent of change. Yet debates about the meaning and purpose of literature, and the role intellectuals should play in social change, are continually evolving, and frequently take place at Dorr-e Dari and on the pages of the *Third Script*.

Although the group of Afghans in Iran calling themselves intellectuals is small—consisting perhaps of no more than a few thousand people in major cities like Tehran, Mashhad, and Qom—the social transformations that have allowed this loose network to emerge have been fundamental and have affected the vast majority of refugees to some degree, just as they have Iranian citizens. A number of important studies have shown how the emergence of governmentality, bureaucracy, and modern discipline, the state's provision of services like public education and health care, the growing pervasiveness of print, broadcast, and digital media, among many other factors, have led to the kinds of changes in Iranian society that have generally characterized industrialization and what is usually called modernity worldwide, albeit with an Iranian twist (Adelkhah 1999, Rejali 1994). These include rising literacy, declining fertility and the rise of the nuclear family, greater emphasis on gender equality, greater individualization, and changing definitions of the public and private spheres—in sum, changing subjectivities and ideas of personhood. Tracing these changes allows us to gain a better understanding of the peculiar combination of opportunities and exclusions experienced by Afghans in Iran, as well as of how top-down policies combine with people's own desires and aspirations to drive change. To be sure, however, the degree of change is not uniform across the whole population. Depending on their location, economic situation, and other factors, Afghans' ability to culturally assimilate and their visibility to Iranian institutions have varied: both have been greater among urban dwellers than, for example, among the more impoverished groups doing agricultural work in rural areas.

In this chapter, I outline the changes in subjectivity and ideas of personhood that have taken place in the wider Afghan population with respect to three key areas, all reflected in the quotation above from Zahra Hosseinzadeh: the rise of modern education, the modernization of religious practice, and the growing pervasiveness of the concept of women's rights. I then show how the best-educated among the refugees have taken on the mantle of cultural pioneers and see themselves as the vanguard of further change. However, it is necessary to look beyond the idealistic claims of these self-described enlightened thinkers to understand the political economy of this situation. Acquiring a new set of cultural dispositions often has its rewards: when being literate and educated (*bā-savād*) carries prestige, identifying as such also signifies an aspiration to upward mobility and a claim to higher status—one that often does not go uncontested.

But to fully understand what it is to be an Afghan poet-intellectual in Iran, we must also delve into the subtler terrain of this vocation's emotional textures. It is inescapable that the majority of the poems written by my friends had an air of disillusionment and despondency about them, and many of the poets admitted to having bouts of depression (*afsordegi*). Although there were certainly personal reasons involved for each individual, this air of melancholy was pervasive enough to allow us to speak of it as a "structure of feeling" in Williams's terms (1977), an incipient, not always consciously articulated set of cultural experiences common to a particular social group; or the kind of collective, historically specific affective experience observed by Navaro-Yashin among the residents of North Cyprus (2012).

This melancholy had various roots and dimensions, and in fact we may speak of several levels of nested sorrows. First, there is a melancholy that has become normative as a model of moral personhood in postrevolutionary Iranian ideology, partly due to the roots of revolutionary culture and mobilization in the mourning rituals commemorating the battle of Karbala: "leaders of the new Islamic Republic decreed sadness to be the appropriate demeanor of its citizens and the paradigmatic emotional tone for contemporary public life" (M. Good and B. Good 1988: 43).[2] Second, there is the justifiable feeling of exclusion and insecurity felt by the majority of Afghan refugees in Iran, not unlike the temporal and spatial limbo felt by North Cypriots due to their territory's unresolved political status (Navaro-Yashin 2012). Finally, there is the ambivalent position of the refugee intellectual who, while believing in the need to speak on behalf of the benighted masses and sharing much of their destiny, feels increasingly estranged from them. Indeed, Williams emphasizes that structures of feeling often emerge from a process of class differentiation or from "contradiction, fracture or mutation within a class" (1977: 134). Sometimes, he says, the first indication that such a process is taking place lies in the new forms and conventions of the art or literature this group produces (133). Thus, it is in the person of the Afghan refugee intellectual in postrevolutionary Iran that these structural sorrows align in the most exquisite fashion, reflected in and in turn nourished by poetry, with its long tradition as a vehicle for the expression of all kinds of longing.

Education and the Making of an Afghan Refugee Intelligentsia

When, in autumn 2004, the Iranian government announced that refugee children could no longer attend public schools without paying a substantial fee—

more than a month's wages for an average laborer—the news dealt a devastating blow to thousands of young Afghans in the country. Many could no longer afford to attend school in these circumstances; according to one estimate I heard, as many as a hundred thousand Afghan children were forced to drop out of school that year.[3] School-aged children described to me how they wept at the sight of their Iranian classmates walking by in their colorful uniforms on the first day of school while they had to stay at home. Their parents reacted with anger, meanwhile, and a number of Afghan mothers were arrested for publicly demonstrating for their children's right to education in front of UNHCR offices in Tehran and Mashhad.

This development, perhaps paradoxical for people who had once fled Afghanistan in protest against the Communist decree of compulsory education for all boys and girls, is a testament to the single most important social transformation that Afghan refugees in Iran have experienced, and to the greatest success story of the Islamic Republic: they have embraced modern education wholesale. Following their exposure to Iranian state discourses promoting universal public education in the service of a just and modern Islamic society, many previously unlettered people came to accept the value of education as a religious injunction, as a means to social mobility, and as a good in itself. Many people tried to remain in Iran at all costs during the Taliban era so that their daughters could be educated (Hoodfar 2004: 169). While literacy was extremely low in prewar Afghanistan, virtually all Afghan children born in Iran are literate, and the young poets of Dorr-e Dari are more likely to be members of the first fully literate generation in their families than they are to be descended from a line of clerics and scholars.

Literacy and learning in prewar Afghan society were restricted and access to them was limited to a fraction of people in urban areas and much smaller numbers, virtually all male, in rural areas.[4] But this restricted nature led some sectors of Afghan society to place an immensely high value on literacy and use it as a marker of power and status, and this emerged clearly in my interviews. Before the introduction of education in Western-style government-run schools (and even after it, due to their limited number), anyone seeking an education would have begun with the local *mollā* (Islamic cleric) at his small *maktab-khānah* (school), and continued at a madrasah (religious school) or with an individual master.[5] Seyyeds in particular valued Islamic learning, and many men I spoke to who had spent their childhoods in the Hazarajat, both Hazaras and Seyyeds, had studied the Qur'an and the Persian literary classics at local *maktab-khānahs*. Despite this decentralization of learning, there existed established scholarly networks of masters and students, as well as a curriculum of set texts that had to be read in a fixed order.[6] These were all great works in Persian verse or rhymed prose, including works by Rumi, the *Golestān* and *Bustān* of Sa'di, the *Khamseh* of Nezami, Jami's *Yusof o Zoleikhā*, Kashefi's *Anvār-e Soheili* (better known internationally as the *Kalila wa Dimna*), and in some places also Hafez and Bidel. A handful of

Seyyed women were also taught to read by their fathers, and the poet Seyyed Reza Mohammadi asserted that his grandmother from Ghazni province was the only woman in the Hazarajat who had studied to a high level in the traditional system.

Those desiring further religious training went on to study in the famous Shi'a *howzeh-hā-ye 'elmiyeh* or religious seminaries in Najaf in Iraq, or Qom or Mashhad in Iran, where they received training in theology, Islamic law, history, and philosophy.[7] One Seyyed cleric, who had been orphaned at a young age, told me that it was his father's dying wish that he should study, so he worked his way out of poverty in the coal mines of Pakistan, studied in Mashhad and then Najaf, and eventually returned to rural Orozgan province to open his own religious school, with a letter of approval from Ayatollah Khomeini himself.

Shi'a graduates of the great seminaries like this man brought new political ideas back with them to Afghanistan, and these became increasingly radical in the 1960s and 1970s. It is perhaps not very fashionable to write intellectual histories of the world's presumed backwaters such as the Hazarajat, but they are critical to understanding phenomena such as that region's internal conflict in the 1980s. Hazara seminary graduates played a major role in social change in the Hazarajat in that decade, when the region was largely autonomous from Soviet rule in Kabul, as Roy has written: "Young, well educated, dynamic and having an awareness of the importance of organization whatever their political loyalties, [seminary graduates] are having a marked effect on traditional society. . . . Hazarajat is experiencing its own mini-revolution" (1990: 145). They achieved this, for example, by opening schools and libraries for children and for women. But these scholars' conflicting political and doctrinal ideas, and in particular their loyalty to ayatollahs with divergent views on the political role of the clergy (e.g., the radical Khomeini as opposed to the politically quietist Kho'i), also played a part in the bloody and little-known civil war in the Hazarajat in the 1980s, although the precise nature of this intellectual influence has not been studied in sufficient detail.[8]

Among Shi'a Afghans who had become refugees in Iran, for young men to study at the *Howzeh* was therefore both natural and highly desirable. It was also significant that their studies were free of charge—indeed, every *talabeh* (religious scholar, pl. *tollāb*) and cleric associated with a *howzeh* is paid a monthly stipend, potentially for as long as he lives. Afghan clerics were also often entitled to other benefits, such as special residence cards and ration coupons. Not all of them attended the *Howzeh* with the intention of becoming clerics, however; for many, it was the means to secure an education in a universally respected field, and hence a degree of social mobility, especially at times when secular education was closed to refugees. It could also be a means of subsistence in a situation where the alternative was to take ill-paid, backbreaking jobs as laborers.

This has had two important consequences. First, it has given a number of Afghans the relative financial security, leisure time, and commitment to be involved in cultural and political activities that have helped to sustain a positive Afghan identity—for example, many of the most important poets of the jihad generation were *tollāb*. The resulting nexus between Shi'a clergy and seminarians, politics, and literature—in other words, the emergence of a politically engaged Shi'a Afghan intelligentsia in Iran—is a significant aspect of the history of the Afghan diaspora, deserving further study in its own right.

Second, study at the seminaries exposed Afghan men to an environment of philosophical debate and questioning and to the wide range of Islamic viewpoints that are discussed in postrevolutionary Iranian religious circles. Certainly, many of these are highly conservative, but some are liberal: many clerics, for example, are sympathetic to women's education and public presence (Mir-Hosseini 1999).[9] According to an artist who headed a refugee art school in Mashhad, the majority of his pupils were daughters of clerics; and one young female poet told me that her cleric brother regularly gave her the free book vouchers he received from the seminary to buy books of poetry and literary criticism for herself, in contrast to other families that opposed their daughters' literary activities. People with formal religious training often expressed their readiness to interact with people from all walks of life, no matter what their religious or political beliefs, for the purpose of broadening their own horizons. The seminaries create an environment in which learning is a value in itself, and indeed the responsibility of every Muslim: I often heard quoted a hadith that enjoins Muslims to "seek knowledge, even though it be in China."

As for secular education in prewar Afghanistan, beyond a limited bourgeois class in the cities, it had not been seen as necessary or desirable, and many people were suspicious of the type of knowledge being disseminated in Afghan state schools even before the Communist coup of 1978. After the coup, when the attendance of both boys and girls at state schools became compulsory, it was seen as an affront to their dignity and to the honor of the men responsible for the protection of daughters and sisters, and thus helped to spur the uprising against Communist rule. Indeed, local clerics preached against government schools, which they (rightly) perceived as instruments of indoctrination (Hoodfar 2004: 156–157).

Conversely, the Islamic Republic of Iran from the outset placed a great emphasis on education and achieved startling success, building schools in poor and rural areas, enforcing single-sex primary and secondary schooling, which made it easier for girls to attend, and reaching near-universal literacy among youths of both sexes (Keddie 2006: 286; Higgins and Shoar-Ghaffari 1994; Abrahamian 2009: 13). Hundreds of thousands of Afghan children and adults have also been able to attend public schools or literacy training programs, partly thanks to educational funding from UNHCR.[10] While many loved their Iranian classmates and teachers, the experience was not always entirely positive, and several poets spoke of the humiliation of going to school with secondhand schoolbags or stationery donated by UNHCR, the prejudice they sometimes encountered, and uncertainty about whether they could attend in any given year. Lina Nabizadeh evoked the experience in an extemporaneous poem when I asked her about the subject:

> Āvāreh ke bāshi
> bāyad yekjā dar ākhar-e saf beisti
> pā-hā-ye nāmotma'enn-at milarzad
> az negāh-e nezhādparastāneh-ye modir-e madraseh del-at āshub mishavad
> Be bakhshnāmeh'i fekr mikoni
> ke hanuz dar rāh ast
> va ma'lum nist ejāzeh-ye raftan-at be madraseh dar ān sāder shodeh bāshad?!
> yā na
> Del-at be hāl-e khod-at misuzad
> Mānto-ye kohneh o rang rafteh-at
> che khub be qiāfeh-ye zār-at miāyad
> Kif-e farsudeh o khasteh'i ke
> mesl-e qalb-at pāreh pāreh ast
> va daftar-e kāhi-hā va qalam-hā-ye
> ehdā'-ye sāzmān-e melal-e mottahed?
> (. . .)
> . . . mitarsi
> mādar-at be madraseh biāyad
> va nāzem kaj-kaj be lahjeh-ye dari-ye mādar-at nishkhand bezanad
> (. . .)

> When you're a refugee,
> you have to wait somewhere at the end of a line,
> your uncertain legs tremble,
> your heart mutinies against the principal's racist gaze.
> You think of the memorandum
> that's still on its way
> and you don't know if it gives you permission to go to school
> or not?
> You feel sorry for yourself:
> your old, faded coat
> goes so well with your miserable face,
> and your tired, worn-out schoolbag,
> ripped to shreds like your heart,
> and your cheap paper notebooks and pens
> donated by the United Nations.
> (. . .)
> You're afraid
> your mother will come to school
> and the vice principal will smirk at her Dari accent.
> (. . .)

(Lina Nabizadeh, unpublished poem shared by the author, 2013)

Yet, so determined are Afghan children and families to pursue an education—even if they lack the refugee documents or, after 2004, the money to attend state schools—that dozens of semi-clandestine schools have sprung up in refugee neighborhoods to cater to them. They are known as *madraseh-hā-ye khodgardān* (autonomous schools) and are run by Afghans for Afghans, employing Afghan university students or graduates as teachers, outside the authority of the Iranian Ministry of Education. They are periodically shut down by the authorities for operating without official permission and their teachers risk arrest and eviction for their activities, but most of the time, their activities appear to be tolerated.[11] Many of these schools, particularly in Mashhad, are run by and for former residents of a particular town in Afghanistan—for example, Herat or Mazar-e Sharif—illustrating the importance of *hamshahri* (townsman) ties in exile. Some receive donations to cover their operating costs from Afghans living in Western countries, allowing them to offer free tuition to children from poor families and to improve their facilities. The facilities are often spartan and improvised, ranging from tiny rooms or bare concrete basements with curtains separating the classrooms, to schools with attractive premises, several computers, libraries, and other teaching aids. Most of them follow the Iranian state curriculum and use Iranian textbooks, which are readily available, while at least one school I visited used textbooks from Afghanistan to teach Afghan history, geography, and the Pashto language.[12]

There is evidence that, besides delivering an education, informal schools have helped to transform young Afghans' sense of marginalization in Afghan society into a positive collective identity, a desire to learn about Afghanistan and to think of themselves as Afghan (Chatty and Crivello 2005: 20). Indeed, considerable dedication was shown by youths wanting to attend these schools. I met one boy who came alone to Mashhad to live with relatives because there were no Afghan schools where his family lived. Another, a twenty-three-year-old who had dropped out of middle school, returned to the classroom with boys half his age, having decided that education was vital to his future. I volunteered briefly to teach English at a bare basement school on the outskirts of Tehran. When it was later shut down by the authorities, the pupils traveled for over an hour by public bus to reach the new premises, even farther out on the hot plain and more rudimentary than before.

The enormous demand for training in a variety of skills has also led to the creation of dozens of educational centers on various scales in Afghan neighborhoods, particularly in Mashhad and Tehran. Due to reports from returnees to Afghanistan that the English language and computer literacy are essential for high-paying jobs there, these two subjects are particularly popular.[13] A number of foreign and Iranian NGOs offer vocational training classes free of charge, particularly in the English language, graphic design, and the use of other specialist

Figure 2.1. A boys' classroom in an unofficial Afghan school, Mashhad.

software, and short medical training courses to address pervasive fears of poor hygiene and lack of health facilities held by those considering repatriation to Afghanistan. Most of the young Dorr-e Dari members I knew had studied at least to high school level, and many (young women in particular) were involved with the Afghan informal schools or training centers, whether as full-time staff in long-term employment, or part-time teachers. Others simply ran their own backyard English language lessons for neighborhood children.

Dorr-e Dari members, like scores of other young Afghans that I met, all harbored dreams of *edāmeh-ye tahsil* (continuing their education), but I was beginning my research at a bad time. Previously, a significant number of Afghan youth who passed the highly competitive *konkur*, the standard national university entrance examination, had been able to study at Iranian public universities in a wide variety of subjects and with no tuition fees.[14] In 2004, however, the new regulations that excluded so many from primary schooling also barred Afghans from sitting the *konkur*. This enactment produced considerable confusion, and universities responded differently to the problem of registering students—even some of these admitted before the rules went into effect were turned away. In recent years, policies have changed frequently, but by and large, Afghan students have only been permitted to apply as fee-paying "foreign students" to a limited number of universities, and youth grapevines are always abuzz with the latest news on which universities are accepting Afghans and how much they charge (up to $1,000 U.S. per semester for tuition fees alone in 2005). Even more painfully, many Afghans whose families are in Iran and who have lived there all their lives have been obliged to give up their residence permits and obtain Afghan passports and foreign student visas that expire when their courses end. Thus, in one stroke, ambitious, educated young refugees are turned into deportable aliens as soon as they graduate. In sum, the promise of education and the disappointment of its thwarting was a crucial defining aspect of the inner lives of the young poets with whom I worked.

Authenticated Islam, Gender, and the Redefinition of the Public Sphere

For many refugees, emigration from Afghanistan in the 1980s was a move imbued with religious significance.[15] Their country had been taken over first by local Marxists and then by Soviet forces, both seen as atheist unbelievers seeking to rend the fabric of society, but they were traveling to an Iran that had just embraced an Islamic system of government. Shi'as in particular, a marginalized group in Afghanistan, now found themselves in a country that not only had a majority Shi'a population but also openly embraced Shi'i values and incorporated them into law and politics. Newly arrived Shi'a Afghans participated enthusiastically in public 'Āshurā processions on the streets of Iranian cities, delighted to be able to do so openly and on a large scale. Required to adopt surnames for the first time, many newcomers from Afghanistan chose names with religious connotations, such as Hosseini or Alavi, in honor of the Imams Hossein and Ali. Some young Afghan men responded to the call for martyrdom in the Iran-Iraq War and went to the front, a fact unknown to most Iranians.[16] In Mashhad, proximity to the shrine of Imam Reza (usually referred to simply as the Haram) was a particular draw with deep spiritual and affective dimensions, and "being neighbors to Imam Reza" was cited by some as reason enough for not wanting to return to Afghanistan (Glazebrook and Abbasi-Shavazi 2007). The veneration of Imam Reza is plain in Kazemi's poem "Return," in which he asserts that when he leaves Iran, he will take nothing with him but a handful of dust from the shrine.

Most Shi'a Afghans continue the vernacular religious practices that they share with their Iranian neighbors. These include both daily observance of prayers and ritual purity, and occasional events such as the *rowzeh* or lament for the martyrs, 'Āshurā processions, *nazr* or the distribution of ritual food in fulfillment of vows, and *ziyārat* or visits to shrines of Imams and their descendants (*emāmzādeh*).[17] The Haram played a focal role in the lives of many of my interlocutors, particularly women. They frequently went to the shrine to pray, to seek solace or intercession in moments of crisis, to release pent-up emotions through weeping, or to pay their respects on religious holidays, often with groups of friends or relatives. Some would also engage in a practice called *dakhil bastan*, which may be roughly translated as "placing oneself under the protection" of

Figure 2.2. An 'Āshurā procession with a portrait of Imam Hossein and boys striking themselves with chains on the streets of Mashhad.

the Imam.[18] This involved tying a string or strip of cloth, or attaching a padlock to the gilded latticed structure surrounding Imam Reza's tomb, or more frequently to a replica of the lattice (the *panjareh-ye fulād*) set up for this purpose in one of the shrine's courtyards. The knot or locked padlock represents the knot of difficulties in the person's life that he or she hopes will be released through the Imam's intercession. Other pilgrims or employees of the shrine often untie the knots or remove the padlocks to hasten the process. Seriously ill people may also physically bind themselves to the lattice with a cord as they pray for a cure. Among my Afghan friends, I heard of many miraculous cures or assistance, for example in important examinations, following an act of *dakhil bastan*. Although this practice may be criticized as *khorāfāt* (superstition) by the religiously orthodox, it is not discouraged in the Islamic Republic, being part of the cult of the Shi'a Imams that is promoted by the state and the powerful charitable foundation that runs the shrine.

Popular religious feeling finds frequent expression in poetry, especially in the form of poems dedicated to the Twelve Shi'a Imams and the Prophet's family, a tradition dating back at least to the beginning of the Safavid era (Rypka 1968: 288–289).[19] Indeed, poetry readings and competitions are a popular way of nurturing the cult of the Imams in contemporary Iran, and they are often held to commemorate the many days in the calendar that mark the births and deaths of the Imams. It is not difficult to find suitable poetry for such occasions, as the addressee of any poem on love or the pain of separation may be transposed from an earthly beloved to one of the holy figures of Shi'ism. The emotive power of a personal connection with Imam Hossein and the vivid contemporary presence of the story of his martyrdom at Karbala are described in part of a poem by Amanollah Mirza'i, a young male Afghan poet originally from Mazar-e Sharif:

(...)
Maryam barā-ye Tāhereh ta'rif mikonad
dar showq-e Karbelā shodeh aghlab, sekāns-e ba'd
tā sobh geryeh mikonad o zār mikonad
Bārān-e chashm-hā-yash morattab, sekāns-e ba'd
mirikht ru-ye dāman-e chinchin o golgoli-ash
Hājat gereft ākhar-e matlab, sekāns-e ba'd
U bud o yek zarih-e tamannā moqābel-ash
bā yek dakhil-e sabz moqarrab, sekāns-e ba'd
Tasvir-e zohr-e hādeseh āmad be khāter-ash
Ān lashkar o sepāh-e mo'azzab, sekāns-e ba'd
(...)

(...)
Maryam is describing to Tahereh how
often, feeling the passion of Karbala—[cut to] the next sequence—
she weeps and sobs until morning.

The rain of her eyes regularly—[cut to] the next sequence—
falls on her pleated and flowery skirt.
In the end her prayers were answered—[cut to] the next sequence—
She was there and the shrine of yearning before her,
approaching it with a green string—[cut to] the next sequence—
The image of the noon of the tragedy ['Āshurā] came into her memory:
that tormented army and troops—[cut to] the next sequence—
(. . .)

(Original in Mirza'i 1385/2007: 39–41)

This fragment mimics the editing of a film as it jumps between descriptions of the battle of Karbala and sequences of a girl in the present day, who weeps as she visualizes the tragic events and intercedes with the Imam to answer her prayers. She also imagines herself at the tomb of the Imam (which is in modern-day Iraq), tying a green string to the lattice.

Despite such continuities in religious practice, it must be remembered that the 1979 revolution entailed a dramatic reformulation of the role and nature of religion in Iran, particularly of its relationship with politics. Clerics were suddenly catapulted to the apex of political power and, as Adelkhah has written, the revolution "triumphed over an illusion: the illusion of a modernity that would have confined religion to the private sphere" (1999: 178). But she states that it is simplistic merely to investigate whether there is "more or less Islam in institutions or in society" (105). Instead, she reminds us that Islam itself has been changing and its role and significance in public life continually shifting. The revolutionary class has become professionalized, bureaucratized and institutionalized, as have certain religious practices like charitable giving, now channeled through state-run welfare foundations (Adelkhah 1999: 53). Debate and fierce contestation of the shape of the polity have continued, despite attempts at censorship and the periodic violent suppression of opposition protests, including the Green Movement demonstrations following the disputed presidential election of 2009 (K. Harris 2012).

Several scholars have stressed that the emergence of political Islam in Iran should not be reduced to a reactionary backlash against a modernity heavy-handedly imposed by the Shah's regime, but rather understood as an attempt to work through the contradictions raised by the uneven social and economic development of the twentieth century. Political Islam should thus be seen as continuous with—and a reinvention rather than a negation of—modernist thought. Vahdat (2002), for example, writes of the clear influences of modernist, positivist writing on the thought of the leading ideologues of the revolution—Ali Shari'ati, Ayatollah Khomeini, and Ayatollah Motahhari—and on postrevolutionary political discourses alike. He puts forward the theory that the idea of individual subjectivity, central to European political theorists such as Kant and Hegel, entered into their works in a modified form—that is, human subjectivity as mediated by God's subjectivity (Vahdat 2002: 134–181). Adelkhah similarly stresses that the Islamic thinkers who influenced the revolution "placed the 'responsible individual,' the rational person, at the centre of their thinking. They criticized the traditionalist view that saw the faith as 'servile obedience,' seeing in it rather a principle of freedom and reason" (Adelkhah 1999: 5). The ideologues of the revolution propagated the ethic of the social person (*ādam-e ejtemā'i*): a person, regardless of gender, who is publicly active (*fa'āl*) and committed to others while maintaining piety and respectability in private life, with particular emphasis on assistance to the poorest sections of society, the *mostaz'afin* (the oppressed or dispossessed; Adelkhah 1999: 5).[20]

These principles are inculcated in citizens (and in refugees attending state schools) through education, among other means. According to a 1987 publication of the Ministry of Education, the goal of education in Iran is to "strengthen the spiritual beliefs of schoolchildren through the explanation and instruction of the principles . . . of Islam and Shi'ism on the basis of *reason*, the Quran, and the traditions of the Innocent Ones [the Prophet, his daughter Fatimah, and the twelve Shi'a Imams]" (cited in Mehran 2007: 54, emphasis added). Secondary school students are introduced also to the revolutionary and political aspects of state Shi'ism. In a high school textbook on the thought of Ayatollah Khomeini studied by Mehran, "pure Islam is the Islam of the weak, the barefoot people of the earth, defiant mystics, and those who have suffered throughout history, and its pioneers are the poor, oppressed, and downtrodden people of the world" (Mehran 2007: 59). The importance of jihad or struggle in the path of Islam, the "bliss" of martyrdom, and the sacred defense of the Islamic Republic are also important principles in these textbooks (59–62). Schools are places "where young Iranians are socialized as pious and politicized citizens" in a "highly ideological educational system" (68).

These changes in religious ethics have not left Iran's refugee population untouched. The importance of education, including education of girls, justified by Qur'anic injunctions, is one example of a pervasive transformation. Another is that certain folk beliefs may be uprooted in the face of orthodox religious knowledge, which is seen as more authoritative. "We didn't know how ignorant we were," a thirteen-year-old female student—a relatively recent arrival from Afghanistan—in my English class told me. "In Afghanistan we were told that God would struggle against Satan on Judgment Day and things like that, which doesn't appear anywhere in the Qur'an. We are much better Muslims now."[21]

Afghan refugees have also adapted to evolving Iranian forms of religious sociability, such as the trend of building communal religious spaces (*hosseiniyeh*) for migrants that double as social spaces for secular events and hometown associations (Adelkhah 1999: 128). The Heratis' relative affluence and the importance of townsman (*hamshahri*) ties are both reflected in the scale and splendor of the *hosseiniyeh* that they built in Mashhad in 1988 as the numbers of refugees from Herat requiring a space to hold religious ceremonies grew. In Herat, on the other hand, such events had been held in private homes, which had generally been more spacious. The *hosseiniyeh* was funded by donations from the Herati community, the vast majority coming from no more than ten donors, two or three of whom were extremely wealthy, and who now form the committee that runs the operations of the *hosseiniyeh*. The *hosseiniyeh* can accommodate three thousand people and, at the time of my visit, ranked as the seventh-largest in the whole of Iran.[22] Its impressive facade of intricate tile work suggests that it was intended to make a statement to the Iranian residents of Mashhad among whom the Heratis live: to make visible their presence, their piety, and their social status. My guide on one visit, the son of one of the founders, proudly told me that even local Iranians frequently hired out the hall for their ceremonies, and some of these had been shown on television.[23]

The promotion of a greater sense of rationality and mindful responsibility in religious practice leads to a spirit of questioning and a lively and perhaps unintended diversification and individualization of practices (Adelkhah 1999). This is similar to what Eickelman and Piscatori (2004: 38) have called "objectified" and Deeb has called "authenticated" Islam (2006: 20–23): a religious practice that calls for greater self-consciousness and personal involvement in the verification of religious truth. My interlocutors exhibited just such a spirit: one female poet told me that when she reached puberty, her working-class parents gave her her first chador and told her: "We will provide you with hijab and explain how to wear it, but you have to think through the philosophy of hijab for yourself." Since then, she said, she has experimented—first wearing a chador, and subsequently rejecting hijab to the extent possible in Iran, wearing colorful clothes and heavy makeup, all the while remaining a Muslim in her heart.

In another case, a group of female Afghan university students, together with some Iranian friends, decided to hold a Qur'an study group, some of which sessions I attended. They tried to read the Qur'an in Persian rather than Arabic, as if they were encountering the words for the first time and without holding any prior interpretation authoritative, to judge for themselves whether they could accept all of its tenets. The sense of curiosity and openness to knowledge about other religions and philosophies is not limited to those in secular education: two Afghan poets, one a student of the *howzeh* in Qom and the other in Mashhad, described to me the dissertations they were writing. One was on the humanist tradition in Islam, and the other on the compatibility of Islam with Frankfurt School critical theory. The latter student was obliged to conclude that the two were compatible (the official line in the Mashhad *Howzeh*), but his private view, he confided to me, was that they were not.

Since the revolution, the public sphere has been transformed into a space that is wholesome by virtue of being Islamic, in which men and women are expected to dress and behave modestly. This has contributed to another remarkable transformation among refugees in Iran, which Afghan intellectuals are quick to emphasize—that in perceptions of gender roles and relations. Many of them speak of it as a "blessing" that Afghan girls and women have been able to "breathe in a cultural environment such as that of Iran," in the words of Mahbubeh Ebrahimi. What is construed as the default Islamicness of the public sphere was illustrated for me by a humorous anecdote told by an Afghan friend: an Afghan husband and wife are traveling on a packed city bus in Iran. The husband stares at a woman whose sleeve has slid down while she clutches the rail over her head, revealing her bare arm. When his wife reprimands him, he says, "*Kheir ast, eslāmi ast* [It's ok, it's Islamic]!" as if the very fact of being in an Islamic country could excuse anything.

Perhaps paradoxically, the Islamization of the public sphere has allowed women from conservative backgrounds to attend school and university, to travel alone, to appear on television, to enter a wide range of professions, to join Islamist organizations, and to choose their own husbands through such contacts (Afary 2009: 295). Osanloo (2009) demonstrates persuasively how women in postrevolutionary Iran increasingly articulate notions of their rights through a hybrid discourse that brings together elements of liberal individualism and Islamic values. Zahra Hosseinzadeh's conversation on the bus shows that this perspective has reached even refugee communities in one of the more religiously conservative cities of Iran. Of course, gender inequality persists, but then it is the responsibility of the so-called enlightened thinkers to lead the way toward redressing it.

A preoccupation with women's rights has been "a persistent trope of modernity" in Iran, as elsewhere (Osanloo 2009: 20), and all intellectuals who claim to be progressive must engage with it: Afghan refugee intellectuals are no exception. The members of Dorr-e Dari were proud of the efforts they had made to include women in their activities, and while most of the older generation of poets and writers were men, the younger generation was more or less evenly divided between men and women. Other Afghan organizations had a similar outlook. The young head of the Mashhad-based Afghan Universitarians' Union was at pains to emphasize that slightly more than half of its thousand-strong membership was female, and women were equally active in the organization of events and administration of the union. He also stressed that extra attention was paid to female members' ideas and proposals. Meanwhile, educated young women often complained vocally about the *ertejā'i* (reactionary, regressive) practices of some of their more conservative relatives, including the injustice of arranged marriage or the displaying of proof of virginity on the wedding night.

To some extent, the change in women's status has been driven by the simple exigencies of refugee life, as the need for extra income pushes women to work.

Figure 2.3. Posters for film and literary festivals adorn a wall alongside women's prayer chadors in a refugee home.

In the first decades of exile, women largely did piecework at home as tailors, weavers, or embroiderers, or by spinning wool or shelling pistachios (Abbasi-Shavazi et al. 2005: 24). But as the Iran-educated generation has grown up, increasing numbers of young women, mostly in Mashhad and Tehran, have turned to work outside the home and away from family supervision either in a variety of informal Afghan institutions or (without legal contracts and social insurance policies) for Iranian institutions, including language schools, hospitals, and research institutes. Just like their Iranian counterparts in an expanding female proletariat (Nomani and Behdad 2006: 199), young Afghan women are also being employed in large numbers in factories. Although unmarried women live with their families and contribute the bulk of their earnings to the household income, they certainly have a bit more spending money for themselves—to pay for clothes and makeup, internet cafes, or bus or shared taxi fares to navigate the city independently.

It is not just young, Iran-educated women whose perception of their place in society has changed. One middle-aged Afghan woman in a study by Hoodfar (2004) justified this change, as with so many things, in terms of a more correct interpretation of Islam: "Before I came to Iran I thought that marriage, work, property and all that, were concerns of men, and we just have to take care of our children and families on a day to day basis. Now I've lived here [Iran] for almost ten years and watched how Iranian women understand their roles and religion and it has changed my views. I am still very much an Afghani, something that I did not think about before, but I also think some of our traditions go against Islamic principals" [sic] (Hoodfar 2004: 156). Most women, young and old, enjoyed increased mobility without requiring the company of *mahram* (related) men. "Here we can move about by ourselves, we can even go to the Holy Shrine in the evenings without having to worry about our security. That would be impossible in Afghanistan," one Hazara woman in her fifties told me. Of the four unmarried daughters of my host family, the oldest was studying alone in Tehran, and the other three were free to come and go and travel throughout Mashhad almost as they pleased. Many other families, of course, were not so permissive, but in general women's mobility in Iran forms a stark contrast to the strict control of women's movements by men that Doubleday, for example, observed in Herat in the 1970s (2006: 4–9).[24] The stigma of women living without men, known as *zanān-e bi-sarparast* (women without protection of a male head of household), who are socially ostracized in Afghanistan as anathema to the image of the male-dominated family, has to some extent been eroded in Iran (Rostami-Povey 2003: 269; Abbasi-Shavazi et al. 2005: 47).

The state family planning campaigns illustrate the ways in which a policy initiated from above can either clash or merge with people's own incentives and interests to bring about change. The state's emphasis on the importance of lower birth rates for the healthy functioning of the Islamic welfare state has been made ethically possible by high-ranking clerics' edicts that there is no religious prohibition on the use of contraception (Hoodfar 1996). Afghans had strongly believed that birth control is against God's will and therefore a sin, but in the 2000s, Iranian health workers began to note an unexpected increase in interest in contraception and family planning among refugees, both men and women (Piran 2004: 285).[25] This interest was driven partly by straitened economic circumstances among the refugees, and partly by the increasing numbers of educated women. But it also freed women from caring for the large families they typically had in prewar Afghanistan and that left many of them worn out (Doubleday 2006: 8), allowing them to pursue their own projects: study, work for a living, or engage in various cultural or political activities. The demographic transition was not unopposed by the older generation, however, and Piran cites stories of often bitter conflicts between youth and elders within families regarding the use of contraception (2004: 288).

In sum, the "relatively emancipated and liberal conditions they have enjoyed" in Iran, as a UNHCR policy document put it, have made Afghan women and youth particularly reluctant to repatriate (UNHCR 2004a: 13). Indeed, some Afghan men jokingly refer to Iran as a *zansālāri*, or femocracy, and threaten their wives with return to Afghanistan if they don't do as they say. Those who do return to Afghanistan bring with them the changed attitudes they absorbed in their host country, and they often appear in news items on female pioneers in various domains, such as the arts, media, sports, or politics.[26] Many men, too, are champions of women's rights. Ali Mohaqqeq Nasab, a Hazara cleric and women's rights magazine editor who was convicted of blasphemy in Afghanistan in 2005 (and later released on appeal), was a recent returnee from Iran and former seminary student. His crime was the questioning of strict Shari'ah punishments and the principle that a woman's testimony is equal to half of a man's (Witte 2005). Unfortunately, female returnees also sometimes appear in statistics on the self-immolation of women who are unable to adjust to a more restricted life in Afghanistan.

Afghan women poets have responded to this situation by writing poetry adopting a specifically feminine voice and calling for a greater recognition of their rights. In one of the earliest poems to speak out against the subordination of women in Afghan society, Maryam Torkamani wrote in 2003:

Man az jahān-e āzādi miāyam
va mojassameh-hā-ye āzādi
mādeh budan-am rā bār-hā busideh and.
(...)
Va kashf kardam
ke behesht zir-e pā-ye mādar jaryān dāsht
hattā zamāni ke
abru-hā-yam bārik o bārik-tar shodand
Behesht ruzi māl-e man khāhad bud
ke man lebās-hā-ye goshād bepusham
va jahannam rā bā tof kardan-e nowzādi
sard konam
(...)

I come from the world of freedom
and the statues of liberty
have kissed my femaleness time and again.
(...)
And I discovered
that heaven was beneath a mother's feet
even when
my eyebrows became thin and thinner
Heaven will belong to me on the day when
I wear baggy clothes
and, by spitting out a newborn child,
cool the flames of hell
(...)

(Original in Sajjadi 1384/2005: 36–39)

Here, Torkamani refers to and questions the popular belief that a woman is most virtuous and blessed when she is a mother, calling instead for a recognition of women's essential freedom to pursue their own happiness. (The reference to thinning eyebrows refers to married life, as traditionally Afghan women do not shape their eyebrows until after marriage).

Despite their eager embrace of many aspects of its ideology, the contradictions of the Islamic regime in Iran have disillusioned many Afghans and have increased secularist tendencies in some, just as they have among Iranians. As Mehran writes, "the sharp contrast between preaching and practice in the larger society has led Iranian youth to question the 'truth' of what is conveyed in the classroom" (2007: 69). I often heard such questioning, particularly in the more open cultural and political environment during the presidency of President Mohammad Khatami (1997–2005), the latter years of which coincided with the early stages of my fieldwork. Indeed, since the 1990s there has been a collapse of faith in many of the ideologies that had provided such a powerful animus for social debate and action in the preceding half century, whether socialism or revolutionary Islam (Jahanbegloo 2000). But Varzi, in her ethnography of postrevolution Iranian youth, has argued that doubt and questioning were also indirect and unintended consequences of the tactics of the revolution itself. By drawing so much attention to surface signs and images, such as veiling, strictly gendered codes of public conduct, prominent murals of martyrs and revolutionary leaders, and ubiquitous photographs of Imam Khomeini and the Supreme Leader Khamenei in public places, she contends that the revolutionary leaders distracted people from inner faith (Varzi 2006: 195). Afghans were as aware of and perhaps more vulnerable to the potential duplicity of politicized religion than many Iranian citizens. As one young poet told me bitterly in 2005, "When hijab was banned in French schools [in 2004], Ayatollah Khamenei offered those French Muslim schoolgirls places in Iranian schools. At the same time, some hundred thousand Muslim Afghan children were thrown out of Iranian schools because fees were imposed that they couldn't afford."

The Melancholy Intellectual and His Poetry

The experiences of intellectual Afghans are marked by such contradictions and liminality of several kinds: if all refugees feel the ambivalence of the long-term exile, who has lost his mooring in his home country but has gained just a precarious foothold in his host country, intellectuals also experience the tension of constantly mediating between diverse sets of cultural values and social circles in their contradictory class position, poor in economic capital but cultivating higher levels of cultural capital. One element of this new structure of feeling seems to be a kind of pained detachment—the eternal melancholy of the sensitive social

Figure 2.4. A slow day at the Dorr-e Dari office.

observer. The examples of two poets will illustrate the spaces that education and intellectual activity have opened up for them, but also the conflicting experiences and inner realities that have accompanied the social positions they have attained.

The liminal nature of the intellectual was already noted in prerevolutionary Iran, when Iranian intellectuals were usually university-educated, middle-class people with secular tendencies. They were well-versed in both European and Persian literature and philosophy, but embodied a variety of contradictions and displacements: "They [were] often angry but politically voiceless, schooled in Western thought yet deeply disturbed about Western cultural penetration, often secular in orientation yet aware of the deep resonance of religion in popular culture, populist yet adopting writing styles and genres not readily accessible to the people they wish to address" (Sreberny-Mohammadi and Mohammadi 1994: 97).[27] Although after the revolution a group of Islamic intellectuals replaced their more secular peers at the forefront of state-legitimated public life, their nativist ideologies and re-embracing of religious identities did not ultimately lead to the tidy resolution of their quandaries. Nor, beyond a basic kind of religious solidarity, did they get closer to "the people." Iranian intellectuals still feel a sense of equivocality in their life and work, akin to the situation of Arab secular intellectuals whom Moroccan social scientist Abdellah Labdaoui has described as "passeurs entre deux rives," ferrymen (or, more evocatively in the other French meaning, smugglers) between two banks, constantly ferrying ideas between their own culture and Western thought (1993: 7). But if this is the case, Afghan refugee intellectuals in Iran are obliged to perform a complicated *triple* balancing act, among loyalty to and the expectations of their own people, the lure of Western thought and lifestyles, and Iranian/Islamic/Shi'i revolutionary alternatives to them.

These tensions were clear in my many conversations, interviews and literature lessons with Seyyed Abu Taleb Mozaffari (b. 1965) the leading Afghan poet, writer and literary critic who is one of the founding members of Dorr-e Dari. He was born in a small village in the province of Orozgan in Afghanistan, arriving in Iran as a teenager with his family in the early years of the war. He is now looked up to as an *ostād* or master poet and mentor by young poets. With his neatly trimmed beard and solemn, reserved demeanor, broken by a mischievous glint of the eye and a sly sense of humor unleashed among close friends, he was a constant, comforting presence in the Dorr-e Dari office and at most of its events. His life story and intellectual development reflect those of many of his literary compatriots of his generation.

He entered the Mashhad *Howzeh* at the age of fifteen, like thousands of other Afghan men, because government schools were barred to refugees for the first five or six years of their mass influx. There he studied to the equivalent of the doctoral level. Yet he was more drawn to literature and philosophy than to *feqh* (Islamic jurisprudence), secretly (*dozdaki-dozdaki*) reading books that were frowned upon by the conservative seminary, such as the works of modernist poets and writers Akhavan-Sales, Shamlu, Sadeq Hedayat, and even Shari'ati. When the *Howzeh* organized a series of poetry congresses for *tollāb* around the country, seemingly making its peace with literature, it was one of the first opportunities Afghan religious students with literary inclinations had to meet others like themselves, scattered around Iran. Inspired by this experience, Mozaffari and a few of his friends created an informal group that met to recite and criticize poetry, usually in private homes. These individuals later formed the core membership of refugee literary associations and were the eventual founders of Dorr-e Dari. Mozaffari has been one of the most prominent figures at Dorr-e Dari and one of the chief editors of the *Third Script* since its founding.

During the political and moral catastrophe that was the civil war in Afghanistan (1992–1996) and the subsequent Taliban takeover, Mozaffari, like his peers, gradually became disillusioned with ideology, politics, warfare, and other grand narratives. Mozaffari describes his own intellectual trajectory as progressing from the revolutionary leftist Islam espoused by Ali Shari'ati, the intellectual godfather of the Islamic Revolution, to the religious pluralism of Abdolkarim

Figure 2.5. Seyyed Abu Taleb Mozaffari.

Sorush, and then to *ma'naviat-garā'i*, or spiritualism, as found in the works of Mostafa Malekian and Seyyed Hossein Nasr (one of the leading figures in the nativist search for Iranian cultural "authenticity" and metaphysical alternatives to Western rationalism before the revolution).[28] Mozaffari now recognizes that an ideological vision of the world was too black-and-white, and says that he and his contemporaries blame blind ideologues for the tragedies that have befallen Afghanistan. This resonates with a broader trend among intellectuals in postrevolutionary Iran, who have experienced a "generalized loss of faith in mobilizing ideologies, especially Marxism and Third Worldism, along with the disappearance of the charismatic principle" of intellectual leadership that was prevalent from the 1950s to the 1970s (Jahanbegloo 2000: 136). There has also appeared a greater tendency toward mysticism and individualized spirituality, seen in the rise of a "postmodern" current among Iranian artists and scholars, what Matin-Asgari calls an "'intellectual style' [that] arguably has occupied the leading place that Marxism enjoyed in Iran a generation ago" (2004: 113).[29]

Nonetheless, Mozaffari recognizes that he and his peers were raised at a time when the dominant vision of cultural activity still included a prominent role for the so-called committed intellectual, as popularized in leftist and lay religious discourse before the Revolution. The rhetoric he uses is still that of the *rowshanfekr* leading the "masses" (*tudeh-ye mardom*) to progress and justice, even though it betrays a hesitation about that intellectual's ability to connect with ordinary people:[30]

> Afghanistan is a developing country that is at a sensitive stage of its history. It wants to transform its previous way of life, a classical and very traditional way of life, to a contemporary or modern way of life. In reality, the instruments of this transformation are intellectuals. Intellectuals can play a role in various respects: laying the groundwork of mental preparedness [*āmādegi-ye fekri*] in order to familiarize people with a new life; with law; with new social ethics; with different types of government; with the rule of law in government. This is the work of intellectuals. The job of educated, industrious people is to make this process of transformation develop from an industrial, administrative, and so on, perspective. Yes, I think that the only hope we can have is from the educated people and intellectuals.
>
> But unfortunately the relationship of Afghan intellectuals with the masses is a little bit cut off. The intellectual is distant from the people, is not among the people, and so over these years—over these several decades—he has not been able to find a deep connection with the people. That's why they have always formed a separate class. The Afghan intellectual needs to remove this gap, the gap between himself and the masses.

Mozaffari did not elaborate on how that gap may be removed, but this conundrum is one that continues to dog the current generation of poets and writers. It seems to me that there is an irresolvable irony here: a modern education inculcates in young people a different worldview from older generations or the nonliterate people around them, but that very difference seems to be a definitive part of what constitutes an intellectual. In a later interview, Mozaffari said that the word *rowshanfekr* is used as an insult by some, to whom it gives off the whiff of moral decadence and *gharbzadegi,* Westoxication or infatuation with the West, a concept made famous by the prerevolutionary Iranian writer Jalal Al-e Ahmad. In 1980s Afghanistan, it was associated with communism and antireligious sentiment, and many people, particularly in rural areas, believed that anyone who studied at a secular government school would inevitably become brainwashed by this ideology. Indeed, the members of Dorr-e Dari have been accused of intellectualism on many occasions by more conservative Afghans. On the other hand, it was clear from my fieldwork that individuals from families that have a tradition of scholarship or that consider themselves open-minded (*bā fekr-e bāz*), for example with respect to their daughters' education or other such innovations, will say with pride that they are *rowshanfekr* or its near-synonym, *farhangi* (cultured), while other people are *bi-farhang:* uncultured, backward, uncivilized. The different moral valences of these terms indicate a culture in which social status has faced upheaval and is still to an extent being renegotiated, such that signifiers of status may be used positively or contested or subverted in different contexts.

One of Mozaffari's best-known poems is a *masnavi* titled "Mādar" ("Mother"), in which the mother is a metonym for the poet's homeland, Afghanistan.[31] It was written in 2000, when the Taliban were in power across most of Afghanistan and the NATO-led military intervention had not yet begun, and reflects the poet's bitterness at the developments in his country. The poem retains the form and many of the rhetorical techniques of the war poetry of the 1980s (e.g., the mix of epic, folkloristic, and religious references and the uses of markedly local words and phrases), but its tone is one of disillusionment with military action and utter despondency at the prospects for political change: it is a lament for the devastated and corrupted homeland. It is presented as a lyrical soliloquy addressed to the mother, but it quickly becomes clear that the narrator is not merely addressing his own mother, and the "we" are not just his brothers and sisters, but a larger collectivity, one that has both suffered and perpetrated terrible violence:

Mādar salām! Mā hamegi nākhalaf shodim
Dar qaht-sāl-e 'ātefeh-hā-mān talaf shodim
Mādar salām! Tefl-e to digar bozorg shod
Ammā darigh, kudak-e nāz-e to gorg shod
Mādar! Asir-e vahshat-e jādu shodim mā
Chashmi gazid va yeksareh badkhu shodim mā
Mādar! Telesm-e daf'-e sharr az khu-ye mā beband
Ta'viz-e mehr bar sar-e bāzu-ye mā beband
Ey māh mā palang shodim o to sukhti
Mā sāheb-e tofang shodim o to sukhti

> Mother! Greetings [peace], we have all become unworthy
> We've wasted away in the drought-year of our emotions
> Mother! Greetings, your child has now grown up
> But alas, your sweet child has turned into a wolf
> Mother! We have become prisoners of magic's horror
> The evil eye has afflicted us and we've become ill-natured through and through
> Mother! Bind a talisman against evil to our personalities
> Tie an amulet of love around our arms
> O moon! We became panthers, and you burned
> We became bearers of guns, and you burned.
>
> (Fragment of "Mother"; original in Kazemi 1383/2005: 285–288)

This opening stanza plays on beliefs and superstitions about magic and protective amulets, probably dating from pre-Islamic times (even though amulets are usually inscribed with Qur'anic verses), that are still current among refugees from the rural Hazara society from which Mozaffari hails. They evoke the concern of a traditional, long-suffering mother for her children; the poet's entreaties to be wrapped in that magical protection are a plea for spiritual healing and a return to the familiar, innocent world of childhood, but they also hint at last-resort desperation when all other solutions have failed. When the narrator says that "we," the collective child, have become a wolf—a fearsome, rapacious creature—he is expressing guilt and self-loathing. The narrator here is clearly presenting himself as a spokesman for the community, engaging in a damning act of moral judgment that slips unsettlingly between blame and partial shouldering of collective responsibility for Afghanistan's crisis.

The final couplet is a haunting, ironic reference to a figure from Persian folktales, the panther that fell in love with the moon, symbol of the eternally beautiful, inaccessible Beloved.[32] "We became panthers" suggests that men became aggressive hunters in pursuit of an impossible ideal, while the Beloved, representing those ideals, burned and was destroyed in the conflagration. In Afghan Persian, the verb *sukhtan* (to burn) also bears connotations of quietly putting up with or tolerating something at one's own expense. The rhyme linking *palang* (panther) and *sāheb-e tofang* (bearer of guns) semiotically equates these nouns, signifying that the pursuit of the ideals was achieved by the taking up of arms, the cause of the conflagration. Meanwhile, the structural and syntactic location of the word *māh* (moon) in these two lines, as an object of address, equates it with the mother, so that the poem is in fact addressed to a combined Mother-Beloved that is a symbol for the homeland, which becomes increasingly clear later in the poem.[33]

Mozaffari's "Mother," then, reflects the disillusionment of the Afghan intellectual milieu; the feeling that ultimately led him and his peers to turn away from overt political engagement and to focus on critique and a more detached aesthetics.[34]

Among the younger generation of poets he has helped train, the melancholic tone is also dominant, but many of them have turned to a more intimate, lyrical style. I call this lyric realism (Olszewska 2013b) because it simultaneously aspires to be highly personal and to achieve a mimetic documentation of everyday life in refugee communities. Its often biting tone of irony, disenchantment and shattered illusions echoes the tropes that have appeared often in European realist fiction since the nineteenth century (Fanger 1965). The following is an example by Gholamreza Ebrahimi, written in 2003 and titled "Tah-e donyā" ("The End of the World"):

In istgāh-e sevvom o labriz-e ādam ast
Sā'at dobāreh shish shodeh ammā kasi kam ast
Howl midahand 'ālam o ādam, dar in miān
Yek piremard goft, Boro! Sandali kam ast.
In bār-e chandom ast ke u dir mikonad
Yā sobh-e zud rafteh va hālā Moqaddam ast.
Hālā savār-e yek otobus-e qorāzeh-am
Bāzār-e chashm-hā-ye tamāshā farāham ast.
Yek sandali-ye kohneh marā dar khod-ash neshānd
Yek sandali ke mesl-e khod-am gong o mobham ast
Bar u neveshteh- and be khatti kharāb o zesht
"Dar in zamāneh 'eshq, khodā, pond o derham ast"
Sad sārebān-e tarāneh o lab-hā-ye khoshk-e man . . .
Sheikhi be ta'neh goft ke āqā, Moharram ast!
*
Khāb o khiyāl āmad o dar man 'obur kard
Āqā boland show! Tah-e donyā, Moqaddam ast.

This is the third bus stop and it's overflowing with people,
it's six o'clock again but someone is [still] missing.
There's a world of people pushing and shoving, and in the midst of this,
an old man says, Get out! There aren't enough seats.
How many times has he [have I] got here late,
or gone early in the morning and reached Moqaddam by now?
Now I'm sitting on a dilapidated bus
and the bazaar is full of spectacle for my eyes
A worn-out seat has embraced me,
a seat that, like me, is mute and vague.
On it, they've written in a broken, ugly hand:
"In this era, Love [and] God are the pound and the dirham."
A hundred caravan-leaders of song and my dry lips . . .
A mullah sarcastically says, Mister, [don't you know] it's Moharram!
*
Sleep and dreams came and passed through me.
Mister, get up! This is the end of the world, Moqaddam.

(Original in Sajjadi 1384/2005: 27–28)

This poem is in the genre known as *ghazal-e now*, the new *ghazal*: meeting the requirements of rhyme and meter of the classical form, but with contemporary, conversational language, incorporating narrative elements, and recounting a mundane activity, in this case the daily journey to work of an Afghan laborer on a rickety old minibus. It is realistic in that it describes the narrator's journey through his external environment, the bus and the throng of passengers as his senses perceive them in vivid detail, but it is also intimately lyrical, as it evokes his inner state: "mute and vague," full of songs that he is unable to sing and dreams from which he is jolted by cold reality.[35]

Gholamreza told me that the poem specifically describes the commute of Afghan laborers in Mashhad, who go at dawn by bus to Chaharrah-e Moqaddam (Moqaddam Crossroads) where many bus lines terminate, to wait with their picks and shovels for employers to pick them up for a day's labor.[36] This practice is known as *sar-e falakeh*, "at the roundabout." He vividly describes the crowding, the competition, and the pessimistic graffiti on the bus seats that mirrors his own pessimism and his own nondescript self-perception. In the penultimate couplet, he tries to sing a song under his breath like a caravan leader (*sārebān*) of yore might have, but his enthusiasm is stifled by a cleric who reminds him that it is the mourning month of Moharram and singing is inappropriate.

The theme of reality baldly reasserting itself over imagination is ever-present in this poem. According to the graffiti on the bus seat, the ideals of Love and God have been reduced to currencies that may be bought and sold. If one sings, one will be cut off by the guardians of public morality, and if one falls asleep, one will inevitably be awakened by a stranger to another day of hard labor at the "end of the world." This shattering of illusions lies at the very heart of the poem, in the ironic confrontation between the formal frame of the poem—the *ghazal*, a poetic form traditionally dealing with earthly or divine love—with its prosaic content, and the cynical assertion scrawled in an ugly hand that Love and God are dead.

The combination of an eye on the external world and the narrator's inner responses to it turns the lyric realist mode into one that allows Afghan poets to document their everyday struggles and reflect on their disillusionment and their small moments of humiliation. But in this poem and others, the intertwining of the narrator's internal and external worlds "gives off" (Goffman 1956: 14–17) some idea of how they would like us to see *them* in that world. The narrator is not a passive passenger, but a keen observer who derives what pleasure he can from the "spectacle" of the bazaar. Yet his daydreaming and songs suggest a romantic sensibility, set apart from the rest of the passengers, forced into manual work out of necessity but dreaming of bigger things. Not all lyric poems necessarily represent the poet's true experiences, but Gholamreza has in fact worked as a laborer. As he told me, "I have lived 95 percent of my poems. That is, I definitely have a record of them in my mind. Some of them I even have in my mind with all of their images, both general and specific." Gholamreza was also an active member of Dorr-e Dari and other poetry circles and editor of an Afghan student journal, and eventually obtained a sociology degree despite considerable obstacles, including a bout of depression. The poem thus represents the contradictory life of the exiled intellectual, who rubs shoulders with his disadvantaged fellow refugees but perceives his own status as different: as a thinker, a dissatisfied observer. Crucially, the contrast between the narrator's imaginings with his moment of disillusionment is necessary to demonstrate the dual qualities expected of the poet-intellectual: sensitivity, thoughtfulness, and empathy, combined with the capacity for clear-eyed and nonideological appraisal of social conditions.

Conclusion

Afghan refugees have responded to, and participated in, the modernizing forces at work in Iran in the last three decades. In the Islamic Republic, Afghans encountered a state and society that many came to see as more *pishrafteh* (advanced) than that of their homeland, but also as more pure and correct in its religious practices. Revolutionary ideas of rational and pious citizenship through education, new ethics of public action including both greater individualism and greater social awareness, the discipline and sanitation of body and mind (whether through family planning or prayer), and the importance of a public role for women, reached Afghan refugees no less than they did the Iranians among whom they lived. The paradox here, however, was that Afghans never were citizens, and have often been one of the groups most vulnerable to the coercive aspects of state rationalization policies and biopolitics, whether through aggressive promotion of contraception, the denial of the right to education because of its drain on the state budget, or roundups and deportation. They both benefited from the Islamic Republic's populism and suffered when the beneficiaries of expensive state welfare policies began to be defined in strictly national terms (Adelkhah and Olszewska 2007). This has had complex effects on the subjectivity of second-generation refugees in particular, who both identify with and feel alienated from their Iranian home, and project feelings of both belonging and terrifying strangeness and backwardness onto their unseen homeland, Afghanistan.

Is it possible to see Afghan refugee intellectuals as "organic" intellectuals in Gramsci's terms (1971: 5–14)? He used this term to describe intellectuals arising from a particular social class, who play a major role in organizing that class. Afghan refugee intellectuals are indeed associated with a fundamental social group, although one defined more by its noncitizen status than by class; and because political and economic organization to defend their interests is closed to them, they have concentrated on educational and cultural organizing, for example through the autonomous schools and institutions like Dorr-e Dari. But it was precisely these institutions that helped to extend the hegemonic project of the state even as the state held them at arm's length, and even as they remained critical of it. Indeed, the extent to which Afghans in Iran, despite their marginal position in society, seem to have internalized various practices and beliefs promoted in wider Iranian society is striking.

But although the intellectuals claim to represent and seek to enlighten all their fellow refugees, some of their compatriots reject these efforts. The reason for this may lie in the gradual process of class differentiation that is taking place within Afghan refugee society. Those refugees who can cultivate cultural dispositions appropriate to educated, aspiring middle-class people can stake their claims to a higher status in Iranian society (vis-à-vis other Afghans *and* Iranians). Being lettered and cultured people or intellectuals—by displaying the appropriate attitudes toward "authenticated" religion and women's rights, for example—is one of the few ways they have of capturing cultural capital when economic capital is scarce. In this way, perhaps they are encouraging the formation of a nascent refugee proto-bourgeoisie in Iran, and their melancholy structures of feeling reflect the many challenges of that position.

3 Afghan Literary Organizations in Postrevolutionary Iran

THE ARENA OF DEATH

Hark! Now is not the time for hesitation, tie up your bundle [and go]
Our patience with the foe runs short, tie up your bundle [and go]
If the foot drags, still you must go
Though your end be at the gallows, still you must go
From the depths of the incident [the battlefield] the smell of battle reaches us
See, the yells of manly [heroic] men reach us
Hark! Set your foot in the arena of death and [be prepared to] die
Come! Now is not the time for hesitation, stand up straight and die
[The foe] thinks each of your numerous wounds a scourge
[The foe] thinks the fury of your blood a river
Since the reins of Rakhsh the danger seeker are in your hands
Your defeat is the defeat of this [whole] tribe's fortress
Hark! The crimson of the dawn sun belongs to us
And the foremost banner of the jihad belongs to us
Tell the enemy that we have no concern for death
"He who is not killed is not of our tribe."

    Mohammad Asef Rahmani

THE BENCH OPPOSITE

I move past all my excuses
on the first bench
my skirt picks up the smell of damp grass
There are always crows here
Stray crows
[There is] neither my shape
Nor the geometry of you
Today I'm a wanderer
so much so that I don't know the taste of an apple.
Your shoulders don't tremble.

> I don't care
> which tree will reach maturity today
> and [that] an apple will fall
> and the flowers on a girl's skirt will be disturbed.
>
> If only the bench opposite [mine]
> were for you
> The pleasure of nonexistence
> rises up to the tree's throat
> and with one sound disintegrates.
> The pungent smell of the grass
> The crows have gone
> The bench opposite mine is empty.
>   Ma'sumeh Ahmadi

THESE TWO POEMS, though written fewer than two decades apart in the same social milieu, could not be more different in tone, style, and authorship. The first is a war poem, written in the 1980s with the aim of mobilizing young men to go to Afghanistan to fight in the war of resistance against the Soviet occupation with one of the armed groups supported by Iran. It is written in a classical form, the *masnavi,* with a strict pattern of rhyme and meter, and is full of archaic, bombastic, and martial words. In this way it harks back to Persian epics through the reference to Rakhsh, the steed of Rostam, one of the heroes of the *Shāhnāmeh.* The doubled-up phrase *na'reh-ye mardān-e mard* (lit. the yells of manly men, with manliness here signifying courage) leaves us with no doubt that it is a hypermasculine poem.

The second poem, however, is the impressionistic reverie of a young girl sitting on a bench in a park or orchard, imagining that someone—perhaps her beloved or an absent friend—is sitting opposite. Rather than thinking of grand historic events affecting tribes and nations, this poet has the luxury of indulging in a fantasy and dwelling sensually on the little things in life: the smell of the grass, the taste of an apple, the sight of some stray crows. The poem is a lyric in blank verse, a self-consciously modern, subjective genre. Unlike the images of the first poem, which function metonymically to invoke epic and religious notions of heroism through conventional images easily readable by all Persian speakers, the images of the second do not seem to have a significance beyond its boundaries. The apples, crows and grass do not have fixed symbolic meanings in Persian; rather, they are examples of what Leach has called "nonce," or private symbols (1976: 15), which are endowed with individual meanings by modernist poets.[1] Appreciating this poem thus requires a shift in modes of reading and interpretation.

Two single poems plucked out of context tell us little, but it is remarkable that at the time the first was written, nothing like the second could be imagined; and by the time the second was written, the first and others like it were considered obsolete. What accounts for this transformation? It is not simply that the war has ended, for the conflict in Afghanistan continues in a different form, although refugees are no longer being called on to fight. It is also too simple to surmise that second-generation Afghan youth have assimilated into Iranian society and prefer other kinds of poetry, because we must account for the fact that Iranian poetry itself has made a similar journey from its own revolutionary and war poetry of the 1980s to a bewildering array of poetic experiments today.

An anthropological understanding of this generic, generational, and gendered shift requires us to consider changes in a web of relations between poets, patrons, audiences, the wider social and political milieu, and aesthetic norms that exist in what Bourdieu (1993, 1996) has called the field of cultural production. Barber's ethnographic work on popular culture in Nigeria also provides useful conceptual tools in her emphasis on the generative relationships between genres and audiences in particular. She argues that literary and performance genres address specific audiences and thus "convene" and "constitute those audiences as a particular form of collectivity" (1997: 354; 2007). Here she draws on Bakhtin's argument that "addressivity, the quality of turning to someone, is a constitutive feature of the utterance. . . . The various typical forms this addressivity assumes and the various concepts of the addressee are constitutive, definitive features of various speech genres" (1986: 99). The same is true of poetic genres; and so the key to understanding the difference between Rahmani's and Ahmadi's poems is the shift in their intended audiences and their sharply contrasting expectations of what poetry is and what it should do.

Yet, for all their differences, the two poems have a commonality: they are both best understood in the context of Persian literary modernism, and their juxtaposition helps to complicate what we mean by this term. I thus begin with a brief account of the emergence of modern Persian poetry, situating postrevolutionary poetry within this narrative to set the stage for the emergence and development of Afghan literary organizations and their audiences in Iran from the 1980s to the 2000s. Drawing on Bourdieu and Barber, I pay particular attention to the politics of patronage, the role of ideology, and the relationships between poets, genres, and audiences. However, there are limits to the usefulness of Bourdieu's theory of cultural production in our context because of his lack of attention to political literature. Nonetheless, his idea of "position takings" is helpful for understanding how and why moral and aesthetic claims often intertwine in the reception and critical evaluations of literature. I show how individual Afghan poets' locations in the field of cultural production, and their creative responses to them, lead them to take certain "positions" on the nature and purpose of poetry and what constitutes artistic merit.

The Emergence of Persian Literary Modernism

From the late nineteenth century onward, Persian literature underwent one of its periodic moments of renewal with the emergence of modernist literature (*adabiyāt-e modern*). With the development of new technologies (notably print), exposure to European culture, and expanding literacy, many new literary genres emerged, often as borrowings from European literature. These included prose novels and novellas, drama, journalism, and literary and social criticism in the European vein.[2] Native literary forms like poetry underwent a concomitant process of change that, although gradual, was retrospectively perceived as a sharp break with the past. These changes reflected a shift in the patronage of poetry and audiences for poetry—or rather, the audiences for the kind of poetry that has been preserved in the national literary canon. *National* is a key word here, because the new poetry was developed by the same *rowshanfekrān* who were simultaneously forging Iranian nationalism and calling for constitutionalism. The emergence of modernist poetry, then, can be seen as reflecting the beginnings of a shift in the center of gravity of political power in Iran.[3]

The standard narrative of the stylistic changes that occurred in poetry reads as follows:

> No more of the moon-faced beauties and their hair-thin waists and intoxicated eyes; no more of the disdainful beloved with the hearts of a thousand lovers enmeshed in her dark tresses; no more of the carefree drinker leaving the mosque for the tavern in search of truth; no more of the almost ritual lament against the fickleness of fate and the frustrations of unrequited love; no more of the age-old metaphors of the nightingale and the rose, the moth and the candle flame. Instead, there was a fresh look at the outside world and a recognition of one's own inner yearnings, conflicts, and sensibilities. (Yarshater 1978: xiii–xiv)

According to this narrative of Iranian literary historiography, which has practically attained the status of a national myth in Iran, it was in the mid-twentieth century that a lone innovator with the pen name Nima Yushij found a solution to the growing discrepancies between literary form and modern experience by creating a distinctively modern genre of poetry. But Karimi-Hakkak (1995) has shown persuasively that the reality was more complex: in fact, a large number of poets had worked over a long period of time to borrow, translate, modify, and appropriate various thematic and stylistic preoccupations from European (mostly French and German) literature, beginning in the late nineteenth century. The appropriations had to be naturalized into Persian poetic language in a way that would be recognized *as poetry*, and thus they involved a number of reworkings. At first, the visible and aural identifiers of the Persian genres—such as rhyme, meter, and types of diction—remained unchanged, but new vocabularies were introduced and given new meanings. This gradual metamorphosis accompanied the appearance of patriotic and political poetry in the years leading up to the Constitutional Revolution (1905–1911), promoting a new relationship between the self and society, the people and the recently conceived nation-state homeland (*vatan*). Traditional poetry was satirized and ridiculed; though ironically, such attacks themselves were usually couched in traditional genres, and no clear formal alternatives were proposed. The long-standing tradition of Persian didactic poetry was put to use, but now to exhort the reader or listener to strive for a reformed society—through education, hard work, and political activity—within an emerging new understanding of historical progress (Karimi-Hakkak 1995).

In Afghanistan, too, a small group of modernist intellectuals arose, associated with the royal court, at the beginning of the twentieth century. A leading figure among them, Mahmud Tarzi, had returned from exile in Istanbul and brought with him many new ideas. In 1911, he established Afghanistan's first biweekly, *Serāj al-Akhbār/The Torch of News,* which became a key vehicle for disseminating modern ideas among the small but growing reading public, most of them educated at the new European-style school founded by King Habibullah, the Habibiyah. They, like their Iranian counterparts, strove for the awakening of their nation through literature, emphasizing a purposive literary practice committed to social and political reform—the creation of citizens rather than subjects—and enabling a "radical cultural critique of the state and society" (W. Ahmadi 2008: 8).[4] In a sign of continued cultural flows between the nascent national spaces of Iran and Afghanistan, similar themes, rhetorical stances, and even expressions may be found in the early-twentieth-century reformist poetry of both countries. Both called for a shift in the expressive mode and the creation of a socially relevant and useful poetry; both vehemently rejected traditional stylistic conventions.

Nima Yushij's contribution in the mid-twentieth century, therefore, should more appropriately be seen as the culmination of a process of intense literary debate and transformation, rather than its instigation (Karimi-Hakkak 1995: 6). His status as a founding father has been so enduring in both Iran and Afghanistan because of his prolific articulation of the theoretical aspects of the new poetry (*she'r-e now*), because he had many ardent followers, and because the changes he made to poetry—such as breaking up the previously uniform line lengths and introducing a selective use of rhyme—were the most readily perceptible to the ear and eye (234–235). Later poets (the first being Ahmad Shamlu) did away with rhyme and meter altogether, creating blank verse (*she'r-e sepid*). It was at this point, Karimi-Hakkak argues, that the previously alien elements that had been brought into Persian poetry came to be accepted as *poetry,* and the system stabilized again around a new interpretive community of poets, critics, and readers.

The major difference in this new system of signification was that the old expressive conventions (the moon-faced beauties, nightingales, and roses, etc.), shared for centuries by the poet and his audience, had been replaced by "a conscious endeavor to construct poetic images of the poet's *own making*" (Karimi-Hakkak 1995: 259, emphasis added). These new images were often closely related to the sociopolitical discourses of the time. Such obscure metaphorical meanings, sometimes transparent only to the poet himself, then required authoritative critics to interpret them for a wider audience. Nima's legacy was that audiences were no longer expected to draw on their own shared knowledge of the classics in order to interpret poetry, but to see the world around them as a continuous source of novel poetic signs: "Nima invites his readers to participate in the act of creating meaning by contemplating the delight in their own observations" (Karimi-Hakkak 1995: 274). Ma'sumeh Ahmadi's poem very much reflects this spirit, but as we shall see, the subjectiveness of this process of meaning making poses challenges for comprehension and interpretation that continue to be debated in poetic forums.

Another unprecedented development in the twentieth century was that the major sources of poetic patronage and arbitration of poetic taste moved away from the royal court and the state as the Pahlavi monarchy showed little interest in poetry. Instead, the interpretive communities of poets, critics, and readers of modernist poetry typically came from middle- or upper-class, educated backgrounds, the people who called themselves *rowshanfekr*. Their gatherings, often connected to oppositional political groups, became the primary locus of literary activity. Writers, journalists, and critics tended to organize in more or less formal groups or associations. The scale of these new bourgeois publics could not have been attained without print technology and rising literacy levels in both Iran and Afghanistan. A number of influential newspapers and journals had emerged in the late nineteenth century, many of them published in exile, to spread the new sociopolitical ideas, and literati tended to cluster around them.[5] Apart from content such as news, political essays, and satire, these periodicals frequently published poetry, often political in theme, and were the cradle of early modernist trends in poetry and prose. (The *Third Script* is thus part of a print periodical culture through which a group of intellectuals finds and shapes a reading public—a tradition dating back more than a century.)

The activities of *rowshanfekr* circles thus included reading, writing, and conversation, and through these they "created and reflected changes in the role of the reader: from that of a passive reader who simply memorized the beautiful classical verses to that of an active reader who vigorously responds to politically significant texts" (Talatoff 2000: 16). Indeed, the literati were seen as the spokespeople for the politicized intelligentsia in general (Dabashi 1985) and poetry was used to transmit important political and ideological messages. The view that poetry should be socially useful and should drive the engines of progress and modernity became so ingrained in Iranian intellectuals, most of whom were left-leaning in the twentieth century, that even a sociologist of literature like Dabashi could permit himself a polemic such as this: discussing twentieth-century Iranian writers, he accuses those who remained aloof from politics and from modernist developments in Persian literature of being "culturally stagnant, socially isolated, and morally indifferent" (1985: 174). "Unable to bear the contradictions of a disenchanted world, they hid behind the thick walls of moral indifference and emotional insensitivity—regurgitating stale enchantments of by-gone days" (175). Talatoff has argued that each literary and ideological movement of the twentieth century in Iran drew on and incorporated, but also subverted and undermined, the discourses, ideologies, and representational strategies that preceded them. Marxist and leftist literature described as Committed (*adabiyāt-e mota'ahhed*) that spanned the 1940s to the 1970s focused opposition to the Shah's rule and eventually helped to foment the 1979 revolution.[6]

Few scholarly studies outside Iran have explored the effects of the Islamic Revolution on literature,[7] but Talatoff's brief survey describes the emergence of modern Persian literature with religious themes and a return to extensive state patronage of literature, particularly poetry. Meanwhile, the Marxist and other secular participants in the revolutionary movement were quickly sidelined by the religious factions, and the prerevolutionary literary circles, which were predominantly leftist, were dispersed and silenced through exile, arrest, assassination, and heavy censorship. Religious writers who supported the new order rose to take their place, providing the ruling elite with political support. The state saw in these writers a valuable resource for the Islamization of the country and for supporting the war effort against Iraq (dubbed the Sacred Defense). Thus, the Ministry of Islamic Culture and Guidance promoted and published work that it considered to be Islamic, and authors who identified as Islamic "enjoyed relative freedom" (Talatoff 2000: 112).

But prerevolutionary aesthetic currents left a deep imprint on such literature: the literature of the Islamic Revolution and the Sacred Defense drew heavily on the imagery and metaphors of Committed literature. As Talatoff shows, "Muslim writers appropriated their rhetoric . . . [and] their notions of commitment, populism, anti-imperialistic sentiments, and justice from pre-revolutionary Committed Literature" (2000: 133). However, there were two major changes. First, while commitment in the mid-twentieth century signified opposition to the state and adherence to left-inspired principles of social justice, after the revolution—which was after all hailed as the victory of such principles—it meant *alignment* with the state and its values (Shams 2015a). Second, while postrevolutionary poetry undoubtedly incorporated earlier themes and rhetoric associated with modernism, poetic *form* became the subject of an ideological clash. Blank verse with no rhyme or meter was seen as a sign of corrupting Western influence and was discouraged, although Nima-style (*nimā'i*) poetry—with meter, irregular line lengths, and sporadic use of rhyme—was still occasionally used (Shams 2015a).

In light of these developments, it is easy to see the kinship of Ahmadi's "The Bench Opposite," in its enigmatic symbolism and dreamlike atmosphere, with the modernist blank verse of the twentieth century. However, it would be a mistake to see Rahmani's "The Arena of Death" as an archaism, a throwback to more "classical" poetic styles. Certainly, in its strict use of rhyme and meter and imagery from old epic poems, it invoked the classical tradition, but the audience it interpellated was a new one: men associated with new types of social organizations, political parties, and partisan groups, structured by ideology rather than kinship ties or home village, and increasingly imagining the Afghan nation-state as its "arena" of struggle. The *masnavi* form itself was a modified version of its classical predecessor, with a longer meter, and was used for political poetry of this kind for the first time. It was thus a new genre of political poetry for a new kind of political subject, and the next section reveals how it came to have its day and why it eventually waned.

Refugee Poets and Literary Patronage in the Islamic Republic

In the 1980s, the Islamic Republic struggled to entrench itself politically and culturally while simultaneously fighting a war with Iraq. At the same time, the war against the Soviets was raging in Afghanistan, as was an internal struggle for power among rival Hazara armed groups. What effects did such an environment have on the literary production of the time, particularly that of refugees? In answering this question, I rely on my interviews with the leading figures of the so-called first generation of Afghan refugee poets—Mohammad Kazem Kazemi, Seyyed Abu Taleb Mozaffari, Seyyed Nader Ahmadi, and Fazlollah Qodsi—as well as on their published writing.

Cultural production in the Islamic Republic is subject to the scrutiny of the Ministry of Culture and Islamic Guidance (MCIG), or a parallel body, the Howzeh-ye Honari (Arts Center) of the Sazman-e Tablighat-e Eslami (Organization of Islamic Propaganda, OIP), founded in 1981. It was—and continues to be—impossible to legally publish any literary work without submitting it for review and obtaining a permit or license (*mojavvez*) from one of these organizations. The Arts Center, which is not subject to the oversight and censorship of the MCIG but is a public body directly responsible to the supreme leader,[8] arguably became the most important and influential cultural institution in postrevolution Iran (Shams 2015b), playing a key role in the emergence of Afghan refugee poetry as a major patron of their literary activities. Its membership consisted of religious supporters of the revolution who were interested in promoting Afghan refugee literature because their ideology was pan-Islamic rather than nationalist. To them, as Mohammad Kazem Kazemi explained to me, "being Iranian was not that important; they more frequently had discussions of the world of Islam or the global Islamic movement, and because of this they were attentive to Afghanistan. But besides this, those who were more prominent among them were the young generation, and our young people got along very well with them." The Arts Center supported Afghan literary endeavors by offering refugees space to organize gatherings and publishing the first anthologies of Afghan resistance poetry and individual poets' first volumes. Its literary journal, *Sureh* (*Verse*, as in a verse of the Qur'an) devoted an issue to Afghan poetry, its members wrote books on Afghanistan, and it has been the most active Iranian publisher of Afghan poetry, which Kazemi described as an "enormous service" to refugee poets.

Within refugee communities themselves, the institutions that defined much of their communal life, including literary production, were the Iranian-backed Shi'a Afghan political parties and armed resistance groups, such as Sazman-e Nasr-e Eslami and the Pasdaran, united after 1989 into a single organization, Hezb-e Vahdat. As Seyyed Abu Taleb Mozaffari explained to me, there was little space for any social or cultural activities at that time that were not under the wing of one or another of the parties: "The first bases of [Afghan] culture and thought in Iran were in the hands of the parties. So if anyone had a publication, published books, organized gatherings somewhere—there were no independent people who could do this and Iran did not give permits for them to do this. For this reason, whether we liked it or not, poetry, resistance poetry in a way developed and began its activities within the parties." The parties would invite poets to their public gatherings, ceremonies, and processions. Sometimes two poets from different parties would read poems for or against a particular idea at the same gathering. These poems were never commissioned, stressed Mozaffari, but were written with the full weight of conviction by their authors and had a great impact on their listeners.

Afghan religious students at the *howzeh*s soon set up their own association, Kanun-e Mohajer (Refugee Association), which published a magazine titled *Payām-e Mohājer/The Refugee's Message* in Qom. The ideology expounded on its pages was anti-Soviet and yet radical, a pro-peasant and pro-worker revolutionary Islam that sought to overthrow the traditional power structures of rural Afghanistan—and specifically those of the Shi'a Hazarajat. It must be remembered that in the early 1980s, a civil war that was simultaneously a social revolution was taking place in the Hazarajat, in which the Iran-supported armed Shi'a parties fought against and eventually prevailed over—although did not quite defeat—the traditional leadership that was largely comprised of Seyyeds, landowners, *mirs,* and *arbāb*s (hereditary state-appointed village headmen). Some of the earliest resistance poetry was published in *The Refugee's Message*, much of it with a strident anti-feudal tone; it was an early forum for Afghan refugees with literary tendencies to hone their polemical and poetic skills.

These forms of literary patronage, as well as the ongoing climate of political engagement through literature and grass-roots organizations that continued after the revolution, affected the form and content of refugee poetry. State-sponsored poetry's primary purpose in the 1980s, among Iranians, was to communicate and encourage moral and political support for the Islamic Revolution, the cultural revolution the state had launched in order to Islamize society, and the need for participation in the Sacred Defense against Iraq. Among Afghans, meanwhile, it aimed to encourage the jihad against the Soviets (or the struggle for political primacy amongst their own rival parties). Seyyed Nader Ahmadi recalled that at the time, refugee poetry mainly functioned as a medium of mass communication for such ideas. As such, it needed above all to keep its purpose and audience in mind: the latter primarily consisted of Afghan refugee men, the majority of whom were from rural areas, nonliterate, and pious.

The diction of resistance poetry was, therefore, straightforward and transparent: "At that time, the simpler the poem, the clearer its message for the listener, the more effective it was," Mozaffari recalled. But it had nonetheless to be rhythmic and rhetorical to appeal to the emotions, to stoke fervor for the revolution and war in a public gathering, and ultimately to cause people to act on these emotions and to participate in political or military action. Perhaps the most significant aspect of rhyme and meter is that they form a recognizable pattern that primes the ear for listening and the mind for committing to memory, as well as being aesthetically pleasing to those versed in the classical tradition. Afghan refugee audiences would have been familiar with vernacular oral poetry as well as with the classical Persian epic poetry that, as we shall see, was traditionally read and recited on winter evenings, both of which adhered to strict patterns of prosody. But very few of them would have recognized as poetry the modernist experiments with blank verse that, in Afghanistan, at least, had never traveled far beyond Kabul.

Anthologies of resistance poetry are thus filled with poems in classical, or to put it more accurately, neoclassical (*now-kelāsik*) forms. The most typical forms of the Persian classical tradition are the *ghazal*, the *qasideh*, and the *masnavi*. The former two maintain strict formal rules, with a monorhyme scheme (aa ba ca, etc.) and a refrain (*radif*), a short word or phrase that immediately follows the rhyming phrase. The *ghazal* has paradigmatically been associated with love, separation, and their mystical elaborations, and is usually short—around six to ten couplets—while the *qasideh* is often much longer and was typically used for praise poetry for rulers. But the most common form used in resistance poetry was the *masnavi*, like Rahmani's. The *masnavi* is a long poem consisting of rhyming couplets (aa bb cc). Unlike the *ghazal* and *qasideh*, it does not maintain a monorhyme throughout, making it suitable for long narrative poems; it was typically used by classical poets for epics and romances.[9]

Afghan poets of the so-called war generation preferred this genre for their resistance writings because, as Mozaffari explained to me, one is able to express philosophical or political thoughts, to argue, to expostulate, to speak one's mind through it. These poets experimented with the form and, finding the classical meter typical of the *masnavi* to be limited in its ability to contain many of the words and phrases needed for contemporary resistance poetry, they modified it. To convey both "the fire of emotion and bravery in the face of the enemy, they needed a meter that lay somewhere between the *ghazal* and the epic" (Hojjati 1378/1999: 67a). To this end, the poets of the time took as their model their Iranian contemporary Ali Mo'allem Damghani (b. 1951) who had created a special long meter for the *masnavi*, and thus the political *masnavi* of this period arguably emerged as an entirely new genre.

Classical metaphors and allusions (*talmih*), like the reference to the steed Rakhsh in Rahmani's poem, were extensively used in resistance poetry because they conveyed deeper layers of meaning through figures familiar to listeners.[10] But they were often used in novel ways, because the political ideas being appealed to were new. A new relationship between the poet, the listener, and the political struggle had to be envisioned, since the war in Afghanistan was represented simultaneously as violating both Islamic propriety and *national* space. As we have seen, the revolutionary discourse of the time—both among Iranians and Afghans—owed much to prerevolutionary Committed literature and its Marxist rhetoric. At the same time, it was Shi'a Islam that molded the defining character of the Iranian revolution and the would-be revolution in the Hazarajat, and a great number of poems were composed that related both the wartime battles and people's everyday struggles to the story of Karbala and to the great Shi'a martyrs.[11] The martial rhetoric of Rahmani's poem, with its mixed metaphors of the "crimson of the dawn sun" and "the foremost banner of the jihad," has echoes of both.

The poetic "I" at the time, therefore, represented a collective rather than an individual I. The tone, diction, and imagery most frequently selected for poetry was the *hamāsi*, or epic or martial, style found, for example, in the battle scenes of the *Shāhnāmeh* or Nezami's romances, also written in the *masnavi* form. Several poets I interviewed recalled that it was not considered appropriate to publish love poetry; even if some wrote it in private, they would not have dared to publish or recite it in public.[12] But *ghazals* with a political rather than amorous theme were often composed, and indeed it became a hallmark of the resistance *masnavi* to embellish it with a *ghazal* in the middle. As with the poetry of the Pashtun refugees of the same era in Peshawar that Edwards documented, "The poet's voice [was] the voice of the culture at large, and his judgments reflect[ed] not an individual's biases but the sensibilities and concerns of the community, as that community [was] defined in any given situation" (Edwards 1986b: 472).[13]

Unlike Edwards, however, I am interested in what was novel about the way that community was being defined. In the work of most Persian-language refugee poets, it was not the tribe that was the primary object of shameful violation by the Soviet invaders, but the homeland (*vatan*), and it was the homeland that had to be avenged through redemptive struggle. Martyrdom was embraced as the most desirable culmination of such honorable struggle to remove "the yoke of servitude" from the neck of the nation; and a whole host of tropes from classical poetry, from the drunken intoxication of libertine dervishes and the mystical pursuit of self-annihilating union with the beloved to laments for the Shi'a martyrs, were engaged and reconfigured to express devotion to, and self-sacrifice for, the *vatan*. The cultural trope of *gheirat*, or jealous protectiveness of one's *nāmus*—traditionally a reference to the women in a man's care—to which a man's honor is closely bound, was also applied to the *vatan*, implying that a man who did not protect the honor of the homeland was no man.[14] This trope is clearly noticeable in Rahmani's poem, which excludes from membership in the tribe those who are not prepared to die.

The conception of the Perso-Arabic term *vatan* as equivalent to the homeland of a group of people occupying the physical and symbolic spaces of a nation-state emerged in both Iran and Afghanistan toward the end of the nineteenth century, as part of the intellectual and political ferment that eventually led to the adoption of constitutional systems in both countries in the early twentieth century (Tavakoli-Targhi 2001: 114–117).[15] A new vision of *vatan* as the nation-state homeland, ailing and in need of rescue, and often personified as a mother, appeared in poetry for the first time concomitantly with these changes (see Karimi-Hakkak 1995, Ahmadi 2008). In the twentieth century, *vatan-parasti* (patriotism) has appeared as a regular concern in the metropolitan poetry of the intellectuals and elites in both countries. However, for audiences of rural origin, whose poetic tradition until then had still mostly revolved around the classics of Hafez and Sa'di and vernacular poetry, these ideas took longer to crystallize. A new subjectivity, a new way of hearing and responding to a new message, and a new sense of political implicatedness had to be inculcated in the audiences of resistance poetry, but its authors came out to meet their expectations mid-way by adapting forms recognizable as poetry and effective for mass communication.

The resistance poets' efforts to appeal to this particular audience appear to have been highly successful. Mozaffari's description of audiences' response to poetry readings illustrates how participatory such events were and how effective they no doubt were in instilling a sense of community through a shared appreciation of particular verses or a common response to vivid rhetoric: "They would have a strong effect on the crowd. . . . The people would praise them and say *bah bah* and *chah chah* [vocal exclamations of admiration] and the poets became well known," he explained. A good audience vocalizes its approval, saying "bah bah" in response to a particularly effective turn of phrase and joining the poet in speaking out loud rhyming words it may have preemptively guessed, or a refrain that is repeated through the poem.[16] Ordinary people in those days knew many poets and many of their lines by heart.

The Birth of Dorr-e Dari

Over time, organizations were formed among the refugees that had primarily a secular literary and cultural, rather than political, focus. In 1984, the Anjoman-e Sho'ara-ye Mohajer (Association of Refugee Poets) was formed in Mashhad by a number of Herati poets under the leadership of Barat Ali Fada'i (Hojjati 1378/1999: 64b). Although its members were supporters or activists of the Afghan resistance parties, the discussions in its gatherings were literary rather than political.

But a younger generation of poets, most of whom had been educated at the Mashhad *Howzeh*, had a more radical cultural agenda and felt the need for a "shedding of the old skin," as Seyyed Nader Ahmadi put it. In 1991, with the support of the OIP's Arts Center, they formed the Anjoman-e Sho'ara-ye Enqelab-e Eslami-ye Afghanestan (Association of the Poets of the Islamic Revolution of Afghanistan). This comprised intellectuals who considered themselves both Islamic and leftist—that is, concerned with social justice and revolution within an Islamic framework. Many of them were supporters rather than active members of the united Shi'a party Hezb-e Vahdat, which was supported by Iran. Their Iranian, rather than Afghan, patronage probably played a role in allowing them to develop a critical stance toward the Afghan armed groups and their not-infrequent abuses of power, which escalated as the 1990s wore on. Their names became well-known among Shi'a Afghans in the 1990s, and out of this group—Mohammad Sharif Sa'idi, Seyyed Nader Ahmadi, Seyyed Abu Taleb Mozaffari, Mohammad Asef Rahmani, Ali Payam, Mohammad Javad Khavari, and Mohammad Kazem Kazemi—all except the last had been *tollāb* or seminary students. Their connection with the Arts Center served them well, as it continued to assist them in publishing their work. Ali Mo'allem Damghani, a prominent poet of the revolution and the Sacred Defense, also lent his support for the first anthology of Afghan resistance poetry (Kazemi and Rahmani 1370/1991) by writing its introduction, and the book was published by the Arts Center.[17]

During Afghanistan's civil war in the wake of the fall of the Communist government in 1992 and the failure of the Mujahideen groups to agree on a future government, refugee writing became more ambivalent. The foreign aggressors and sources of financial support had withdrawn, leaving behind a fratricidal war for political primacy. Although many refugees continued to support particular parties and the idea of Shi'a power itself—for example, supporting Abdol Ali Mazari, the Hazara leader of Hezb-e Vahdat, in the terrible fighting in West Ka-

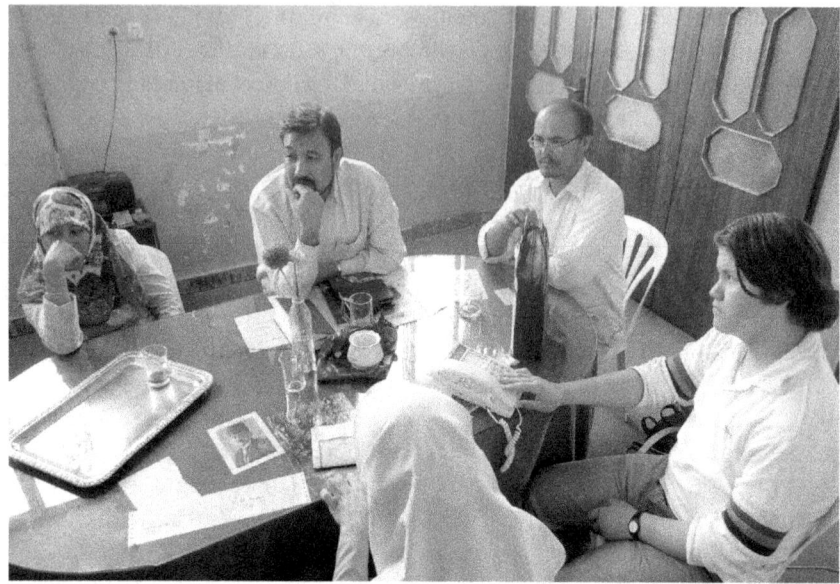

Figure 3.1. An editorial meeting of the *Third Script*, 2007.

bul that culminated in the Afshar massacre of Shiʻa civilians in 1993—others began to question their own role in backing military force, whose effects had fallen far short of their promise. On the other hand, while some politicians were for conciliation and peacemaking, many poets, including Kazemi, Qodsi, and Mozaffari, opposed the disarmament of Shiʻa troops and urged them to fight on. But it was no longer simple to typecast good and evil as native and foreign oppressor, believer and communist infidel, respectively. As one Afghan commentator put it, "Judgment was and is not so simple in civil war. Perception of reality requires a strong sensitivity and more than anything it requires courage. For this reason [story-writing and poetry declined during this period], even though the biggest misfortunes and most painful disasters occurred during the time of the civil war" (Hojjati 1378/1999: 68b).

As several poets recalled in our conversations, people found themselves increasingly disillusioned by a situation of inter-ethnic warfare and bloodshed that was becoming difficult to praise. It was in such a context that another "shedding

Figure 3.2. Covers of Afghan publications. Top row: issues of the *Third Script*, cover design by Wahidullah Abassi. Bottom left: an issue of *Farkhar* published by the House of Afghan Literature in Tehran, cover design by Majid Akbarzadeh. Bottom right: Fatemeh Sajjadi's edited anthology of refugee youth poetry, *Tangled Locks*, cover design by Wahidullah Abassi.

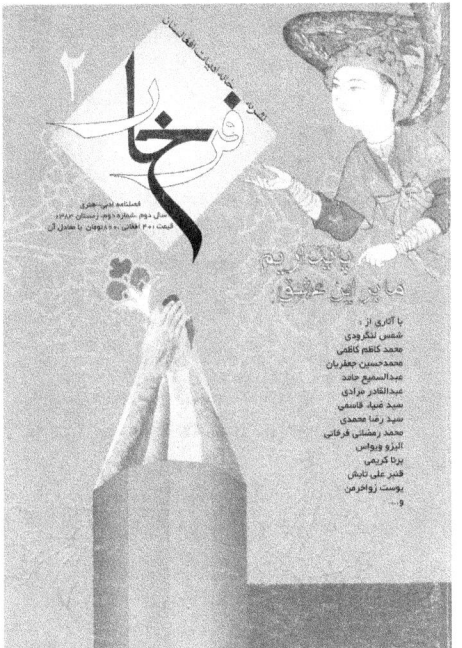

of old skin" took place and the foundations for a multi-ethnic literary organization were laid in 1997, devoted solely to cultural rather than political work. Its own publicity material states: "During the two decades of the refugee presence in Iran, a generation of intellectuals had the opportunity to arise which protested against the current of factionalism and discrimination dominant in their country, and saw the solution to the crisis in independent, specialist cultural work, focused on national unity. . . . They did not divide their homeland into north and south, nor did they want their patriotism to be partitioned into Pashtun, Hazara, Tajik and Uzbek" (Dorr-e Dari n.d.: inside front cover). This organization, the Markaz-e Farhangi-ye Nevisandegan-e Afghanestan (Afghan Writers' Cultural Center, based in Qom), published *Dorr-e Dari/The Pearl of Dari*, a quality cultural and literary magazine with the editorial board primarily located in Mashhad.

The Mashhad-based group parted ways with the Afghan Writers' Cultural Center in 2002, establishing a group with the name Mo'asseseh-ye Farhangi-ye Dorr-e Dari or the Dorr-e Dari Cultural Institute, and retitling the magazine *Khatt-e Sevvom*/the *Third Script* (also, third line). Mozaffari explained that this phrase, taken from classical mystical poetry, communicated that the group would try to steer an independent, alternative course in the minefields of Afghan politics, which, following the U.S.-led invasion in 2001, was entering a new phase. Dorr-e Dari has now grown into the foremost cultural institution among Persian-speaking Afghan refugees, surpassing in its range of activities smaller literary associations in Tehran and Qom. Despite its all-inclusive outlook, in practice the vast majority of its members are Hazaras and Seyyeds from the Hazarajat, with a few Shi'a Tajiks from Herat and isolated individuals from other ethnic groups or sects. Although its leadership is still drawn from the renowned poets and writers of the resistance generation, including Abu Taleb Mozaffari and Mohammad Kazem Kazemi, the bulk of the attendees at weekly poetry readings or lectures are young, raised and educated in Iran, and with a very different set of life histories, concerns, and poetic expressions.

Second-Generation Refugees and the Fall of Political Poetry

Ma'sumeh Ahmadi's generation, the first generation of Afghans born or raised in Iran, had come of age just before the time of my research, and this was clearly a generation riddled with paradoxes. As we have seen, they have had opportunities for advancement alternately offered to them and taken away without notice. Many have been educated at secular Iranian schools and universities but have been denied the opportunity to practice their professions in Iran (although some do informally). They have absorbed many of the values and practices of Iranian modernity such as the pursuit of social progress and individual upward mobility through education, and the pursuit of social justice through religious, political, and cultural engagement. Though outwardly most of them are pious Muslims, many also suffer from the same disillusionment and crisis of faith (or the pursuit of a more individualized and rationalized faith) that has emerged among their middle-class Iranian peers (see Varzi 2006). More than anyone else, they are also keenly aware of the failures and paradoxes of the 1979 revolution, as a group that might have benefited most from its stated commitment to the welfare of the *mostaz'afin*, or downtrodden, but that has been increasingly excluded from its purview due simply to its nationality. Despite the pressure to repatriate, along with a desire to participate in the reconstruction of their homeland after 2001, most of them would prefer to stay in Iran if at all possible, balking at the thought of the insecurity, lack of basic medical and educational facilities and employment prospects, and the social restrictions they would face in Afghanistan, particularly in the case of women.

Poets from this generation are experiencing a period of ferment, experimentation and competing attempts at self-definition that remove them from the concerns and poetic styles of previous generations, particularly those of the resistance era. The elevated language, epic and romantic styles, religious, patriotic, pro- and anti-war stances of that era are for the most part gone; in their place has come a much more personal, introspective, intensely lyrical, and also socially conscious poetry. Elements of irony, alienation, disillusionment, and protest are noticeable, and there is an emphasis on *hanjār-gorizi* (flight from convention) and *now-āvari* (innovation). There is a preoccupation both with the lost, victimized (and increasingly abstract) homeland and the liminal status of the refugee, and a lyrical focus on individual emotions and experiences, many of which were rarely voiced in public previously. Indeed, lyricism appears to be the chief characteristic of this generation's poetry. Fewer topics are taboo for them, and they are most concerned with developing an individual style (Mozaffari 1384/2005).

Writing poetry is, for some, an intensely personal activity—a means of emptying (*takhliyeh kardan*) oneself of sorrow and disappointment in the privacy of one's own notebook, or for a few confidantes. One of the students in my English class at the informal Afghan school in south Tehran, which was facing the threat of closure, told me that everyone in her class had become a poet because it was the only way to deal with the tensions and difficulties of life as a teenage refugee girl. A number of young people told me that writing poetry was a good, cathartic outlet for their *dard-e daruni*, their inner pain, and for the difficulties of exile. This reflects the prevalent ethic of stoicism and patience (*sabr*) in the face of emotional distress, which, it is believed, ought to be released somehow but without risking *āberu-rizi* or loss of face for the sufferer.[18] Zahra Hosseinzadeh told me: "The reason that young Afghans take an interest in poetry, I think, is that it is a world in which they can take shelter, and free themselves from the difficult moments of exile; and it is an opportunity for them to speak their own minds, or to find their own thoughts in the words of other poets they read." As a teacher at an informal

Afghan school, Zahra frequently had to respond to the fears and anxieties of her students, including questions like "Why wasn't I born Iranian?" She encouraged them to write: "I tell them, in this wide world, you too have the right to a fresh point of view, to discover everything for yourself, and to tell the world of your discoveries—with words, through poetry."

But such experiments increasingly spill out of private notebooks as many poets attempt to tap into a growing reading public. Almost every one of the many grassroots cultural, educational, and political organizations in Golshahr, Kuy-e Tollab, and Sakhteman (the Afghan-dominated areas of Mashhad) publishes its own weekly or occasional magazine with essays, poetry, and short stories. Afghan university students, women, and young writers' groups also have their own publications. Besides the *Third Script* and *Farkhār/Ornament* (published in Tehran; also the name of a town, river, and district in Afghanistan), which are high-quality literary magazines, I have collected a number of minor publications, including *Hamvatan/Compatriot*, *Hekāyat/Story*, *Payām-e 'Asr/Message of the Age*, *Nedā/Voice* or *Song*, *Hirād* (a river in Afghanistan), and *Bānu/Lady*, all published in Mashhad.[19] New genres and media, including short-story writing, theater, visual arts, filmmaking, and blogging, are also increasingly popular. Both the compulsion to document and to narrate the experience of living as an Afghan in Iran, and the new possibilities offered by film, are evident in a screenplay idea described to me by an Afghan filmmaker, Reza Heidari: a young, uneducated Afghan boy working in a menial job gets hold of a video camera and turns it on himself to document his everyday life.

This ambivalent situation, which some young Afghans described as their "identity crisis" (*bohrān-e howviyat*), combined with the general political climate in shaping their poetic output. Following the gradual liberalization and diversification of the Iranian cultural sphere since the late 1990s and particularly after the 1997 election of the reformist President Mohammad Khatami, refugee poetry has now opened up thematically and stylistically. After the propagandistic and highly politicized literature of the revolution, the Sacred Defense and the Afghan-Soviet war, the 1990s heralded a time of questioning, stylistic proliferation and linguistic experimentation. Even nominally conservative entities like the Arts Center sometimes pushed the boundaries of what was acceptable in a bid to produce commercially successful works in this period, and its policies shifted with every new director (Shams 2015b).

Thus we find ourselves in a period that, according to Anushiravani and Hassanli, "is probably a unique period in which all trends of Persian poetry in a wide . . . spectrum from traditional classical to post-modernist poetry are actively engaged in literary production" (2007: 164). As a result, when the spring 2006 issue of the *Third Script* devoted a section to youth poetry, in an attempt to define its characteristics and give it the official recognition its authors felt they deserved, what emerged was a sense that it is easier to describe what young people's poetry *is not* than to define its common characteristics. Nonetheless, young poets echo wider trends in Iranian poetry, which include "a rejection of romantic, epic, and mystical language and expressions. . . . A conscious effort to evade lofty language and search for a language that is surprisingly close to spoken language. . . . Looking for new horizons and subjects which have been neglected in the past. . . . Use of bitter and harsh satire" (2007: 160–161).

In the transcript of a roundtable discussion published in the youth poetry section of the *Third Script,* Zahra Hosseinzadeh mentioned the challenges of these evasions for contemporary poets:

> Today's poet is an errant, confused [*sargardān*] poet. She does not have the right to choose of the poets of the past. She does not stand by the sea looking to pull out a single seashell. She is someone who has fallen into a whirlpool, and this whirlpool torments her such that she doesn't want to return to a point she has already passed before. Because of this she clutches at different things, whatever she can get a hold of. One day she seeks structure, another day it is form she follows, another day she clings to language, and so on. In any case, what torments her is [the fear of] being repetitive. (Mirza'i 1384/2006: 94)

All of this points to a generation that has lost its aesthetic and perhaps also its cultural moorings, and is forced to create them for itself. Indeed, Zahra emphasizes that one of the primary impulses for contemporary poets is originality and experimentation.

Part of the creative work these young artists have to engage in is not merely that of expression but of finding and establishing connections with sympathetic audiences for their works. In fact, many of their parents' generation (and many older Iranians likewise) find it difficult to identify with their poetry and to see what is poetic about blank verse or other such innovations. Blank verse is intended to be read silently more than it is to be recited, and its emergence is connected to growing levels of literacy. Learning to apprehend it *as poetry* also requires training in the skills of deciphering this new "code" (Bourdieu 1993: 225–226). In embracing such forms of poetry, then, young Afghan poets were unwittingly turning their backs on their own less-educated compatriots and instead cultivating claims to membership in an emerging stratum of intellectuals. If not quite a class, they constitute a stratum of young people with aspirations to upward mobility; many of them could quite easily have joined the ranks of the Iranian lower-middle or middle classes if not for the many exclusions of their nationality. As a result, they gravitate toward institutions like Dorr-e Dari to find other likeminded refugees. Since 2001, the Qand-e Parsi literary festival has been held by the Khaneh-ye Adabiyat-e Afghanestan, or House of Afghan Literature, in Tehran (a group that operates with the support of the OIP's Arts Center and meets on its premises) to present and reward the works of the most promising Afghan poets below the age of thirty. But the Afghan community is no longer the sole audience they have in mind: many also attend Iranian poetry circles and enter their work into Iranian local, provincial, or even national literary competitions, in which many have achieved great success.

But after this new audience is found and the creative process adjusted to meet its expectations, successful artists can eventually gain respect (and acceptance for their new genres and styles) back in their own social milieu. This was illustrated for me by the case of Elyas Alavi. Elyas only wrote blank verse in simple, rather spare language, and typically dwelled on the sorrows of being Afghan and of exile. He often played up his Afghanness when reading his work for an Iranian audience, telling folksy anecdotes and adjusting his accent, apparently to the delight of the crowd. He described to me how his father—a religious scholar trained in classical Persian and Arabic literature who spent much of his time writing religious commentaries in his own private notebook—initially had been vigorously opposed to his poetic activity and thought it worthless. Elyas recounted how, after he had won the first of his several prizes at Iranian competitions and appeared on television, his father had telephoned to congratulate him. He had been embarrassed to hear the latter address him for the first time with the formal "you" (*shomā*) that conveys respect. His father made his peace with Elyas's poetry then and, now continuing his poetic career with parental approval, Elyas became an inspiration for his peers and younger siblings in their own pursuit of artistic activities.

In summary, then, the shift between resistance poetry and second-generation lyric poetry might be explained in terms of a move away from poetry as a medium for the transmission of a political message to a wider audience of refugees, and a reorientation toward a new, more restricted audience—Iranians and Iran-educated Afghans with intellectual leanings. This change of the audience for poetry was often described as *bohrān-e mokhātab*, or "crisis of the audience," because it represented the loss of the mass Afghan audience. To rephrase Marshall McLuhan, the audience had *been* the message, because every Afghan refugee had been addressed by the war poems and encouraged either to physically fight or to otherwise support the resistance. Once the Soviet occupation and the civil war were over, the resistance-focused political message simply dropped out of the equation, and nothing appeared in its place to maintain a link with that audience. The breakthrough to the intellectual Iranian audience, while potentially larger and more prestigious, was a very difficult and long-term process that not all poets were able to make.

Fissures in the Field of Cultural Production

The narrative of the emergence of modernist Persian literature in the twentieth century—and even, in microcosm, the move from resistance poetry of the 1980s to the lyric poetry of the 2000s among Afghan refugees—seems to reflect, at first glance, Bourdieu's account of the "autonomization" of the intellectual and artistic fields from the field of power in nineteenth-century France. While all writers and artists remained subordinated to political power, they now enjoyed a greater degree of autonomy because they were no longer directly dependent on wealthy patrons as in the eighteenth century, allowing the creation of "disinterested" art and eventually "art for art's sake" (Bourdieu 1996: 49; 1993: 36–37). One of the victories of the movement for artistic autonomy described by Bourdieu was the appropriation of the right to define artistic taste and the value of a work by the producers themselves rather than by patrons, and it seems that both twentieth- and early twenty-first-century Persian poets have gained this right to a large extent, censorship notwithstanding.

Bourdieu identifies two opposing poles within this modern field of cultural production that determine hierarchies of value. At one end, in the subfield of large-scale production, producers cater with formulaic products to large audiences with unsophisticated tastes, and such production is driven by commercial forces and evaluated in terms of material profit. At the other end is the subfield of restricted production whose audience tends to be limited to other producers or connoisseurs, which makes it conducive to experimentation and innovation in form and content. The practices of restricted production systematically invert the principles of other fields, disavowing, for example, the pursuit of profit or institutional honors. What is at stake instead is *symbolic capital* that operates according to its own logic, often the inverse of the economic world. One can imagine the kind of symbolic capital to be gained by an independent U.S. filmmaker, for example, by refusing to do big-budget movies with commercial studios and decrying the "junk" that Hollywood produces (Ortner 2013: 30)—indeed, the aura of authenticity around the term "independent filmmaker" comes from such disavowals. Writers at this end of the spectrum may not make much money from their work but instead may be praised for their commercially untainted vision.

However, as in other cases where scholars have tried to apply Bourdieu's theory in non-European contexts, the modern Persian literary field presents conundrums. Where, for example, does one locate the twentieth-century Iranian Committed poets who vehemently insisted that poetry must have a message and contribute to political and social change, and that poetry failing to do so is both bad art and morally reprehensible? Were the revolutionary poets of the 1980s, both Afghan and Iranian, reverting to a premodern state of direct dependence on patronage and merely acting as a mouthpiece for the state or resistance groups, as Bourdieu might lead us to believe? Or were they creative innovators with deep personal convictions who experimented with form until they found a formula that had mass appeal and sometimes even led to material profits for them?[20]

Literary theorist Zimbler found similar anomalies in the South African literary field under apartheid because a significant proportion of literature there was written "neither for the sake of art nor for money" (2009: 604), but was avowedly political. A major hierarchy of value was based on commitment to critiquing the injustices of the apartheid regime. And yet, for Bourdieu, art intended to convey a political message (he calls this social art) is a vestigial category that does not fit neatly into his dualist structure; he even claims it is a disguised form of commercial art. In South Africa, as in Iran, political engagement drove the experimentation with new forms that Bourdieu associates with the autonomous pole, while state censorship meant that there was little money to be made even from notoriety as a radical author. Thus, Zimbler argues, in the South African context, "it is as difficult to reduce the political principle to the principle of the market as to reduce the autonomous principle to either" (2009: 606).

I agree with Zimbler that it is not enough to simply change the dyadic structure to a triadic one by reinserting a political hierarchy of value into it. Instead, we need to recognize that a literary field may be "characterized by a variety of distinctive, overlapping and contradictory principles of evaluation [and] in which agonistic relations are often complex and multi-directional, rather than Manichean" (Zimbler 2009: 612). Zimbler concludes that autonomy should mean not so much the artist's right to choose to create art for art's sake, but rather the artist's freedom to choose a hierarchy of value for herself, even if the apex of that hierarchy is something other than "pure" art. It might be art based on political commitment, usually critical of the state (as was the case in prerevolutionary Iran). Although Ortner, in her ethnography of independent filmmaking in early twenty-first-century America, does not mention the political gap in Bourdieu's too-neat schema, it appears that she reads Bourdieu in the same spirit as Zimbler, showing how one of the hallmarks of independent film is implicit cultural critique (Ortner 2013: 3). But Winegar takes a critique of Bourdieu one step further in her ethnography of modern visual artists in Egypt, showing that aesthetic values are *always* tied to power, ideology, and a range of interests even when they masquerade behind a "fantasy of [artistic] autonomy" (Winegar 2006: 4). It is Egyptian artists' training and relationship with various state and international institutions and audiences, she argues, that shape the form and content of their work, as well as their diverse ideas about how to be true to themselves and what counts as good art. Similarly, I believe that arguments about the necessity for artistic and literary autonomy in contemporary Iran are inherently political and ethical statements.

Afghan Poets' Moral and Aesthetic Positions

Rather than attempting to shoehorn Afghan poets, institutions, and genres into a schema that can be represented visually in two dimensions and in terms of a series of dualisms as Bourdieu does (see 1993: 49), it is more fruitful simply to take up Bourdieu's idea that the field of cultural production is a site of assertions of and struggles over artistic value, and to examine the rhetorical claims and counterclaims of its agents. Within this modern field of literary production, artists and other agents compete with one another for prestige and recognition. The struggle to defend or change one's position in this matrix, or to challenge someone else, manifests itself as what Bourdieu calls *prises de position*, or position takings. Bourdieu acknowledges that there are many possible forms of cultural production in the spectrum between the perfectly autonomous and the perfectly market driven, and they are all subject to contentions by actors located in various positions in the hierarchies of symbolic and economic value. Sometimes the conflict is between established traditions and the challenge posed to them by new genres. The idea of the field helps us to mediate between the poet's position in relation to power, for example her class background, and the likely forms and aesthetic standards of her poetry. Literary critics (who, in the case of Iran, are usually also poets or writers) are those with the authority to determine the criteria by which a literary work may be judged and whether or not it constitutes literature, so their positions matter. How, then, is the value and purpose of poetry defined by contemporary Afghan poets?

A number of common positions may be identified, and some of them reveal interesting correlations with certain features of the poets' biographies, gender, ethnicity and class background. At two extremes are Committed poetry and postmodern poetry, and a wide array of poetic experiments that fall somewhere between.

The first category represents a modified form of the Committed literature of the 1980s—no longer overtly propagandistic, but not departing from state-sanctioned norms on the appropriate themes and forms of poetry. Such poetry may be highly personal, but unlikely to cross boundaries of propriety by, say, dealing with sexual matters. Moreover, it often highlights social problems, criticizes the oppression of the poor and continues the tradition of speaking on behalf of the downtrodden. The interesting thing about Afghan refugee poets is that most of them do not need to consider themselves strongly aligned with the Iranian state to write about such things, because simply by describing the poverty and marginalization they witness in their own communities, they willy-nilly show their commitment to the revolutionary cause of supporting the *mostaz'afin*. Similarly, writing about exile and the ravages of war in Afghanistan is an implicit (and sometimes explicit) criticism of U.S. predation in the region. In terms of form, both blank verse and neoclassical forms are represented, although the *ghazal* is now the most common of the latter. This kind of poetry is most likely to be published with little or no censorship and wins accolades at state-sponsored festivals. Its authors may be invited to participate in poetry readings by various state cultural organizations, at the pinnacle of which are the annual poetry readings held by Supreme Leader Ali Khamenei.

Zahra Hosseinzadeh's poetry and biography are perhaps the clearest example of this position. Born in 1979 to a family of illiterate and landless Hazara farmers in Ghor Province, Afghanistan, her life is a striking example of the social advancement made possible for Afghans by migration to Iran. Zahra has a degree in Islamic Studies from a Shi'a university in Mashhad; she is a pious Muslim who maintains impeccable hijab at all times, and she considers herself someone who has managed to reconcile the tensions between tradition and modernity. A much-loved teacher in an informal Afghan school, she is also active on the editorial board of the *Third Script*. She has won first, second, and third prizes in consecutive years in the Qand-e Parsi literary festival, and was invited to participate in a poetry evening held by Supreme Leader Ali Khamenei (see Shams 2015a). She was the first poet to have a second printing of her work by the Afghan publisher Ebrahim Shari'ati, and I heard it said that her book was one of his few profit-making titles. She has an unusual talent for writing metric and rhyming verse, and uses the *ghazal* form with particular skill. Her poetry is neither overtly political nor ideological, although she is concerned with women's rights and seeks to portray the injustices and indignities suffered particularly by refugee women. Her poems are remarkable in that they take the little tragedies of everyday life and elevate them, in a metric yet fluid and conversational language. Her poetic world is filled with sad, tired protagonists, usually women from the margins of society who are often the victims of poverty or abuse, as in the following *ghazal*:[21]

> *Mo'arefi kard khod rā: man-am kabutar-e chāhi*
> *Marā forukhteh mādar be panj sekkeh-ye shāhi*
> *Medād-e sabz o goli-am kenār-e madraseh jā mānd*
> *Va khatt-e chashm badal shod be sāyeh-hā-ye siāhi*
> *Davāzdah sālegi-am do bacheh dar baghal-ash dāsht*
> *Pesar ke mesl-e pedar shod—sholugh, har che bekhāhi*
> *Va dokhtari ke az avval dorost nimeh-ye man bud*
> *Be jā-ye sorsoreh bāzi neshast khireh be rāhi*
> *Sokut, geryeh, va showhar talāq-nāmeh ferestād*
> *Vali be didan-am āmad barā-ye maskhareh gāhi*
> *Man az khodā geleh dāram khabarnegār! Neveshti?*
> *Dochār mishavad emshab be rudkhāneh se māhi*

She introduced herself: I am the pit-dwelling pigeon.
My mother sold me [into marriage] for five pennies.
My green, flowery pencil was left behind beside the school,
and eyeliner was exchanged for black shadows [black eyes].
In my twelfth year I had two children in my arms:
a son who became like his father, aggressive, whatever you can imagine,
and a daughter who, from the beginning, was exactly half of me.
Instead of playing on the slides, she sat, staring at the road.
Silence, weeping, and then my husband sent a divorce paper
(but he would come to see me sometimes just to mock me.)
I have a complaint against God, journalist! Have you written it?
Tonight three fishes will be entangled in the river.

(Original in Hosseinzadeh 1390/2011: 31–32)

This poem represents a dialogue between a despondent young woman and a journalist. It describes the sad life of a young woman who was married off by her mother against her will and at a young age, while she was still going to school. The mention of black shadows around her eyes suggests domestic violence, and her early motherhood by the age of twelve also suggests a cruelly early sexual initiation. Although she put up with the abuse and with her aggressive son and passive daughter through silence and weeping, the last straw seems to have come when her husband nonchalantly divorced her and, to rub salt into the wound, would come to visit her simply to mock her. Now she finds no solace in religion, blaming God for her misfortune, and appears to be on the brink of killing herself and her children. But although she has no desire to live, she refuses to vanish without a trace. She wants to tell her story and checks to make sure that the journalist has recorded it.

When I discussed the poem with Zahra, she said that she had wanted to give a voice to the suffering women she saw all around her, noting that suicide among Afghan women has become a common tragedy. She used the metaphor of a "pit-dwelling pigeon," she said, to signify "a creature condemned to [a life of] loneliness and darkness." While the element of protest in the poem remains within the domain officially sanctioned by the state, it nonetheless shows how even Committed literature has opened up spaces for formal experimentation (such as the use of heteroglossia and colloquial language in a *ghazal*) and social critique, including feminist critique and an assertion of women's voices. While she may not be the most radical poet in any of these domains, she is universally admired and respected by the other Afghan poets.

Other Afghan poets have found themselves celebrated as Committed poets almost by accident. Elyas Alavi's poetry, for example, was honored by the revolutionary poet Ali Moʻallem Damghani in his speech at the award ceremony of an Iranian festival at which he had won a prize for his *bidāri-ye vahshatnāki* (terrible vigilance) toward the suffering of Muslims in the region. After the abuse at Abu Ghraib prison in Iraq was made public, he wrote a poem in which love is more powerful than being kept in solitary confinement or being chewed to pieces by dogs. In another, he highlighted abuses against Muslims worldwide, referencing the 2003 U.S. assault on Fallujah in Iraq, the 2005 Paris riots (in which immigrants of Arab and African origin protested poor living conditions and unemployment), and the alleged torture of detainees at Guantanamo Bay:

Āh, sheʻr-e man
to niz āvāreh-i
Yek ruz dar Fallujeh dud mishavi
yek ruz dar Pāris be zendān mioftī
Ruz-e digar dar Guāntānāmo
band band-at pāreh pāreh mishavad.
(. . .)

Figure 3.3. Zahra Hosseinzadeh.

Oh, my poem
you, too, are a refugee.
One day you go up in smoke in Fallujah,
one day you are thrown into jail in Paris,
another day in Guantanamo
your verses [joints] are torn, torn apart.
(...)

(Original in Alavi 1386/2008: 11–12)

In a poem inspired by witnessing scenes from Palestine on television, he ends on a sardonic, often-quoted note: "*Mā mimirim tā ʿakkās-e* Times *jāyezeh begirad*": "We die so that the photographer of the *Times* can win a prize." The irony is that Elyas was equally critical of the Iranian government's treatment of refugees, but his poetic references to this were often veiled. Over time, he also gravitated more to writing love poetry, some of it of an implicitly erotic nature. He also experiments with form, using only blank verse and playing with repetition, disrupted syntax, and puns, as in the poem above, in which the word *band* means both "verse" and "joint" (of a limb).

On the other side of the spectrum is postmodern poetry (*she'r-e postmodern* or *pasāmodern*), which lacks a consistent definition but is generally characterized by a stance of opposition to many of the social and aesthetic values of Committed poetry. It may deal with sexuality and other taboo topics and is very open to formal and linguistic experimentation. The closest thing to a manifesto for such poetry was written by Mas'ud Hasanzadeh, a young poet from Herat who, although not a refugee, was a frequent visitor to Mashhad and a close friend of many members of Dorr-e Dari. In a blog entry titled *Adabiyāt-e Badi* (the "literature of evil," which I gloss as "Bad Literature," first print publication in Hasanzadeh 1383/2004), this is the name he bestows on the work of some members of his generation that, he claims, holds nothing sacred—neither language, nor social norms and values that have stifled the authentic voice of the youth: "Bad Literature is the product of the failure of official literary discourses that are humble, well-behaved, humanist-oriented and ideological. Bad Literature has appeared in the empty space left by the stifled instincts of a generation that has to supplicate, murmur and seek permission in order to satisfy its most natural needs. [It] is an unconscious, non-collective process of a generation that is contradiction and rebellion from head to toe. Rebellion against the self and within the self!" (Hasanzadeh 1383/2004: 103).

Authors of Bad Literature, according to Mas'ud, have no concrete solutions to propose, but they are tired of the "oppressive" dominance of official literary discourse propagated by the academy (*dāneshkadeh*) and of formal structures such as universities that, he argues, have taken on the role of the former arbiter of taste, the royal court. Bad Literature poets negate moral taboos and generic rules, and he argues that this brings them close to a movement such as Dadaism. Mas'ud has since founded one of Afghanistan's first rock bands (Morchah, or the Antz Band) and put on an exhibition of satirical and provocative drawings in Herat. He is one of the few who actively seeks to embody the lifestyle of a bohemian rebel, craving artistic autonomy and the right to create art for art's sake, but also to engage in political criticism. However, his aesthetic position is interesting in light of his social pedigree: his maternal kin are a well-established Herati family with a long history as performers of high art music (described in Baily 1988, Doubleday 2006), who offer him encouragement and support. Mas'ud has also carved out a measure of autonomy for himself through his income as a journalist, a form of commercial writing.

But the kind of poetry he describes is roundly denounced by the established poets of the Islamic Republic. In an interview published in 2007, Ali Mo'allem Damghani laments what he perceives as the total subjectivization of today's poetry, which has altogether removed its universal meaning and value: "Everyone writes poetry, everyone is pleased with their own poetry, and everyone agrees that the world no longer has anyone like Hafez" (Baqeri 1386/2007). In such a situation, literary criticism has no meaning, he says, because there are no longer any standards an external critic could apply to poetry: "Today everyone modifies poetry according to his own taste in form and meaning, in the name of innovation [*now-āvari*]." He sees the root of this situation in a distancing from universal conceptions of truth and beauty, to be replaced by particularism that itself is linked to humanity's arrogant sense of god-like control over the world rather than a respect for a higher power. He reiterates his oft-repeated message about the need for poets' social responsibility and vigilance: "Those who do cultural work and the literati [*ahl-e qalam*, lit. people of the pen] have the duty of creating awareness and consciousness [*āgāh-sāzi va hoshyāri*] among the people." Otherwise, poetry will be worthless: to be read today and discarded tomorrow, because it was written in and for the moment and has no enduring message—precisely the qualities that postmodern poets embrace.

The sexual frankness and other private matters that make their way into postmodern poetry make it extremely difficult for poets writing this kind of work to get published without significant alterations of a kind they usually find unacceptable. Appropriateness of poetic expression is cast as an issue at once moral and aesthetic; and excessive frankness is seen by some as definitively unpoetic and is described as *ebtezāl*, a word meaning triteness, commonness, or baseness, which may be glossed as vulgarity. But many of the more moderate poets themselves also balk at these trends. Amanollah Mirza'i, one of the youngest poets at Dorr-e Dari, told me in an interview:

> They [postmodern poets] have taken some issues they believe in and brought them into poetry . . . some things that would be better left unsaid, because

otherwise they drag poetry toward vulgarity [*ebtezāl*]. . . . If I come along and talk about dirty sheets, white thighs, or sludge . . . or, I don't know, bras, underwear, and so on, this doesn't raise the conceptual weight of my poem, it doesn't attract the reader/listener, it draws poetry toward vulgarity. If we want to ensure that our poetry will have an audience and will have an effect on that audience, we need to do better than that. We can work in the postmodern [style], we can turn to the particular, we can turn to many other things, but not be drawn into these sexual things or vulgarity.

Finally, state patronage is criticized by some and aspersions are cast on those who benefit from it, once again in both moral and aesthetic terms. Indeed, there was a thin line between *sheʿr* (poetry) and *shoʿār* (mere sloganeering), and all poets writing anything vaguely political had to tread it carefully. Afghan poets, too, were not immune to such accusations. Anyone who wrote too obviously in praise of a government or political figure risked being labeled a *shāʿer-e darbāri* or "court poet"—a position once held in high esteem in the Persianate world but now used as an insult. When a number of refugee poets attended the 2013 poetry soiree hosted by the Iranian supreme leader, they were attacked on Facebook by other Afghans for selling out to an oppressive state for personal gain. But there were also defenders who posted that, whatever one's view of the government, the poetry reading was one of the few avenues available to Afghans to draw attention to their plight as refugees and to present themselves as educated, cultured people.

We have seen here a number of positions that young Afghan poets can claim, from outright rebellion against received aesthetic conventions to a more cautious approach in which originality is prized but excessive boundary pushing is criticized. We have also seen that, in addition to political commitment and artistic purity, morality is also a value with its own hierarchy, playing a role in structuring the official literary field of the Islamic Republic. As for market forces, none of the poets discussed here has great commercial appeal, with the exception of one or two of the older revolutionary-era poets who have excellent connections with Iranian institutions and whose poetry has even appeared in public school textbooks. One such poet, Mohammad Kazem Kazemi, is probably the only one who is able to make a living solely off literary activities, although he supplements his income by working as a professional editor.

The rest of the poets, particularly the young ones, seek instead the symbolic capital of being a poet-intellectual, and perhaps from time to time receive a small monetary prize and recognition at a literary festival. Even if their books are published, they mostly give them away for free to their friends. They can either choose to toe the line and write poetry that promotes various religious and ideological causes (such as poems for the martyred Shiʿi imams or in support of the Palestinian cause), or they can avoid ideology altogether and adopt the poetic subjectivity common in Iran today: that of the sensitive but alienated observer, critical of what they see as oppressive social convention and skeptical of all ideology, but uncertain about what to suggest in its place. By expressing such a subjectivity through their poetry, young Afghan refugees wish to show that they are abreast of intellectual and literary developments in Iran and to tap into the cultural capital they offer. But even refugee poets who are not consciously writing postmodern poetry are moving toward more individualized poetry, rejecting grand narratives, placing themselves at the center of their poems, and adopting new techniques even in classical forms. Originality has become a central feature of poetic authenticity.

Their artistic autonomy, moreover, is highly context dependent. They are most free to experiment in their own circles, particularly among their own peers. At the poetry criticism sessions, they must be careful to stay within the bounds of public propriety, as there are social consequences to breaking too many taboos of frank expression. Nonetheless, these circles are still relatively liberal and a wide variety of poetic positions are represented at any reading at Dorr-e Dari, highlighting the important role it has played in creating and buffering a semipublic sphere of more autonomous expression. It is certainly more liberal than the state censor, to whom any work seeking a wider audience must be submitted, and who frequently removes vocabulary or other material deemed immoral or improper before a publication license can be released. This process is now changing as more people self-publish their work online, but the extent to which the internet will allow people to sidestep the guardians of public taste and morality and become entirely autonomous artists remains to be seen.

4 The Social Lives of Poets and Poetry

It is a Friday early afternoon at Dorr-e Dari, between the weekly poetry reading and criticism session held in the morning, and the afternoon short-story writing class. Some of the poets are still around, catching up with friends, sipping fragrant black tea, rereading their latest poems for any latecomers, and asking for their friends' informal feedback. More experienced poets give beginners useful tips on how to improve. A female poet and chess champion challenges a male short-story writer to a game of chess in a corner (see fig. 4.1); others head to a nearby park for a round of badminton. A heated debate has emerged in the kitchen, where the smokers have gathered, over whether a poem read in the morning was too provocative in its feminism or not. A group of university students uses one of the back rooms to discuss the upcoming issue of their magazine. The office contains a substantial literary library, and poets can borrow books to brush up on their knowledge of the classics.

There is also a steady stream of visitors. People who have repatriated to Afghanistan but are back in Iran for business or family visits drop by to see old friends and to exchange news and blog addresses. Some bring the latest newspapers or magazines from Afghanistan; many are now involved in media, politics, or education in their homeland. A recent Afghan graduate from an Iranian university comes by to share her good news and distribute pastries to those present. Meanwhile, Mozaffari, after giving a radio interview by telephone, leans back into his office chair and hums a traditional *dobeiti* (folk quatrain) from his birthplace in the Hazarajat.

(from my fieldnotes)

IN THIS CHAPTER I give an ethnographic description of poetry as a social practice among contemporary Afghan poets in Iran. I examine the ways in which poetry is learned and taught, composed and disseminated, performed and listened to, published and read, bought and sold, and used as a means of communication among Afghans. Current literary activities at Dorr-e Dari create an interpretive community (Fish 1976) for poetry, particularly for emergent genres that are still in the process of crystallization; and a community of practice wherein a group

Figure 4.1. A game of chess at Dorr-e Dari, 2005.

of like-minded people learn their craft through participation, interaction, and emulation (Lave and Wenger 1991). The poetry criticism sessions are a pedagogical forum in which a few older "master" poets impart the skills of composition, interpretation, and appreciation of classical and modern poetry and the rules of prosody. But they are held in an open format, so they also encourage experimentation, originality, and receptiveness to new audiences, and the master poets themselves have admitted to being influenced by the younger generation. Therefore, poetry criticism sessions may be seen as an interactive site for the collective formation of individual creativity and aesthetic taste—or training in the production and reception of aesthetic codes, in Bourdieu's terms (1993: 225–226).

At Dorr-e Dari gatherings, the old poetic tradition is still much revered, but it has now been bracketed off as classical poetry (*she'r-e kelāsik*), whose genres and conventions have undergone many stylistic shifts but whose basic verse forms have existed for a millennium. The so-called new poetry (*she'r-e now*) that developed in the twentieth century is seen as radically different. Not only verse forms but ideas about the purpose and nature of poetry and the proper relationship between the poet and the *mokhātab* (addressee or audience of a poem) have undergone similar shifts. Despite the diverse positions they take, all poets agree that classical poetry can and should still be learned, interpreted, and appreciated, and classical *forms* may continue to be used, but their *content* must be modern and ideally relevant to contemporary life, often for the purpose of making ethical critiques of society. These days, attempts to replicate classical diction and imagery without a very good reason for doing so are frowned on.

It is interesting to consider Dorr-e Dari's poetry sessions in light of the argument of a number of anthropologists of the Middle East that mass education has irrevocably altered both pedagogical models and conceptions of self in the region (e.g., Eickelman 1992, Messick 1993). This certainly seems to be true of Iranian state schools and universities with their standardized curricula. But in a small-scale, more informal setting such as Dorr-e Dari, there are echoes of the older, highly personalized traditions of knowledge transmission between a master and a pupil that were once prevalent in the Middle East. The central role of a small number of charismatic master poets at Dorr-e Dari, and the esteem in which they are held as embodiments of a literary tradition, suggest interesting continuities in older pedagogical styles and forms of authority, even as they interplay with changes in the ways poetic texts are interpreted that are explicitly understood as modern.

Formal Training and Individual Talent in the Formation of a Poet

One is not born with a grasp of the meter, rhyme, vocabulary, and stylistic conventions that are the building blocks of poetry; but neither are these necessarily taught formally or learned consciously. The life histories of the poets I interviewed revealed that most of them grew up in environments where poetry was read or recited and enjoyed from a young age, and this exposure primed their ears to the rhythms and conventions of classical verse. This was especially true of those with literate fathers (mostly Seyyeds or clerics in the case of those coming from the Hazarajat, and merchants in the case of those from Herat), but only one poet, Mohammad Kazem Kazemi, was born into a family with a long literate poetic tradition in Herat. Calling into question any simplistic narrative of Persian literary modernism as a sharp break with the past, many poets mentioned oral recitation of the classics, oral folk genres, and nonliterate oral poets as the greatest influence on their early careers.

Oral folk poetry (and oral transmission of classical poetry that elsewhere is written down) remains a flourishing art form in Afghanistan. The Hazaras and Hazara Seyyeds, together forming the largest Persian-speaking group in the country, have a tradition of memorization of great bodies of classical Persian poetry by certain individuals, known as *maddāh*, as well as the creation and transmission of oral poetry in their own dialect, Hazaregi (Mousavi 1998: 83–88, Khavari 1382/2003). Some poets, including Mozaffari, mentioned that their first contact with the poetic "sweetness" of the Persian language was with the lullabies sung by their mothers, and one mentioned an uncle who was a gifted composer of *dobeiti*s. Many of the poets I interviewed who had spent their childhood in rural

Hazarajat described the tradition of reading or recitation of classical poetry in men's gatherings on winter evenings. In some areas, the favored material was an old text called the *Hamleh-ye Heidari,* an epic religious poem in praise of Imam Ali, his descendants, and their glorious deeds and tragic fates. In other areas, the *Shāhnāmeh* was recited according to a particular repetitive melodic pattern, more a chant than a song. The Qom-based poet and religious scholar Qanbar Ali Tabesh, who was born in a Hazara village in Ghazni province in 1969 and learned to read from a book of Hafez in the religious school (*maktab*) in the village, gave this account of the environment in which he and many others learned to appreciate poetry:

> In our village, on winter evenings, the people would gather in the mosque or one of the houses, and two or three people who could read [*savād dāshtand*], they would read books of poems and stories. These were either Najma and the King's Daughter, or Yusuf and Zuleikha, or *Hamleh-ye Heidari,* or the *Shāhnāmeh* of Ferdowsi.[1] They would read one of these, and since I had learned to read early, and apparently had some talent, they would ask me to read these poems too and interpret them [*ma'nā kardan*]. So my first interest in and familiarity with poetry began from there.

Those born or mostly raised in Iran, too, often reported being encouraged by their parents to recite poetry from memory. Elyas Alavi, for example, described how he and his siblings were encouraged to perform for guests:

> At home, I remember, we used to have a lot of guests.... All of our neighbors used to say, "Your house is a caravanserai!" ... And when we were children, *Bābā* [Dad] used to say—whatever you know how to do, whether it's poetry, or acting, do it in front of the guests. And we used to climb up onto the window, onto the windowsill, and recite whatever we knew—we recited poetry, not our own but things we had memorized. We told jokes/riddles [*latifeh*], things like that, and everyone would laugh.

Literature classes at school were mentioned as an encouragement by some and as completely irrelevant by others. Maral Taheri, for example, complained that the approach to teaching literature at her high school had not been scholarly or given much importance, and instead was just teachers repeating outdated and clichéd notions (*harf-hā-ye konserv shodeh va kelisheh*).[2] Instead, she learned to appreciate poetry from the Sa'di that her father—a laborer originally from Herat—loved to read and recite, and the Hafez beloved by her mother. Like thousands of other Persian-speaking youth, particularly girls, she entered adolescence finding comfort in the words of the mid-twentieth-century Iranian female poet Forugh Farrokhzad, most of whose *divān* (collected works) she had memorized by the age of fourteen, and whose style has left an indelible mark on the poems of many young women today.[3]

The idea that a poet's basic training occurs through reading or recitation and memorization of the poetry of others is as old as Persian poetry itself. Medieval didactic works, such as the twelfth-century *Chahār Maqāleh/Four Treatises* of Nezami Aruzi of Samarkand, advised the aspiring poet to "memorize 20,000 lines from the poets of old . . . and 10,000 words/lines . . . from the recent poets. . . . He should be constantly perusing and learning the divans of the masters to see how they handled the difficulties and subtleties of language" (translation by Franklin Lewis in Lewis 1994: 200). Only after "the methods and genres of poetry are etched in his brain and his nature" was a poet supposed to study the rules of poetics and prosody and literary criticism in a more "scientific" manner (ibid.). Although this emphasis on study and—to a lesser extent—memorization remains today, greater emphasis is placed now on the creative autonomy of the poet, as we see in this chapter.

Many poets told me that they first began to write or compose verses of their own ("although I don't know if I would call it poetry today," they would add modestly) in their teens, often in the first flush of romantic feeling or other intense emotions. These compositions were not uncommonly addressed to classmates of the same sex and usually were not shared with more than a few confidantes. The next step in becoming a poet for contemporary Afghans in Iran usually involved developing an awareness (often through others' encouragement) of their talent and gravitating toward other poets and literary circles or associations of varying degrees of formality. During the jihad years, as we have seen, these included politically oriented groups and publications; at present, there are apolitical Afghan literary circles in Mashhad, Qom, and Tehran. Other platforms for young poets included school pupils' statewide or nationwide competitions (*mosābeqeh-hā-ye dāneshāmuzi*) or congresses of seminarians' poetry (*kongreh-ye she'r-e howzavi*), which enabled Afghan poets resident in different cities to meet for the first time in a literary context. Major Iranian poetry festivals at which young Afghans have done well in recent years include the annual *Shab-hā-ye Shahrivar*/September Nights festival held in different cities, and the *Shākh-e Nabāt* festival in Shiraz, named after the great beauty who was Hafez's beloved (the name means Branch of Sugarcane).

The most active and successful poets, or those most determined to have a poetic career, usually try to develop a personal relationship with, or seek feedback from, one of the Afghan master poets; that is, those like Seyyed Abu Taleb Mozaffari and Mohammad Kazem Kazemi who are accorded the title of *ostād*. *Ostād*, meaning "maestro" or "teacher," in this case is not a title conferred by any institution (unlike that of university professors, though the same word is used for them). Rather, it represents a collective consensus that the person in question has achieved a high level of proficiency and renown in their field. It is also relational: a master poet is not necessarily addressed by the title *ostād* by all persons at all times, and one may recognize someone as one's *ostād*, or not.[4] An *ostād* is treated with the appropriate respect. Seating is reserved for them in front rows, and even a speaker on stage will nod in greeting and place his hand on his heart, partly rising from his chair if seated, if his *ostād* enters an auditorium while he is speaking.[5] Mozaffari, Kazemi, and a few other individuals are the spiritual, scholarly, and artistic "godfathers" of the Afghan literary scene in Iran: they are involved in publishing and editing, are prolific critics, attend Iranian and Afghan poetry readings and festivals, and organize criticism sessions and lectures on various literary themes. As such, they are not only *ostād*, but also *sāheb-e nazar*, the "keepers of opinion," people whose views on important issues count.

In pursuing relations with *ostāds*, young poets are once again following the advice of Nezami Aruzi, who recommended literary study with a "capable master" so that one may someday become worthy of the title oneself (Lewis 1994: 200). However, the range of activity by such figures today partially overlaps with that of aristocratic patrons of poetry in the past, who used to preside over literary gatherings and reward poets for their efforts—as we see in this chapter—without necessarily being poets themselves. Rather than the strictly hierarchical relationship of an *ostād* with his *shāgerd* (pupil) in the past, akin to a relation of apprenticeship in the learning of a craft, or the relation between a Sufi master (*pir*) and his disciple (*morid*), Mozaffari told me he preferred to think of himself in more egalitarian terms as a friend to the younger poets. The younger poets, on the other hand, would sometimes speak of him as something akin to a father figure, both loved and respected.

And what of individual talent and predilection for poetry? A number of poets told me that, from a young age, they were introverted (*tu-ye khod-am; gushe-gir*) and perceived as crazier (*divunetar*) than others, spending time by themselves, playing in the mud, or working long hours alone at solitary jobs such as carpet weaving to support their families. I frequently heard the opinion that poets are *ādam-hā-ye 'ajib-o-gharib* or "weird people." One friend, an editor with a student magazine, grumbled when she heard that a young poet we both knew had been elected as her managing editor: "He's a poet—I don't know how good his managerial skills will be." She perceived him as too dreamy and disorganized, though I was not sure to what extent she was basing her judgment on her poet brother, who usually stayed up all night and slept all day and was probably more disorganized (*bi-nazm*) than most. In fact, it was my impression that some poets (but by no means all) played up their disorganization and lack of punctuality and seemed not to be too apologetic for them, as if society was a little more forgiving of their flaws out of respect for their art. This to some extent echoes Caton's observation in Yemen of the belief that "the poet suffers more than the rest of mankind by having to forgo sleep and peace of mind" (1990: 39).

Poets themselves stressed their unique individuality, saying that they most definitely were different from ordinary people: more sensitive, and with a more acute perception of people and the world. Indeed, female poets, perhaps still feeling the need to justify their relatively high participation in poetic activities in recent times, often played up these qualities, claiming that women naturally possessed them to a greater degree than men and could thus become better poets. Mahbubeh Ebrahimi, a well-known poet and one of the organizers of the Qand-e Pārsi Afghan literary festival in Tehran, explained women's strong showing in the 2005 edition of the festival thus: "The quality of the women's work was much higher than that of the men. Because of their sophisticated visions of life, the natural world, and their environment, and their feminine sense and perception, women interact with their environment more comfortably and easily, and these encounters are expressed in their poetry." Rahimeh Mirza'i, whose poem about the *Mona Lisa* so inspired me, was one of the women poets receiving an award at the festival. She similarly claimed that "Women's sensitivity toward events and to the external environment is much higher than that of men. Of course, one can't say that male poets don't have such a spirit, but women have a greater aptitude because of their natural temperament." Basi Gol Sharifi, another member of the organizing team, also stressed that "the poetic spirit is much closer to women than to men. They are much wittier and more elegant."

Poetic training was thought to deepen these qualities of perception, giving a poet a greater ability to see through social convention, and to observe and gain a more profound insight into one's own and others' inner lives. Elyas Alavi put it this way (in his characteristic manner of nonchalant despondence) when I interviewed him:

> The most important [change created by poetry in my life] has been this. Something like writing, writing poetry, brings one closer to oneself. You understand yourself better, comprehend yourself better. . . . For me this has been more of a bad thing. Before this, you didn't really . . . you were a more ordinary person. You were happy with your friends, you laughed, and so on. You had a simple life. After it, you . . . it's as if you interfere with your own inner self [*darun*], both your own inner self and the inner self of others. When, for example, your friend lies to you, you realize he's telling a lie. And it's difficult for you to put on an act in front of him, say that you believe it. It's a bit difficult for you. And then, so to say, you realize how far you've sunk, that you've fallen into a hole. This makes continuing on with your life a bit difficult.

The Social Life of a Poem

Having absorbed, unconsciously or through study, the principles of *vazn* (meter) and *qāfieh* (rhyme), a poet will begin to compose when the appropriate inspiration strikes. Mozaffari described this process to me as follows, noting the unconscious nature and spontaneity of the original inspiration, while stressing the creative autonomy of the poet:

> My method of writing poetry is not such that I sit down somewhere and pick up a pen and write a poem. Stories—yes, I sit down and write stories, or articles. But poetry... several couplets [at a time], in an unconscious, very natural way from an ordinary incident, an ordinary feeling, come to me and I write them down—whether they come in my sleep, or at work, or on a bus. Wherever I may be, I write them down, and then I complete/perfect it [*takmil-esh mikonam*]. The coming of a poem, the process of a poem, is very natural in my mind. And I think that these things don't need any external factors. Rather, it's just those inner feelings of a person that combine with his experiences in a single moment and flow from his tongue [*bar zabān-e ādam jāri misheh*], that's all. In older times, people thought some kind of deities or jinn—the Arabs thought that jinns would suggest poems or that there was some kind of supernatural inspiration [*elhām-e gheibi*], but I don't believe that. It's not an external thing, but the emotions of a person himself that in one instant, cause something of a particular form to take shape and emerge.

Elyas Alavi, too, described the moment of inspiration as a "spark" that could be produced by any event. One of his poems, for example, arose after he saw an elderly man's gaze follow a young girl with striking eyes as she walked down a lane: "She had beautiful eyes / and the old men of the quarter all wished / that they had been born later." He was inspired to write the line from his most famous poem, "We die so that the photographer of the *Times* may win a prize," after seeing images from Palestinian leader al-Rantissi's assassination on television in 2004, although the poem itself developed into one about Afghanistan. He described the creative process evocatively, comparing the first poetic inspiration to a feeling, a spark, an insect that eats away at your mind compulsively until you do something with it:

> At the beginning, a feeling reaches out to you [*yek hessi be ensān dast mideh*]. It can come from seeing an event, a poor person, a beggar, a photograph. Or for example it can be something in your mind, something that comes into your mind at one particular instant. After that... a spark is struck and then usually one couplet, or one sentence, or one word... comes from somewhere and then it keeps on, like a... we say *khoreh*—it's something that—I think it's an insect—it doesn't stop, it keeps eating—so like a *khoreh*, it eats at your mind and keeps on eating. And you can't stop anymore and you're obliged to do something to it, you play with it and play with it and keep adding words. And this is transformed into a poem. And then when that moment is over and that feeling has ended, when you have returned to your normal state, you can look back at it and change some parts of it a little bit.

Maral Taheri's description of poetic inspiration provides an interesting insight into the imaginative work that is done in the poet's mind as she responds to ordinary events in her surroundings and tries to give voice to some of the most private emotions and sensations experienced not only by herself but by those around her:

> Today I was walking around the house—my sister is pregnant and she was in pain. I said to her, "How are you feeling?" She said, "I'm not bad, but the baby is kicking in my stomach and it's a good feeling." At that very moment this morning something came to my mind, *Harekāt-e gij-e janini ke darun-e man ast / talkh ast o banafsh,* "The giddy movements of the foetus inside me / are bitter and purple." It comes at a moment like that, an essence, and then it cuts off. That was all it was. I can't say exactly where I get inspiration from. It's not clear at all, but it can come to me at any time—in the street, on the bus, in my bed, anywhere.

The spontaneity of the inspiration is reflected in the phrase commonly used by poets *she'r āmad soragh-am,* "a poem came to me." Most poems still tend to be composed in the mind rather than on paper, at least in their early stages. The oral origins of poetry are reflected in the verb used for the act of composing poetry, which in Persian is not "writing poetry" but *she'r goftan,* or "saying poetry," even when it is actually written down. The relative weight given to the two different stages—spontaneous creation and more conscious, rational tinkering or correction later, as described by Alavi—differed among poets. I heard some poets asking each other if their poems were more *jusheshi* or *kusheshi*: literally, those composed "while in a state of boiling" or those composed "through effort," respectively. While most poems are almost inevitably a combination of the two, and *bedāheh-sarā'i* or extemporaneous composition is not practiced or appreciated as much as it was in the past, I did witness some rather startling examples of original poems taking shape almost automatically before my eyes during online chats with poet friends, sometimes with near-perfect rhyme and meter that they only lightly modified later.

This emphasis on autonomous inspiration, individual creativity, and originality was often highlighted as a feature of contemporary poetry, but scholars of classical Persian literature stress that individual talent and originality were always admired, and particularly celebrated in some historical periods (Losensky 1994, Lewis 1994). But they were also always situated in the context of a highly intertextual literary field in which certain forms of poetic dialogue and imitation were permissible, even desirable, if they demonstrated the poetic mastery of the challenger. Losensky argues that although in the modern West, we have the "illusion of radical originality," no text is ever produced in a vacuum. The Persian classical tradition recognized "a more dynamic dialectical relationship between originality and imitation" (Losensky 1994: 228). The genre of *esteqbāl*, for example, was "plagiarism done openly and decorously (honouring or vying with an earlier poem and its creator by imitating, alluding to, or pastiching it)" (Lewis 1994: 199–200). It would be wrong to see this as a sign of the stagnation or derivativeness of classical poetry, particularly court poetry. Rather, poets took up certain refrains or mimicked meters as a test of their ability, while also responding to audiences' demand for tried and tested formulas with commercial appeal (Lewis 1994: 211–212). Even twelfth-century poets had to be vigilant about lifting particularly choice turns of phrase from others without introducing some innovation into them or improving them in some way (Lewis 1994: 199). But these days, *serqat-e adabi* (literary plagiarism) is seen as much more pernicious, and being accused of it can lead to public shaming and the withdrawal of honors and awards.

Besides responding to everyday or unforeseen events, poems may also be composed to mark particular occasions (known as *she'r-e monāsebati*) or for particular people. Losensky (1997) has noted that the tradition of "occasion poetry" had fallen into disuse throughout the twentieth century but was revived under the state patronage of the Islamic Republic; for example, over three hundred elegies were written after the death of Ayatollah Khomeini in 1989. Afghan poets embraced this tradition: Hossein Heidarbeigi composed a poem for the occasion of his father's departure from Mashhad to return to Afghanistan, a poem that meant a great deal to him because it marked what proved to be the last time he saw him. Poems are frequently dedicated (*taqdim*) to particular people, sometimes but not necessarily one's beloved (and love poems are usually not dedicated publicly, except perhaps with initials). Often these are close friends, particularly after memorable or moving shared experiences, or as declarations of love and admiration. I was delighted and felt honored when some of my poet friends dedicated poems to me during my fieldwork. Elyas Alavi dedicated a poem to Ostad Mozaffari at a literary festival where the latter was feted; his friend Asef Hosseini dedicated a poem to Elyas when the latter was accepted for resettlement to Australia, in a friendly admonition not to forget his homeland and not to misuse it in his poems for personal gain.

Following the initial inspiration, composition, and recording of a poem, usually in a notebook (but increasingly typed on a computer or other digital device), if one is seriously trying to improve as a poet, one tries to get feedback on it, either from like-minded friends or from a more experienced poet. This usually involves attending a poetry criticism session (described in greater detail below), and, if well-received, sending the poem to a magazine for publication or entering it in a competition. Festival competitions can be effective for improving one's exposure, developing a name and a reputation, having one's work appraised by leading literary figures, and also—in the case of the biggest talents—winning prizes.[6] Since about 2006, many young (and some older) poets have also started blogs and regularly post their new poems and other writings on the internet, offering a particularly dynamic forum for feedback, as readers, both friends and strangers, are able to post their comments, praise, and criticisms. In this way, they have begun to form a "blogging community" (Alexanian 2006).[7]

Once one has accumulated enough poems of a relatively high standard, one may consider publishing a book. There has been a spate of book publications by the young poets of the first generation to be born or raised almost entirely in Iran. Most were published by the Erfan publishing house in Tehran (headed by an Afghan, Ebrahim Shari'ati) in its Contemporary Poetry/Stories of Afghanistan series, and some by Iranian publishers.[8]

Literary Gatherings

Jalasāt-e naqd-e she'r, or poetry criticism sessions, are one of Dorr-e Dari's principal activities, and are considered a distinctly modern form of engagement with poetry. While this sort of gathering emerged as an institution of poetic sociability in the twentieth century, it has deep roots: assemblies in which poets read, recited, and discussed poetry have long been an important site of poetic sociability in the Persianate world. In centuries past, one of the principal arenas for institutionalized literary activity was the *majles* (pl. *majāles*), a formal or informal social gathering held by a patron of literature and scholarship, who was often a high-ranking courtier or a member of a royal family.

Subtelny describes the *majles* of the Timurid court in Herat in the late fifteenth and early sixteenth centuries, where "the customary forms of entertainment could include musical performance and singing, wine-drinking, engagement in witticism and the relation of anecdotes, and the recitation and discussion of poetry. When this last activity constituted the chief focus, the term *majlis* carried the connotation of a literary assembly, a kind of literary 'soirée,' and it represented the main forum for literary, particularly poetical, expression in the late Tīmūrid period" (Subtelny 1984: 144). Subtelny presents vivid vignettes of a literary *majles* presided over by Mir Ali Shir Nava'i (1441–1501), a poet and great patron of the arts in the court of the Timurid prince Sultan Hossein Bayqara (1469–1506) in Herat. It was also a forum for the appreciation or criticism of poetry, and for the display of verbal virtuosity in the solving of riddles, the impromptu composition of poetry (*bedāheh-sarā'i*) or quick-witted ripostes to the poetic challenges of rivals. Other contemporaneous sources note that women poets, too, were active in such gatherings, and even composed teasing jibes addressed to their husbands (Arbabzadah 2002: 45–47). Dull wits were ridiculed and soon disposed of. The ultimate aspiration of all accomplished poets was to be introduced to the patron, but competition was great, for "a very large number of poets . . . were active in [Herat] at that time and [one] critic . . . even complained that, 'Wherever you listen, you hear the murmur of a poet'" (Subtelny 1984: 150). One poet quoted by Subtelny, a precocious young talent who had memorized the Qur'an and mastered the *mo'ammā*, one of the riddle-poem genres popular in the day, recalled his trepidation when he was to be presented to Ali Shir in a formal gathering (1984: 140). The *majles* as a site for the royal patronage of literature and other forms of learning persisted at least until the end of the nineteenth century in both Iran and Afghanistan.

More recently, formal civic associations of writers and poets following a Western model, such as the Kanun-e Nevisandegan-e Iran (the Iranian Writers' Association, founded in 1962), were also created, and played an influential role in cultural and political life. Literary congresses and festivals have been important venues for literary exchange and sociability since the first Iranian Writers' Congress in 1949. But more fluid gatherings of poets and writers at which they read and discuss their work have remained an important venue of poetic sociability. An important example of such gatherings in the twentieth century is the *dowreh*, an informal circle of intimates, "men or women basically in intellectual and emotional sympathy" (Mottahedeh 1985: 271), who meet periodically and rotate the venue among the homes of members (Bill 1973: 132).[9] Sometimes there is a leading intellectual, religious, or political leader at the core of the group, who may regularly host the meetings, like the *majles* patron of old. *Dowreh*s may have a literary focus, and poetry and short fiction may be read and discussed at them. Many such gatherings, unlike the *majāles* of the past, came to be associated with opposition to power rather than with its praise. In contrast to formal institutions, like the Iranian Writers' Association that was forced into exile in Paris in 1983, informal groups, as Eickelman argues, have flourished in Iran because they have no "effective center or formal leadership for state authority to co-opt, coerce or suppress" (Eickelman 2002: 319). Rather, they have helped to contain the excesses of governments and on occasion helped bring about their downfall.[10]

In Mashhad, a circle of regulars (between fifteen and twenty people) has developed at the Dorr-e Dari Cultural Institute around the person of Mozaffari (and Kazemi, who is less frequently present), who participate almost every week in the Friday poetry criticism sessions, write articles for or assist in preparing the *Third Script* for publication (e.g., by transcribing interviews or designing page layout), and generally just drop by the office in their free time to drink tea and chat with anyone who is around. They are also the ones who are invited to outings or special meals. A few of them are entrusted with answering the phone or keeping the keys when Mozaffari is not there. Several of them have taken turns as moderators of the poetry criticism sessions and have been invited to prepare and deliver lectures on various themes. The respect accorded to Mozaffari means that families' concerns are usually allayed and young women are able to participate in these activities just as actively as men, although not without certain restrictions

Figure 4.2. Dorr-e Dari regulars share a picnic during a winter daytrip to the mountains, 2005.

on their movements. For some, the Dorr-e Dari office has become their second home where they might nap, pray, play chess, or just hang out on slow days.

Commensality, travel, and shared outings are an important part of the sociality of Dorr-e Dari. The regular attendees are invited to special meals in the office (e.g., *eftār*, or fast-breaking meals during Ramadan), which they chip in to pay for and then prepare together. The institute's kitchen is in many ways the beating heart of the enterprise, and even the men participate in cooking. A large water kettle is almost constantly simmering, and endless cups of black tea (and sometimes green tea with cardamom, which is favored in Afghanistan) are served to visitors and regulars alike. Visitors who have good news to celebrate (completing their degrees or announcing a marriage) arrive at the institute with a customary box of pastries to share with everyone present.

Among the social highlights for the poets, however, are group day trips to the mountain valleys outside Mashhad, a time-honored practice among urban Iranians wishing to leave behind the bustle of the city and relax in a natural setting. Strict codes of behavior are also relaxed somewhat, as girls dress more colorfully and wear looser headscarves; and as the picnic site is usually near cool, flowing water, wading and splashing are part of the fun on hot summer days. There

Figure 4.3. Young women in a flowering orchard during a spring outing, 2010.

are games of volleyball and badminton, and scrambling up the steep mountains, usually followed by a picnic lunch and more tea, steeped in the trusty kettle over an open fire (see figs. 4.2–4.4). As such, even though the main goal of these trips is wholesome fun for a group of young people deprived of many opportunities to have it, this is a good example of a liminal setting outside the framework of everyday life that engenders what Turner (1969) calls *communitas*. It encourages greater trust, solidarity, and a feeling of social equality to develop among the members of the group; a factor that is very important for gender equality and for my later discussions of love and the limits of appropriate self-expression in poetry.

While garden and river meadow settings were once sites for poetic *majāles* (Brookshaw 2003), the Dorr-e Dari poets' main venues for poetic discussion are not outdoors but rather the formal Friday morning criticism sessions in the office. A table is set up at one end of the room, behind which are two chairs, one for the poet, one for the moderator. There is usually a plastic flower arrangement on the table, and above it hangs an oil portrait of Ostad Rahnavard Zaryab, the celebrated Afghan short-story writer, based in Kabul and a friend of the institute. Opposite this table, which functions as a podium for any speaker presenting in

Figure 4.4. A water fight during a day trip to the mountains, 2007.

the room, are rows of white plastic chairs. Senior poets and invited guests usually sit in the first rows, behind them the women, and the men sit across the aisle from them. This gender segregation, however, is largely spontaneous and not necessarily strictly enforced, and the arrangement can vary depending on the size of the crowd.

The moderator is usually a young but promising poet selected by Mozaffari, who holds this responsibility for several months at a time. He opens and closes the session with a reading from a famous poet, either Iranian, Afghan, or other. After this, he calls members of the audience up one by one to read their poetry. If someone is new or a beginning poet (which they usually reveal, with humble apologies, at the start), they are invited to read without having their work subjected to criticism. Those who have read before, on the other hand, usually read their work once and then the floor is opened to anyone wishing to comment, praise, or critique the poem or any of its parts (often in the context of the poet's work in general, if people in the audience are familiar with it). Usually one or another *ostād* who is present will offer his thoughts first. Others then raise their hands and add their own comments, often disagreeing with previous speakers. The poet may be asked to read specific parts of the poem again if they were seen as particularly interesting or problematic. At the end of such a turn, the moderator asks for a round of applause before calling up the next person. The only ex-

Figure 4.5. A poet (Lina Nabizadeh) reading her work at a poetry criticism session chaired by Hossein Heidarbeigi, 2005.

ception to this is during the month of Moharram or other mourning occasions, when clapping is not appropriate. At such times, there is no applause following individual turns, but the session is closed by a collective chanting of the *salavāt*, an Arabic invocation of blessings upon the Prophet and his family (typically used in group situations such as prayers, ceremonies, or journeys—e.g., the beginning of intercity bus rides).

Poetry is usually read, and sometimes also recited from memory. There is a specific intonation and rhythmic pattern adopted in the case of classical or other metric verse that highlights the meter. Since Persian meters are quantitative (based on long and short syllables rather than on stress), some syllables are elongated rhythmically while the voice is either kept rather monotonous or modulated expressively, in a manner that would seem unnatural in everyday speech. Such recitation is a learned skill in itself.[11] Audience members react to particularly effective turns of phrase by exclaiming out loud *"ahsant!"* or *"āfarin!"*—"well-done" in Arabic and Persian, respectively. It is the unspoken prerogative of more senior members of the audience, as well as the moderator, to make the loudest exclamations and thus be arbiters of aesthetic judgment. Experienced poets with a good ear for meter will immediately hear any mistakes, and this is often one of the first criticisms offered in these sessions: *"vazn-esh kami kharāb bud"*—"the meter was a little wrong." Persian meters are extremely complex and there are

Figure 4.6. Mohammad Kazem Kazemi attends a poetry criticism session at Dorr-e Dari, 2007. *Photo © Najieh Gholami, reproduced by kind permission*

many different patterns, so they represent something of a minefield for beginners. There are also various rules and exceptions for the suitability of different rhymes.[12]

In their critiques, which usually attempt to be friendly and constructive (the moderator reminds people of this if their comments are out of line—especially when they begin to make moral criticisms of the content rather than the form, or even of the character of the poet), the listeners draw attention to language and the ways in which it is used for "creating a poetic space" (*fazā-sāzi*). They also comment on the extent to which the poet has succeeded in building a relationship with the audience (*mokhātab*, lit. addressee; this can be either a listener or a reader, depending on the context); in other words, the extent to which the poet has expressed his or her personal concerns in a way that the listener can relate to. They may comment on the suitability of the particular form used to express the content—for example, is the neoclassical *ghazal* the best way to convey a particular sentiment or idea, or might blank verse work better?

It is recognized that such criticism sessions, and literary criticism in general, are a relatively new innovation in the history of Persian literature, being imported from the West and dating back no more than a century or so, as I was told (see Karimi-Hakkak 1995, Parsinezhad 1380/2001). However, they are viewed as a positive and necessary rational development, enabling poets to improve their work and for common literary trends to evolve. One poet compared criticism to surgery (*jarrāhi*), which ultimately helps to cure the patient, unlike the flaying (*sallākhi*) that failed poets might have been subjected to in the past. Criticism is of course also written and published, in the form of reviews of new books, or in response to the body of work of a particular poet—typically in journals such as the *Third Script*.

Following are excerpts from a transcript of one poetry criticism session that I recorded on 27 July 2007, and the criticism of a poem that was not seen as among the poet's best. This criticism reveals both the difficulties that the subjectivism of modern poetry still presents for poets and audiences, and the attempts to shape an interpretive community. The sessions could be seen as a collective training in both the production and appropriation of poetic codes, both those used for classical forms and the conventions of blank verse. These excerpts are responses to a rather opaque poem in blank verse by a young woman whose images included a tree, a chirping bird, and a blushing sun and seemed to obliquely hint at some kind of amorous encounter. The comments from the audience suggested that its meaning was unclear, and some asked the poet to explain what she meant, while others said that it was fine for the poet to be ambiguous and for every listener to interpret the poem in her or his own way.

> [*The moderator invites a poet to read a poem, and she moves to the front to take a seat.*]
>
> POET: The spring that started with your branches
> and my chirping
> made the cats sleeker.
> I would reach you,
> and you me,
> and how far is it from us to intoxication?
> The sun was red,
> redder when it looked at us.
>
> The spring that started with your branches
> brought summer into fruition.
> Your branches shook
> but the ripe grapes
> were in the eyes of a little girl who was leaning against you.
> I chirped,
> louder, louder;
> opened and closed my wings,
> dug my claws into your branches
> and the grapes one by one made the little girl sweeter.
> Your branches shook,
> the ripe grapes [fell] into a pleated skirt,
> and I am no longer chirping.

MC: A poem from Ms. M. Friends, let's discuss it then.

AN UNIDENTIFIED BEGINNER: Excuse me, Ostad. It's really difficult for beginners like us [modest form of "me"] to understand the message of this "new poetry," in particular. Could we hear a brief description of the general message of the poem?

MC: Usually poets don't do that; they don't say what the general meaning of their poem is. It's not right, either, for example for a poet to limit her poem to one interpretation.... Besides that, the conception that exists in the poet's mental world and the way it enters a poem: perhaps each *mokhātab* [listener or reader] might have a different reception of it from different points of view, perhaps they would agree only on one part and diverge on other parts.

SEYYED ABU TALEB MOZAFFARI: Well, if somebody does do it [explain the meaning of their poem], it's not a problem!

MC: Well, I don't know if Ms. M ...

POET: [*laughs with embarrassment*]

MOZAFFARI: Can you read it again, bit by bit? A little bit louder?

MC: Please read it a little bit slower and more clearly.

POET: The spring that started with your branches / and my chirping / made the cats sleeker ...

MOZAFFARI: This "The spring that started with your branches"—does it have an answer anywhere? The spring started with your branches, and then what?

[*A discussion of the images of the tree and chirping bird ensues.*]

(...)

POET: The sun was red, / redder when it looked at us.

MC: The intention of the use of the word *red* and *turning red* is not quite clear here.

POET: The meaning of blushing?

MOZAFFARI: No, it doesn't really come across, it's not worthy [*shāyesteh*] of the other images ... you have an intention, but I don't think the sentence gets it across [*resānā nist*]. Even the first sentence had that difficulty. In order for it to come across, the image needs further elaboration. Because here, "when it looked at us" is the only phrase that tells us that the sun's turning red suggests blushing. "It looked at us" is not anything special, what happened to make the sun turn redder? This part limps a bit [*lang ast*].

UNIDENTIFIED MALE IRANIAN GUEST: *Jenāb* Mozaffari, excuse me please, something just occurred to me.[13] This message that you have just talked about is what in fact she said with simple words. If we want a poet to explain what they said in their poem and what they meant, in my opinion it's not only useless but wrong. As Mowlana [Rumi] says, *"Har kasi az zann-e khod shod yār-e man / Az darun-e man najost asrār-e man"* [Everyone became my friend for his own reasons / He did not seek my secrets within me].[14] I think this is no less than an offense to the poet. (...) Let's assume that I'm in a gathering where someone gives a speech, but my education is not up to the same level. (...) This exact thing happened to the great Ostad Ja'fari. He was giving a speech and somebody said, "You're speaking at a really high level, we can't understand what you're saying." He said, "Well, it's not my fault! I can't come down to your level, you need to pull yourself up to my level." Sometimes, a poet uses complicated language. We don't have the right to interrogate her and say, "What did you say? What did you want to . . ." What's important is what *your* perception [*bardāsht*] is. She says the sun was red and when it looked at us it got redder. Let's assume that you attribute this to jealousy, it turned red with jealousy. Or attribute it to embarrassment, it turned red with shame. Or to the arousal of excitement, it turned red with excitement. If you read a poem of Hafez for ninety people, they will have ninety different interpretations. We don't have the right to ask a poet "what did you want to say, and did you manage to convey it or not?" I think that in criticism, what we should focus on more is where are there grammatical problems, or problems with the structure of language? What technical mistakes are there? But as far as content and ideas are concerned, as far as the imagination of the poet is concerned, we'd have to interrogate [*be salib bekeshim,* lit. crucify] every single poet and say, "What did you mean?" Sohrab says "When my father died, all the policemen were poets" or "I do my ablutions with the heartbeat of windows,"[15] and many other such poetic phrases. If we . . .

ANOTHER UNIDENTIFIED MALE [SKEPTICALLY]: If there are seventy different understandings of a poem, and the poet has a different understanding, that makes seventy-one different understandings, . . . whereas I think . . .

IRANIAN GUEST, INTERRUPTING: The beauty of poetry is its multidimensionality. Look, the poetry of Hafez is read by both a wine drinker and by the one who prays in the mosque and says all his prayers on time. If we say something bare and stripped of its skin [*lokht o pust kandeh*; forthrightly], throw out a text, well, that's not poetry. The beauty of poetry is in these very complexities, and the thoughts and imaginings that it creates in different people. The very thing that makes you think, what did she have in mind? Why did the sun turn red? It's important that it persuades you to go after what she meant to say. (...)

MC: Good. Very good.

MOZAFFARI: I have a point to make to follow up. We . . . I think that the work of poetry is not quite so free. You know, we . . . the poet has to follow several things. One of them is the grammatical rules of the language; another, an aesthetic principle, whatever it may be; and another, the logical and cultural rules of a society, right? In any case, these are the things that enable us to understand a text. When a poet is constructing an image, he has to keep two things in mind. One is the principle of aesthetics, one is the principle of communication. That is to say, a poem should be both beautiful, and communicate effectively. If these two principles are not followed, we can disagree with the poet if he says that his vagueness [*ebhām*] is so deep that we might not get the meaning. We have the right to say to a poet, this image you've constructed is neither beautiful, nor communicative. Why? Because in the old rules of the language, in metaphors and allusions, we used certain symmetries and analogies. These symmetries and analogies and so on existed only because the *mokhātab* wanted them from the poet—he would test him, in any case, the test of a poet was the mind of his listeners. It's not free and unbounded, in my opinion. Even now, if we criticize a poet, it has to be at these levels, too. If I say, the sun turned red, I have to have an analogy behind it to guide the mind in a certain direction. If it doesn't guide, then I don't accept this poet, even if he claims to be the greatest philosopher in the world.

UNIDENTIFIED GUEST: Let's interrupt the discussion here with an example. If we put a person's face in the place of the sun and say his face was red, when he saw us he blushed even more—do we need to explain any more?

MOZAFFARI: Yes, I think that even if we include such explanations a hundred times over, we won't get anywhere. He made us blush—what does that mean? He saw us and blushed out of shame, out of embarrassment, out of fear, out of what? [*Speaking rapidly and slightly raising his voice.*] In poetry, we want to guide the reader toward something, not abandon him in the middle of a barren wasteland. I, with my poem, am guiding the reader toward something, I'm showing him the way, even if he has a different perception. But these codes that I use as a poet are important. I, as the poet, whether seeing me was like seeing a bogeyman that frightened the other party [the sun], or a kind mother that drew him to her, or was like what— if the poet doesn't communicate this and claims that you can take from it what you want, in my opinion we cannot accept such words from a poet. Because if we behave in this way, we are destroying the basis of language.

MC: Good, very good. Please go on, Ms. M.

POET: The spring that started with your branches / brought summer into fruition

(...)

MOZAFFARI: I think the branches have been repeated too much. It's as if you're helpless because you don't have another image—but a tree has many other things you could talk about. You shouldn't just be stuck on the branches. It's not just through branches that we know trees. In your poem the main image is a tree, and its [other] axis is a bird that is among the branches. You want to repeat this relationship, but whenever we return to the tree we have the branch, and whenever we return to the bird, we have the chirping. This indicates a limited vocabulary. Look for other images. For example, in the poems of the Indian Style, in every poem in which Bidel has a drop of water, a dewdrop, he looks at it from a different point of view, as if the creation of imagery [*tasvir-sāzi*] around this dewdrop was never ending. It's just that a limited use of language is noticed very soon.

MC: That was a very interesting point about this section. Right, you've finished then?

This lengthy excerpt illustrates the kinds of discussions that take place in poetry criticism sessions and the kind of standards against which poems are judged—which are themselves subject to debate, particularly in the case of blank verse, as with this poem. Mozaffari here, as in many other criticism sessions that I attended, is insisting on the need to refer to some recognizable aesthetic system, "whatever it may be," which is necessary for a poem to be an effective medium of communication within a given context. He is criticizing the poem for being too obscure and not forming a coherent, meaningful series of images in the listener's mind. As the senior poet in the audience, he appears to become mildly irritated when the Iranian guest contradicts him but gives little indication of this other than a slightly raised voice. The guest is clearly knowledgeable about classical and modern poetry and readily drops poetic quotes into his speech to emphasize his authority and support his argument. Later, Mozaffari urges the poet to expand her vocabulary and broaden the range of images she uses, giving the example of the classical poet Bidel and his treatment of a dewdrop. In other sessions, too, I could observe a trend in which younger poets read poems with obscure metaphors that did not immediately convey their intentions to the audience. Older poets like Mozaffari regularly emphasized the need for the poet to connect with the audience by referring to universal concepts and values, rather than their own subjective experiences. Nonetheless, he also encouraged them to try to develop a distinctive style of their own and a fresh (*tāzeh*) perspective.

The established format of another kind of poetic gathering that I witnessed at the time of my research, the *shab-e she'r,* or poetry evening, likely developed during the course of the twentieth century. Most were held in purpose-built auditoriums at state-run cultural centers or universities and organized by officially-recognized groups. The programs and speakers were introduced and moderated by one or several masters of ceremonies (*mojri*), and usually amplification technology was present to enable a large audience to hear the speakers. Sometimes, light Persian classical music was played in the background while a poet read his or her work. A master poet might also be invited to give a keynote speech on some aspect of poetics. During breaks, tea or fruit juice and fruit or cakes were the de rigueur refreshments, either distributed to the seated audience by ushers or served in a foyer outside the auditorium. Lunch was also served in an adjoining cafeteria or restaurant in the case of better-funded or longer programs.

Another type of event, the literary festival or competition (*jashnvāreh*), is one of the foremost forms of state literary patronage and is extremely popular and common in the Islamic Republic. Festival participants are selected on the basis of their submitted works (which must be preapproved and relevant to the festival theme); they are hosted at a hotel by the organizers, and travel expenses are usually reimbursed. Thus, festivals provide a forum for poets and writers from all over the country to meet and spend several days together, discuss their work, and exchange ideas. Prizes usually include gold coins (*sekkeh*) of different sizes, readily exchangeable for fixed amounts of cash.[16] They are thus costly to organize, and except in a few rare cases, involve cooperating with one of the various state cultural organizations, such as the provincial branches of the Ministry of Culture and Islamic Guidance (MCIG) or the Organization for Islamic Propaganda.

Ultimately, the institution of a cultural center such as Dorr-e Dari is a fascinating hybrid of two literary traditions. On the one hand is the personal relationship with one's *ostād,* not unlike the relationship between a mystic and his disciple or a master craftsman and apprentice, although it has become far less exclusive and binding today. On the other hand are open criticism sessions in which anyone can participate and offer their opinion, as long as it is reasonably argued. And the contemporary *ostād* encourages his students not to follow or mimic him in any way, but rather to break out of the mold and develop their own original voice and perspective. In fact, some of the people most criticized for the overly iconoclastic form or content of their poetry in these group sessions have been the ones most encouraged by Mozaffari to persevere and find their own way. On the other hand, he also always encourages beginning poets to study the classics as often as possible, in order to achieve new things by drawing on the rich resources of the Persian literary tradition.

Poetry in Social Interaction: The Magic of Quotation and Divination

Poetry, as the most aesthetically refined form of language, holds the attention of listeners or readers and enables them to tap into shared cultural repertoires in an elevated and moving register. Thus, in the Persianate world, with its ongoing interpenetration of oral and literary registers (Mills 2013: 230), it remains in daily circulation: quoting individual lines from famous poems at appropriate times is a skill still widely practiced and admired by Iranians and Afghans. Beeman has noted the importance of the aesthetic dimension in Iranian interpersonal interactions and described the efficacy of language as a kind of magic, through which Iranians "are able to negotiate and even transform an uncertain world with skill and grace[, rising] above mere pedestrian conversation and into the realm of art" (Beeman 1986: 20). Poetry, full of "deeply anchored, association-rich metaphors," may be deployed as one of the cultural forms that give ritual its efficacy. For in the end "it is not the ceremony, but how the ceremony is done. It is a kind of powerful magic, not just linguistic or rhetorical, but a magic of cultural form" (Fischer and Abedi 1990: 287). Socially awkward situations can be smoothed over and relationships transformed simply by saying the right thing at the right time, complete with appropriate quotations from classical poetry. Poetic quotes are an example of what Bakhtin (1986: 88) calls "authoritative utterances" of others that are brought into speech.[17] Calling on the authority of past figures to bolster one's argument is one of the functions of quotation identified by Morawski; it also fulfills the aesthetic function of adding ornamentation to speech, and of establishing the erudition and cultural expertise of the speaker (Morawski 1970). Audiences, too, can establish their erudition and membership of an interpretive community when they are able to correctly interpret allusions and recognize literary sources, which are often not given attribution (Mills 2013: 232).

Many people (I heard of both schoolgirls and soldiers) compile notebooks of their favorite poems or couplets extracted from them, although the ability and desire to store vast amounts of poetry in one's memory seem to be declining. However, I was told that truly great poetry, or at least individual couplets from it, may be recognized by its ability to remain in the memory after a single hearing or reading. Conferences often begin with appropriate and edifying quotes, and people often quote poetry or proverbs to illustrate particular points even in informal conversation, at the same time presenting themselves as educated people with mastery of verbal forms and a powerful memory. I once remarked to the poet Seyyed Reza Mohammadi that the media were foretelling a bloody battle between NATO and Taliban forces in southern Afghanistan in the spring of 2007. He replied by quoting a poem by Mahbubeh Ebrahimi, in which she begs the spring not to come so that the war season will not begin (M. Ebrahimi 1386/2007: 24–25).

Quotes may be skillfully deployed to take on a very different meaning in their new context than they had in the original poem (this is the fourth of Morawski's basic functions of quotation); and such versatility, too, may be a criterion for gauging the depth and beauty of a verse. Mills (2013) has argued that Persian poetic quotations, like proverbs and other pithy verbal formulas, are compact but elliptical carriers of cultural knowledge, allowing a speaker to claim authority but leave interpretation open-ended. The polysemy of Persian literature allows for great creativity on the part of the contemporary quoter. In modernist poetry, the Beloved is likely to have originated as a real person of flesh and blood, albeit rarely named or described with specific characteristics. However, as we shall see, even such poems may readily be quoted in other contexts: in which, for example, the absent, longed-for one becomes a semi-divine being such as the Mahdi, the Hidden Twelfth Imam of Shi'ism, or even a metaphor for a historical event, such as a revolution.

Poetic quotes are used in the most everyday of events to give them additional resonance of meaning. At a surprise birthday party thrown in 2006 by the members of Dorr-e Dari for Ostad Mozaffari, the two-tiered cake they had prepared was decorated with the words "*Nimeh-yam ze Ferghāneh, nimeh-yam ze Torkestān*" (Half of me from Ferghana, half of me from the land of the Turks), a single couplet from Rumi's *Divān of Shams of Tabriz*.[18] This was as much a tribute to the double heritage of Mozaffari, who has spent his adult life in Iran but whose childhood memories and literary work are rooted in Afghanistan, as it was a statement of the double identities of almost all of those present. Another occurrence involved the appearance of a mysterious anonymous blog titled *Gand-e Parsi* (the rottenness/stink of Persian). This was a mocking play on the name of the Qand-e Parsi (the Sweetness of Persian) literary festival and accused its organizers of corruption in selecting the winners, under the alleged influence of wealthy opium-trading Afghan sponsors. Many people left comments vociferously protesting such an unseemly attack, but none with the pointed dismissiveness and economy of Ostad Kazemi, who quoted a single couplet from Bidel: "*Tā chand be har 'eib o honar ta'neh zani hā? / Sallākh na-i, sharmi az in pust kani-hā*" (How long will you go on ridiculing every fault and virtue? / You are no tanner, shame on you for this flaying of skins!).

Poetic quotes may also be used in serious, public contexts, including political campaigns, for the rhetorical power of their reserves of meaning. Asef Hosseini, who grew up in Mashhad but returned to Afghanistan in his midtwenties to work and attend university, was idealistic enough to become one of the youngest candidates in the parliamentary elections of September 2005. He ran in Kabul on a patriotic, pan-ethnic, nonsectarian, progressive Muslim and slightly populist platform, seeking to attract the vote of youths, women, students, and intellectuals. The slogan that appears on the front cover of his small campaign booklet, over a picture of a thoughtful Hosseini, is notable. "*Dobāreh misāzam-at vatan*" (Again I will build you, my homeland) is from a *ghazal* by the late Simin Behbahani (1927–2014), until recently Iran's leading contemporary poet, which has been set to music by Iranian pop singer Dariush and a number of Afghan singers. If one is familiar with the subsequent lines, what emerges is a sense of a visceral patriotic zeal in which the citizen forms an organic bond with the nation and his fellow citizens; a sense that is strong in Iran, and that Hosseini certainly aspired to, but that remains a distant dream across much of Afghanistan:

Dobāreh misāzam-at vatan, agarche bā khesht-e jān-e khish
Sotun be saqf-e to mizanam, agarche bā ostokhān-e khish
Dobāreh mibuyam az to gol, be meil-e nasl-e javān-e to
Dobāreh mishuyam az to khun, be seil-e ashk-e ravān-e khish
(...)

I will rebuild you, my homeland, if need be with bricks of my own life
I will raise columns to [support] your roof, if need be with my bones
Again I will smell your flowers, in the desire of your young generation
Again I will wash away your blood, with the flood of my own flowing tears.
(...)

(Original in Behbahani 1377/1998: 327)

According to Hosseini, the poem and Behbahani's works in general were familiar to many people in Kabul, so the slogan would have held a deeper resonance for them. Indeed, this is one variation on the classical *ghazal*, in which the *vatan* takes the place of the Beloved. Even without this context, however, the phrase has a poetic ring to it, and this elevated tone also gives it force as a patriotic slogan.[19]

A year later, having predictably lost the election and much of his faith in the possibility for rapid positive change in Afghanistan, Hosseini became even more despondent when Seyyed Mohammad Yunos Hosseini, another parliamentary candidate who had later become a member of the Kandahar provincial assembly, was gunned down by unknown assailants in October 2006. Contemporary Iranian poetry made its way again into a letter he wrote about his reaction to this news, later posted on his blog. He had seen Yunos Hosseini's old campaign posters while traveling by bus through Kandahar on his way to Iran to see his family after the elections, and had felt a surge of excitement at their shared ideals: "Once again an extreme idealism raced through my body. I became radical again. Once again I gave myself hope that I was not alone. I thought that we were like the scattered pieces of one puzzle, and if we were to gather in one place, the ideal state [*madineh-ye fāzeleh*] would be nigh.[20] (. . .) All the way to Herat and Iran and to the middle of nowhere, I was thinking: '*Lahzeh-ye didār nazdik ast*' [The moment of the meeting is near] . . . Afghanistan will be rebuilt" (Hosseini 1385/2006).

The quoted line is from a poem by the modern Iranian poet M. Omid (Mehdi Akhavan-Sales), in which the poet begs his trembling hand not to cut him while shaving, and his beating heart not to embarrass him, so intoxicated is he by the thought of his imminent rendezvous. With whom, or with what, is left unstated—and this is an example of the openness to interpretation and polysemy common to both classical and modern Persian poetry. The original was in all probability a simple love lyric, but the Beloved could be interpreted as human or divine (as in classical mystic poetry), or could be a metaphor for a fateful event or destiny itself, even for a political revolution—a singularly modernist development.[21] I recognized this line as one another poet friend had quoted to me at our first reunion after having not seen each other for some time; in its simplest sense it is an expression of affection. But Hosseini clearly meant it in a loftier sense—he imagined he was approaching a tryst with the political destiny of Afghanistan as he and the slain man had envisioned it, his utopian city. The poem is in fact a perfect reflection of his political fervor, and of his despondency on hearing of the assassination. He ends the piece with the same line, this time with several ironic question marks: "The moment of the meeting is near??"

A final example worth remark is the title of Dorr-e Dari's magazine itself, the *Third Script*. This is taken from one of the mystical sayings of Rumi's friend and spiritual master:

Ān khattāt se guneh khat nevesht
Yeki rā khod khānad va lāgheir
Yeki rā ham khod khānad va ham gheir
Yeki rā na khod khānad va na gheir
Ān khatt-e sevvom man-am.

That scribe wrote in three kinds of script:
one that he himself might read and no one else;
one that he himself might read and others too;
and one that neither he nor others might read.
That third script am I.

(Original in Saheb al-Zamani 1351/1972: II:39–40)

Although this is a mystical verse reflecting the esoteric enigma of the mysterious dervish Shams, and of the mystic in general, it might be read in this context also as a statement on the liminal situation of a group of exiles: their mixed identities not entirely legible to themselves, nor to others. Yet, in a certain sense, this is a privileged position: while, like mystics, they may be feared and difficult for others to comprehend, they view society from a vantage point outside it and offer new perspectives. I should stress that this was my own interpretation, though Mozaffari, the magazine's editor in chief, said it was an interesting one. It echoed one made by Mozaffari himself in an interview with the Mashhad-based daily *Qods*: "The literature of exile is another way of seeing" (Ravankhah 1383/2005). For the members of the magazine's editorial board, the title had been chosen to reflect their desire to carve out a new path in Afghan culture and politics.

One major body of classical Persian literature, the *Divān of Hafez of Shiraz*, has another special application that is popular and widespread in Iran and Afghanistan. It is consulted for divinatory purposes by people facing difficult decisions or dilemmas, or desiring guidance as to the unfolding of their destinies. Hafez is called *lesān al-gheib* (Tongue of the Hidden) for his power to convey arcane knowledge from the mystic realm, *'ālam al-gheib* (the world that cannot be perceived with the senses, where angels are believed to reside, and where human destinies are already known). One holds a question in one's heart, then opens the volume of Hafez at random. The first couplet one's eye falls on is thought to hold the answer to the question, while the rest of the *ghazal* further clarifies its meaning.[22] This is known as *fāl-e Hāfez*, or divination with Hafez. *Fāl*s written on slips of paper in small envelopes, containing a single couplet or a complete poem together with an interpretation, may also be bought for a small sum from itinerant peddlers at tourist sites, particularly Hafez's tomb in Shiraz, or at traditional teahouses. Divination can be an entertaining activity among family or friends on special occasions such as birthdays or Nowruz, the Persian New Year, to see what the coming year holds in store, particularly if there is a chance that a marriage may be involved. It may also be done individually and privately, for guidance and reassurance when weighing different courses of action, and is taken very seriously by many.²³

Among Afghans, I heard of several life-changing *fāls*. In one case, Elyas Alavi's father, a cleric and religious teacher once well-known in the Hazarajat, had faced pressure from the different Shi'a political factions present in the Hazarajat during the Soviet war to declare his support for them, and he was persecuted when he insisted on remaining apolitical. His wife resisted leaving her home village and possessions, however, and flight would expose his large family and small children to other kinds of hardship. Having survived an assassination attempt, he gathered his family and turned to Hafez for counsel. The *ghazal* to which the book fell open—could it have been a well-thumbed page?—was uncannily appropriate and optimistic, indicating that they should joyfully begin a new pattern of life, and although there may be many dangers along the way, they could defeat them together:

> *Biā tā gol bar afshānim va mey dar sāghar andāzim*
> *Falak rā saqf beshekāfim va tarhi now dar andāzim*
> *Agar gham-lashkar angizad ke khun-e 'āsheqān rizad*
> *man o sāqi sāzim va bonyād-ash bar andāzim*
>
> Come, let us gather flowers and pour wine into the cup!
> Let us break through the vault of destiny and lay down a new design
> If the army of grief should arise to spill the blood of lovers
> The cup-bearer and I will join together to overthrow its foundation.

Indeed, the last line of the poem quite literally refers to moving to another country: "*Biā, Hāfez, tā khod rā be molki digar andāzim*" (Come, Hafez, let us take ourselves to another country). This was seen as an auspicious *fāl*, and so Elyas's father and his family decided to go to Iran. He still enjoys telling the story, which has become something of a family legend. No doubt it is the uncanniness of the *fāl* that makes the story memorable, but it also reinforces belief in the ability of Hafez to communicate the intricacies of human destinies that have already been written in the *'ālam al-gheib*.

What explains the power of Hafez? One answer is the ambiguity of the text, making it open to interpretation and applicable to a wide range of life situations. In Hafez's poetry, "the use of rather complicated, though highly competent, metaphor and imagery ... gives it an ambiguous, sometimes even enigmatic, character. This accounts for much of the fascination of readers for his poetry, including its regular use by them in a fortune-telling text" (Katouzian 2006: 38). Another factor lies in the didactic and reassuring tone of many of his *ghazals*, including the frequent use of imperatives: such as *biā* (come) and *beshekāfim* (let us break) as in the examples above. This guiding quality offers solace to people making difficult decisions, as do horoscopes and other forms of divination: "Divination, like religion, is invoked when one relinquishes control of one's own destiny" (Varzi

2006: 1–2). Turning to poetic divination need not always mean relinquishing control, however: the act of interpreting a verse, especially one whose meaning is not readily apparent, offers one a chance to further analyze and actively reflect on the choices available.

Poetry as Ethical Intervention

Poetry's rhetorical power to communicate in specific circumstances is not only in the hands of one who creatively quotes it. It may also be composed in specific situations as a vehicle for criticism or protest, in the most personal or the most public of circumstances, and it has been used in this way throughout the Persianate world and in neighboring languages for centuries.[24] For example, poetry's powerful rhetorical and socially generative qualities were described by Nezami Aruzi in his *Four Treatises*. Poetry is

> that art whereby the poet arranges imaginary propositions, and adapts the deductions, with the result that he can make a little thing appear great and a great thing small, or cause good to appear in the garb of evil and evil in the form of good. By acting on the imagination, he excites the faculties of anger and concupiscence in such a way that by his suggestion men's temperaments become affected with depression or exaltation; whereby he conduces to the accomplishment of great things in the order of the world. (Cited in and translated by Browne 1906: 14).

It is for this reason that poetry has been called "lawful magic" (*sehr-e halāl*) (Browne 1924: 196).

Persian poetry, then, has long had a powerful rhetorical function and was often designed to provoke affect and action. The poet's eloquence may persuade the listener, or provoke silencing or repression, depending on the stakes of the given situation and the effectiveness of the rhetoric. The poetic career of Nadia Anjoman, a young poet who became famous in Herat in Afghanistan, for example, was launched when she was barely a schoolgirl. Believing a teacher in her school was discriminating against her and lowering her grades, she wrote a rhyming, metric poem in very formal language protesting this.

> *Vasileh'i davā-ye dard-e shāgerd!*
> *Cherā hargez nayāi su-ye mā to?*
> *Hami khāham ke bā man yār gardi*
> *Dahi pāyān-e in ranj o balā to*
> (. . .)

> You are a remedy for the pupil's pain!
> Why do you never come to our side?
> I keep wanting you to become my ally
> To bring to an end this suffering and misfortune
> (. . .)

(Original in Nurza'i 1385/2006)

She gained the admiration of the other teachers and the situation was redressed (ibid.), showing that a kind of verbal magic can be worked successfully even by an intelligent little girl. This particular case, however, was a conflict with relatively low stakes. Another example from Afghanistan ended rather differently. In 2006, at the popular *Gol-e Nārenj* (Orange Blossom) poetry festival held in Jalalabad every spring, one young poet, Taher Shah Safi, read a poem critical of Pakistani policies toward Afghanistan. However, he was interrupted and "violently brought down from the stage" by the provincial governor, Gul Agha Shirzai (Media Watch Afghanistan 2006: 3). The governor later insisted that the poem had been of a "poor morality and not worth listening to," despite the fact that it had been approved by the festival's organizing committee, itself appointed by the authorities (ibid.).[25] However, this incident shows that the powerful can and do retaliate with intimidation or violence when a poet's criticisms strike close to home.[26] The poets fought back in any way that was available to them: some participants tore up their works and left the festival, using their silence and absence as forms of protest.

Although there are limits to its power, then, poetry, like other arts, offers an artistic convention for the transmission of criticism, protest, and entreaty that can potentially shield the poet from the negative consequences of such outspokenness. If aesthetic and rhetorical elements are used skillfully, an audience can be persuaded, or at the very least be induced to admire. Poetic rhetoric is particularly effective when the poet is able to tap into a general social sentiment, to uncover a general truth, and to speak for his or her community. This was certainly true of resistance-era poetry among refugees in Iran. But, as with the quotation of proverbs, metaphor and allusion also allow for a "safe margin of deniability... where the speaker's desire to criticize may outweigh his or her power or authority to do so" (Mills 2013: 242).

The tradition of *esteqbāl*, also known in the past as *javāb* (answering) or *nazar-guyi* (speaking opinions) described by Lewis (1994) and Losensky (1994) continues in the context of political poetry today. When a poem presents a particular claim or argument, and in particular when it is addressed to a particular person or group of people, it may be responded to in kind, leading to an elevated form of debate or dialogue.[27] Mohammad Kazem Kazemi's "Return" is an example of this. Its six sections encapsulate the essence of the poetry of resistance and exile, and include accusations of indifference on the part of Iranians to the plight of poor refugees. It concludes:

(...)
Agarche mazra'eh-ye mā dāneh-hā-ye jow ham dāsht
Va chand boteh-ye mostavajjeb-e darow ham dāsht
Agarche talkh shod ārāmesh-e hamisheh-tān
Agarche kudak-e man sang zad be shisheh-tān
Agarche motahham-e jorm-e mostanad budam
Agarche lāyeq-e sangini-e lahad budam

Dam-e safar mapasandid nāomid marā
Valow dorugh, 'azizān! Bahal konid marā
Tamām-e ānche nadāram, nahādeh khāham raft
Piādeh āmadeh budam, piādeh khāham raft
(...)
(...)
Although it's true: upon our farms, among the barley grains,
there also grew some thorny weeds deserving to be culled;
although perhaps at times your sweet repose would be disturbed;
although perhaps my children broke your window with a stone;
although I was unjustly blamed for documented crimes—
but if at times I well deserved the silence of the tomb,
on my departure's eve, dear ones, do not wish me despair.
I ask for your forgiveness, even if but half-sincere,
and taking the possessions I don't have, I will go.
On foot just as I once arrived, on foot I will go.
(...)

(Fragment of "Return"; original in Kazemi 1384/2005b: 40)

The bitterness in Kazemi's poem provoked a series of replies, also in verse, from Iranian poets (many of them his personal friends), published in newspapers or sent directly to him. They expressed pain or indignation at his accusations and reassured him of their solidarity, friendship, and shared destiny, using words that are not frequently heard in defense of refugees in the Iranian media: "*Qabul kon ke dar in borheh mā mehak hastim / va yād-emān naravad in ke hamnamak hastim*"; "Accept that in this era, it is we who are the touchstone / and let us not forget that we break bread together" (lit. eat the same salt) (Ekrami 1380/2001). Kazemi's poem became so popular among Afghans, and aroused so much interest and embarrassment among Iranians, because it succeeded in coalescing and expressing the painful experiences of his and subsequent generations. Thus, Kazemi was able to say in verse what few others had been given the right to say in a public forum, and to engage in a critical dialogue with his Iranian counterparts and Iranian society in general. Since that time, Afghan poets have increasingly contributed works to Iranian national newspapers and more specialized poetry magazines, participated in and won awards at Iranian literary festivals, and invited Iranian poets to their own. Through this process they have consistently projected a positive image of themselves as educated and urbane and successfully conveyed their concerns to the public.

Poetry continues to permeate much social interaction in Iran and Afghanistan, drawing on deep reserves of meaning that afford those in their interpretive community the pleasure of recognition. We have seen how poetry criticism sessions combine elements old and new, from the poetic *majāles* hosted by eminent patrons in the past, to the modern civic model of a cultural organization that is more democratic, enduring, and less dependent on the personalities of its leaders. The contemporary pedagogic model is also less bound up in a hierarchical relationship between a master and an apprentice poet but is more a matter of friendly encouragement, debate, and constructive feedback, not only from more experienced poets but also from one's peers. The *ostāds*, nonetheless, remain highly respected and influential—quintessential eminent personalities or *chehrehā-ye barjasteh* (lit. prominent faces). While beginning poets are still encouraged to study both classical and contemporary poetry, imitation is no longer considered a form of flattery but as plagiarism. Although it would be inaccurate to claim that originality was never prized in the premodern Persian poetic tradition, it is stressed now at the expense of many other considerations. In these senses, contemporary poetic sociability in Iran reflects the increasing institutionalizing and individualizing trends in Iranian society, but like any poetic quotation used in a new setting, such sociability continues to carry echoes of centuries of tradition.

5 Modern Love

Poetry, Companionate Marriage, and Recrafting the Self

I hadn't spent any time with Zarifeh and Sorayya away from the office until my visit to Zarifeh's house. Her room was actually a small, one-room concrete structure built in the corner of her family's courtyard (I later learned that many people build these to rent out for the extra income). Zarifeh's mother wanted to rent it out, but for now it was her personal haven in which to read, study, and entertain her friends: a room of her own, whose vital importance for women's ability to write Virginia Woolf once emphasized. We sat on the carpet while Zarifeh served us tea, homemade cakes, *ājil* (dried fruit and nuts), and candy. I flipped through the photo album she showed me—mostly pictures of various trips and outings to places outside Mashhad with the Dorr-e Dari kids, both young men and women—waterfalls, villages, woods, picnics, badminton games. Quite a few pictures were of fully clothed people standing knee-deep in water flowing by them.

We shared news and stories about people we knew, and then they got down to business. Looking at me with a smile at once shy and mischievous, Sorayya asked me, "Have you ever been in love?" Slightly taken aback by the solemnity of the question, I told both women a bit about my past relationships. Then they told me about their early heartbreaks, and the nights they spent sobbing into their pillows until they were wet with tears. In some cases their feelings had been for cousins, or even for female classmates in their single-sex schools. They hesitated to give me specific details of their current objects of affection—I didn't push the matter, as I sensed they might be people I knew—but the two of them seemed to know each other's secrets. The striking difference between my stories and theirs was that their passions were intense but unrealized. We then talked about marriage: hardly anyone here marries the one they love, they said. Marriage is something you tolerate. Most people still have little choice in who they marry—for many, a partner is still selected by their parents without them ever meeting in person. I knew from their poetry that neither of them relished this prospect. Yet things are changing: Sorayya's oldest sister was married in the traditional way, but her second sister had the chance to talk to her suitor and had accepted him.

> We ate a delicious meal of rice with chicken and *tahchin* (crisped potato from the bottom of the rice pot)—Zarifeh has a reputation as an excellent cook. The three of us sat next to each other on the floor to eat off one large plate, which I enjoyed, because it seemed like the perfect expression of friendship.
>
> (from my fieldnotes)

THAT EVENING WAS not the first time the young female poets had asked me about relationships: the topic came up frequently, but our previous discussions had been more abstract. It struck me that the more intimate question about love had come in the context of a small, private, single-sex gathering, in which we were getting to know each other better, and we trod carefully as we disclosed some details and held back others. Yet deep passions seemed to motivate so many of the poems the young people recited, and indeed it should come as no surprise that love (*'eshq*) should maintain in the present day its status as one of the most celebrated and cherished themes of Persian poetry's long history. But there have inevitably been shifts in how love is defined and expressed, for whom, and to what purpose.

The young women's chafing against the expectation that they should marry suitors selected by their families was illustrated by Zarifeh's *Mona Lisa* poem: she contrasted the "feverish and impassioned love" that led to the painting's creation with her own likely "exile in the confines of an unknown man's chest." This articulation of dissatisfaction is of a piece with what some anthropologists have argued is a revolution taking place all over the world: a discourse of romantic love and companionate marriage is being equated with modernity and is actively being sought as a project of modern self-fashioning by young people (Hirsch and Wardlow 2006, Padilla et al. 2007, Cole and Thomas 2009). This shift can be described as global because it is enabled by demographic changes themselves associated with modernity and globalization (e.g., falling family size and increased levels of women's education; Giddens 1992), and by changes in communication technology, the most basic and influential of which is growing literacy. Ahearn (2001), for example, has demonstrated how new conceptions of selfhood are set in motion when newly literate Nepali villagers begin to have the means and skills to write love letters to one other. While the discourse is increasingly universal, however, with mass media providing the images and the "proto-narratives of possible lives" (Appadurai 1996: 36), the extent and manner in which it can become a reality varies from one locality to the next, being affected notably by socioeconomic conditions and existing kinship patterns, including continuing gender inequality (see Hirsch and Wardlow 2006).

Romantic love itself is certainly nothing new, nor is it Eurocentric to speak of it: anthropologists have demonstrated that passionate love is a human universal (Jankowiak and Fischer 1992).¹ It is certainly difficult to imagine the Persian cultural inheritance, above all its poetry, without it. However, in a little-known but elegant essay, Gell (2011) notes that in many nonindustrial societies love is an "extra-structural" phenomenon: it is acknowledged and possibly sought after by many, but it exists outside the institutions of social reproduction represented by marriage and family, and, as in his New Guinean example, may be associated with death and destructive forces such as bewitchment. Meanwhile, marriage is often a "structurally predestined" social institution, in that the selection of one's marriage partner is dependent on numerous factors intrinsic to one's position in society, but beyond one's control (ibid.).

This distinction is extremely useful when exploring what at first seems to be a contradiction in the role of love in Persianate societies. On the one hand, there is a powerful and exalted "culture of love" with an extensive vocabulary, repertoires of affect and practice, and a pervasive presence in literature that is still revered.[2] On the other, the highly idealized and mystically inflected nature of that love was distant from the more practical exigencies of married life. Marriages in Persianate societies were for centuries "structurally predestined" through the favoring of consanguineous or politically advantageous marriages arranged by parents. In both folk and classical literature, most of the star-crossed lovers were unable to marry and many died, while the love described in classical literature reflected courtly or mystical practices that combined earthly (usually homoerotic) desire with reflections on sacrifice for the ruler or union with the divine.[3] This love was certainly extra-structural in relation to social reproduction through marriage, but Gell's dichotomy should not prevent us from noting the crucial ethical and didactic role that the discourse of love played in courtly culture at the very centers of power (Meisami 1987, Andrews and Kalpaklı 2005).

What happens, then, when a cultural system built on structure-dependent marriages and extra-structural love confronts new ideas of companionate marriage, as Iranian travelers to Europe did in the nineteenth century, and as Afghans in Iran are doing today? Gell contrasts structure-dependent marriages with modern marriages, the latter of which are based on a sentiment (romantic love) between two individuals who consider themselves uniquely suited to one another. The ideal of romantic love in modern marriage obscures the fact that such marriages may be based on largely arbitrary choices that their participants convince themselves are essential, predestined, and irreplaceable. Romantic love is the tool that is used to "convert the arbitrary into the inevitable" (Gell 2011). His flippancy about such unions, which he calls relationships founded on the "whims" of young people influenced by "love-fictions" peddled by the modern media (ibid.), is presumably an ironic device intended to disrupt their naturalness for the Western reader.[4] While Gell discusses the substantial emotional work that individual romantic couples have to put into constructing their relationships as central and irreplaceable (through the sharing of confidences and indiscretions), he does not mention the immense amount of imaginative work that a transitional generation needs to put into the larger cultural project of legitimating such relationships.

Afghan refugee intellectuals in Iran respond to ideals of romantic love and companionate marriage by working—not on a whim but with thoughtful, self-conscious, and stubborn deliberation, and sometimes at considerable risk to themselves—to make such fantasies a reality in their lives. Here, I want to focus on the role of creative practice by exploring the case of one poet, the relationship between her cultural activities and her eventual love marriage, and the love poetry she wrote as a result. To place the emotional resonance of that poetry within its proper context, I first trace the historical trajectory of the culture of love in the Persianate world and the transformations it has undergone in the modern period.

A Brief Cultural History of Love and Marriage in Afghanistan and Iran

Iranians consider themselves a romantic people, and many observers have agreed (Afary 2009: 19).[5] Love is a "core symbol" in Persianate society (B. Good 1977: 38–39). It is related polysemically to a number of other symbols and gives meaning to a wide range of affective experiences and social relationships in a dense "semantic network" similar to what Good has charted for its somatic relative, "heart distress" (1977). Typically, being in love (*'āsheq*) means being in an altered mental and physical state involving intense attraction for and attachment to a beloved (*ma'shuq*). It physically manifests as a set of symptoms compared in negative terms to illness or madness, or positively to intoxication (*masti*). The sense of intoxication or excitement arises in the beloved's presence or in anticipation of it, whereas melancholia and longing are associated with separation. The heart flutters, one is struck dumb; sometimes this transformation occurs in the blink of an eye after setting eyes on the beloved for the first time. Because poetry has traditionally been the art form in which love was celebrated, the association between the two has come to work both ways: a poet is a prototypical lover, and the art of poetry is often compared to loving (*'āsheqi*).[6]

Persian love poetry is everywhere in contemporary Iran in the form of romantic snippets from the poems of the modernist poets that grace posters, or the many classical love lyrics that are set to both art and pop music. While during my fieldwork I most often encountered such posters on bedroom walls in private homes, romantic images and poetic quotations now also regularly feature on the virtual walls of many of my young Afghan and Iranian friends on Facebook. Many, however, are not aware—while others perhaps choose to overlook—that the meanings and contexts of the ubiquitous word *'eshq* have changed since they were so extensively elaborated in the medieval period.

The discourse of love in medieval princely courts was a pedagogical tool for inspiring devotion to a ruler among courtiers and subjects (Meisami 1987, cf. Andrews and Kalpaklı 2005). Meisami highlights poetry's didactic and ethical functions: poets were often advisers and boon companions, rather than simple entertainers or flatterers, to their rulers—a function probably dating to pre-Islamic times—and attempted to guide both courtly audiences and the ruler toward the good. Court poetry's primary topic was the love relationship, representing an ideal to aspire to and mirroring the self-abnegating relationship of the courtier to the prince (Meisami 1987: 38–39), while the beloved was invariably represented as a superior being, noble and untainted, and holding the power of life and death over the lover (254–355). Devotion to a royal person, whether male or female, was sometimes even expressed in an erotic idiom (Brookshaw 2013: 24).

Persian poetry, useful as a didactic medium for the transmission of philosophical thought and many other kinds of esoteric knowledge, also developed a deep connection with Sufism, where it was used as a hermeneutic device for the transmission of mystical secrets to novices.[7] Many of the great canonical poets were Sufis, including Rumi, Saʻdi, and Hafez, and for them, union with the Beloved became a way of speaking about a mystical union with God and the oneness of all creation. The Sufis adapted court poetry, and in turn, court poetry integrated many mystical elements, contributing to many difficulties of interpretation in later eras (de Bruijn 1997: 4).[8] De Bruijn points out that the blurring of the boundaries between profane and mystical love was quite conscious: poets recognized that they were "sublimating" the earthly emotions felt and understood by human beings in order to metaphorically describe a higher spiritual state (51–53). Thus arose a complex constellation of meanings and practices called the religion of love (*mazhab-e ʻāsheqān*; Lewisohn 2010). Gazing at the "heart-stealing" beauty of young boys was used as a "witness" to the divine in a practice known as *shāhed-bāzi*, intertwining homoerotic practices with a complex Sufi metaphysics. Women were often explicitly excluded from the exalted purity of such love (Najmabadi 2005: 158).

Emerging as they did from the milieus of Sufi orders and princely courts, then, a significant proportion of all the love lyrics of premodern Persian poetry were based on same-sex attachments, although the gender-neutral third-person pronoun *u* disguises this fact in contemporary interpretations and translations to other languages. Indeed, the archetypical *maʻshuq* or beloved of classical poetry was a male slave who worked as a soldier and a wine server (*sāqi*) and hence combined warlike and refined, sociable attributes (Yarshater 1960). Without this knowledge, "many aspects of Persian love poetry, and for that matter, much of Ottoman, Urdu and Islamic Arabic poetry remain puzzling" (52). Indeed, in what Andrews and Kalpaklı have called the Age of Beloveds in Ottoman poetry (1550–1622), "deployments of desire were homoerotic, mystical, and reflections of and on courtly power relations" that were "persistently eroticized" (Stokes 2010: 29; Andrews and Kalpaklı 2005: 28).

Marriage operated according to a different logic altogether. In the past, in both what is today Iran and Afghanistan as in many parts of the Middle East (or indeed the world), marriage was largely a procreative contract between two families. Married couples often lived with the husband's parents while they were alive, and the conjugal bond was not the strongest tie in a marriage. Men's unequal rights to divorce by repudiation, to polygyny, and (in Shi'ism) to temporary marriage undermined couples' emotional investments in each other, although it should be noted that these phenomena were much more common among wealthier urban classes than rural residents and the poor (Afary 2009: 19–42).[9] Much of a woman's time was spent caring for her many children in the company of other women. Often, the bond between mothers and sons was stronger than that between spouses, and the meddling of coresident mothers-in-law was the scourge of many a bride. This fact only encouraged women to develop a close bond with their own sons, thus reproducing a cycle whereby middle-aged matriarchs finally attained a degree of power through their authority over their children, daughters-in-law, and other junior members of the household (see, e.g., Grima 1992 on Pashtun women in Pakistan). As a result, even if passion blossomed between newlyweds, it was difficult to sustain with the scant privacy afforded to them, nor was it necessary for the success of a marriage. This is not to say that courtship never arose out of infatuation (particularly in the case of more powerful individuals, or men marrying second wives). Similarly, a strong attachment could develop over time between spouses through a lifetime of cooperation and shared experience. I saw such situations among the older generation of Afghan refugees, although they were unlikely to express it openly except through kindness and everyday acts of consideration.

In Afghanistan before 1979, marriages were traditionally arranged by families, often between patrilateral cousins or cross-cousins, and frequently for the purposes of cementing a political or economic alliance through the exchange of brides, or for settling a feud (N. Tapper 1991). The bride and groom had little or no say in the matter. In urban prewar Herat, for example, cousin marriage was preferred in most cases, and cousins would often be betrothed as infants. Marriage negotiations and wedding arrangements were conducted by senior women of the families, and the bride and groom usually saw each other for the first time at their engagement party, though some might have remembered playing together as children if they were related (Doubleday 2006: 25–30).

Since ethnic groups in Afghanistan were and still are largely endogamous, marriage has been a central and highly politicized institution of social reproduction and boundary maintenance (N. Tapper 1991; Monsutti 2005b: 77–82, 2004: 223). Indeed, among the Hazaras in Afghanistan, most marriages traditionally took place within patrilineal descent groups and were determined by kinship, "so much so that in the event of the death of her husband, a Hazara widow is automatically married off to her brother-in-law, regardless of age or suitability" (Mousavi 1998: 61). Hazara women have, however, often married Seyyed men, leading to the formation of a distinct group, the Hazara Seyyeds. As this group claims a higher status than Hazaras, the rule of hypergamy has meant that Hazara Seyyeds would refuse to "give" their daughters to Hazaras in marriage, although they could "take" Hazara women as daughters-in-law.[10] Challenges to the prevailing order and even interethnic elopements were not unknown in prewar rural Afghanistan, but these could end tragically in revenge killings or open warfare (N. Tapper 1991: 63, Boesen 1983).

The treatment of passionate love in oral folk literature in Persian and other languages reflects its extra-structural nature. Folk poetry in Afghanistan, particularly that by women, possesses a strong strand of rebellion and provocation, often expressed through the praise of a beloved who is explicitly not the woman's husband. Examples are the following *landay*s translated from the Pashtu.

> I love! I love! I shall not hide it. I'll not deny it.
> Even if that's why you with your knife will cut off all my beauty marks.
>
> Last night I was close to my lover, oh evening of love not to return again!
> Like a bell, with all my jewels and deep into the night, I was chiming in his arms.
>
> (Majrouh 2003: 5)[11]

The Hazaras, too, have a similar tradition in their own dialect of pithy couplets with amorous themes:

> My love, do not make any noise, I am in the middle of cooking
> Kiss me discreetly, so that my husband may not see.
>
> The old man could be my grandfather
> The young man, the light of my life.
>
> (Mousavi 1998: 84–85)[12]

Such verses in the vast majority of cases were simply wishful imaginary scenes, given the high costs of adultery. The phrase "I shall not hide it" in the Pashtu *landay* is an implausible expression of defiance, given that the consequences of revealing such a secret could indeed be as harsh as the second line suggests. Perhaps, as Abu-Lughod (1986) suggests, they were generalized rhetorical critiques of the patriarchal system by women, either recited by the poet only in the safe presence of intimates, or repeated by others without knowledge of the particular context in which they were composed (see also Boesen 1983).[13] Whatever the case, there is a remarkable number of recorded Hazaregi oral poems in a variety of genres, by both female and male poets, depicting sometimes bawdy and often unsuccessful nocturnal trysts between former sweethearts now married to other people (Mousavi 1998: 85–87).

Meanwhile, many of the love stories in both folktales and classical poetry ended tragically with the death of one or both lovers, such as the story of Leili and Majnun or Shirin and Farhad. Majnun (the Madman), the prototypical love-crazed protagonist of an old Arabian tale popularized by Nezami Ganjavi's twelfth-century Persian verse rendition and scores of imitations, lived out the rest of his days in the wilderness, wild animals and his own poems his only company, after his beloved Leili was married to another man by her family.

In contemporary Afghanistan, a popular pop song of the prewar period, recorded by the celebrated female Afghan singer Mahvash and later also by the Iranian singer Hayedeh, describes the more acceptable trajectory of passionate love as a feeling that is acknowledged, even desired, but that must be reined in rather than acted on:[14]

> *Waqti 'āsheq shavi rāz-e deleta gofta natāni*
> *Cheqadar sakhta khodāyā! (×3)*
> *Delbar-et khanda kona bā digarān*
> *Tu besuzi va bar-esh gerya koni*
> *Delbar-et biāya, beporsa ke cherā?*
> *Tu bar-esh gofta natāni,*
> *cheqadar sakhta khodāyā! (×2)*
> *Ruz-e nawruz bechini gol-e sorkh*
> *Bar sar-e rāyeh negār farsh koni*
> *Delbar-et biāya, beporsa kār-e kist?*
> *Tu bar-esh gofta natāni,*
> *cheqadar sakhta khodāyā! (×2)*
> (. . .)

> When you fall in love, you cannot tell your heart's secret
> How difficult it is, O God! (×3)
> If your beloved [lit. the one who has stolen your heart] laughs with others
> You'll burn for him/her and weep.
> If your beloved asks, Why?
> You won't be able to tell him/her.
> How difficult it is, O God! (×2)

> If on New Year's Day you pick red flowers
> And spread them like a carpet on the road
> If your beloved comes and asks, who did this?
> You won't be able to tell him/her.
> How difficult it is, O God! (×2)
> (. . .)

This song, and countless others of a similar tone, were the favorite listening material of many of my friends, and in some cases I know that they chose to listen to them while dwelling on their own impossible love affairs. Even today, much love poetry and a vast body of popular love songs speaks of the suffering of unrequited love, or of the agony and euphoria of keeping forbidden love secret.

Yet, despite this traditionally extra-structural nature of love both among urban sophisticates and remote highland dwellers, the nineteenth and twentieth centuries saw dramatic transformations of love, sexuality, and marriage in the context of the emergence of modernism and nationalism in Iran (Najmabadi 2005, Afary 2009). Contact with Europeans led to the denouncement of anything but monogamous companionate marriage as backward and harmful by the modernizing intellectuals. The homoerotic and homosocial practices that had played such an important role in premodern Persian culture were repudiated, and the "heteronormalization of love was central to the shaping of a number of political and cultural transformations that signify Iranian modernity" (Najmabadi 2005: 7).[15] Marriage also began to be reimagined as a romantic rather than procreative contract. These changes at the level of individual practice may be linked to the wider political context: at the same time, the homeland was being imagined as a female beloved, meaning that companionate marriage became simultaneously a romantic and a patriotic endeavor. Women began to demand of men equal emotional and erotic investment (Najmabadi 2005: 177).[16]

The Pahlavi period was a time of progressive modernization and expansion of women's rights, and by the 1970s companionate marriage with individual selection of partners had become the norm among educated, urban people in Iran, although not necessarily other social classes (Afary 2009: 219–220). However, gender reforms also caused profound anxieties, not only among the religiously conservative but also among educated intellectuals. After the revolution, the Islamic government was particularly concerned with reversing some of the gender-related reforms of the Shah, reinstating a social order based on men's greater sexual freedom, encouraging polygyny and temporary marriage, and once again weakening conjugal bonds. Family life was to be based on male authority and a gendered division of labor (Afary 2009: 265–278). The Islamic Republic overturned the Pahlavi-era Family Protection Law, for example lowering the minimum age of marriage back to nine, though it had been progressively raised to eighteen in the Pahlavi period (277). Arranged marriages and cousin marriages continued in many parts of the country, and with the stricter gender segregation of public spaces after the revolution, extended family gatherings and introductions by relatives once again became essential tools for finding spouses (281).

However, various cultural changes had already taken root in Iran: in practice, the average age at first marriage did not fall even in the first decade after the revolution, but rather kept rising until it reached twenty-four in 2007 (Afary 2009: 360). Although people in large urban areas—especially Tehran—were the front-runners of change, the desire for (if not always the reality of) companionate marriage reached even less affluent rural communities (Afary 2009: 346, Friedl

2009, Hegland 2009). A survey conducted in urban Iran in 2000 and 2005 found a significant shift even in that short time in attitudes to spouse selection, with an increasing emphasis on personal choice and love.[17]

The polysemic pervasiveness of the discourse of love in Persian poetry lends it to use in other contexts where a language is needed to describe passion, longing, devotion, and commitment. Thus, someone committed to a political cause may be described as *'āsheq* (a lover) or *fadā* (one who is devoted), as in the Fada'in-e Eslam, the prerevolutionary militant group. We have already seen how this reserve of meaning was used in the political writings of the parliamentary candidate, Asef Hosseini. The language of passionate love was also prevalent in the poetry of the Sacred Defense, which drew on the mystical homoerotic genres of the past and largely returned to classical verse forms. The poetry of the battlefield described "a longing for the scent and the sight of the lover and promise[d] the union of the martyr with the lover at the end of the path where the lover awaits" (Moallem 2005: 116). War veterans and Basijis continued to remember the war in ecstatic terms in their various publications, including their websites: "They describe the war as an 'epic event where brave young men created passionate scenes of love and devotion.' They also define a Basij veteran as one who 'takes responsibility,' 'shows passion,' becomes 'drunk' with ecstasy, and ultimately 'unites' with his 'beloved' as a result of such sacrifices" (Afary 2009: 288).

Such discourse was not limited to Islamists, however. In the protests following the contested presidential election of 2009, secular activists opposed to the allegedly fraudulent reelection of the conservative president Mahmud Ahmadinejad used similar rhetoric to counterpoise the "tyranny" of the president with the purity and sacrifice of the opposition:

> *Ān khas o khāshāk to-i*
> *Doshman-e in khāk to-i*
> *Shur man-am, nur man-am*
> *'Āsheq-e ranjur man-am*
> *Zur to-i, kur to-i*
> *Hāleh-ye bi-nur to-i.*
> *Dalir-e bi-bāk man-am*
> *Mālek-e in khāk man-am*

> You are the one who's dirt and chaff,
> You are the enemy of this land.
> I am the passion and the light,
> I am the suffering lover.

> You are [illegitimate] force, you are the one who's blind [to the truth],
> You are the lightless halo.[18]
> I am the fearless warrior,
> I am the owner of this land.

(Anonymous poem of unknown origin)

After being spotted on a placard, this poem was set to music and recorded by a number of artists, including California-based Hamed Nikpay. These songs, edited over montages of photogenic young protesters, subsequently circulated widely as YouTube clips. The praising of the protesters as ardent and passionate was on the one hand an affective appeal to people to participate, and on the other hand a fair reflection of the "libidinal" energy that could be sensed at mass demonstrations (K. Harris 2012: 439). Both the conceptual language and the affective experience of love, then, can be harnessed as a political tool, and earthly love can be rhetorically sublimated to these higher causes, particularly in eras when puritanism is in the ascendant. In the film *Vorud-e Āqāyān Mamnu'/No Men Allowed*, Rambod Javan, 2010), the character of a prim headmistress of a girls' high school, Ms. Darabi, can be seen as satirizing such puritanism. Her response to the predicament of a pupil expelled from the school because she fell in love and married is revealing. She says curtly, "There are only two kinds of love. The love of a mother for her child, and the love of a person [*bandeh,* lit. slave] for God. The other kinds of love are *majāzi* [worldly, metaphorical, transient] and arise as a result of hormonal disturbances."

Changes in Afghan Refugee Marriage Practices

Afghan refugees' close interaction with their Iranian neighbors in cities, as well as their exposure to new ideas about love and personal choice in marriage pervasive in Iranian and global media, have led to a number of changes in these practices. I focus here on a few selected aspects: the role of families and individuals in spouse selection, the material aspects of marriages, and challenges to former norms of ethnic endogamy.

Choosing a Spouse

Although many marriages are still arranged by parents, and many still occur between first cousins or more distant relatives, there is a clear trend toward the greater involvement of the prospective bride and groom. The spectrum now ranges from families that persist in the traditional style, to those that consult their children and allow them to get to know each other before making a decision, to couples in independently initiated love relationships who seek to gain the approval of both families, and finally to rebellious elopements (but even these ultimately force the families to negotiate). Some degree of consultation is now definitely the norm, according to a small sample I collected, and is justified in Islamic terms.[19] In some cases, as with Sorayya's sisters, the change has come in the relatively short time between an older and a younger sibling's marriage, and older siblings who stand up for their right to choose a spouse often set a precedent for all their younger siblings.

The most common form of spouse selection among Afghan families today is the contemporary Iranian style of *khāstegāri* (marriage suit), which retains the emphasis on the family as a corporate unit and marriage as a union between two families. Typically, a young man's family (often his mother, sisters, or aunts) seek out prospective brides among their friends, relatives, and acquaintances, though not necessarily people they know very well, and visit their families to assess their financial, status, and ethical compatibility. A large number of factors are assessed in this mutual selection, including the amount of money and goods to be transferred between the families and other conditions for the marriage, comparative levels of education, future plans, personality, outlook on life, and physical appearance. It is usual for both sides to conduct behind-the-scenes investigations of the other party's character and background, and a large number of actors may be involved in the decision making. In some cases, almost any family member on either side can veto the proceedings (including, in one case, a young man's sister living in Holland, who had once quarreled with a family member of the prospective bride). Young women consult their close friends on the comparative merits of suitors.

This situation may be compared to marriage negotiations in other parts of the contemporary Middle East and reveals continuities with the process in urban prewar Afghanistan described by Doubleday (2006: 27–42), particularly in the motivation to ensure both happy unions between the spouses and good relations between families. However, young people now have more voice in the process and the range of potential spouses is broader. Since kin groups may be separated in exile, cousin marriages are less common and compatibility must be scrutinized on every level, very much as documented by Hoodfar (1997) in the working-class quarters of Cairo in the 1990s. Hoodfar shows how newly urbanized Cairenes had to contend with social change, limited finances and rising costs, and varying expectations of families from different regional or economic backgrounds, leading to protracted negotiations and clever strategizing to secure the material and emotional security of their children and the stability of future unions (1997: 72).

Khāstegāri is used in the selection of brides for young Afghan men living in other countries, in Europe, the Americas, or Australia, a practice that Centlivres and Centlivres-Demont suggest helps to ensure ethnic endogamy and the reproduction of the community in exile (2000: 167), and also makes it possible to speak of Afghans as a transnational community (Omidian 1996: xii–xiii). In one case I heard about, the brother of one of my language students, a young Hazara man living as a refugee in Belgium, visited Iran with a group of other Afghan men. His family in south Tehran set up *khāstegāri* visits with the customary bouquet of flowers and a box of pastries to the families of over thirty young women in their circle of acquaintance, but he did not find anyone whose personality suited him. Although he did not find a bride during his short visit, all of the other young men in his group did. One study found that almost a quarter of households in its Mashhad sample had arranged for an Afghan woman in Iran to marry an

Afghan abroad, and it was said that Afghan men living in Western countries preferred as brides Afghan women living in Iran, since they were considered to be more modern and adaptable to life in the West than women in Afghanistan. For their part, families in Iran counted on extending their social networks through marriage and perhaps receiving future assistance from abroad (Abbasi-Shavazi et al. 2005: 35).

The significance of this style of *khāstegāri* is that it gives the prospective bride and groom the opportunity to meet and size each other up, and it potentially gives young women greater bargaining power in their choice of a husband. Girls with a number of suitors (*khāstegārs*) could play them off each other or use the threat of one sealing the deal to mobilize into action another whom they preferred. Some of my male friends even complained that they had been duped into thinking a girl really liked them when she was in fact just flirting with them to make another suitor jealous. Certainly, there was both an art and a political economy to courtship at which some were particularly skilled and successful. It should be noted that *khāstegāri* visits also take place between the families of young people who independently initiate their relationships, as the exchange aspect of marriage must still be negotiated and formalized.

The *'aqdnāmeh,* or marriage contract, in which both sides can stipulate conditions for the contracting and termination of the marriage, and whose use was rare among rural families in Afghanistan, has gained importance and evolved over the years, under the influence of the rationalization of religious law in Iran. It, too, is enabling many young women to expand their rights and entitlements in marriage and family life in a way unheard of among previous generations.[20] The following statement I heard from a twenty-four-year-old educated Hazara woman, working as an English teacher, illustrates the combination of individual preference in marriage and the continuing importance of family, and the pragmatic bargaining that is involved to balance the two:

> I am engaged to my *pesar khāleh* [mother's sister's son]. He lived in another city but visited my family from time to time in Mashhad, and during these visits we gradually fell in love. I think he's a good person and he thinks the same of me. We decided to get married after we sat down to discuss our plans for the future and expectations of each other, and found that they were compatible. I insisted that I want to work outside the home, and he agreed, but on the condition that he can visit my workplace first and decide if it's suitable for me. I want only two children, and he agrees. I insisted that we must never live far away from my parents. I would not have agreed to marry him if he hadn't accepted these conditions. We have bought a house in Herat—my father and my fiancé chose it together.

Young women in particular try to make their decisions by combining pragmatic and affective considerations, on the assumption that affection will blossom in an appropriate match. "I want to choose with reason, and live with love," said one young woman trying to choose between suitors, who ended up marrying a distant relative living in the United States. As in Hoodfar's study of urban Egypt, psychic and socioeconomic compatibility were important characteristics sought in spouses, while love was mistrusted as "blind" and unreliable (1997: 62–63). In other words, family-negotiated and companionate marriage were not seen as mutually exclusive, but rash decisions based on infatuation were warned against.

Nonetheless, these days, even young couples who first meet during the *khāstegāri* process try to cultivate romance after marriage. Certainly the smaller family size and neolocal residence that are now common, as well as the geographic dispersal of refugee extended families, enable a stronger emotional bond between spouses (see Giddens 1992: 26). In 2010, I visited one such couple who were celebrating the first anniversary of their wedding in Sakhteman. It was the first time I had heard of an anniversary being marked. The young woman had been a friend of the man's younger sister, who had suggested her as a potential bride. She was twenty at the time, and he was almost a decade older, having spent years working in construction to save up for his marriage. For the party, she prepared a spread of pastries and a cake with a candle in the shape of the number 1, and also bought a gift for her husband: a lilac-colored button-down shirt. (She undoubtedly took pride in unusual aesthetic choices, as the complete set of dinnerware that she had chosen for her *jahāz,* or trousseau, displayed prominently in a wooden cabinet, was in a similar lilac color decorated with cherry blossoms). Notably, however, the anniversary was not a private affair between the two of them and seemed like a slightly modified birthday party: the man's sisters and I celebrated with them by eating cake and clapping as they danced together while their baby slept nearby. The man was not shy to show physical affection for his wife in front of us, embracing her as I took photos and kissing her cheek to thank her for the gift.

The Costs of Marriage

One of the reasons families continue to play a corporate role as marriage brokers is that marriages in this region have long been occasions for exchange and consumption practices on a vast scale, helping to display status, seal alliances, and secure the material welfare of the newlyweds. There are usually two wedding parties (an *'aqd*, a gathering at which the couple is formally married, and an *'arusi* or wedding party, often months or years apart) that must be paid for, specified amounts of goods and money to be exchanged between families or promised for later, and the bride and groom must be established with all the equipment necessary for their new lives. The number, size, and splendor of the parties the amounts of money and goods, the significance of each individual payment, and the understanding of who must pay for what are all subject to cultural changes, themselves susceptible to numerous demographic and socioeconomic factors.

Figure 5.1. Young women carry a decorated henna cake to the bride's house for a henna ceremony before a wedding, 2007.

One major difference exists between Iranian and Afghan marriage practices, namely the payment of the *shirbahā* (lit. price of mother's milk, or bride-price), known in some regions of Afghanistan as the *galeh* (lit. flock, presumably referring to its origin as gifts of livestock), in cash to the bride's family before the marriage contract can be drawn up and the *'aqd* ceremony carried out. The bride's family typically uses the money to prepare the bride's trousseau, which now includes all the soft furnishings and kitchenware for the new couple, although the groom is expected to provide the large appliances and furniture. The practice of *shirbahā* payments has all but died out among Iranians; for them, the *mahr*, or specified amount of money owed to the bride, which can be claimed by her at any time but especially in divorce, has skyrocketed in recent years. Among Afghans, the *mahr* is often low while the *galeh* is very high.[21] The latter had reached about 2 million tomans in Mashhad and even 3 million tomans in Tehran (ca. $2,200 and $3,300 U.S., respectively) when I first gathered data in 2005, but by 2013 it had spiraled to 6 million tomans in Mashhad and 12 million in Tehran (ca. $4,900 and $9,800 U.S.). These costs, along with the customary expectation that the groom's family will cover most of the costs of the many ceremonies and parties leading up to and immediately after the wedding, as well the house and furnishings for the new couple, mean that the total cost of marriage for young Afghan men is prohibitive—on average, 8 million tomans in 2005 and 15 million in 2013 ($8,800 and $12,200 U.S., respectively).

These costs, which were already rising in the 2000s but have been compounded in recent years by the lifting of government subsidies on basic goods, inflation, the global rise in the price of gold, and the 2012 collapse of the Iranian rial due to the Western sanctions on Iran, are having a number of effects. They push some Afghans to seek Iranian women as brides because they do not request a *shirbahā* payment: "*dokhtar-e Irāni rāyegān*" (Iranian girls for free), as the saying goes. For most Afghans, these economic conditions simply push up the age of marriage as young men work longer to save up (exactly as in Egypt; see Hoodfar 1997: 69). On the other hand, combined with the perceived increasing impatience and rebelliousness of young people, they are leading to an increase in elopements among infatuated youngsters. In these cases, the couple arrange for the girl to run away and move into the boy's family home. Faced with a fait accompli that puts their honor on the line, the families have no choice but to enter into marriage negotiations and marry them off quickly and without ceremony. In one case I heard about through a friend, the teenaged girl and boy had spoken on the phone a few times and met in person just a few times before they eloped, obliging their parents to negotiate their marriage; perhaps unsurprising, this hasty match soon ended in divorce.

Another reason why the family retains significance brokering marriage is that, although divorces do take place, divorced women are still stigmatized. I heard about a woman who eventually managed to successfully divorce her physically abusive husband, but she was later ostracized by the community and blamed for the breakdown of the marriage. Divorced women are also unlikely to be able to remarry well, and the low importance placed on the *mahr* payment by Afghans means a woman may not have the means to support herself and her children after a divorce. At best, she might become the second wife of an older man, or marry a widower with many children who need to be looked after. This explains young women's need to sustain strong ties with their natal families, to take their wishes seriously in marriage negotiations, and to make well-reasoned choices rather than merely follow their hearts. Conversely, it encourages the families of young women to take particular care in investigating their suitors and to negotiate well on their behalf (see Hoodfar 1997: 71).

Challenges to Marriage Boundaries

While the socioeconomic compatibility of families continues to play a significant role in marriage, ethnic origin is declining in importance in an appropriate match. Perhaps more than ever before, young Afghans in Iran have more opportunity to interact with people of the opposite sex from outside their families—in educational centers, universities, student organizations and publications, literary or drama groups. Given these circumstances, young women are finding suitors who previously would not have been acceptable to their families. Marriage between Sunnis and Shi'as, interethnic marriages and hypogamous marriages between Hazaras and Seyyeds used to be taboo. "They won't admit to it in public, but it is there in private," one Hazara man, the director of an English language school, remarked to me bitterly in 2004 after his son's marriage proposal to a Seyyed girl was rebuffed.[22] In the mid-2000s, several such courtships I heard about appeared to be doomed, while in one case a marriage ended in tragedy: a Seyyed girl and a Hazara boy had eloped and reportedly got an Iranian court to register the marriage on the basis that the girl's father had opposed it on unreasonable grounds. The couple then moved in with the boy's family, but the girl's uncles plotted the groom's murder. The boy was killed, the perpetrators fled across the border to Afghanistan, and the Seyyeds of Mashhad banded together to raise the blood money to be paid to the victim's family. Other Seyyed families who permitted such marriages at the time were ostracized by their relatives.

A close friend of mine, a highly educated Seyyed woman, had a Hazara suitor at the time: a man she had interacted with when they were members of an Afghan student group and admired for his erudition and principles. She couldn't believe her luck when his family visited hers in a formal *khāstegāri,* but her joy was short-lived as her parents refused outright. The pair got in touch by email and developed a close bond as he persisted in courting her for five more years, despite her parents' intransigence and several more formal rejections. We spent many an afternoon in her room sighing about the situation, and she was often ill and depressed. She chafed against the inegalitarianism and sexism she perceived in the norm of hypergamy:

> I used to be very proud of being a Seyyed, a descendant of the Prophet. Now I think it's wrong to say that we're superior to anyone else. My grandmother was a Hazara—was she any worse? It's wrong to focus on someone's origin, who their father and mother were. What's important is a person's mind, their thoughts and outlook, and their compatibility with you. Also it's unfair that boys can marry whomever they want, while we can't. I no longer accept my family's reasoning, and we have had many conflicts and difficulties.

She told me that some Seyyed women remained unmarried—a highly undesirable situation for a woman—when no suitable Seyyed suitors were found and non-Seyyeds were rejected by their parents; others still had been coerced into unhappy marriages with Seyyed men they did not care for. The norm of ethnic endogamy or hypergamy was one of the pieces of the old social order in Afghanistan than refugees struggled to maintain in Iran, although the fact that it had already lost much of its importance for urban Iranians made it a site of intergenerational conflict for families with children raised in Iran.

Yet this edifice that caused my friend so much despair crumbled with a speed none of us could have predicted at the time. One day in 2009 I got the news that her parents had relented, having accepted her brother's reasoning that the match was an excellent one in every other way, and the pair are now happily married with a young son. While the Seyyed relatives in Afghanistan initially protested, the family stood their ground and ignored them. When suitors came to ask for her younger sisters' hands, the question of whether or not they were Seyyeds simply no longer arose, and two of them eventually married non-Seyyed suitors with whom they had independently struck up relationships. My friend laughed wryly and said she wished she had known through all those years of suffering how easy it would eventually be, and what a battle she would win for her younger sisters—and indeed, for many other couples, as the story quickly became well-known in Golshahr.

Fatemeh and Abbas
Beautiful Emotions

If marriages are still largely family negotiated for the average Afghan family in Iran, how are the self-described intellectuals who consider themselves cultural pioneers responding to these changes? Below I present a detailed case study of the courtship and marriage of Fatemeh, a poet and Dorr-e Dari member, with Abbas, a young man who was a refugee and student of mathematics in France. I unwittingly played a role in their courtship when Fatemeh asked me to meet her secret internet suitor, whom she had never seen, while he was visiting friends in London. Both of them wanted to hear about the other through a neutral third party who had met them in real life. A few months later, when I was back in Mashhad, Fatemeh came in to the office one day, very flustered. She confided in me and another friend that she had just met Abbas for the first time—he had come to Iran to ask her to marry him and to seek her family's approval. "I set him a test in my mind," she told us. "I thought to myself that if he tried to shake my hand, I would call the whole thing off!" Fatemeh was a pious young woman who usually wore a black chador in public, while Abbas was a self-declared socialist, but he had the sense to keep his hands by his side, thus earning her trust and gratitude. They were eventually married, and Fatemeh joined Abbas in France. I caught up with them recently via online chat to hear the full story. I present it here in Fatemeh's words, edited for chronology.

> At the time, I was very passionate and full of ideas for my future. I'd decided to go back to Afghanistan and help my compatriots, for example as a teacher. I wasn't thinking of marriage at all, because Afghan men want a wife for cooking, cleaning, and bearing children, not for progress [*pishraft*]. I knew that with my personality I would not be able to tolerate a life of slavery and servility [*zendegi-ye kanizi o nowkar-mānand*]. Most Afghan men prevent their wives from studying and advancing. In short, with these idealistic thoughts of mine, I decided to publish my second book [*Gisuān-e gij/Tangled Locks*], and this was not an easy decision because of the financial issues. I decided to seek help from culture-loving people living in Europe.

One of my friends introduced Abbas; he had met him through an Afghan chat room. So I got Abbas's ID [username] and sent him a message saying something like: "Hello, I'm so-and-so. I wanted to see if you could help me with a cultural project." At that time, Abbas had just been in France for a year or two. He was depressed and didn't know much French, so he spent a lot of time on group chats, which were popular at the time. But when he got my message, he politely declined because he didn't know me. I'd been quite abrupt in bringing up my project, as well. But I thought, how selfish these Afghans in Europe are! Somehow I wanted to provoke this boy a bit, to put him in his place a bit [*kami ādam shavad*]. Abbas, meanwhile, thought, "Who on earth was that? No preliminaries, just like that! How impertinent. She needs to be put in her place." So both of us wanted to take the other down a notch!

Anyway, for months I didn't contact him again as I was busy with the book, but eventually we became good friends in the course of our chats, and he encouraged me in my work. For almost two years we just chatted without there being anything between us—mostly about the news, culture, Afghanistan, women's rights issues. Then I gradually came to feel that Abbas was an honest and kind boy [*pesar-e sādeq o mehrabān*], that he had a big heart. He took a liking to me too, even though he hadn't [yet] seen my photo.

Let me tell you, I never sent him my photo because I believed that if someone likes you [*dust-et dāreh*], they should like you for your thoughts and your actions, for who you are. Also, I was very slow to believe him and didn't trust him, especially because I'd heard lots of stories about girls who were deceived through the Internet. I investigated everything Abbas told me. At the time, this kind of relationship wasn't common among Afghans. If someone had found out [about our online communication] they would have gossiped, saying so-and-so has a boyfriend. Because of that, neither I nor Abbas said anything to anyone. It was a secret. I didn't know Abbas and had no way of knowing if he was an honest person. How was I to know that he didn't already have a fiancée? I couldn't trust anyone [to know about our communications] . . . , not even my family, because I knew they would worry about me.

Eventually I realized that Abbas was in love with me [*'āsheq-am shodeh*], but I tried not to let on to him that I knew. He didn't tell me, but if I asked anything of him, he wouldn't say no—he would do it to make me happy. . . . I was very pessimistic, but he cured me of my pessimism throughout our acquaintance. He really helped me from a psychological point of view.

Anyway, eventually he told me he loved me, but I hid my own feelings and told him I needed to think about it. I really messed with him [*aziyat-esh kardam*]. As he puts it, I made his hair go gray! I knew he had a big and kind heart, but I wanted to know the extent of his love. He, on the other hand, already understood that I was a hard-working girl, that I was sincere and had big dreams. But let me tell you, Abbas is a very moral [*bā-akhlāq*] and extremely patient person. I confess he was much better than me in this regard. I'm not patient. I wanted to test Abbas to see how much he loved me. Because of this, I told him that my family would never accept him, because we are Seyyeds and he is a Hazara. My father had held such views before, but life in Iran gradually changed him. My parents had faith in me, just as Abbas's family respected his choice. I knew that if I wanted Abbas, nobody would be able to stop me. But I discouraged him. When he said he wanted to come to Iran, I told him it would be pointless—my father would never give me to him.

Nonetheless, although I had told him there was no hope, he traveled to Pakistan to seek his parents' blessing. Then he came to Iran. When I realized he was coming, I told my parents about us. They didn't agree [to the marriage] because they didn't know Abbas. I had to go to a lot of trouble to convince them. My father is a very good person, and he eventually accepted.

First Abbas stayed in a hotel, but then I told [one of the senior poets about our situation], and he [Abbas] went to stay with him. Because of the law in Iran, as a woman I couldn't just meet him in a hotel. Poor Abbas thought he might get killed by Seyyeds, because he had heard the story of that incident in Mashhad [when the Hazara groom had been killed]. So he stayed with Ostad, who played a very important role. He was like a kind father; he helped me. Those were really tense days before I gained my father's support.

I hadn't told anyone [outside my immediate family] about Abbas. Only once our *'aqd* was official did I tell everyone. What we did was contrary to tradition in a traditional society: a breaking of the Hazara-Seyyed [marriage] taboo, a struggle against ethnic prejudice. In addition, I wanted to be the decision maker in my own life. Usually, girls don't have the right to choose in Afghan traditional society. That's why I kept quiet. If I had said something, my family, Abbas, and I would have faced harassment. We wanted only our families to know and to present everyone with a done deed, telling them only after we were formally married. My brother and sisters were very happy, but my parents were very worried. Other Seyyeds harassed my father after the wedding, making malicious comments that he had given his daughter to a non-Seyyed. [My other relatives] weren't happy and they still aren't; they wanted to break our union. But I don't care at all. My family is important; they love me and support me. The others don't matter.

[In the *khāstegāri* process,] Abbas came to our house a few times, once with a friend of mine. My brother, my sisters, and my mother were in favor, but my father wasn't. He spoke to Abbas a few times. Eventually he said that Abbas's kindness had pleased him [*be del-esh neshasteh bud*], and he accepted. You're making me cry as I remember those days!

I made my *mahr* very low, and my *shirbahā* was low too. Our wedding was very simple because Abbas was a student, and in any case he paid for all our living costs. Now when I see the wedding expenses and *mahr*s [of others] I'm amazed [at how high they are].

After we were married, Abbas had to give up his studies, since in order to bring me over [to France] he had to work—it was part of the [French immigration] rules. It took two years for the paperwork to be sorted out. Those were hard days, being apart from each other, both for me and for Abbas. Abbas could come to visit only during the summer, and for a short time, since he was working. We had our wedding party ['*arusi*] the following summer [2008] and in early spring 2010 I came to France.

Letter writing played a very big role in our courtship. Abbas sent a lot of emails and letters. Oh, what nights we had when we chatted [via instant messaging] till dawn! Abbas was always the one to phone me, and after our marriage he called every day, as well as chatting all night. We chatted so much that my parents were amazed at the phone bill, as in those days our internet connection was through our phone line.

[*What role did poetry play in your courtship?*] I wrote a lot of poems. I had beautiful emotions. When we became engaged, I dedicated a number of poems to him. Our love was not like in a Hindi film where it starts with a single glance; our love came from knowing each other, from understanding each other. And now we're very content. I have a very deep feeling of happiness/ good fortune [*khoshbakhti*].

[*Did you always want to marry for love?*] I didn't want to marry at all, because I know my personality [*akhlāq*]. But when I chose Abbas, it was definitely for love. A love that grew stronger and stronger with time. [*What's your definition of love?*] Love has been talked about and talked about by so many, but I've come to the conclusion that love is an unconscious bubbling, a wellspring of affection/tenderness [*mohabbat*], without any hows or whys. Abbas was more in love with me at first, and then I fell in love with his *mohabbat.*

[*What happened to your ideals? Do you still want to work in Afghanistan?*] Yes, and now I can do it better because I have studied. I am also helping Afghans here in France, for example in preparing their asylum applications so that they succeed. I've recently contacted a few Afghan associations and have lots of plans, although my studies are important to me and my exams are coming up. I also want to continue my poetry. All we can do here is grow. Both Abbas and I still have a long way to go.

I talked to Abbas, too, and asked him how he fell in love with Fatemeh when he had never seen her. Like Fatemeh, he stressed the importance of shared conversations and experiences, a virtuous character, and the uniqueness of the other person.

We chatted [online] a lot, we talked about lots of things. Our virtual life seemed like real life. I fell in love with her—I liked her character. She was special, not like other Afghan women or girls. The most important quality for me that Fatemeh had was honesty [*sedāqat*]. It was very important that she was a poet, because I love literature and especially poetry. Her poetry talked about the conditions of her life, the condition of exile that she was living in, her humanism, her feminism. I trusted Fatemeh, and she did the opposite—meaning she was extremely cautious, and in this way we learned a lot about each other.

Abbas found it difficult to define love, saying jokingly that the word was synonymous with Fatemeh. He simply said, "To me love is everything." He also called the fact that young people were now marrying for love a "revolution," a "radical" act, and explicitly associated it with modernity. His two older sisters had chosen to marry in the "traditional" way, but his two unmarried younger ones were "armed with technology," as he put it, and like him were busy looking for love online.

Fatemeh and Abbas's accounts confirm some of the trends already mentioned, and they permit a number of other interesting observations. For one, Abbas's courtship of Fatemeh was a good example of a deliberate and consciously articulated challenge to the traditional rules of group endogamy or hypergamy. Fatemeh explicitly cited her father's time in Iran as leading him to change his thinking on the subject, despite the threat of pressure and harassment from their extended family. The family's faith in and support of their headstrong young daughter could also be attributed to social changes experienced in Iran. The principles that replaced endogamy and kinship-based marriage were a deep knowledge of and respect for each other's personalities built up over time, and a perception of uniqueness (neither Fatemeh nor Abbas saw each other as being "like other Afghans") that led to a strong bond of emotional intimacy. A great emphasis was placed on virtues such as patience, perseverance, being a moral (*bā-akhlāq*) person, and above all honesty.

Another striking aspect of the story is Fatemeh's tactical approach to the relationship. No doubt her caution and pragmatism would have been advisable anywhere simply due to the medium through which they had met, as the stories of internet deception Fatemeh describes are in no way unique to Afghans. The difference between her and Abbas—who said he chose to begin from a position of trust while Fatemeh did the opposite—may also have been down to personality differences. However, when considering the many tests of his devotion to which Fatemeh subjected Abbas, I find it impossible to ignore the comparative disadvantage of Afghan women relative to Afghan men with regard to reputation and the ability to leave a bad marriage. It also explains the pragmatic approach of other young women, and the weight given to positive character traits and virtues like patience and honesty.

Once sure of Abbas himself, Fatemeh continued to manage the situation carefully with regard to secrecy and disclosure. If she revealed too much too soon, there may have been more vocal opposition to their plans from the Seyyed relatives, and the couple may have faced malicious gossip and attacks on her honor for having a "boyfriend." I was one of the few people who knew about the situation relatively early precisely because I was an outsider with little stake in the matter, and I had a useful role to play by meeting Abbas in London. Fatemeh's close friends and the senior poet she enlisted for fatherly advice and support were other people she could trust.

There are parallels here between Fatemeh's slowness to reciprocate Abbas's feelings and the "reluctance" of young women in the Philippines to marry suitors chosen by their families described by Cannell (1999). It was precisely this reluctance followed by grudging acceptance that accorded Philippine women a measure of power vis-à-vis their natal families later on, a kind of emotional debt, as if to say, "I did this for you, so you must look after me if something goes wrong." In this Afghan-Iranian case, however, reluctance allowed Fatemeh and other young women to protect their honor and emphasize their own worth, showing that they were not quick to lose their heads for just anyone. Not only did this discourage less than serious suitors, a pragmatic approach based on mutual compatibility rather than feeling was important when persuading their families of the soundness of the match in a context where the suitor and his background were unknown to them. Fatemeh stressed that theirs was not a Bollywood romance of love at first sight but one built on a solid foundation of a deep emotional intimacy and thorough knowledge of the other person. Although founded, therefore, on very sensible reasons, such pragmatism is precisely what encourages the investment of a good deal of time and emotion into cultivating the relationship of unique private intimacy between courting couples.

New communication technologies are clearly playing an important role in allowing young people to communicate and get to know each other. At the time of my initial fieldwork, people would try to get each other's email address or instant messaging user name, and then either email or chat online with each other. It was just as often young women who initiated such contacts. Others spoke on the telephone or tried to arrange secret meetings. Later, many set up blogs and communicated via their comments sections, both publicly and privately. Most recently, however, Facebook has become a popular way for people to get to know each other, with people "friending" many individuals whom they have never met and have no connection to. While Facebook is filtered in Iran and requires a cumbersome filter-breaking process to access, a 2013 article on Facebook's popularity in Afghanistan reveals some common themes. The number of Facebook users in Afghanistan has jumped from 6,000 in 2008 to 470,000 in 2013 (Najibullah 2013), and the site is often used by young people seeking love and marriage partners. While young men are little concerned with online security, young women take greater precautions, rarely posting their own photographs (a favorite substitute is pictures of Bollywood actresses). While some such relationships end in marriage, in other cases online deception leads to heartbreak, as many female profiles turn out to be fakes set up by other men to prank their friends.

Finally, for idealistic young people of an intellectual bent such as Fatemeh and Abbas, the will to support each other in making a contribution to their homeland and their people becomes a highly desirable quality in a life partner. I heard many sad stories from Afghanistan about poetically talented and educated young women whose husbands insisted that they put aside their creative activities or their work outside the home after marriage, so as not to impugn their honor, and who suffered violence if they tried to resist. So doubtful was Fatemeh of her ability to find a mate who would permit her more than a life of "slavery and servility" that she did not initially want to marry at all. In Abbas, however, she found a companion who admired her precisely for those qualities and encouraged her to study, continue her poetry and her activities on behalf of Afghan refugees; he even suspended his own studies to meet the French visa regulations on financial support of a spouse. Fatemeh further signaled her intellectual status by revealing her disdain for gifts of gold, which are still part of wedding exchanges for most brides; she considered electronic goods more useful and prestigious. For young Afghan intellectuals, then, companionate marriage has become a patriotic project in the name of progress, greater rights for women, and ultimately of a healthier society, much as it was for the patriotic Iranian intellectuals and a more limited circle of Afghan elites a century earlier.

Fatemeh's Poems

Fatemeh shared with me some of the poems she had written for Abbas and published on her blog. While poetry provided Fatemeh a language and emotional framework for her cultivation of companionate love, as well as a form of release for its frustrations, love certainly also provided her fodder for her poetic practice, as it did for many of the other young poets—whether that love was requited or not. Her poems were a revealing example of the ways in which idioms of love from the Persianate literary heritage were being co-opted and transformed. For example, written when Abbas was returning to France after their ʿaqd, one poem evokes the age-old trope of separation from the beloved in a farewell poem that is almost becoming a genre of its own due to the frequency of departures in this transnational community. In another, she expressed how much she treasured the letters he wrote to her during their long separations:

> *Bist sāl*
> *na*
> *Chehel sāl baʿ d*
> *Nāmeh-hā-yat rā negah midāram*
> *Nāmeh-hā-yat bu-ye kohnegi nemigirand*
> *Sedā-ye gozashtegān dar ān jaryān dārad*
> *Bu-ye tisheh-ye Farhād*
> *Majnun o biābān*
> *Tāgur sheʿr mikhānad*
> *(. . .)*
> *Nāmeh-hā-yam rā fosil mikonam*
> *Tā sad sāl*
> *Na*
> *Sad qarn-e digar*
> *Shāyad dirinehshenāsi shavi ke marā az nāmeh-hā-yat*
> *Kashf koni*
> *Man miravam*
> *Be hamān khāki ke jodāyemān kard*
> *qasam*
> *Benevis . . .*
> *Be dam-e vāzheh-hā-yat man zendeh-am tā abad.*

> For twenty—
> no,
> forty years
> I'll save your letters
> Your letters won't smell musty with age
> The voices of those who have passed are alive in them:
> The smell of Farhad's ax,
> Majnun and the wilderness,
> Tagore singing his songs.
> (. . .)
> I will fossilize your letters
> for a hundred years—
> no,
> a hundred centuries—
> perhaps you'll become a paleontologist who'll discover me in your letters
> I will disappear
> [but] by that soil that will separate us
> I swear:
> Write to me . . .
> I will live in the breath of your words for eternity.
>
> (Original in Sajjadi 1385/2006)

This poem metonymically references the tragic love affairs of Leili and Majnun and Shirin and Farhad, neatly incorporating the emotional intensity and the cultural weight of these stories into Fatemeh and Abbas's own narrative (while presumably hoping for a happier outcome). World literature, too, is enlisted into this project through a passing reference to Rabindranath Tagore. Fatemeh suggests that her love will be as enduring as that of her legendary antecedents and even more so: should civilization itself collapse, the fossilized remains of their letters will still tell the tale of their love and hold something of the unique essence of these two young lovers "for eternity."

These separation poems are perhaps the single clearest thread binding contemporary love poetry with that of the past. Love was frequently expressed in a wistful mode—an aching, bittersweet longing for the beloved in the face of separation (*hejrān, ferāq*) or a cruel, heedless or coquettish beloved, often manifested as various physical symptoms such as weeping or inner burning. Among the Afghan poets, love poems were still usually written by young people in the process of courtship or other situations of separation or uncertainty, and such output typically dropped off once they married. Indeed, a senior poet once asked me in genuine confusion what we wrote love poems about in the West, since we could be with whom we wanted and did not need to endure separation. Poetry inspired by marital bliss is still rare: Ahmad Shamlu was the only twentieth-century Iranian modernist poet to specifically name his wife Aida as the addressee of his love poems (Papan-Matin 2005). There are, nonetheless, also poems about desire and union, and these are increasingly written by women, owing much to the space opened up for such expression by the incandescent love poetry of Forugh Farrokhzad. However, women's poems of this type are as often about the need to express desire as about desire itself. Another of Fatemeh's poems is interesting to us here because of what it reveals about young Afghans' struggle to make modern ideas of love more socially acceptable. In this poem, Fatemeh attacks the traditional society that prevented her and Abbas from freely expressing their love even after they were legally married. Newlyweds do not usually live together and are still known as *nāmzad* (betrothed) until after the *'arusi*, the second wedding party, which may sometimes take place months or years after the *'aqd*. Consequently, the period between the two events is an awkward transitional time in which the couple is afforded a limited amount of privacy for physical intimacy (*nāmzadbāzi*), but must still be circumspect, and becoming pregnant during this time is frowned upon.

> *Bāyad vānamud konam*
> *khoshhāl-am*
> *va labkhandi nemibāyest marā*
> *va hattā negāh-e dozdāneh-ye dokhtari 'āsheq*
> *be mu-hā-ye mardi bi-e'tenā.*
> *Bāyad be otāq-e kuchaki panāh bebaram*
> *ke panjareh'i nadārad*
> *va dastmāl-hā-ye ābi ke ruye tāqcheh por az 'aks khābideh and*
> *va dastān-e kuchak-at rā barā-ye fardā zakhireh konam.*
> *Nemibāyest marā chonin khoshhāl.*
> *In chandomin bār ast ke khod-am rā gul mizanam*
> *to rā*
> *va in jahān-e gerd rā*
> *va ādam-hā'i ke dust-eshān dāram*
> *Adā-ye zan-e khubi rā dar miāvaram!*
> *Bedun-e dar nazar gereftan-e gerdbād-hā-ye mokhālef-e sāhel*
> *be takhteh-ye chubi delkhosh-am*
> *Āh!*
> *Marā bozorg kon*
> *becharkhān dar dastān-at*
> *ke az ruz-e avval zan in guneh budeh ast.*
> *Panjareh rā bāz kon*
> *sorkh nashow az bu-ye ham-āghushi-mān*
> *Bogzār bu begirad fazā-ye ta'afon-e nafas-hā-yemān*
> *ke az kohnegi-ye jadd-emān be ers resideh ast.*
> *Bogzār bu beresad be mashām-e marzbānān-e mast*
> *ke man o to rā*
> *barā-ye buseh-hā-ye payāpey tab'id kardeh-and*
> *In chandomin bār ast ke vahshat dāram ke bedāni*
> *hameh chiz-e yek zan-e tanhā rā*
> *Bogzār farāmush konam*

talkh labkhand bezanam
tā habbeh habbeh berizi-am dar chāy-at.

I have to pretend
I'm fine,
but for me to smile is not proper,
nor [is] even the stolen glance of a girl in love
at the hair of an indifferent man.
I must take refuge in a small room
with no window,
with the blue handkerchiefs in the alcove full of photographs
and your small hands that I have to save for another day.
It's not proper for me to be so happy.
How many times have I deceived myself now,
and you,
and this round world,
and those I love?
I will pretend to be a good woman!
I won't pay attention to the storms ravaging the coast,
I am content with my wooden bed.
Oh
Enlarge me,
turn me in your hands;
for woman has been like this since the first day.
Open the window!
Do not blush at the smell of our embraces
Let the air fill with the pungency of our breaths
that we've inherited from the staleness of our ancestors.
Let the smell reach the nostrils of the drunken border guards
who exiled you and me for our continuous kisses.
How many times have I felt horrified that you should know
everything about a lonely woman?
Let me forget,
smile bitterly,
and pour me like sugar cubes into your tea.

(Original in Sajjadi 1386/2007)

The veiled but unmistakable reference to *nāmzadbāzi* owes much to Forugh in terms of tone and diction. Perhaps its most interesting aspect for an anthropologist is its vivid depiction of the conflict between two habitus: one that requires the narrator to act with proper reserve, "like a good woman," and another that gives primacy to self-expression, including the expression of female desire. The narrator makes it clear that it is not just society's "border guards" and obsolete ancestors who demand modest behavior, but that she herself is struggling against her own upbringing. She admits to feeling "horrified" at sharing the most private details of a woman's life with her new partner. In enjoining him (and perhaps herself) not to blush and to "open the window," she is wishing away a lifetime of embarrassment and awkwardness with the opposite sex, and longing for openness. Indeed, the final lines present a beautiful metaphor of yearning for a union as sweet, natural, and total as grains of sugar dissolving in tea.

In this case, poetry appears to be used as a "technology of the self" (Foucault 1986), a tool used to know the self and to intervene in it to bring about the transformations the poet aspires to, and to provide a model or a script for other young women around her to do the same. This is very much in keeping with Foucault's original use of the term in relation to the self-knowledge that is connected to vigilance over desire and sexual prohibitions, though this particular project of the self requires changing the boundaries of what is permissible.

Gender and the Idealization of Love

Although the pressure to marry and have a family weighs on both young men and women, men have a little more freedom to idealize love and indulge in it, and perhaps even to have one or two relationships before marriage without much harm to their reputations (although this is easier in practice for those who live in countries other than Iran or Afghanistan). Some young male poets described themselves as *'āsheq-pisheh* (romantic, amorous, one who makes a vocation of love) and prided themselves on pushing the boundaries of social convention. Love was a dominant theme in the poetry and life story of Asef Hosseini, for example, who was the author of the following *ghazal*:

> *Digar lozumi nadārad pish-am bemāni 'aziz-am*
> *Bā ghosseh-hā-yam besāzi bā mehrabāni 'aziz-am*
> *Man mitavānam bemānam bā enfejār o tanaffor*
> *Ammā to jām-i, bolur-i, key mitavāni, 'aziz-am?*
> *Bogzar ke ātash begirad in jangal-e ru be pāyān*
> *Qoqnus-e man par begiri, ruzi, zamāni, 'aziz-am*
> *Man ettefāqan do ruzi dargir-e yek ettefāq-am*
> *Tā sādeqāneh beguyam bā bizabāni 'aziz-am*
> *Key mishavad jā begirad dar qarieh-ye kuchak o sard . . .*
> *Vaqti ke shahr-i, jahān-i, yek kahkeshān-i, 'aziz-am*
> *Ey she'r-e nābāvar-e man, ey lahzeh-hā-ye setarvan*
> *Man nāmeh'i nātamām-am, tā to bekhāni 'aziz-am*
> *
> *In ruzegār-e jozāmi bi-chehreh-am kardeh ammā*
> *Bā in hameh ru-ye pelk-am gol mitekāni 'aziz-am.*

> It's no longer necessary for you to stay with me, my dear;
> to put up with my sorrows with kindness, my dear.
> I can stay [here] with explosions and hatred,
> but you are a wine glass, a crystal; how could you, my dear?
> Let this forest facing its last days catch fire,

so that someday, sometime, my phoenix, you can fly away, my dear.
Actually for two days I've been preoccupied by an event [a thought]
That I should honestly tell you without words, my dear—
How could you find a place in a small, cold hamlet
when you're a city, a world, a galaxy, my dear?
O my unbelieving poem, O [these] barren moments,
I am an unfinished letter for you to read, my dear.
*
This leprous age has made me faceless, but
despite all this you make flowers flutter on my eyelids, my dear.

(Original in Hosseini 1391/2012: 199–200)

This *ghazal*, written in 2007 while Hosseini was living in Kabul, is a conventional love lyric in the sense that it is true to the *ghazal* form, and the poet elevates his beloved while abnegating himself. But there is a twist: it is not the beloved who is cruel and inaccessible, as in many classical ghazals; rather, the poet preemptively turns her away. The *radif*—'*aziz-am* or "my dear"—focuses attention on the beloved as the addressee of the poem and provides a paradox: the poet is turning her away precisely because he loves and admires her and does not think she can tolerate life in Kabul. The last couplet, however, suggests that his attempts to distance himself emotionally are futile. Despite the fact that the relationship seems doomed from a practical point of view, he continues to idealize her. For his own unworthiness, he blames the accidents of history and geography: a "leprous age" that has made him mediocre and nondescript (*bi-chehreh*, lit. faceless), and a city full of hatred and suicide bombings that resembles a small, cold hamlet (*qarieh-ye kuchak o sard*). The references pass through a dizzying array of the mythical bordering on the bombastic, and the mundane (the beloved is compared to a phoenix, a glass or a crystal, a city and a galaxy; while the poet is a faceless man, an incomplete letter, a dying forest, a potential victim of suicide bombing). When read in the context of Hosseini's other poems, one sees a distinctive personal style and imagery emerging: he frequently jumps through an array of seemingly unrelated images drawn both from contemporary life, myth, and classical poetry, while putting his own stamp on them. The image of a forest set on fire, for example, recurs frequently in Hosseini's poems, a metaphor for himself under the influence of passionate love—a force represented both as destructive and redemptive (the phoenix rising from the ashes).

Conclusion

Despite the passion with which young women like Fatemeh are now pursuing love and companionate marriage, the material presented here shows that the kind of individualistic "pure relationship" that Giddens has argued has emerged in the West—a relationship that serves the emotional interests of each member of the couple and lasts only as long as it satisfies both (1992: 58)—is very far from being a reality among Afghan youths in Iran. The kind of sexual equality that would enable both men and women equal freedom to enter into *and* leave such relationships does not exist; nor is it really possible for relationships to exist other than as a preamble to marriage and within a dense framework of kinship obligations. The practical and material aspects of the relationship are never far from young people's minds, but this is particularly the case for women. They disproportionately value young men who not only seem serious about marriage but who also clearly state that they will continue to grant their wives certain freedoms after marriage.

Many of the marriages described here are happy and still in their early stages, but others I heard about had already ended sordidly when the romantic illusions of young lovers soured in the face of extended family demands, domestic abuse, or infidelity. Indeed, my more mature friends are aware of a fact familiar to anyone who has seen rising divorce rates both in Western countries and in Iran: that marrying for love bears little ultimate relation to marital satisfaction, and indeed such marriages may suffer from their inability to live up to the ideal. They know that love marriage is not a destination but an ongoing journey.

Nonetheless, more and more educated young Afghans are deciding to follow this path. Within a few years of our conversation, Sorayya and Zarifeh did in fact marry for love, and their husbands are both poets. Having met at Dorr-e Dari, Zarifeh and Alireza were friends for several years. Her parents were putting pressure on her to marry, and she had another suitor that she'd met online. But Zarifeh thought Alireza would make a suitable husband because they already knew each other well and she valued his sanguine, level-headed, and rational approach to life, and his honorable, modest attitude to women. She tactically sought Alireza's advice regarding the other suitor to plumb what he might be feeling; he advised her against the match, in this way signaling his own interest. They fell in love and had a relationship for a time before informing their parents of their wish to marry. Both sets of parents were opposed to the match at first, on the grounds that the families did not know each other, but with time they came around. Zarifeh and Alireza now have two young children, but when I last met them Zarifeh sighed that conjugal contentment was not conducive to writing poetry. Sorayya, meanwhile, recently wished her husband, Enayat, a happy birthday on her Facebook wall, calling him the "most important person in [her] life."

6 "When Your *Darun* Speaks to You"
Ethics of Revelation and Concealment in Lyric Poetry

In midwinter in early 2006, I attended a Friday poetry session at Dorr-e Dari with Zeinab, one of the granddaughters of my host family, who was beginning to take an interest in poetry. We were sitting in the second-last row, so I couldn't see the poets who were reading very clearly, but I had a good overview of the room. One of the young women who wrote more daring poetry had put in a rare appearance at the session. She wore colorful, distinctive clothing and a lot of makeup, including dramatic sweeps of black eyeliner. Her poems were equally forthright, dealing with women's sexuality and the problems attached to it. On this occasion, she read her poem before the audience: it was long and in blank verse, and I couldn't follow all of it, as I was still having problems catching all the intricacies of poetic language.

But I noticed that the reactions of the people around me were increasingly agitated. Some of the women in the back row behind me were whispering among themselves and muttering muffled curses. Suddenly one of them got up, pressed past the others in her row, and hurriedly left the room, having to walk through most of the audience and pass demonstratively close to the speaker to reach the door. One by one, a handful of other people also got up and walked out. The poet's eyes flicked to the door, but she retained her composure and read to the end of her poem. Twelve-year-old Zeinab watched the scene wide-eyed, thoroughly enjoying herself, and later recounted it gleefully for her aunts back home. The poem ended and there was a scattering of applause. I had not understood much of the poem, except for a fragment that went something like, "And God and his girlfriend Madonna sat eating pizza at the breakfast table." I tried later to get a copy of this poem, but the poet was reluctant, and I unfortunately had not recorded the session.

(from my fieldnotes)

This vignette illustrates the delicate ethical terrain that poets often have to negotiate when they compose and perform poetry. The current generation of poets places a strong importance on self-expression—on the expression of their *harf-e del* (words of the heart), by which they mean their innermost, most individual, and genuine thoughts and feelings. Even refugee poets who are not consciously writing postmodern poetry are moving from the general to the particular, rejecting grand narratives, placing themselves at the center of their poems, and adopting new techniques even in classical forms that they believe allow for freer expression. I have suggested that the world-weary attitude that many of them display in their behavior or self-presentation—including in the writing of self-consciously unconventional, avant-garde, or socially critical poetry—represents an aspiration to the status of a *rowshanfekr,* or intellectual, whether religious or secular. This involves projecting oneself as a sensitive but alienated observer, critical of what they may see as oppressive social convention and skeptical of all ideology, but unable to suggest anything in its place. By expressing such a stance through their poetry—and by becoming such persons—young Afghan refugees wish to show that they are abreast of intellectual and literary developments in Iran and that they are ready to tap into the cultural capital these offer. This is one of the few resources available to them to project themselves as *khodsākhteh,* or self-made, a quality to which many of them aspire.

But this position is not without its perils. The modernist poetry of the *rowshanfekr* often requires the critique of social conventions seen as repressive and a degree of self-disclosure and emotional openness that is variously interpreted, revealing how contested the shifting contours of personhood still are in this social milieu. Casting oneself as an honest social critic sometimes cuts against other ethical norms current in the communities in which they live, such as guarded and discreet comportment in public and sexual modesty. Most of the poets in my study, both men and women, were unmarried when I began my research and thus still lived with their parents (with the exception of those who were studying in other cities and thus lived in university dorms). The need to obtain a certain kind of prestige through a certain form of self-expression came at the expense of a different kind of symbolic capital: proper behavior within the relational moral universe in which they remained embedded in daily life, and in which the individual's actions reflected on the reputation of her whole family. This tension involves daily tactical performances, the forging of alliances with other like-minded people, and the necessity of periodically confronting moral censure.[1] Young poets in essence "edit" their expression, the early drafts of their poems, and their own physical appearance to make them fit for public display in different contexts, in the sense used by Manoukian (2011: 62–106).[2] Although everyone confronts this necessity, the consequences of mistakes are usually more serious for women.

Exploring these issues requires us to confront a recurring trope of self and personhood in Persianate culture, that of the symbolic divide between the *zāher* (the public, exterior self) and the *bāten* or *darun* (the private, interior self) that each person is said to possess. It is both an emic trope with roots in Sufism, and one that has been extensively elaborated in the cultural analysis of Iran (e.g., Betteridge 1985; Beeman 1986, 2001; Milani 1992; Graham and Khosravi 2002; Varzi 2006). Many of these accounts (e.g., Beeman 1986: 34) place the origins of this dichotomy in a history of "despotic" government in Iran and the Shi'i practice of *taqiyyeh* or religious dissimulation, according to which it was acceptable to conceal one's true faith at times when Shi'as were persecuted. But the idea that this is a natural or essential Iranian trait has been criticized (Manoukian 2011: 103), and a comparative anthropological perspective shows an abundance of ethnographic examples from around the world of a duality between private and public behavior, or between true feelings and their socially acceptable expression, in a wide range of sociopolitical systems.[3] Indeed, one of the classic sociological studies of North American social interaction posited that all of life is a performance and that individuals constantly adjust their appearance and communication to their audiences in order to avoid embarrassing themselves and others (Goffman 1956).

While acknowledging the persistence and productivity of this "paradigmatic bifurcation" in scholarship and journalism on Iran, Manoukian argues that processes of subject formation *everywhere* should be recognized as being "intrinsically connected to the dialectic between public and private" (2011: 9). This theme is also explored by Adelkhah, who has argued that shifting concerns in the management of the boundaries between public and private have been central to the experience of modernity, in Iran as elsewhere (1999: 160, 172). Thus, while the language of *zāher* and *bāten* provides a ready vocabulary for such dichotomizing, it is important to note that their meaning and content are continually evolving. As was my aim with the concept of personhood itself, I seek here not to fix a particular meaning of these terms or fetishize them as somehow essentially Iranian, but simply to show how they are used by people in contemporary Iran to reflect on and contest ideas of appropriate expression.

Modernist poetry is often portrayed as allowing the poet to express her true self more freely. It has also redefined the *kinds* of persons who can publicly express themselves in poetry: for example, the participation of women in mixed-gender poetic activity with a wide public audience has now risen to a level with few precedents in Persian literary history. The question that most concerns us here, then, relates to how young Afghans talk about self-expression in poetry and how they relate this to a quest for greater individuality. Poetry, in fact, may help us to reformulate the terms of the debate about the "bifurcated self" because it has arguably always provided a mechanism for allowing some of what is hidden into plain sight, all the while granting the poet a degree of plausible deniability.

Inner and Outer Selves in Persianate Culture

For Beeman, who has extensively considered it, the symbolic dichotomy of *zāher* and *bāten* underpins much of the ritualized, aesthetic dimension of interpersonal interaction in Iran, requiring much skill to negotiate adeptly. The *zāher*, the outer self or public facade that one wears, is a form of calculated, restricted expression and politeness in situations of uncertainty, between status unequals, or simply when confronting the so-called corrupting everyday reality of the outside world. The *bāten*, one's inner or true self, is the seat of one's deepest emotions and is typically concealed except in situations of free, unguarded expression, such as in the secluded realm of the family sphere or between status equals and intimate friends (Beeman 1986: 11, 2001: 38). God and saints may also be included in the range of intimates who have insight into one's true self (Betteridge 1985: 198). Perceiving the difference between situations that call for each type of expression calls for subjective judgment, as any given social interaction falls along a continuum between absolute "inside" and "outside" (Beeman 1986: 12). Beeman further argues (2001) that in some situations, such as the inhospitable *birun* (outside) when one is among strangers or status unequals, one's *bāten* must be deeply concealed and protected. Communication will thus be restrained and reveal little of it *unless* there is a need for a particularly strong emotion to be expressed or sincerity to be performed. In this case, various communicative strategies from the *andarun* (the secluded realm of home and family) are employed, including less formal diction or physical displays of grief or anger. Betteridge (1985) argues, therefore, that this distinction lies at the core of the Iranian conception of the person: the *zāher* involves a kind of flattening out of individuality, while one is seen in one's fullest individuality by those few who have access to one's *bāten*.

The inside/outside dichotomy maps on to a great many binary categories and practices in Persianate society, regulating differences in the ways strangers and intimates interact.[4] But two important points should be remembered here. The first is that boundaries between the two have varied historically, especially with regard to various physical markers, such as the veiling of women, or spatial distinctions. For example, Iranian women have successfully renegotiated the spaces and boundaries of their symbolic seclusion, such that the veil is now used as a tool for *de*segregation rather than segregation, allowing them to participate in a wider range of activities in public space than in the past. As elsewhere in the Muslim world, homes in Iran used to be divided into a *biruni*—an "outer" space for the entertaining of male guests—and an *andaruni*, an "inner" sanctum of women's and family quarters. This division used to be structurally encoded in architecture, but in most newer homes all over Iran, this is no longer the case: there is a preference for function over form, with open-plan kitchens and individual bedrooms if space permits (Adelkhah 1999: 157).

The second point about this dichotomy to consider is the question of how these divisions are enforced. The content of one's *darun* that must be suppressed in various "external" contexts is tightly correlated to diverse moral, ethical, and political considerations in society at large, so that the repercussions that may meet one who does not adhere to the proper decorum are diverse, ranging from social incomprehension or ostracism (as in the chapter epigraph) to legal censure, or, in religious terms, damnation of the soul. As in most other Islamic contexts, the idea of proper conduct as a marker of individual morality and the moral health of society has been prevalent in Iran, supervised by an officer (or office) for "enjoining good and forbidding evil" (*amr-e be ma'ruf va nahi az monkar*). This office has been institutionalized in the Islamic Republic as a branch of the police and was assisted by the Komiteh, the informal revolutionary committees that arose in mosques during the revolution and acted as moral police, until they merged with the armed forces in 1991. Institutionalized censorship (*sānsur*, from the French *censure*) of written material has also existed in Iran since the advent of print publishing in the second half of the nineteenth century (Karimi-Hakkak 1992). But the imposition of these norms is not merely external: it becomes an internal impulse, a component of one's habitus, proper socialization, and personal ethics. Indeed, it is common in Iran today to describe the act of refraining from saying or doing something inappropriate that one was tempted to do as self-censorship (*khod-sānsur*). Yet because Iranian society is diverse and there is no single habitus in which all the people in the country are raised, particular care must be taken by social analysts when describing the relationship between people and state-imposed norms: the law prescribing public veiling, for example, may be experienced as onerous by some but as an entirely internalized, legitimate and natural ethical behavior by others. Thus, many Afghan (and Iranian) women voluntarily veil before unrelated men, also in the confines of their homes.

We may ask what effect the inside/outside dichotomy has had on Persian literature. Literary historian Farzaneh Milani argues rather dramatically that a "pernicious" state of self-censorship and many forms of concealment have arisen in Iranian culture as a result of official censorship and political oppression (1985: 326–328), which "evolved over centuries of living in a state of terror in an uncontrollably repressive environment" (1985: 338). "External constraints," she continues, "give way to inner bonds, control to self-control, deception to self-deception. Walls are internalized; lips locked; emotions veiled; spontaneity imprisoned; and pretense unleashed" (343). In writing, Milani claims, this is manifested in a lack of a Persian-language tradition of frank autobiographical writing (a feature that Mines also identified in South Indian autobiographies [1994: 3–4]), as well as a lack of personal detail even in the lives of characters in works of fiction.[5] However, even in poems praising notable individuals in the past, there was rarely any mention of specific attributes of the people in question. Rather, they were praised for their adherence to idealized character traits and stereotyped markers of beauty (Brookshaw 2013). I suspect that the lack of a tradition of confessional or realist literature in the past is more related to poetry's public ethical, ritual, and didactic functions than to life in a constant "state of terror."

Although Milani draws on Freud and Marx to make her point, perhaps she is tapping into a deeper and far older critique in Persianate culture of hypocrisy. One of the most admired character traits in Iran is *safā-ye bāten* (inner purity or sincerity), indicating continuity between behavior and intention, and it is a compliment to say of someone that *zāher o bāten-esh yeki-e*—his or her outer and inner selves are the same (Milani 1992: 338). This is consonant with the general presumption of the unity of outward behavior and inward intention in Islamic law (Rosen 1999: 37). But it is recognized that the appearance of virtue may often be duplicitous. This is a critique frequently found in Sufi mysticism and poetry, for example in the trope of the outwardly pious but inwardly corrupt *riyākār* (hypocrite), of whom the preacher (*vā'ez*, like the biblical Pharisee) is the classic example. Its inverse is the pure-hearted *rend* (libertine) who gleefully embraces bad behavior in order to make no claim to virtue, the ultimate antidote to hypocrisy. Hafez, for example, wrote "*Jām migiram o az ahl-e riyā dur shavam / Ya'ni az khalq-e jahān pāk-deli bogzinam*" (I take the wine cup and distance myself from the hypocrites (*ahl-e riyā*) / Thus from all of the creation of the world may I choose pure-heartedness).

Manoukian has been particularly critical of the idea that such a bifurcated self is a natural Iranian trait supposedly arising from the country's history of despotic government (2011: 103). He stresses that the practice of editing or adjusting appearances for public display is found worldwide, both in its mundane varieties and in more momentous incidents of violent iconoclasm, censorship, and coercion. (Indeed, the Colombian novelist Gabriel García Márquez told his biographer that "all human beings have three lives: public, private, and secret.") Yet, seizing on the practice of *taqiyyeh* or other examples of divergences between public and private life in Iran, both scholars and international media "concur in producing and enforcing a bifurcated view of Iran as a country that is the opposite of the 'rest of the world.' The structuring of a bifurcation between underneath and surface is at the core of the dominant discursive formation on Iran" (Manoukian 2011: 103). In the reality of everyday life, things are more complex. Betteridge, based on her material from the 1970s, argued that although the separation between *zāher* and *bāten* was often regretted, "rules perpetuating it [were] scrupulously observed" (1985: 200). If that was true then, we may be witnessing a change now: there is certainly still a difference in the way people behave with strangers and intimates, and in spaces and situations that are more or less formal, but there is also a degree of fluidity between them, and many of the boundaries are being challenged. Poetry and other art forms have always provided a controlled way to bring private thoughts into public discourse, but the so-called "red lines" or inviolable boundaries of what is appropriate are pushed back and forth, debated and contested, and there is certainly no firm consensus on where they should lie. The "bifurcated self" itself is the subject of internal cultural critique and debate, and is increasingly pathologized by some (in the vein of Milani) as a form of repression or what they call schizophrenia.[6] This critique is class based to some extent, since it is wealthier, more secular people who define their identities in part by the rejection of veiling, gender segregation, ideas of sexual modesty, and other attributes of what they see as a backward lifestyle imposed by the government (see Mahdavi 2009). What is perhaps more remarkable is that such arguments have traveled even to economically deprived and socially conservative communities like those of Afghan refugees.

Ethics of Self-Expression among Afghan Youth

The character judgments of other people routinely made by young Afghans, expressed in Mashhadi youth slang, show that a certain degree of restraint in one's behavior is still valued as a component of ethical conduct that was not merely religious in origin. This was emphasized through the negative adjectives *susul* or *lus*—words that were so self-referential that it took a group of young people some time to come up with a suitable definition for me. Someone who is *susul* is like a spoiled child; that is, she demands attention, uses various ruses to get what she wants, may be pretentious, is soft (untempered by hardship), and is not sufficiently restrained in the expression of emotion. Such behavior may be tolerated in children, but in a grown person it may arouse anger or irritation in others. *Susulbāzi*—acting *susul*—refers to actions that make a person appear *susul*; these might include flirtation with the opposite sex or coquettishness in general, dressing provocatively, laughing or complaining too loudly, or, in the realm of cultural activities like poetry, engaging with something in a pretentious or shallow manner. Conversely, someone who is *sangin* (solemn or serious) is praised for his or her reserve. Young people themselves were often ambivalent about which characteristics to assign negative or positive value to, and gossiped about other people who acted not too differently from themselves. People who were *fa'āl*, or active in various social and cultural activities, were praised, including young women. But *āberu* (a core concept in Persian society that may be glossed as "face"—good name or reputation) had to be maintained through restrained behavior and sexual modesty.[7] One young woman, a talented actress and active in an Afghan theater group in Golshahr, criticized one of her fellow group members, a young woman who had apparently gained so much self-confidence from her acting that she had begun wearing short, tight *māntos*. My friend, shaking her head, said that this woman had "lost herself" (*khod-esh rā bākhteh ast*). Indeed, watching a rehearsal of this theater group gave me an insight into the way that young Afghans wove together two ethical codes in their daily life, that of "cultured" people interested in creative expression, and that of modesty: while moving around the room in a warm-up exercise to focus their minds on their acting, the young women were constantly adjusting their headscarves and overcoats if they had slipped.

The factors determining appropriate behavior in social situations, as Beeman observed, were highly contextual. I witnessed stark personality differences in some of my friends depending on the situation. A young woman who was always talking, laughing, and joking among her family members was quiet and reserved when she came to Dorr-e Dari, though she knew most of the people there relatively well. Once, after she had applied a lot of makeup and we were on our way to a wedding, we bumped into her father in the lane and she quickly pulled the corner of her headscarf over the lower part of her face so he wouldn't see her lipstick, as this would have embarrassed both of them. As noted above, domestic space is usually no longer structurally divided into an *andaruni* and a *biruni,* but, depending on the situation, it can sometimes still be used in this way. Most Afghan homes follow Iranian architectural fashions and have open-plan kitchens, but blinds are sometimes positioned over the counters, allowing them to be converted into women's secluded space if unfamiliar guests or unrelated men are visiting. Main living spaces often consist of large rooms furnished only with wall-to-wall rugs and seating consisting of thin mattresses with cushions lining the wall.[8] Male and female family members share the same single space in most of their activities, including sleep, for which they spread out their bedrolls wherever they like on the carpet. But once, when a large number of distant relatives stayed with my host family, a clothesline and makeshift curtain divided the main living space into men's and women's sides.

The Dorr-e Dari premises themselves were an excellent example of the shifting, contextual boundary between inside and outside behavior. The Friday poetry reading and criticism sessions represented the highest degree of formality, with people sitting in orderly rows, greater gender segregation, controlled postures and expressions, formal introductions by the moderator, and silence on the part of everyone not called on to speak. These qualities would be even more heightened in the presence of high-ranking guests. After the session, the participants would disperse to the remaining rooms to talk and drink tea, with a cluster perhaps still holding a formal conversation with any official guests or the more infrequent visitors. Once these people departed, the regulars, most of whom were good friends, would stay and make themselves at home in an atmosphere of greater *samimiat* (intimacy, informality)—some would nap in a back room, others would smoke together in the kitchen (mostly men, and one or two women), play chess, tell jokes, listen to music or play instruments such as the *dotār* (a two-stringed lute) or the *ney* (reed flute), go for a game of badminton in the nearby park, or read early drafts of their poems to their closest friends. These are all markedly inside activities; that is, to be shared only with status equals or close friends (Beeman 2001: 46–47). Although this example seems to reinforce the idea of the dichotomy, in fact it shows how far the boundary has shifted: for many other Afghans, such activities should certainly not be shared by men and women who are not *mahram* (related and unmarriageable), if at all.

On a few occasions, we experienced an even greater *samimiat* when the core group of young poets held a *shabneshini*, or night vigil, party in the Dorr-e-Dari office. While only the men had done this previously, some of the women and I asked to join in out of curiosity. It was difficult for the women to obtain permission from their families to spend a night away from home; some of those who did come had told their parents that they were going to the Haram with their friends that night, while others had to return home by taxi before midnight. We started with an evening meal, which I cooked in an attempt to return the hospitality I had so often enjoyed. Afterward, some of the men smoked a *qalyān*, or water pipe, and several of the women took single timid puffs.[9] We spent the night talking, playing chess, and reading poetry in various groups in different rooms. Toward dawn, all those who remained—about ten of us—gathered in the small room housing the main office and library, sitting on chairs around its perimeter, and decided to play a game of truth. One by one, we were asked to give our true opinions of each other's characters, whether or not we had been in love, and what kinds of characteristics, physical and personal, we found attractive in other people. There was a thrill to this kind of testing of the boundaries, so not wishing to disrupt the atmosphere, I did not record the conversation or take notes. Most of the answers given were interesting, but still not particularly revealing—it was still a mixed-sex, medium-sized group, so despite the friendship among most of the participants and the intimacy of the setting, they were not necessarily party to each other's secrets. One young man was asked about the identity of the recurring female addressee of his love poems. He looked embarrassed and wriggled his way out of giving a direct answer—other than to say that it wasn't who everyone thought it was.

It seems, then, that alongside the pervasive nature of the inside/outside dichotomy and most people's unconscious adherence to the rules governing appropriate expression, there is a deep curiosity about the *bāten* of others, and some people make a hobby of attempting to penetrate and influence the inner selves of people around them.[10] The email accounts, blogs, and Facebook pages of my Afghan friends were hacked into with an alarming frequency—not by strangers but by people known to them, in attempts to defame them or to pose as them in chats in order to uncover their secrets. The best protection against such manipulators was not to confide one's secrets—for example, one's loves, or secret trysts with them, which occurred more frequently than anyone would admit—to more than one or two close friends or siblings: otherwise one risked being *rosvā* (revealed, disgraced) and suffering *āberu-rizi* (loss of face). Nonetheless, gossip, backstabbing (*gheibat*), and rumors (*shāi'eh-hā*)—some of them quite unfounded—spread like wildfire, as I discovered to my chagrin on more than one occasion. Indeed, Rejali has written that before the advent of modern governmentality, these were once major mechanisms of social control and power in Persian society: "Each individual struggled to protect the purity of his or her *batin* from being violated by others and simultaneously tried to uncover and gain access to the *batin* of others through social dissimulation" (Rejali 1994: 136). If the hacking is anything to go by, I would argue that to some extent this remains true.[11]

But a critique of the so-called schizophrenia of bifurcated selves, like the one voiced by Milani, is gaining salience in Iran and is also expressed by Afghans. While the social and religious values of their parents' generation may be largely congruent with the official stance of the Islamic Republic, many educated second-generation Afghans, like their Iranian peers, feel that the sharp distinction between their private behavior and that required by the state in public is oppressive, or a form of *riyā* (hypocrisy).[12] Various external markers of piety, including strict forms of hijab such as the black chador, are increasingly questioned even by self-professedly pious Afghan youth. In the Afghan neighborhoods of Mashhad, black chadors are still the norm for many women, with schoolgirls and students tending to wear plain-colored *mānto*s and *maqna'eh*s. But over the years of my fieldwork in Iran (2005–2010), I noticed that several of the female poets I knew had gradually changed their appearance, no longer wearing chadors, for example, or wearing discreet amounts of makeup and colorful headscarves rather than the formal, neutral-colored *maqna'eh*. They themselves professed to having developed a more open (*bāz*) outlook on the world, and had simultaneously, they said, become more forthright in their poetry.

Dialectics of Truth and Falsity in Persian Poetry

Persian poetic genres that to some degree cohere with the lyric genres identified in classical Greek and later European poetry (i.e., those that express the personal thoughts and feelings of the poet, notably the *ghazal* and modern blank verse) are a form of expression that may be seen as another means of "performing sincerity" in Beeman's terms (2001). But as an art form and a convention, poetry is even more highly mediated and carefully controlled than everyday speech and behavior. As such, throughout history it has either been idealized as uncontrived truth that is effectively conveyed and moves people to the right kinds of action or emotion, or derided as a device for manipulation, deception, or sycophancy. In fact, much of poetry's aesthetic and social efficacy seems to have been produced in the ambiguous terrain between these two ethical extremes. These value judgments have also regularly provided the moral language for the championing of certain literary styles at the expense of others: those to be rejected are said to be contrived, deceptive, and pernicious, whereas the ones being advocated are direct, truthful, and good representations of reality. Recall Nezami Aruzi's claim that poetry had the power—indeed, the purpose—of amplifying both the good and the bad and of rousing people to action. Another twelfth-century poet, Nezami Ganjavi, was more skeptical: in the epilogue to his famous work, *Leili and Majnun*, he admonished his fourteen-year-old son thus: "*Dar she'r mapich o dar fann-e u / Chun akzab-e u-st ahsan-e u*" (Do not embroil yourself in poetry and its craft / For the more full of lies it is, the better it is).[13] Both Nezamis recognized that poetry is, by its very nature, a contrivance, and in some cases the more contrived it is, the more effective it will be.

This conception of the rhetorical and highly mediated nature of poetic expression has survived through the centuries, despite the efforts of modernist literary theorists to promote a simple, unfettered poetic language. Poets themselves are highly conscious of the degree to which their thoughts are mediated: when I asked a poet with philosophical leanings, Seyyed Reza Mohammadi, to help me understand what poetry was, the conversation was remarkably layered:

> SRM: That's difficult, Zuzanna, that's difficult. By the Qur'an, I don't know what to say. I told you I'm really stupid. Poetry, you know, I think . . . what I said before, poetry is a kind of revelation. (. . .) The interior [*darun*] of a person is the place where he establishes contact with the world, and the world means God—God is not external to the world, but when we take the whole world together, that is God, that living spirit of the world. And it's that spirit of the world that speaks to you. When a stone speaks to you, it's God that's speaking to you. When your *darun* speaks to you, God is speaking to you. God is not a singular creature, he is an entirely tangible creature—everything in nature is actually God. (. . .) In poetry, you are in touch with the living spirit of the world. (. . .)
>
> ZO: So is poetry the truth?
>
> SRM: No. Poetry is nature, as I said. Poetry is the word—yes, each word that is produced is the truth. But no, poetry is a mystery. A mystery doesn't have to be the truth.
>
> ZO: Does a poet reveal himself or hide himself in a poem?
>
> SRM: A person hides himself. You said it very well, you hide in your writing, hide behind the words. Rather than revealing secrets, you weave secrets. For centuries we've been reading Hafez in Persian poetry . . . and we still haven't understood the mystery of Hafez.

In another informal conversation on the subject, Asef Hosseini put it more succinctly, but no less metaphorically: "Poetry is a truth which is told in the guise of a lie. It is a truth from which you distance yourself through embellishment and to which you then return. And that journey is full of spectacle (*tamāshā*)."[14]

Poetry is thus the truth of the world and nature speaking to your *darun* or inner self, woven into a mystery or *zāher* behind which the poet hides; it is a truth expressed in the guise of a lie. It is the dialectic between these two that, when adeptly tapped, allows poets to say much that must otherwise remain unsaid. The thousand-year-old tradition of Persian poetry, with its myriad genres, tropes, and poetic personas, gives poets a rich variety of precedents for revealing concealment and concealed revelation.

Although Persian-language poets recognize that it is the highly mediated nature of any kind of poetic language that forms part of its aesthetic appeal (its "spectacle," in Hosseini's words), there is a tendency in literary criticism to accuse whatever kind of poetry one is opposing of being contrived, and conversely, to praise one's favored kind as natural and direct.[15] This has particularly been the case in clashes between proponents of traditional and modern (or today, postmodern) poetry: blank verse is praised for allowing the poet to speak freely and naturally, while even in contemporary neoclassical poems the meter is expected to allow a conversational tone to flow throughout rather than pose an obstacle to it. I suspect that there is a greater tendency to hold up "naturalness" as a paragon for poetic expression in the modern era than in the time of the two Nezamis, but naturalness may now be discovered and praised in older genres, too—notably in folk poetry. For example, in his introduction to a collected volume of Hazaregi *dobeitis,* or folk quatrains, Dorr-e Dari senior member Mohammad Javad Khavari wrote: "If we wish to find the most uncontrived [*bi-takalloftarin*] whisper of man's loneliness, without doubt we should mention the *dobeiti*; for it is not created out of either knowledge of letters or reading of [books of] wisdom, but the source of its creation is the burning and endurance of the heart" (Khavari 1382/2003: 7).

Similarly, two Islamic literary critics detected the same quality in the *marsiyeh* (threnody, or mourning lament), which had become one of the most common expressive genres in the poetry of the Sacred Defense, in their introduction to a collection of war poetry: "Threnody is the most original and natural speech which comes from the spring of a poet's feeling. Threnody is the language of the heart, a poem which comes from the depth of the soul of those overtaken by a calamity. (. . .) Threnody is the natural utterance of a human's pain and suffering" (Shahrukhi and Kashani, cited in Talatoff 2000: 124). It is the tension between the original thought of the poet and the rhetorical embellishment required to create the desired effect on the audience that characterizes poetry's appeal and mystery—indeed, the fundamental mystery of artistic communication, on which we seem able to shed light only with further metaphors.

The more time I spent with the young poets of Dorr-e Dari, the more I realized that even—or perhaps especially—the most abstract lyric poems with the most subjective metaphors often represented real emotions and people in the poets' lives. Many of my friends had secrets (usually related to clandestine love affairs) that they were at pains to conceal because they could have dangerous consequences if revealed, but they were nonetheless interested in bringing some of these emotions to the surface in their work. The "true" meaning was only clear to me in the case of one or two people whose secrets I knew, and even then I did not know much. For the rest, the glossy exterior of the poem was held up in public for others to admire: poetry itself seemed to have a *zāher* and a *bāten*. Then again, poetry is a work of the imagination, and it would be wrong, my friends insisted, to conclude that all poems that seemed to abstract real events were actually based on them, particularly love poems. Indeed, getting to the poet's true intentions at the heart of a poem was often infuriatingly and intentionally slippery. In the one or two poems I composed and read at the Friday sessions during my months of fieldwork, I found myself beginning to apply these qualities, unconsciously at first. Nobody was mentioned by name; I found myself weaving together real events and emotions and imaginary ones, holding impossible dialogues and collapsing together several individual addressees at the same time, so that nobody's *āberu* would be at risk, least of all my own. Anthropologists, it must be said, have an acute understanding of the need for this kind of concealment of identity despite their simultaneous need to establish authority and ethnographic sincerity, and I have had to use similar evasive tactics in writing this ethnography to protect people's identities. My Persian poems were thus very different to the frank attitude I adopted in English-language ones written at the same time, and not only because they were far more halting and rudimentary.

Women's Poetry and Its Perils

Another issue that must be considered in discussing appropriate expression in poetry is gender.[16] As we have seen, one of the key elements of Iranian modernity identified by anthropologists and other scholars has been the increased public presence of women, beginning in the late nineteenth century. Milani emphasizes the connection between restrictions on women's movement and expression, noting that the pervasive outside/inside dichotomy is analogous to other binaries—including masculine/feminine, culture/nature, reason/passion, self/other, subject/object, law/chaos, day/night, and rational/emotional, among others—and gives women central symbolic power and heightens the need for their control (Milani 1992: 5). Thus, she argues, it is no accident that the beginning of a serious women's literary tradition in Persian coincides with their attempts to unveil 150 years ago (1–2).

Woman have been a part of the Persian literary tradition from its recorded beginnings, although it seems that literary canonization processes in this region have been more resistant to the acknowledgment of women's accomplishments than society itself at any given moment. It is instructive to explore both the limitations that women authors have faced and the exceptional nature of those who were able to rise above them. Today, many Persian speakers remember the chilling legend of the first recorded poetess of the Persian language, Rabeʻeh of Balkh, a tenth-century noblewoman who was murdered by her brother for the crime of falling in love with a slave. She is said to have written her last poem with her own blood on the door of the bathhouse in which, her throat cut, she was left to die. It is regrettable—but perhaps no accident—that far fewer people remember the remarkable women of the Timurid era in Herat. That dynasty yielded not only the powerful queen Gowhar Shad, one of the instigators of Herat's fifteenth-century cultural renaissance, but many other aristocratic ladies who were active patrons of architecture, music, painting, and literature—or themselves notable poets (Arbabzadah 2002).

The literary gatherings of that time included female as well as male poets. Some of them, married to other poets, composed teasing jibes to their husbands in verse: mocking them, for example, for their old age. Female poets of the Timurid era included Mehri, Moghol Khanum, Afaq Jalaher, and Bibi Esmati. They were educated noblewomen, well-known for their intellect and wit, and were able to participate in intellectual exchanges with men. One, Nija Monajjemeh (the Astronomer), was highly accomplished in that field and wealthy enough to endow several mosques, even engaging in a rivalry of mosque building and a contest of wits with the great Sufi poet Jami. These poets' verses circulated throughout Herat and remained in people's memories long after their deaths—sadly, from this culturally effervescent time, Jami is the only one commonly remembered today, whether male or female (Arbabzadah 2002: 32–47).[17]

Throughout Persian history, it was typically women of the aristocratic classes or members of the court who had the education and sufficient leisure time to pursue literary and artistic activities, and they account for most of those whose names have survived in literary histories (Milani 1992: 54–55; Sadr 1335/1956; Brookshaw 2005, 2013).[18] However, even they were not above the ideal image of a woman as *sangin o sāmet* (solemn and silent), secluded, invisible, and suffused with shame and modesty (*sharm*), such that even the wives of kings who could read and write sometimes hid their literacy from others. Before the twentieth century, women's education was thought to be useless and corrupting, with the potential to cause them to lose control over their sexuality (Milani 1992: 55). Thus, female poets across the Persianate world had to take special care to protect their reputations, and in this their choice of noms de plume is telling: popular ones include Makhfi and Mastureh, both mean the Hidden One, while Mahjubeh means the Veiled/Modest One. Such pseudonyms perhaps functioned like symbolic veils in allowing these women's words to enter the public arena, the world of the *birun*, while safeguarding their honor and modesty to the extent possible. In a similar vein, nineteenth-century praise poems for royal women (including some by female poets) had to perform a delicate double act between extolling their power on the one hand and their chastity and modesty on the other (Brookshaw 2013).

But the twentieth century and the advent of modernist poetry produced a rich crop of female literary role models for today's young poets, including Parvin E'tesami, Forugh Farrokhzad, and Simin Behbahani, as well as a number of female fiction writers such as Simin Daneshvar.[19] Indeed, the post-revolutionary period has yielded a surprisingly assertive group of women writers in Iran, including the late Behbahani, whose post-revolutionary writings represented a new concern with the daily lives of ordinary women. Yet barriers to expression remain, and they still echo the triple bind that faced Parvin E'tesami over a century ago, which Milani summarizes as three challenges: "The first, the difficulty of self-assertion for women; the second, the necessity for self-assertion for the poet; and the third, the cultural unfamiliarity with and unconventionality of public self-revelation. Torn between admiration for her poetry and scorn for its results, between such values as *Sharm* (modesty/shame) and self-expression, Parvin E'tessami in her poetry eloquently expresses the push and the pull between self-acknowledgement and self-censorship. Indeed, the very ambivalence toward absence and presence, voice and silence is one of the central paradoxes of E'tessami's poetry" (Milani 1992: 124).

Despite this need for greater care in negotiating appropriate expression, women now comprise approximately half of the active poets, not only at Dorr-e Dari, but at other Afghan institutions in Iran, as well. Afghan poet and student of sociology Gholamreza Ebrahimi wrote the following appraisal of his female contemporaries in an issue of the *Third Script* (and his very interest in them is symptomatic of a sea change in Afghan refugee society):

> The broad and active presence of women in refugee youth poetry has led to variety and metamorphosis in refugee poetry. This presence has led to the creation of fresh new spaces and images, and allowed the hidden and untouched dimensions of refugee life to be brought to light. It is in this arena that the Afghan refugee woman arrives at self-awareness and embarks on rebellion, revolt, and revelation against male-oriented social structures and thought systems; she speaks of her rights and dues; she creates beautiful images of her pain and suffering; she ridicules existing conventions and imaginings; and she even dares to fall in love. She takes herself down from the flimsy pedestal of the beloved and becomes the lover. Refugee youth poetry has manifested these in a variety of forms; at times with harsh forthrightness, at times with vagueness, ambiguity and metaphor, at other times in the form of images from the everyday life of a refugee woman. (G. Ebrahimi 1384/2006: 115)

Hoping to gain a better understanding of these tensions in the case of female poets in particular, I spoke with two of the young women who wrote self-professedly feminist poetry, and asked them to what extent they were able to be present in their poetry. Maral Taheri told me that although she often began with the pronoun "I" and most of her poems were based on personal experiences, she was also often inspired by the experiences of her friends and other women around her: "I think that until a poet has gone through the emotions that are in a poem, she cannot show them to the listener. . . . The effectiveness of the poem would decrease. If I haven't been in love, I can't talk about love. If I haven't put my hand in the fire and seen that it is hot, I can't speak about the fire's heat. I need to have experienced it to convey it to the listener . . . otherwise it's artificial."

Her friend Maryam Torkamani disagreed, and in the discussion it was always she who was more cautious. She said it was enough to observe something in your surroundings from close at hand and to feel something deeply, which a poet has the power to do: for example, to sympathize with the pain of a friend. She said the truth in her poems was more of a social truth, a condition and set of problems common to all women. She also noted that many people "who have not arrived at the same level of understanding" might look at her poems and condemn them as bad or *zesht* (ugly—a word that can be used in both an aesthetic and a moral sense), thinking that she herself must have experienced these things, but the fact is simply that she has been able to empathize with another woman.

When I asked them to what extent they considered their audience at the moment of composing a poem, their reactions once again differed. Maral said she didn't think of them at all during composition but was extremely sensitive to their reactions when reading her poems, and it often ended badly for her. She has found it impossible to publish her poems in journals without some degree of in-house censorship, and entirely impossible to entertain the idea of publishing a book of her work in Iran. She finds it hurtful that publishers do not consider it worthy of reading, let alone publication. I heard more than one educated man saying it was "vulgarity, and anything but poetry" (see Doostdar 2004). Meanwhile, Maryam said she often did a brief edit and tried to keep her expression under control even at the moment of poetic inspiration, in order to preempt an audience's negative reaction when reading for them. In the past, Maral's poetry has been poorly received in criticism sessions, particularly by other women but also one or two men, who would walk out, refuse to listen, and even phone her afterward to threaten her. But they have gradually witnessed a change among the women who attend the poetry sessions. Maryam said: "But now, for all of them, *māshā'allāh* [an expression of praise, here used ironically], cigarettes are something natural, they all speak openly about their loves. I think both of us had an effect on them." Yet she was pained at the fact that all the other regulars of Dorr-e Dari had had their books published, but not the two women. "Our poetry has to pass through the Seven Trials [*haft khān*] of Rostam in order to become the type of poetry that they like, but we're not willing to do that." Similarly, noted Maral, you have to walk and dress the way society wants you to, not the way you want to.

She seemed to be doing her best to fight against this, but again at a personal cost: her unconventional look often earned her stares, harassment, and teasing comments (*matalak*) in the poorer and more conservative parts of town.

Maryam responded to my question of whether it was possible to express the self more easily through poetry.

> In poetry, everyone is more *samimi* [close, intimate] with themselves, in poetry nobody has *ru dar bāyesti* with themselves, and you can put on paper whatever comes to mind, just because that poem is coming out from your *darun*, so you can express yourself more comfortably.[20] When you want to bring it out into society, though, it will be understood and some may not like it, and some may like it. But I think that whatever comes from the heart, will naturally find its way into the heart of others.[21] Since you are freer, your hands are less tied, you can speak more comfortably [*rāhat-tar*]. You can use metaphor to say some things that in the ordinary world might be bad, but in poetry might be beautiful and find a suitable place.

Maral said that she tried to reveal herself (*āshkār kardan*) through her poetry, but this was more of a challenge, an invitation to the *mokhātab* to see if their understanding was subtle enough to grasp what she was trying to say. Sadly, she said, most often they did not understand. Maryam added that even if in their hearts they understood, they may feel compelled to suppress such feelings for social reasons: they have to maintain their public face. (I suggested that this was why people sometimes walked out of poetry readings when something made them uncomfortable, rather than to be seen to approve of it, and they agreed, noting that this fear is always present in their traditional Afghan society.) Nonetheless, both women cautioned me against trying to "know" someone from their *zāher*, and this included their poetry. You cannot assume that someone who is critical of religion in their poetry is antireligious, and neither can you assume that the author of an erotic poem has sex on the brain (or even sexual experience, in the case of unmarried people), although many poets suffer from such accusations.

That the old ethic of emotional restraint is being subjected to questioning by the younger generation became clear from Maral's critique, seemingly affected by the spread of a certain kind of popular psychology in Iran that has begun to ascribe negative value to such behavior.

> I have no expectations of traditional society right now. Since they themselves are so subject to extreme self-censorship and don't express their [true] emotions or reactions, they don't let things out [*takhliyeh nemikonan khodeshuno*]—they're suffering from extreme complexes [*oqdeh-hā*] . . . unlike many societies, European or American, that we see in films—when they feel that they want to laugh right now, they laugh, when they feel that they want to cry right now, they cry. But the boundary between laughter and tears for Afghan

kids at least has been lost, for example when they laugh it's hysterical, nervous laughter or hysterical weeping. So I don't blame them.[22]

This tension between self-expression and concealment, the appropriate expression of feelings without being seen as hysterical, the ability to release the emotional tensions that build up inside and communicate them to society, but most importantly, the need to cast oneself as an intellectual woman hoping to have her voice heard in the public arena, is clearly one that is still consuming many female Persian-language poets. The performative aspect of negotiating these boundaries, and the fluid and shifting personas that women adopt both in poetry and in life, is demonstrated by Maral's names. She has three: in official documents, she is Fatemeh, a popular religious name, after the Prophet's daughter and the wife of Imam Ali. As is typical in Afghan families, however, she has another name used only by her family within the confines of their home. Maral, the third and the name by which she is commonly known, both in literary circles and in everyday life, is a name she chose for herself.[23] It is the name of the female heroine of *Kelidar* by Mahmud Dowlatabadi (1978), a novel in twelve volumes, considered one of the finest in Persian literature. At the beginning of the novel, Maral, a young Kurdish girl, rides proudly into town on a horse to try to get her father and her fiancé released from prison. Maral Taheri said she chose this name for herself because she was impressed by the character: "This was the name that I grew with as I was beginning to form a distinct personality, and it influenced me. It really has an effect, what people call me—when they call me Fatemeh I become a humble, downtrodden girl, but as Maral I am someone who tries to live her own way and takes her life into her own hands."

Three "Revealing" Poems

I turn now to a discussion of three poems that adopt varying strategies of revelation and concealment. The first is by Maral Taheri and may be seen as an example of the so-called Bad Literature discussed in chapter 3. Maral's poems are always in blank verse; use a colloquial language, some repetition, and broken syntax; and are heteroglossic in that they incorporate lines of dialogue, sometimes also in English. This particular one deals with sexual domination, and as such places Maral in the small group of Afghan poets (and one or two male visual artists who are now based in Afghanistan) who seek to uncover the problems related to human sexuality in their work:

Va mard ke ru-ye zan istād
Tekkeh-hā-ye khod-ash rā tekānd
Injā tekkeh-ye banafsh khābideh
Va in āqā dar kenār-ash istādeh
Siāh motamayyel be qermez

Khānum, cheqadr rang-e qermez be shomā miāyad!
Goftam rang-e qermez?
Gusheh-hā-ye dahān-at larzid
Injā yek nafar zir-e sefid
Zir-e zir-e sefid
Gisuān-ash az tars larzid
Khānum, muhā-ye beham bāfteh shodeh ham be shomā miāyad
*
Aslan begozarim az in tekkeh-hā-ye ezāfi-ye mard
Khānum shomā?
Baleh man hastam!
Hālā borideh gisu-ye marā be zur be shenāsnāmeh-at sanjāq kon.

And when the man stood on top of the woman
he shook the pieces of himself.
Here a purple piece is resting
and this man is standing beside it.
Black tending toward red.
Ma'am, the color red really suits you!
I said, the color red?
The corners of your mouth twitched.
Here a person under the white
under the under the white.
Her locks trembled with fear.
Ma'am, braided hair also suits you.
*
Actually let's leave these extra bits of the man
Ma'am, [are] you?
Yes, I am!
Now forcibly pin my cut-off lock of hair to your identity card.

(Unpublished poem by Maral Taheri, 2007, shared by the author)

This poem seems to describe a close but rather emotionless encounter between two people who appear to be strangers, given the use of the titles *āqā* and *khānum* (mister/sir and ma'am, respectively; neither indicates marital status). The man appears to be trying to flatter the woman, but she is afraid, perhaps hiding under a white sheet. It is not clear whether this is a description of prostitution or another kind of unequal sexual relationship.[24] The final line, however, conveys the full force of the poem. *Gis borideh* (shorn locks) is an expression for a disgraced woman, for example an adulteress, who has been humiliated by having her long hair—a woman's most seductive trait—cut off (see Bromberger 2008: 390). In this case, a lock of hair is cut off from the woman, symbolizing the loss of her chastity and honor, but it accrues to the man and to his identity (pinned by force to his identity card, itself possibly a metaphor for the sexual act), perhaps as a trophy of another sexual conquest.

The poet attempts to observe the scene from a number of different perspectives, including that of the female victim. The third-person references, meanwhile, may be seen as evasive tactics to avoid too strong an identification with the victim and suspicions of writing from personal experience. The poem weaves and dodges around the scene, viewing it from above, below, and to the side; the colors shift as often as the perspectives and pronouns, as if to give the scene a surreal quality—in other words, to highlight its *imaginary,* mediated nature while at the same time describing a real and bitter fact of life.

It is not just women who sometimes face problems for too-revealing poetry and lifestyle. Men must also be restrained in their behavior and may equally be accused of *susulbāzi* (immature, unrestrained behavior) or worse, immorality. Anonymous commentators in blogs sometimes accuse some of the male poets of *dokhtarbāzi* (playing around with girls), of using their poetry to seduce women, or of drinking alcohol. Usually such accusations were directed at their characters with little relation to the content of their poetry. Sometimes, however, attempts to guess at the true inner (*daruni*) meaning of a poet's work also amounted to intimations of immorality. The tension between self-expression and too much revelation was thus a delicate matter for men just as much as for women.

I witnessed one such event, and an instance of "editing," in Manoukian's terms, in the blog of Asef Hosseini. It concerned a short poem in free verse that he had posted, in the highly abstract style typical of his work, dedicated (*taqdim*) to someone indicated only by two initials:

> *Hichkas tul o 'arz-e donyā rā nemidānad*
> *Āghush-at rā bāz kon*
> *Tā tamām-e in hādeseh rā baghal koni:*
> *In bāgh-hā-ye ālbālu*
> *In pichak-hā-ye kudakāneh*
> *Va āftābi ke tā nok-e pestān-hā-yat bālā āmadeh ast*
> *Man hanuz*
> *Ru-ye shākheh-ye boland-e kāj istādeh am*
> *Va montazer-e khabari hastam*
> *Ke jangal rā bekhābānam*
> *Dokmeh-hā-yat rā bāz kon*
> *Rusari-at rā pas bezan*
> *Hich kas tul o 'arz-e donyā rā nemidānad*

> Nobody knows the length and breadth of the world.
> Open your arms
> to embrace this event in its entirety:
> these cherry orchards,
> these childlike morning-glory vines
> and the sun that has come up to the tips of your breasts.
> I am still
> standing on a high pine branch

and I am waiting for the news
that will put the forest to sleep.

Undo your buttons,
pull off your headscarf.
Nobody knows the length and breadth of the world.

> (Original republished in Hosseini 1391/2012: 38–39)

Despite the ending suggestive of an intimate encounter, the poem has a contemplative rather than erotic mood to it, and its overall message seems to be that the author is awaiting a piece of news, or an answer, from the addressee of the poem. *Pestān* is an archaic word for "breast" and thus has a markedly literary quality to it, which the author evidently hoped would neutralize its connotations and not intrude on the reflective mood.[25]

In the comments window of the blog, a number of readers seized on a rather more sexual interpretation of the poem. One suggested that the poem is not so much erotic as pornographic (though, as a close male friend of Hosseini, the reader is likely teasing him), and another admonished him to "Please be cautious with the name and reputation [*nām o āberu*] of others," meaning the addressee of the poem, whose identity he or she appears to have guessed. Hosseini then added the following sentence below the poem in his entry, "This is not at all an erotic poem! Why do you think so, brother?" This invited a number of comments praising the poem and reassuring him that, erotic or not, it was still beautiful, enjoyable, and thought provoking. The most interesting comment reads as follows: "You don't need to pin yourself to your poem [*lāzem nist khod-et rā be she'r-et sanjāq koni*]! A poem that has been composed no longer belongs to the poet, and anyone can have any interpretation of it. You have to endure the criticism and not try to justify yourself!" Hosseini did not publish any further rejoinders, but subsequently disguised the initials by adding a third letter.

This incident illustrated for me, on the one hand, the hermeneutic difficulties posed by the increasing subjectivism of poetic imagery in Persian new poetry discussed earlier. On the other hand, it demonstrated that many readers welcome the invitation to interpret the poet's images any way they please. Poetry's communicative power is oblique: a way of communicating subtle nuances of feeling (love, uncertainty, anticipation) stripped free of most contextualizing information that might incriminate the poet, the addressee, or the reader. The conventions of Persian poetry were perhaps always used in this oblique, ambiguous way. Nonetheless, those close enough to the poet to be able to guess at the context and inner meaning of the poem still subject him or her to moral scrutiny. Ironically, due to the capacity of some blogs to accept anonymous comments, the internet enables not only those who would be more open but also those who would condemn them for it—a fact by no means unique to Iran.

Self-revelation in poetry need not, of course, always involve sexuality or those aspects of corporeality that fly most obviously in the face of ideals of modesty; indeed, for authors of so-called Committed literature, it rarely does. It may also involve seemingly trivial details of one's everyday life, including aspects that may once have been hidden from public view, such as the mental health of a loved one. The following *ghazal* by Zahra Hosseinzadeh is an example of lyric realism that gives insight into the daily life and struggles of a refugee woman and her sister:

Belit, noskhah vo yak mosht pul-e pārah begir
Beist ākhar-e saf, shambah-hā shomārah begir
Dobārah Tayyebah hāl-ash bad ast, zang bezan
Morakhassi-e khod-at rā az ān edārah begir
Be shekl-e part o palā, harche did, howselah kon
Az āstin-e khod-ash māh yā setārah begir
Kharid chiz-e badi nist, rang-e delkhoshi-ash
Lebās, kafsh, alangu o gushvārah begir
Havās-etān naravad az pey-e parandah o sang
Begu be Tayyebah az mardomān kenārah begir
Agar ke doktor-e 'asāb bāz vaqt nadāsht
Do qors-e kuchak-e mashkuk rā dobārah begir
Na, sinamā bebar-ash, yā bezan be kuh o kamar
Feshār-hā-ye jahān rā to hich kārah begir
Az in ketāb-e moqaddas bepors khāhar-e man
Dobāreh khub mishavad yā na, estekhārah begir
Belit, noskhah vo yak mosht pul-e pārah begir
Beist avval-e saf, shambah-hā shomārah begir

Take a ticket, the prescription, and a handful of torn money;
stand at the end of the queue on Saturdays, take a number.
Tayyebah's unwell again, make a phone call,
take a day off from the office.
In her haphazard way, whatever she sees, be patient:
take the moon or a star out of her sleeve.
Shopping isn't bad, the colors that make her happy;
buy her some clothes, shoes, bangles, and earrings.
Don't waste time pursuing a bird or a stone.
Tell Tayyebah to keep away from people.
If the psychiatrist has no time once again,
take two small, suspicious pills again.
No, take her to the cinema, or head for the hills!
Don't give in to the pressures of the world.
Ask this holy book if my sister
is going to get well again, do a divination.
Take a ticket, the prescription, and a handful of torn money;
stand at the front of the queue on Saturdays, take a number.

(Original in Hosseinzadeh 1390/2011: 23–24)

Here, the poet appears to be talking to herself, going through the steps she needs to care for her sister, who appears to be suffering from some kind of mental distress. Caring for her, however, involves confronting a bureaucratized, psychiatrized world: getting a day's leave from the office, taking a number and standing in a queue with a prescription, going to a doctor for mental disturbances (rather than blaming them on jinns and fairies, as was common in Afghanistan, see Dupree 1980: 106–107), and taking pills, no matter how suspicious. The monotony of this world is underscored by the repetition of the first line in the last, with the only difference being standing at the front of the queue—perhaps with a greater resolve to get there early.

It may not be obvious to the casual reader, but it was clear to those who knew Zahra that this poem had an autobiographical element, since her sister Tayyebeh is a real person. When reciting the poem for me, too, Zahra made it clear that she was speaking as an Afghan refugee by adjusting her pronunciation to a more Afghan one, for example saying "Tayyebah" rather than "Tayyebeh." The poem is clearly set in Iran, given the presence of a psychiatrist and commonplace acceptance of a psychiatric discourse (Behrouzan 2010), the vocabulary (e.g., a ticket is *belit* in Iran, but *tiket* in Afghanistan), and the apparent freedom of movement of these two young women. The narrator's poverty is suggested by the "handful of torn money" and the ticket, which no doubt refers to a city bus ticket, the cheapest mode of transportation in Iran. The narrator appears to have tried everything to make her sister feel better when she has a bout of illness, from medication to shopping to watching films or going on an outing away from society and its "pressures," and although she speaks as if she is giving herself instructions, we imagine her acting on them in narrative form. Ultimately, however, as she grows increasingly desperate or weary, she turns to religion of the traditional kind and does a divination (*estekhāreh*) from the Qur'an. It is interesting that this is seemingly a last resort, although Zahra herself is pious and a graduate of Islamic studies. Perhaps the most striking things about the poem are what it reveals about the degree of responsibility this woman has for her family and how adept she has become at single-handedly negotiating the institutions of modern life.

Zahra, as we have seen, keeps the themes of her poetry within the bounds of mainstream, officially sanctioned discourse in Iran. Nonetheless, she, too, subtly reveals the degree to which the mundane details of personal life can be considered poetic, especially when expressed in the medium of the *ghazal,* which itself conveys a high degree of poetic mastery. Maral Taheri is aspiring to a different image—that of a young woman, like the heroine of the novel who inspired her, who defies social conventions, uncovers their hypocrisies, and is determined to find her own way in life. Such an ethic would resonate more closely with secularized Iranians and her behavior and appearance would not be out of the ordinary in upper-middle-class areas of Tehran. Both Zahra and Maral grew up as refugees in Mashhad, both their fathers were laborers, both achieved a degree of independence by working outside the home, and both were brave, strong-willed women. But I suspect that it was easier for Maral to seek to identify with the values and lifestyle of that group because she mingled with Iranians, worked as a receptionist in an Iranian company, and eventually married an Iranian man. In addition, she is a Herati Tajik, not visibly distinguishable from most Iranians. Zahra is noticeably a Hazara and must take additional care to avoid unpleasantness in Iranian society in general. She has sought the officially sanctioned route to social advancement for women, by embracing religious study, personal piety, and modest comportment, but not surrendering the possibility of creative expression. Because of this, she is safer in Afghan refugee society and in the official public sphere of the Islamic Republic, and enjoys a success and aesthetic recognition that poets like Maral who push the boundaries in the other direction are still dreaming of.

But the fact that poems like Asef's and Maral's have their defenders, too, is noteworthy, and suggests that at least some people in their audiences are willing to dissociate artistic production from personal morality. Incidents like the one with which I opened this chapter notwithstanding, the atmosphere at Dorr-e Dari was generally encouraging of such experiments. In 2014, Ostad Mozaffari expressed his stance well in a Facebook defense of a Kabul-based artist who had stirred up controversy with his paintings of nude men and women engaged in sexual acts. The language of his comment is interesting: it urges viewers not to pay attention to the *zāher* of the works, but to interpret the message of social critique at their heart:

> The aim of such works is not the documentation of the external reality of the subject, and in a way is even unconcerned with it, but rather seeks to make another side of reality stand out. The repellent exterior of the work leads the judgment to form in the mind of the ordinary viewer that the artist is sneering at the moral conventions of society. Traces of this artistic style can be seen in other art forms and also in Persian poetry, which these days smacks of corporeality and speaks grimly of genitalia and sexual relations between men and women, and may be analyzed in this vein. Talking about moral conventions in art is a difficult thing to do and I don't want to get into it, but I want to say to that handful of friends who will probably take issue with this kind of artist that they shouldn't fixate on the smutty exterior of these sorts of works. The aim of these works is not what [these people] think, but rather exposing the hidden sicknesses that arise from the corporeality of human beings and cannot be seen when clothed by convention. Their ugliness is obvious but eyes habituated to the fence of convention will not see it.

We have seen that Afghan poets and artists engage in an ongoing debate over creative expression with respect to conventions of appropriate conduct. But regardless of whether they are pious or consider themselves secular iconoclasts, it is apparent that they believe that it is the poet's job to expose truths normally cloaked by social convention, the main disagreement being over how directly and graphically this ought to be done. Some of those who have made a career out of being more forthright are well-known and have defenders as well as detractors. Thus, the poet seeking to carve out a space of individuality faces the same balancing act as Adelkhah's *javānmard* (1999: 45–56). She must strike a strategic and sometimes paradoxical balance between discretion and self-display, and pitch her behavior at just the right level, embodying society's values but also sometimes taking them to extremes.

Conclusion

Throughout this book, I have reflected on a number of tensions, dualities, and contradictions, both in the way personhood is conceived in cultural representation and analysis, and in the way it is experienced by Afghan refugees in Iran. These have ranged from the contradiction of being a long-term resident of Iran and fellow Persian speaker while being denied citizenship, to being an educated person with high levels of cultural capital but no good employment prospects. I have also explored the negotiation between public and private modes of comportment and expression, between discretion and self-display, and between family interdependence and social propriety, and individual aspirations and self-expression. I may thus have given the impression that the people I have described are themselves walking contradictions, bundles of tension ready to snap; certainly, if this were true it would represent an almost unbearable psychological burden. I suspect it would be overstating the case to say that their selves are cloven into irreconcilable fragments in this way, as for the most part people have a remarkable capacity to get used to things and go about their daily business without a constantly looming sense of psychic rupture. But these facts are inescapable: young Afghans in Iran *do* live in a structurally ambiguous situation from a legal point of view, they *are* living at a time of intensified cultural flux and transformation, and they are certainly conscious of both. All it takes is for a passerby to look askance, or an official to demand documentation, or an elder to comment loudly that one is improperly dressed, for the tensions to be brought cruelly into hard relief.

This point was echoed in countless interviews, and was very much part of the lived experience of the subjects of my study. Asef Hosseini described it to me as follows in an interview in 2006:

> I think that being a refugee [*mohājerat*] really has an effect. It's a feeling inside a person that he can't tell anyone about, and nobody can understand it. You live in this society, but you don't belong to this society. This feeling of not-belonging always exists in my mind, its pulse keeps beating. On the other hand, you don't remember anything from your own past. You say "Afghani-

stan," but which Afghanistan? You have no background, you have nothing from your own country. Except war—and even that you hear on the news—war, conflict, and so on, and so on. And your childhood memories are marked by *mohājerat*, by work, sometimes by insults, sometimes by restrictions—in particular by restrictions.

Interesting comparisons may be made of this state of suspension to the situation of intellectuals marginalized or culturally dominated in various ways by other societies, including minority and colonized populations: for example, Franz Kafka's description of the plight of assimilated Jews in Europe: "This means that I don't have a moment of peace, that nothing has come easily to me, not just the present and the future, but even the past, that thing that each man receives as his birthright: even that I have to conquer, and perhaps that is the hardest task."[1] Or one may compare the complex dual identities and inferiority complexes of the educated colonial subject subtly described by a range of anticolonial and postcolonial writers, including Fanon (1967) and Nandy (1983). Such cognitive dissonance perhaps inevitably leads to resistance and attempts at cultural, literary and spiritual as well as political liberation, as elegantly described by Said in *Culture and Imperialism* (1993).

Hosseini himself explicitly made the connection between this situation and his creative work: "All these things in a way lead you to take refuge in something, something is created inside you." Indeed, the tradition of Persian poetry, accessible both to the literate and the nonliterate, has provided a ready outlet for this impulse to creatively work through all the contradictions in refugees' lives. Several anthropologists have written of the license apparently granted to poets (or artists in general) in some societies to express the otherwise unsayable—for example, to countenance independent female sexuality and extramarital romantic love in an honor-bound society defined by male control of female sexual modesty, or to slander other tribes without fear of retribution (Abu-Lughod 1986, Boesen 1983, Edwards 1986b). For Afghans in Iran, too, poetry has been able to capture the risks, ambiguities, and hidden costs of social upheavals. It is one of the few media through which they are able to describe the phantoms that haunt them and their sense of loss. Poetic traces of these emotional costs might perhaps be called "the ghost in the machine," to borrow a metaphor used by Varzi (2006: 175–193, coined by Ryle 1949) when describing the way the profound losses and dislocations caused by the Iran-Iraq War are subtly represented in the Iranian cinema of the war, even as the Sacred Defense is ideologically glorified.

To what extent, then, is it possible to speak of poetry as providing a heterotopic space par excellence, one in which the exile may at least temporarily feel whole again? In Foucault's use of the term, heterotopias "are something like counter-sites, a kind of effectively enacted utopia in which the real sites, all other real sites that can be found within the culture, are simultaneously represented, contested, and inverted" (1986: 24). These sites offer "a space of illusion that exposes every real space . . . a space that is other, another real space, as perfect, as meticulous, as well arranged as ours is messy, ill-constructed, and jumbled" (27). This concept is useful for thinking about alternatives to dominant ideologies, reflecting the multiple strands of identities and ethics that govern the lives of people at the geographical and political margins of nation-states, as Stokes (1998) has shown in a study of *Arabesk* music in an Arab-inhabited region of Turkey near the border with Syria (see also Caron 2013).

The answer is that this might be so, but within limits. The space opened up for creative expression, including literary expression, is always itself mediated by existing conventions, genres, tropes, and the power of patrons, critics, and other arbiters to shape an understanding of what is tasteful, what is appropriate, what is beautiful, and what ought to be silenced. Some genres have developed to be intentionally oppositional, such as the leftist Iranian poetry of the mid-twentieth century, but others have served to praise and support of powerful persons and institutions. Tropes such as that of the *rend* or libertine provide symbolic potential for opposition to conventional morality and fodder for cultural critiques, such as the current criticism of hypocrisy or a disjuncture between the inner and outer selves, but rebellious writing may equally be offhandedly dismissed as unappealing vulgarity. Thus, a poetic heterotopia can never represent absolute escape—it is itself subject to the workings of power.

Nonetheless, the very existence of such a space external to mundane discourse opens up the possibility for acts of creative invention that test new boundaries and sometimes enable social reformulations. It is what allows new worlds to be imagined as a result of hybridization, or the seeping in of new elements into systems of signification, as Karimi-Hakkak so compelling argued (1995). Or, as Salman Rushdie has put it, "[*Mélange*] *is how newness enters the world*. It is the great possibility that mass migration gives to the world and I have tried to embrace it" (1992: 394, original emphasis).

A respected cultural tradition with a pedigree as long and splendid as Persian poetry has another benefit, however. Refugee poets and other educated Afghans have consistently sought access to the cultural capital of the status of the *farhangi* (cultured) person or the *rowshanfekr*. The precise definition of this figure has gradually shifted, from the revolutionary, religious "Committed" intellectuals of the 1980s, to the far more ambivalent and skeptical postmodernists of the turn of the twenty-first century, but it has always represented an elevated, if contested, status. Afghans' disillusionment in part stems from the empowering possibilities offered to them by Iranian populist policies in the 1980s, and their gradual retraction in the following two decades. What cannot be taken away from them, however, are the new scope of their knowledge and abilities, and their new subjectivity, the latter of which feeds a sense of entitlement to aspirations more commonly (but erroneously) associated with the middle classes, foremost among which is education and intellectual life. It is through this kind of intellectual and creative labor, often alongside their far less satisfying menial day jobs, that Afghan poets recuperate a sense of pride, aspiration, or achievement, much like the moonlighting nineteenth-century French working-class writers and intellectuals described by Rancière (2012).

Indeed, I often heard from poets that poetry had been a way for them to discover themselves. Gholamreza Ebrahimi put it evocatively in an interview in 2010: "I know Gholamreza Ebrahimi [myself] only from when I began writing poetry. Before that, there was no milestone in my life to let me say that I'd achieved something, or had a life I was proud of—no. At least, this feeling that I exist and have existed, I've only felt it since I entered the world of literature and poetry. Before that, my life was, as the poet says, a kind of 'gradual death.'" Moreover, when Gholamreza traveled to Afghanistan when he was feeling particularly suffocated in Iran, he was amazed to learn that people he had never met before knew and loved his poetry. One ministry official he contacted to sort out some paperwork before he could return to Iran even knew many of his poems by heart, and helped him solve his bureaucratic problem. Gholamreza had become a *mashhur* (famous) individual in a time-honored way—through the circulation of his poetry—and this gave him unexpected privileges and a new confidence to take his life into his own hands. After receiving a master's degree in sociology in Iran, he went on to marry a fellow poet for love and became a magazine editor and lecturer in Kabul.

This story confirms the major theme that I have explored in this book: that the individualism Afghan refugee poets seek and champion feeds on both old and new cultural practices that are difficult to separate into "traditional" and "modern," even if those referents are frequently used rhetorically to celebrate or oppose those practices. In the same way, one cannot become an accomplished author of new poetry without studying the classics; poetry criticism sessions are an amalgam of old and new pedagogical and interpretive practices; and individualistic romantic love and companionate marriage can be mediated by highly relational extended family structures. Several models of personhood and relationality coexist in this society, then, and the lines between them are not clearcut. What young refugees understand very clearly, however, is that it takes great effort to become a true individual, and education and intellectualism are among their few resources to achieve this.

We have seen a number of examples of poets lyrically identifying with Afghan manual laborers, with young girls forced into unhappy marriages, or with women in exploitative sexual relations. While they may not have personally experienced some of the extreme situations they describe, the major difference with bourgeois intellectuals is that they are not engaging in fanciful or patronizing imaginings of the lives of the poor: they *themselves* are the urban poor, and many of their forefathers were the rural poor of one of the most deprived and war-torn regions on earth. If Afghan poets' string of literary awards is any indication, it seems that Iranians are beginning to pay attention to them. There may still be a long way to go before they can have a tangible effect on government policies toward them, but at least they are increasingly being heard, rather than appearing merely as mute images in Iranian art films. That such a group exists at all—with all its achievements, suffering, and contradictions—is testament to all that is best and worst in postrevolutionary Iran.

Epilogue

Much has changed in the decade since I first began work on this project. The most significant development is that a large number of the key members of Dorr-e Dari have remigrated to other countries, some of them having first returned to Afghanistan and having found that the high hopes they had for rebuilding their homeland were difficult to realize with the continuing insecurity in the country. Of the poets and others mentioned in this book, half are now living in Western countries, and a further handful in Afghanistan. Some were resettled by the UNHCR; some paid people smugglers to transport them via terrifying overland and sea routes; some won prestigious scholarships for higher education; some sought asylum after receiving invitations to attend cultural events; and some of the women married Afghan men based abroad. There are now Dorr-e Dari members in Australia, the Netherlands, Sweden, France, Germany, and the United Kingdom, and many of them have continued their cultural activities, aided partly by the sudden flowering of social media toward the end of my research, particularly blogs and Facebook. Those in Australia were mostly clustered in the southern city of Adelaide, and they opened an informal chapter of Dorr-e Dari there in 2007. A more official branch opened in Kabul in 2010 and remains active, holding regular poetry evenings and criticism sessions. Such literary activities thus continue to provide a resource both for networking and for personal development for young Afghans, now on a global scale.

Meanwhile, under Iran's ongoing economic crisis, exacerbated by U.S.-led sanctions against the country and economic restructuring that wiped away many of the social safety nets and subsidies on which the poor once relied, life for Afghan refugees is becoming increasingly untenable and the trickle of those seeking a better life in Europe or Australia at great risk to themselves has turned into a stream. But amid the sorrow there has been a glimmer of hope: following the 2013 election of the reformist President Hassan Rowhani, it was announced in July 2014 that in the coming school year, the 350,000 Afghan refugee children attending state schools in Iran would no longer have to pay registration fees. The measure came about after the Ministry of Education recognized that the fees were causing many children to drop out of school, and the president agreed to the ministry's request for a budget increase to solve the issue. The news was greeted with joy and will certainly have a life-changing impact on a whole generation of Afghan children—many of whom will no doubt go on to become poets.

August 2014

Notes

Introduction

1. The *Behār al-Anvār* (*Oceans of Light*), a collection of narratives of the prophets and the Shi'a Imams in 110 volumes, as recounted by Allameh Mohammad Baqer Majlesi (1616–1689), an important Shi'a scholar and cleric of the Safavid era.

2. For this reason I take issue with Talatoff's "episodic" view of literary history (2000), which identifies four distinct periods in twentieth-century Iranian literature, analogous to four ideological movements that attracted the support of intellectuals. Each episode is defined by a cluster of canonical texts that are closely associated with the dominant ideological discourse of the time and share key metaphors with it. Talatoff simply ignores those works that do not fit into his "dominant" discourses and ideologies, and gives the impression of a monolithic, unitary literary field that does not exist concurrently with any other. A more complete approach to Iranian literary historiography would allow for a greater diversity of literary voices at any one time and include those nonelite, non-ideological, non-innovating (i.e., "traditional") and even non-Persian voices that were never admitted into the twentieth-century Iranian canon. Literary change would also not be so easily and discretely periodized (see Karimi-Hakkak 1995).

3. There is in fact a growing literature on creativity and expressive genres among refugees, exiles, migrants, and other people living on the margins of states in non-Western countries, often with a focus on the way in which the homeland is imagined, remembered, or reinvented through visual art, film, music, dance, and various verbal arts (e.g., Gow 2002, C. Harris 1999, Stokes 1998, Baily and Collyer 2006, Barkan and Shelton 1998, Lavie 1991, Edwards 1996, 1986b, Naficy 1991, and Powles 2000, 2004, 2005). Some of these focus specifically on the literature of refugees and exiles, discussing the ways in which they construct and reconstruct the notion of the homeland in their work (Bowman 1994, Siddiqi 1995, Said 2002 [1984]).

4. See, for example, R. Tapper 2002, Naficy 2002, Varzi 2006, Fischer 2004, Dabashi 2001, 2007, Sadr 2006, and Khosronejad 2012.

5. For example, Khosravi 2008, Mahdavi 2009, and Nooshin 2005, 2007, 2009, 2011.

6. For example, Graham and Khosravi 2002, Doostdar 2004, Alexanian 2006, Sreberny and Khiabany 2010, and Akhavan 2013.

7. There are countless historical examples. To mention a few from modern Afghanistan: Gholam Mohammad Tarzi was exiled to Karachi and then Istanbul in 1881 with his whole family; his son Mahmud Tarzi was exiled to Iran in 1929; and Seyyed Baha' al-Din Majruh was assassinated in Peshawar in 1988.

8. The critical importance of performative context (such as the relative social status, political ideology or gender of the storyteller and the audience) has likewise been highlighted by Mills (1991a, 1991b) in the interpretation of oral folktale performances in western Afghanistan.

9. See Sax 2002 on how the self is constructed in and through performance, particularly dance and oral epic recitation in India.

10. The use of the word *subject* to mean "the active mind or the thinking agent" is paradoxical given its other, older meaning of a "passive subject of political dominion" (Williams 1988: 310), but both meanings have evolved from their Latin roots through linguistic and philosophical developments in European languages, which Williams traces in an illuminating entry in his dictionary of social "keywords" (1988). See also the discussion of the word's etymology and philosophical history in Rorty 2007.

11. See Ortner (2005: 31–33) and Sax (2002: 6–7) for useful summaries of such work. Although Foucault's work is usually included in the antihumanist category, Foucault himself expressed regret at this perception and sought, late in his life, to draw attention to the importance of self-fashioning as a kind of freedom (see Laidlaw 2002: 321–325; Foucault 1984).

12. Much of the comparative anthropological debate on personhood has taken place among scholars of Melanesia, India, and Africa (see Lambek and Strathern 1998; Carrithers, Collins, and Lukes 1985; Busby 1997; and for summaries of the Indian debates, Mines 1994: 4–10 and Sax 2002: 9–11). Comparatively little work has been done on Iran and the Middle East more broadly, but the relevant texts are introduced throughout this book.

13. There are, nonetheless, an increasing number of ethnographic works on postrevolutionary Iran exploring a wider range of social groups that implicitly complicate the analytical models described by Khosravi, Varzi, and Mahdavi and deserve more attention. These include pious women (Kamalkhani 1993, Kalinock 2003, Sadeghi 2009); women in lower-income urban areas (Sadeghi 2009, Hoodfar 2009); people in rural areas or small towns (Hegland 2009, Friedl 2009); Qashqa'i tribesmen and women (Beck and Huang 2006, Huang 2009), feminist clerics (Mir-Hosseini 1999); and various constituencies involved in the memorialization of war martyrs (Khosronejad 2013). Behrouzan (2010; 2015) presents a dynamic model of subject-formation from "above" *and* "below" in the context of the growing ubiquity and internalization of psychiatric and biomedical discourses in Iran.

14. See Hoodfar 2009 and Sadeghi 2009 on how volunteer female health workers in poor areas, and *Basiji* women, respectively, are redefining concepts of citizenship and enacting their beliefs in the importance of social and political engagement for women.

15. See, for example, Hooglund 2009 on the effects of rural development policies.

16. Afghans have long been defined in international humanitarian jargon as one of the largest "refugee caseloads" (Colville 1997), or as "one of the world's largest and most prolonged refugee emergencies" (HRW 2002: 4). However, much of the international funding and assistance, and with it academic or media attention, has hitherto been devoted to camp-based refugees in Pakistan, most of whom were Pashtuns (Edwards 1986a: 313). See, for example, Edwards 1986a, the contributors to Anderson and Dupree's 1990 volume, and Centlivres and Centlivres-Demont 1988.

17. See Adelkhah and Olszewska 2007 for a fuller account of the complex interactions, formal and informal, between Iran, Afghanistan, and their peoples.

18. As of late 2005, Shi'a Hazaras at 47 percent constituted the single largest ethnic group among Afghans in Iran, followed by Tajiks at 30 percent, Pashtuns at 13 percent, and the remaining 10 percent divided between small numbers of Baluch, Turkmen, Uzbeks, and others (UNHCR/BAFIA 2005). The proportion of Hazaras had risen by 6 percent since the beginning of 2004, suggesting that they are the ethnic group that is most reluctant to repatriate (ibid.). The majority of Afghans lived in the large cities or surrounding rural areas in the provinces of Tehran (27 percent), Khorasan (16 percent, including the city of Mashhad), Isfahan (12 percent), Sistan and Baluchistan (11 percent, including the city of Zahedan), Kerman (7 percent), Qom and Fars (6 percent each, the latter including the city of Shiraz). Figures for

the year of arrival indicate two major departure waves, with 40 percent arriving in the years 1978–1985 (the early years of the Soviet occupation), and 36 percent arriving between 1996 and September 2001 (the years of Taliban rule). The gender balance was 44 percent female and 56 percent male. Almost half (46 percent), were children aged seventeen or younger.

19. See Mousavi (1998: 43) and Gawęcki (1983: 86) on the fraught patron-client relationship between the Hazaras and the group that Mousavi calls the Hazara Seyyeds in central Afghanistan. Seyyeds were considered to have extraordinary power or *barekat*, and their prayers were believed to be more effective. They were thus seen as predisposed to religious functions and many became clerics. Each Seyyed family would have several Hazara client families, from which they collected *khoms* (tithe), providing religious services in return. This arrangement could be benign but in practice was often exploitative, leading to political strife in the 1980s.

20. *Howzeh* can refer to an individual religious school, also know as a *madraseh*, or it can be used as an umbrella term to refer to the collectivity of seminaries in a given area. Thus the Mashhad *Howzeh* is made up of a number of *madraseh*s, clustered around the shrine, as well as the Razavi University of Islamic Sciences, a modernized version whose degrees and teaching methods are modeled on Western-style universities, but whose curriculum remains similar to the more traditional seminaries. In this book, I refer simply to "the *Howzeh*" in general in deference to the standard practice among my informants.

21. The Shariʿatis' views, for which they were criticized by conservatives, emphasized modern education, women's literacy, and rational explanations for natural phenomena (Boroujerdi 1996: 103). Ali Shariʿati's prolific writings, which were influenced by French and German social philosophy following his studies in France, offered a solution to the predicament of the Iranian intellectual's *gharbzadegi* (intoxication with the West), which he termed *bāzgasht be khishtan* (return to the self), through a modernist reinterpretation of Shiʿa Islam (for an in-depth discussion of Shariʿati's oeuvre, see Boroujerdi 1996: 105–115).

22. As in many other cities in Iran, however, the inhabitants of Mashhad could enjoy the slightly more relaxed atmosphere of nearby pleasure spots in the hills, such as Torqabeh and Shandiz, where many open-air restaurants sometimes offered live music performances.

23. There are some echoes in my experience of the difficulties in doing Middle Eastern fieldwork that Dresch found in Yemen, which he likens to a "wilderness of mirrors" (2000). This is a world, he argues, in which privacy structures and defines social groups, preventing the outsider from knowing many things (111). Where some might see this as an obstacle, however, these are in themselves social facts, teaching us much about the way ideas of the public and the private are structured.

24. See Gardner (1995), who went through a similar process while working in rural Bangladesh.

25. Such moments also figure in twentieth-century Iranian fiction, such as the short story by Jalal Al-e Ahmad, "Gonāh" ("Sin"), which is critical of an excessive insistence on female modesty and shame in a patriarchal culture that goes far beyond what is required by Islam.

1. Border Crossings and Fractured Selves

The opening epigraph by Hossein Heidarbeigi (original in 1386/2008: 29–32) mentions a number of place-names, explained here: The Pamirs are a mountain chain in northwest Afghanistan; Helmand is the name of a river and province in the south. A *dobeiti* is a folk quatrain often sung by Hazara shepherds (see chapter 4). The town of Bamyan is the economic and cultural center of the Hazarajat, while Ghazni is a city at its eastern edge. Baghchar and Sangtakht are villages in the Hazarajat. The Jeyhun or Amu Darya, known by the Greeks as the Oxus by the Greeks, is the river that demarcates the border between Afghanistan and Tajikistan in the north. Also, Ali and Masih are the names of the poet's young sons.

1. The border between Afghanistan and Russian Central Asia was not clearly defined until 1887, when it was demarcated bilaterally by the Joint Anglo-Russian Boundary Commission in St. Petersburg. The Durand Line, establishing the boundary between British India and the kingdom of the Durrani Amirs, was first defined by a treaty between the British and Amir Abdur Rahman in 1893, while the border with Iran was fixed in 1904.

2. See Monsutti 2005b: 102, 125, and Mousavi 1998: 148–150. On other historical forced relocations and the flight of populations both out of and into Afghanistan, see R. Tapper 1983: 35, Centlivres and Centlivres-Demont 1988 [1983], Balland 1978, and Shalinsky 1979.

3. Information on this population is limited because research in Iran was made difficult by the political situation in the years of the Iran-Iraq War in the 1980s, and statistics from that time, if any were gathered, are not publicly available. A number of policy-oriented reports appeared later, and sociological and ethnographic studies began to appear from the 1990s onward, both in Iran and abroad, e.g., Pahlavan 1379/2000 and a special *Iranian Studies* issue (vol. 40, no. 2, April 2007). See Abbasi-Shavazi et al. 2005: 15–18 for a discussion of Iranian policy toward Afghans, including details of legislation passed to encourage repatriation and limit welfare provision, and debates with the UNHCR. For a general overview of the situation of Afghan refugees in Iran, see also Olszewska 2008.

4. According to Shahrani, the Arabic-origin word *mohājerin* (singular *mohājer*) designates "those who leave their homes in the cause of Allah, after suffering oppression" (Qur'an 16:41). *Mohājerin* should therefore be rendered in English as "Muslim refugees" (Shahrani 1995: 192), and their flight ought to be seen as inherently political. This self-designation carries with it the concomitant appeal to a host country to act as hospitably as did the Ansār, the inhabitants of Medina who gave the Prophet shelter. For in-depth accounts of the origins of this paradigm in Islamic tradition and its significance throughout history, see Ansari 1990 and Abu-Sahlieh 1996.

5. The word used by UNHCR in Iran as its official translation for "refugee" is *panāhandeh*, which denotes a person seeking asylum or shelter. It is this word that is used in the name of their own offices in Iran, and also by Afghans when speaking about people who have been resettled by the UN to third countries or who have sought asylum in the West. Iranian official discourse avoids this term, possibly because of the international legal obligations it suggests.

6. The international refugee law and domestic laws are, respectively, the 1951 Convention Relating to the Status of Refugees and its 1967 Protocol, and Iran's Refugee By-Law of 16 December 1963.

7. UNHCR's difficulties in Iran have partly been due to its limited funding compared to the vast sums spent on refugees in Pakistan ($1 billion U.S. were spent in Pakistan between 1979 and 1997, but only $150 million in Iran, for geopolitical reasons; Loescher 2001: 216). When the UNHCR cut its educational subsidies in 2004, Iran promptly imposed school fees for refugee children.

8. Analysts have differed on the dominant motives: Hanifi (2000), Monsutti (2005b, 2004), and Centlivres and Centlivres-Demont (2000) have argued that the Afghan presence in Iran bears the hallmarks of labor or economic migration, such as frequent movements back and forth across the border and a majority of single young men, rather than a classic scenario of forced migration. Shahrani, meanwhile, argues that for the majority of Afghans fleeing the invasion, the decision was one of political defiance and moral commitment to Islam (1995: 192).

9. In the early 1980s, both Sunni and Shi'a clergy faced persecution at the hands of the People's Democratic Party of Afghanistan government and many were arrested and killed (Dorronsoro 2000: 114–121).

10. The first repatriation agreement had been signed after the fall of Afghanistan's communist government in 1992. During 1993, over 300,000 Afghans repatriated under this program, and close to 300,000 returned "spontaneously" (Turton and Marsden 2002: 12). In 2002, Iran, Afghanistan, and UNHCR signed a new agreement to provide assistance to refugees wishing to repatriate voluntarily, running from April 2002 for a year, and henceforth renewed at new Tripartite Meetings on an annual basis. By 2012, some 902,000 refugees had returned to Afghanistan from Iran with UNHCR assistance (UNHCR 2013).

11. Currently, an average of 1,000 Afghan and Iraqi refugees are resettled outside the region each year. The main resettlement countries are Australia, Canada, Sweden, and Finland (UNHCR 2007: 1–2).

12. Afghans contributed an estimated 4.4 percent of a GNP of $161 billion U.S. (i.e., more than $7 billion) in 1994–1995 (Farhang 1375/1996: 43–49); more recent figures are not available. In 2000 and 2001, Iran considerably tightened its legislation on the employment of foreign nationals, imposing heavy penalties on those employing illegal foreigners and restricting Afghans with residence cards to sixteen categories of work, mostly manual labor (Turton and Marsden 2002: 31; Abbasi-Shavazi et al. 2005b: 17). Afghan workers in Iran are in high demand in certain skilled construction jobs, such as installation of steel building frames, masonry, tiling, or decorative stuccowork on facades and interiors, and they are known as efficient and reliable. First jobs on arrival in Iran were largely in the construction sector or other unskilled labor, but over time Afghans increasingly found their way into occupations requiring skills or assets, including tailoring, bricklaying, hawking, or grocery shopkeeping (Abbasi-Shavazi et al. 2005b: 23–24). Some moved on to educational or cultural work as teachers, translators, writers, or publishers (necessarily based on informal arrangements, given employment restrictions). Poverty also obliges many Afghan women and children to work (Chatty and Crivello 2005: 16), and I knew of whole families employed at brick kilns.

13. Such sentiments and tactics were not used uniquely against Afghans: they had also been directed by urban health professionals toward Iranian villagers during the vigorous family planning campaigns of the 1980s (Orkideh Behrouzan, personal communication, July 2013).

14. The narrator of this story, a young mother of two, then recounted with awe and approval that this man was apparently met with divine retribution when all of his family members died one after the other in a series of freak accidents. His accurate eye aside, mistakes are also sometimes made, as in the case of one Iranian citizen of the Khavari ethnic group I heard about, who was deported to Afghanistan after being stopped by the police when not carrying his identity card.

15. The Sefid Sang incident is the subject of a recent Afghan feature film (*Hamsāyah/ Neighbor*, Zubair Farghand, 2010). The film was initially banned by the Afghan Ministry of Information and Culture, reportedly under Iranian pressure (APAP 2011: 1), but has since had limited screenings in Kabul.

16. A number of serial killers active in the 1990s and 2000s were wrongly presumed to be Afghan in initial media reports (Adelkhah and Olszewska 2007: 160). In fact, Afghans were instead often victims, most notoriously of one pedophile who raped and murdered up to twenty-two children at Pakdasht near Tehran in 2004; tellingly, Afghan parents had failed to report their children's disappearances to police for fear of being deported.

17. See also Boroujerdi 1996: 13. Matin-Asgari (2004) has seen in this tendency to consider the *sharqi* (Oriental) self as irrational, mystical, religious, and poetic, the reason for the recent popularity of loose interpretations of postmodernism as an "intellectual style" in Iran.

Note that this dichotomous thinking has many analogues in Persianate culture: '*aql*, reason, is a masculine trait, whereas *ehsās*, emotion, is feminine.

18. This is not to say that there have not been intellectual efforts to de-essentialize the West in Iran: there have been such attempts among reform-oriented Muslim thinkers, secularists, and feminists (Tohidi 2002: 220–221). Notably, these are groups critical of the government and its love of political slogans based on binary opposites.

19. This echoes Tavakoli-Targhi's observations on the "self-refashioning" of Iranian identity over the past few centuries, for which identification or dis-identification with various geographies and cultures provided creative rhetorical devices or alternative "scenarios." Both Europe and Iran's pre-Islamic past were set against the dominant Islamic discourse and Arab cultural-linguistic influence (2001: 103).

20. Afghanistan is sometimes also cast as the location of a purer, older, more authentic self, as when Iranians express delight at the musicality of Afghan Persian or Dari, which purportedly contains fewer loan words. However, they just as frequently make fun of the Afghan accent, the way hillbilly or redneck speech is ridiculed in other parts of the world—charming but rustic and inferior.

21. See also Fischer, who argues that even when Afghan refugees are sympathetically portrayed in Iranian films, they "are incidental vehicles for Iranian ethical self-reflection" (2004: 325). He argues that this changed when the lens was turned on Afghanistan itself, for example in Mohsen Makhmalbaf's *Safar be Qandehār/Kandahar* (2001). However, a film so replete with reductive symbolic imagery (of burkas, desert wastes, and prosthetic limbs) is difficult to see as anything more than an Orientalist vision of the country and its misery.

22. For a detailed discussion of Persian literary historians and critics and the development of a "project of literary history" closely linked to national space and identity, see Clinton (1372/1994).See also W. Ahmadi's (2004a) rejection of the "exclusionary poetics" of the Iranian critical discourse that marginalizes the literature of Afghanistan.

23. More generally, see Tavakoli-Targhi 2001 on the cultural "refashioning" and Kashani-Sabet 1999 on the "frontier fictions" involved in the creation of the modern Iranian nation-state.

24. This is not to say that this space was completely undifferentiated in terms of regional or political identities, but merely to say that Persian was a *Kultursprache* that facilitated communication and the exchange of ideas (Fragner 1999). Indeed, classical Persian poetry is replete with pejorative or satirical attacks on other ethnicities (notably Turks and Arabs) or rival cities. I thank Oliver Bast for drawing my attention to this issue.

25. Karimi-Hakkak notes that the overwhelmingly negative value assigned to the "complexity" of the Indian style originated with the nineteenth-century poets of the Literary Return movement in Iran and is associated with the growing pains of the Iranian nation-state (1995: 28).

26. Even poets who for the most part lived and worked near their places of birth also frequently undertook extensive travels throughout the region and left detailed travelogues, e.g., Sa'di and Naser Khosrow (1004–1077). The latter undertook a seven-year journey from his native Balkh through Khorasan, Armenia, Syria, Egypt, the Arabian Peninsula, and back through Persia, and documented it in great detail (Hunsberger 2000: 5).

27. While he is best known in the West by the epithet Rumi (after Rum, "Roman" Anatolia or Byzantium where he lived), Afghans proudly refer to him as Balkhi, after his birthplace. To both Afghans and Iranians, however, he is usually known simply by his religious sobriquet, Mowlānā or Mowlavi. While acknowledging this usage, for the sake of simplicity I refer to him as Rumi.

28. From the thirteenth century onward, many other people from Iran and Central Asia sought to improve their fortunes by emigrating to India, including Shah Jahan's own stepmother and his wife Mumtaz Mahal, whose mausoleum is the Taj Mahal.

29. Attempts at promoting the Pashtu language included the establishment of a Pashtu Literary Association in 1932, replaced by the Pashtu Academy five years later. Their activities included research into the history, grammar, and etymology of the language, translation into Pashtu, and publication of Pashtu books, textbooks, and periodicals (Nasar 2000). Dupree notes the absurdity of the prewar government policy requiring all official documents to be translated into Pashtu when neither the sending nor the receiving official could understand that language (1980: 66, 70).

30. Nonetheless, heated debates on which language should dominate returned to Afghanistan after 2001, when the Pashtun minister of information and culture, Abdul Karim Khurram, decreed that a number of Pashtu words (including many neologisms and, ironically, words of English origin) would replace Persian words in official discourse, such as *pohanton* instead of *dāneshgāh* (university) or *gāleri* instead of *negārestān* (gallery). These moves were widely condemned in Persian-language media and blogs, the ensuing confusion being satirized, e.g., by Navisa 1387/2008. On these trends before the war, see Dupree 1980: 93–94.

31. Of course, there was more rhetoric than substance to this claim, given that seventeen years after publishing this poem, Kazemi is still living in Iran and has little intention of going back to Afghanistan.

32. This translation is literary rather than literal, aiming to preserve the formal structure of the original by using a familiar English meter and maintaining the *radif,* or "over-rhyme," the phrase that is repeated at the end of certain lines. All of the images, however, have been preserved as faithfully as possible, although the meter necessitated some additions.

2. The Melancholy Modern

The opening epigraph is from Zahra Hosseinzadeh (original in 1382/2003: 102).

1. In Iran, men and women are segregated on public buses, with the women's section the rear third of the bus.

2. This paradigm has subsequently been challenged and sadness has been increasingly pathologized and defined by psychiatric discourses as *afsordegi* or *depreshen* (depression), particularly in the context of the ongoing trauma and social effects of the Iran-Iraq War (Behrouzan 2010, 2015). This has, however, merely further entrenched the presence of various kinds of dysphoria in the Iranian public imagination.

3. This is a reasonable estimate or even an underestimate, given that there were around 340,000 Afghan children aged seventeen or younger legally residing in Iran as documented refugees in October 2005 and entitled to public schooling, not all of them would have been attending school, and some of them may have been able to afford the fees (UNHCR/BAFIA 2005). See also Harrison 2004.

4. The first government school was established in Kabul in 1907, but even by the late 1970s, there were fewer than 900,000 school pupils for a population of 14 million (Kakar 1995: 79). Literacy rates in the late 1970s were estimated at between 5 and 10 percent of males and about 1 percent of females (Mills 1991b: 3).

5. Compare Messick's evocative account of village Qur'anic schools in highland Yemen, followed by lesson circles in a city mosque for a select few (1993: 75–92). See also Eickelman 1978 on Islamic education in Morocco.

6. See Ghani 1988: 430–431 and Edwards 1996: 36; Elphinstone describes almost exactly the same set of texts used in pedagogy more than a century earlier (1839: 248–50).

7. For a vivid historical and ethnographic description of life and studies at the Qom *Howzeh* before the revolution, narrated through the recollections of one ayatollah, see Mottahedeh 1985; see also Fischer 1980 for the role of the Qom clergy and scholars and their intellectual and political activities leading up to the Revolution.

8. On the Hazara civil war and the changes it wrought in Hazara social and political structures, see Emadi 1997, Kakar 1995: 94–95, Harpviken 1995, Mousavi 1998, Canfield 2004, and Ibrahimi 2006.

9. Mir-Hosseini gives a fascinating account of the shifts in Shi'i thought and jurisprudence that enabled greater attention to be paid to gender issues, through debates she held with feminist clerics at the Qom *Howzeh*. Indeed, she writes of the creation, in postrevolutionary Iran, of a "space in which a critique of the fundamental gender assumptions in Islamic law can be sustained in ways that were impossible until very recently" (1999: 10). Increasingly, women are also taking theological classes in their own right: both Iranian universities, and a number of Afghan religious centers offer them degrees in Islamic studies or shorter courses in the reading and interpretation of the Qur'an—including a seven-year university-equivalent degree course specifically aimed at women, offered by one Afghan religious foundation in Mashhad.

10. According to a UN report (Squire 2000), some 137,334 Afghan children were enrolled in Iranian public schools in 1998, of whom at least 47 percent were girls—these represented less than a third of the estimated number of Afghan children in Iran. Over 18,000 Afghan children and over 300,000 adults were taught basic literacy skills between 1985 and 1999 in the Iranian national literacy campaign. A household survey of refugees in Mashhad found that literacy rates and education levels rose after arrival in Iran, with 90 percent of household heads being literate, but no illiteracy among children born in Iran (Abbasi-Shavazi et al. 2005: 21).

11. See ICRI 1999, Squire 2000, Sarhaddi-Nelson 2001. A UN report estimated that in 1998–1999 approximately 14,000 students were attending informal Afghan schools in Tehran and Mashhad (Squire 2000).

12. The fees of the informal schools were substantially lower, ranging from 1,000 tomans to 6,000 tomans per month in 2005, depending on the level (approx. $1.10–$6.60 U.S.). The diplomas issued by these schools were being certified by the Afghan embassy so they could be recognized in Afghanistan once the children repatriated.

13. Classes are also offered in first aid, basic pharmacology, midwifery, Pashto language, journalism, filmmaking, design, and handicrafts including rug weaving and artificial flower making.

14. No statistics are available on the total number of Afghan university students, but between 1996 and 1999, a German scholarship fund disbursed over seven hundred scholarships to Afghan refugee students in Iran, the majority of whom were studying medicine and engineering (Squire 2000). The Mashhad-based Afghan Universitarians' Union, created as a guild organization and support group for Afghan students and graduates, had a thousand members as of November 2005, scattered across various parts of Iran and Afghanistan.

15. Since the poets with whom I worked were all Shi'a Muslims, I restrict my remarks here to a discussion of Shi'a Islam, rituals, and practices among Afghans in Iran.

16. See Emadi 1997: 377–378. A short documentary by a young Mashhad-based Afghan journalist and filmmaker, Reza Heidari, includes an interview with the father of two martyred Afghan volunteers (*Mādar marā āvāreh zā'id/Born an Exile*).

17. See also Doubleday's description of the religious life of Herati Shi'a women in the 1970s, whose major forms of religious sociability were visits to a saint's shrine outside the city, supplication for the granting of wishes and leaving votive objects, and the cooking and distribution of a ritual sweet, *halvā*. Another regular activity was the weekly singing of a *rowzeh* for the women of a house by a blind sheikh and the distribution of another sweet food, in fulfillment of a vow (Doubleday 1988: 45–54). Compare Kamalkhani 1993 on women's *rowzeh* and *nazr* gatherings in postrevolutionary Iran and their sociopolitical dimensions; and Kalinock (2003, 2004) on other ritual gatherings of Iranian women.

18. *Dakhil* means one who has entered, an intimate or also, conversely, an intruder. This paradoxical lexical range comes from its usage in Arabic and the practices of Arab tribes, for whom strangers who entered a group's territory would become guests entitled to hospitality, protection, and asylum. Physical contact with a person (even an enemy) or his tent or belongings was often enough to become his *dakhil* (see van Gennep 1960: 32, who classifies such acts as rites of incorporation into a group; for parallels in other Semitic groups and the common semantic links between "stranger," "enemy," and "guest," see Derrida 2001: 380–402). The practice of leaving something at a shrine is also common among pilgrims to the tombs of saints in Afghanistan, where trees in shrine courtyards often become thickly enveloped in threads or studded with nails, considered to be a cure for toothache (see Dupree 1980: 104–105). It also has clear parallels with the ex-voto offerings of Catholic pilgrims.

19. Notable early examples included Baba Feghani (d. 1519), who "did penance at the grave of the Imam [Reza], to whom he dedicated a *qasida* that subsequently became famous" (Rypka 1968: 288) and Lesani, a Sufi who composed a hundred thousand verses in honor of the Imams (289).

20. Compare Deeb 2006 on similar developments in the Shi'i community in Lebanon.

21. Other beliefs that are shared by Iranians persist, such as belief in the "evil eye" and the various practices used to ward it off.

22. This figure includes 1,500 men, who use the *shabestān* or large domed hall of white marble, and an equal number of women, who use the women's section in the basement (or, for some occasions, the smaller gallery overlooking the *shabestān*). All events are strictly gender segregated, and women were allowed in the *shabestān* only for rare secular events, such as official polling for Afghanistan's presidential elections in 2004, or an unprecedented series of poetry evenings that were soon abandoned. At a mourning ceremony for the former king of Afghanistan, Zahir Shah, which I tried to attend in 2007, women were not allowed on the premises at all.

23. Refugees from other towns, including Kabul, Kandahar, and Mazar-e Sharif, also have their own places of worship, community schools, and other institutions in Mashhad.

24. Doubleday reports that with the exception of a few educated schoolteachers, almost all the women in Herat observed complete segregation from unrelated men in most situations, including full veiling with a burka in public and remaining in women's quarters when male guests were in the house. They sometimes complained of the restrictions of their *qeit* (confinement), but generally accepted it (1988: 4–9). I was told that Hazara women from rural Afghanistan, meanwhile, did not cover their faces, often performed agricultural work outside the home, and led a less gender-segregated existence, but men were still responsible for them in almost every aspect of their lives.

25. One nationwide study found that around 40 percent of married refugee women are using some form of birth control, compared to 80 percent of urban Iranian women (Mehryar et al. 2004: 18). Another study found that 61 percent of Afghan families of different ethnicities and across rural and urban areas in a smaller sample used family planning (Tober 2007: 271).

26. See, for example, Arnoldy 2005 on a girls' karate club established in Kabul by returnees from Iran. The youngest female candidate to stand in the first postwar parliamentary elections was a twenty-six-year-old who spent twenty-three years in Iran.

27. For thorough histories of intellectuals and intellectualism in Iran, see Boroujerdi 1996, Gheissari 1997, and Mirsepassi 2000.

28. See Boroujerdi 1996: 120–130 for a detailed and critical discussion of Nasr's influence on contemporary Iranian philosophy (120–121).

29. Matin-Asgari is dismissive of the intellectual rigor of this trend, noting the many contradictory views to which the term is applied (2004: 113–114).

30. In this at least, Mozaffari had not departed significantly from the ideals espoused by his erstwhile source of inspiration, Shari'ati, who held Third World intellectuals responsible for enlightening their compatriots and finding solutions to their nations' ills (Boroujerdi 1996: 111).

31. The poem was considered representative enough to be included in Kazemi's survey of a millennium of Persian literature (1379/2000: 455–458).

32. This metaphor was famously used to great effect by Bijan Mofid, a prerevolutionary Iranian playwright, in an allegorical verse drama representing the doomed idealism of Prime Minister Mohammad Mosaddeq's democratic movement that confronted American and British imperial designs on Iran, only to be defeated by a CIA-orchestrated coup in 1951 (Houshmand 2007). The "leopard king" represents Mosaddeq, and the moon, his democratic ideals, which, Mofid seems to contend, were still inaccessible to Iranian society.

33. Compare the representation of the homeland (*vatan*) as a long-suffering mother to all her citizen-children in late-nineteenth-century Iranian discourse leading up to the constitutional revolution, as described by Tavakoli-Targhi (2001: 113–133).

34. Interesting comparisons may be made here to the disenchantment with diverse certainties and orthodoxies felt by a generation of European writers and poets following the senseless tragedy of trench warfare in World War I, which left an indelible mark of world-weary irony on English literature (Fussell 1975), or to Arab poets' disillusionment with the political failure of Arab nationalism and pan-Arabism, which led to a similar despair and bitterness in their poetry (Ajami 1998).

35. This poem is but one example of a trope often found in lyric realist poems, that of the melancholy wanderer in the city, a kind of Persianate *flâneur* (Olszewska 2013b). It appears to be a common trope in the region, with a long pedigree, for example, in Turkish literature, from nineteenth-century poetry to the postmodern novels of Orhan Pamuk (Stokes 2010: 147).

36. Moqaddam is now officially named Meidan-e Shahid-e Gomnam (the Unknown Martyr's Square). This is a popular place for the police to arrest Afghans without (sometimes even with) Iranian residence permits. One of the minibuses was nicknamed *Tābut*, the Coffin, by the Afghans who rode it every day: they could not be sure if they would return home in the evening or be detained and deported.

3. Afghan Literary Organizations in Postrevolutionary Iran

The two epigraphs are "The Arena of Death" by Mohammad Asef Rahmani (original in Kazemi and Rahmani 1370/1991: 42–43) and "The Bench Opposite" by Ma'sumeh Ahmadi (original in Sajjadi 1384/2005: 30–31).

1. The red apple stands for wholesome beauty and health in the *haft sin,* the spread of seven auspicious foods and objects traditionally assembled to welcome Nowruz, the Persian New Year. Apples appear frequently in the metaphysical lyrics of Sohrab Sepehri (1928–1980), usually evoking similarly wholesome associations with life, sweetness, beauty, and the sun, and it seems to be this usage that Ahmadi is following here, but Sepehri's symbolism remains more enigmatic and multivalent than the well-established conventions of classical poetry.

2. See Ahmadzadeh 2003 on the rise of the Persian novel, Parsinejad 2003 for a history of literary criticism in Iran from the mid-nineteenth to the mid-twentieth century, and Browne 1914 for a discussion of early Iranian journalism.

3. It should be noted that national literary histories are usually restricted to developments among these very groups, and little light is shed on literary developments among the working classes, ethnic or religious minorities, rural and nomadic people, or nonmainstream literary trends in general. Yet developments were certainly taking place, unbeknownst even to the elites—see Fatemeh Keshavarz's surprise when, as host of a radio program in Shiraz in the 1970s, she was asked to invite an illiterate, "toothless old man in peasant clothing" who had memorized the entire works of the first major woman poet of the twentieth century, Parvin E'tesami, and was able to hold an articulate conversation about her with callers to the show (Keshavarz 2007: 43–45).

4. Ahmadi describes this as an alternative form of modernity achieved by creative adaptation, among others in the literary sphere. Tarzi, for example, advocated the spread of rationalism and patriotic loyalty to Afghanistan among all its diverse peoples, but also believed in Islam as a primary unifying factor for the nation-state and a core part of people's identity. For a detailed discussion of Tarzi's and his associates' values and interpretation of modernity, see W. Ahmadi 2008: 21–37.

5. These included *Akhtar/Star* (published in Istanbul 1875–1894), *Qānun/Law* (published in London 1890–1905), *Habl al-Matin/The Firm Cord* (Calcutta, from 1892), *Sur-e Esrāfil/The Trumpet of Esrafil* (a weekly newspaper printed in Tehran 1907–1908 that played an important role in the Constitutional Revolution), and Mahmud Tarzi's *Serāj al-Akhbār* (Kabul, 1911–1918) (see also Atabaki 2008, Browne 1914). In the mid-twentieth century, the publications around which literati tended to cluster included *Sokhan/Speech, Majalleh-ye Musiqi/Journal of Music,* and *Kāveh* (the name of a mythical hero from the *Shāhnāmeh*) (Talatoff 2000: 16).

6. This was an appropriation of Sartre's idea of *littérature engagée,* which represented a call for the use of literature to advocate a particular social or political cause and a protest against art for art's sake in post–World War II France.

7. Notable exceptions include a series of articles by Karimi-Hakkak (1985, 1986, 1991, 1994, 1997), Losensky 1997, and an ongoing doctoral project by Fatemeh Shams on the relationship between poetry and power in the Islamic Republic (Shams 2015a, 2015b).

8. This has led to conflicts between the MCIG and the OIP in the past over various cultural products sponsored by the Arts Center, such as the film *Ādam Barfi/The Snowman,* which involved transvestism, leading to attacks by the radical group Ansar-e Hezbollah on cinemas that showed it in 1997 (Naficy 2002: 55–56). Another example was the music album *Toranj/Bergamot Orange* (2007) by avant-garde singer Mohsen Namjoo, the only one he managed to produce with a state license before going into exile. The Arts Center was heavily criticized by the MCIG for granting the license (Shams 2015b).

9. Some of the most significant poems in the history of Persian literature have been written in *masnavi* form, including Ferdowsi's mythic-historical epic *Shāhnāmeh/Book of Kings,* written in Ghazni a millennium ago. Nezami Ganjavi's (d. 1203) *Khamseh/Quintet* of romantic epics, including the archetypical stories of Leili and Majnun, and Khosrow and Shirin,

were also written in this form, as was Attar's (d. 1220) mystical *Manteq al-Teir/Conference of the Birds* and Rumi's *Masnavi-ye Ma'navi/The Spiritual Masnavi*.

10. See Zarkub 1371/1992 for an exhaustive analysis of the religious and mythological imagery, much of it shared with classical poetry, used in the resistance poetry of Afghanistan. For more examples of such poetry from the time of the Soviet war, see the anthology in which Rahmani's poem was published, *She'r-e Moqāvemat-e Afghānestān/The Resistance Poetry of Afghanistan* (Kazemi and Rahmani 1370/1991).

11. For a discussion of the prevalent use of the Karbala story in Iranian Islamist literature, see Talatoff (2000: 114–119).

12. Majrouh likewise noted a thematic shift in the oral and written Pashtu literature that was flourishing in the refugee camps and the bazaars of Peshawar, with less love poetry, and more religious and martial poetry and nostalgic poetry of exile being produced (Majrouh 2003: 42). In close to one hundred *landays* that he collected, women pine for lovers fighting in the homeland, ridicule men who do not wish to fight and praise those who do, and rhetorically offer sexual reward to those who prove most courageous (38–72).

13. Edwards (1986b), focusing on the work of Pashtun resistance poets based in Peshawar, shows how they invoked the logic of tribal honor in their verses as a rhetorical strategy to incite listeners to participate in resistance against the infidel invasion. Alternately shaming and praising different tribes, poets used the oppositional character of the tribes and the game of challenge and riposte to goad them into action, addressing a specifically Pashto consciousness in their listeners. By allowing one to speak with the voice of cultural conscience, not as *a poet* but adopting the persona of *the Poet*, convention also enabled him to shame particular tribes without consequence to himself.

14. For a discussion of these and other dominant themes in Afghan resistance poetry, accompanied by many examples from refugee poets living in Pakistan and Iran, see Zarkub 1371/1992, in particular 63–103. I have not found examples of poetry in which an ethnocentric rather than nationalist stance is adopted, although such political tendencies existed among the Hazaras (and much resistance poetry is Shi'a-centric). Most poems still take the nation-state as their basic framework, and where another ethnic or political group is attacked, it is frequently as *"vatan-forushān"*—traitors to the common homeland. Perhaps more ethnocentric sentiments were expressed in Hazaregi folk poetry, as they appear to be in the Pashtu poetry described by Edwards, but this is beyond the scope of this book.

15. Before the early twentieth century, the term *vatan* simply meant someone's home, though it also had an aterritorial, metaphysical resonance as the originary home of the human soul (Tavakoli-Targhi 2001: 115–117).

16. Compare Barber (2007: 137) on the visible and audible responses of African audiences to performances, and Schimmel (1992: 51) on the effect on the audience of poets in Pakistan, who can bring their listeners to a state of near-ecstasy and induce political fervor in them.

17. This is an interesting document in itself, describing the anti-Soviet resistance as an Islamic revolution in Afghanistan (while ignoring the divisions among Afghan parties) and locating this within the broader movement of Islamic and so-called Eastern awakening and casting off of the bonds of imperialist exploitation. Still, Mo'allem places much of the blame for the situation on a lack of consciousness in the "slumbering" Islamic world and on "traitorous rulers and sell-out [*khod-bākhteh*] intellectuals" (1370/1991: 7–8).

18. Fischer writes that one confides the "pain of one's heart" usually not to a person, but to "a mountain, a light, a shrine, a well, the Qur'an" (Fischer 2004: 216).

19. These are often improvised and can be rather flimsy, reproduced by photocopying, hand-assembled, and stapled together. Most are produced with desktop computers and have simple digital or hand-drawn graphics. Some publications have short life spans due to lack of

funding. Some that manage to attract sponsorship have a more solid appearance, but are often accused by rivals of being political because they are undoubtedly disseminating the views of their sponsors—in some cases, it is alleged, the government of Iran. They are reminiscent of the chapbooks of Pashtu poetry published in Peshawar, as described by Heston (1991), but have much broader aspirations to cultural critique.

20. In any case, Meisami's (1987) study of medieval Persian court poetry has dispelled the misconceptions that patronage was not conducive to creative autonomy and that court poetry was repetitive, artificial, and bombastic. Instead, she points to its didactic and ethical functions: poets were often advisers and boon companions, rather than simple entertainers or flatterers, to their rulers. Sharlet (2011) meanwhile, has shown that the tension between poetry as commodity and as aesthetic and ethical product also existed under medieval court patronage.

21. In this, Hosseinzadeh is following in the footsteps of the late doyenne of Iranian poetry, Simin Behbahani (1927–2014), who writes about ordinary, contemporary people and their everyday burdens in the ghazal form (Talatoff 2000: 161; Brookshaw 2008).

4. The Social Lives of Poets and Poetry

The vignette in the epigraph is a composite account based on regular participant observation over a period of six months in 2005–2006. Several changes could be noted over my subsequent visits, notably the addition of a large television tuned to satellite channels (among others, from Afghanistan) that the regulars frequently watched.

1. Also known as *Najmā-ye Shirāzi*, "Najma and the King's Daughter" appears to be a folktale told in verse (or a cycle of love quatrains) known across Afghanistan, which may have been published as a chapbook in Peshawar, but I have not yet located a copy.

2. Despite this particular opinion, the Iranian school curriculum inevitably plays a major role in familiarizing children with poetry, since classical and modern Persian poetry, including religious and political poems, is plentiful in textbooks (Mehran 2007: 57) and children are frequently asked to memorize poems for homework.

3. On the ongoing poetic and personal resonance of Forugh Farrokhzad for generations of Iranians, told as a moving memoir, see Keshavarz (2007: 33–58): "Before, during, and after the revolution, Farrokhzad's poetry has sold like hot cakes" (41). See also Brookshaw and Rahimieh 2010.

4. Compare the consensual process by which a cleric or religious scholar is gradually awarded the title of ayatollah by his circle of followers, as described by Mottahedeh (1985: 343, 390).

5. Compare the treatment of master musician Ostad Latif Khan in Herat in the 1970s: "Heads turned as he made his way to the front of the audience, greeting friends as he passed, and from the stage the singer pressed his hand to his heart and bowed to him as he sang" (Doubleday 1988: 20).

6. The financial incentive is also there, of course. Although it would probably be impossible to live solely from one's prize earnings, Elyas Alavi's friends joke that he has come close to doing this by winning almost every possible prize in the festivals he entered or was invited to in 2005–2007, totaling several gold coins.

7. There have been many studies of the dramatic takeoff of the phenomenon of blogging in Iran and the way it is reconfiguring conceptions of public and private, the public presentation of the self and emotion, and even ideas of political participation and mobilization; see

in particular Graham and Khosravi 2002, Doostdar 2004, Alexanian 2006, Sreberny and Khiabany 2010, and Akhavan 2013.

8. Some have also tried to self-publish with sponsorship from Afghan businessmen, but such books suffer from poor distribution.

9. According to Bill, *dowreh*s may be organized around "professional, familial, religious, recreational, political or economic" ties, and thus help to hold together Iran's social and political fabric (1973: 132). See also Mottahedeh (1985: 337).

10. See Bill (1973: 133) and Tavakoli-Targhi (2001: 121–122) on societies founded to oppose Qajar rule, and Mottahedeh (1985: 356) on the role of informal religious groups in the 1978–1979 revolution.

11. Schimmel notes the importance of the "purely acoustical qualities" of Persian poetry but suggests that modern Persian speakers pay less attention to rhythmical stress when reciting poetry (1992: 51). This was not my experience—rather, recitation style seemed to differ from person to person, and was a matter either of taste or skill.

12. Classical Persian adopted the sixteen meters of Arabic verse, although some of these were never used and others were adapted. For an engaging and accessible introduction to the genres, metres, imagery and rhetorical devices of classical Persian (and Urdu and Turkish) poetry, see Schimmel 1992. For a more thorough treatment of the various meters used in Persian, see Elwell-Sutton 1976 and Thiesen 1982.

13. *Jenāb* is the polite title of address for a man, "Sir."

14. The sixth couplet of the famous lament of the reed flute, the introduction to Rumi's *Spiritual Masnavi*. Rumi's meaning is that everyone is drawn to the flute's melody for their own reasons, without needing to know how or why the flute is being played and its secrets.

15. Lines from Sohrab Sepehri's famous long poem in blank verse, *Sedā-ye Pā-ye Āb/The Water's Footfall*, 1964.

16. One *sekkeh* is worth approximately $150 U.S.; they also come in denominations of a half-*sekkeh* and quarter-*sekkeh*. The first prize at a festival could be anything from one to five *sekkeh*s in the mid-2000s.

17. See Bowen (1991: 141) on the role of maxims among the Gayo of Sumatra.

18. Ferghana is a valley in Central Asia, today falling between Uzbekistan, Kyrgyzstan, and Tajikistan.

19. A later publication, Hosseini's memoir of the election campaign (1386/2007a), is similarly peppered with poetic quotes from both contemporary and classical Persian poets.

20. The concept of *madineh-ye fāzeleh* comes from the tenth-century Muslim philosopher and polymath Abu Nasr al-Farabi, of Persian or Turkic origin, considered to be among the foremost Islamic commentators on the Greek philosophers and the "founder of Islamic Neoplatonism" (Fakhry 2002). In his Arabic-language work *Al-Madina al-Fadila* ("The City of Learning/Virtue") he presented a theory of an ideal state as in Plato's *The Republic*.

21. A similar repositioning of the polysemy of classical verse occurred in another heir of classical Persian verse, twentieth-century modern Urdu poetry, for example in the *ghazal*s of Faiz Ahmed Faiz. Faiz introduced politics and the longing for social justice into love poetry, in which revolution at times competes with the beloved for the poet's attention, and at times itself becomes the beloved: "For the love of your flower-like lips / We were sacrificed on the dry branches of the noose / For the desire of the candles of your hands / We were killed on half-dark paths / And with revolutionary dignity: / On our lips the words of the ghazal / And the torch of misery in our hands / Gather our banners from the place of murder / Caravans of other lovers will emerge / For whose path our feet have shortened the distances of pain." Translation at http://www.faiz.com. See also Faiz 1995.

22. A similar divination technique using the Qur'an, also seen as a means of access to the Tongue of the Unseen, has a different name: *estekhāreh gereftan*. It is usually carried out by those with religious training.

23. Legend has it that this tradition dates to the death of Hafez himself, when the orthodox clergy of Shiraz argued that he should not be given a Muslim burial (as recorded, e.g., by Gertrude Bell, 1928 [1897]: 48). His many followers protested, however, and the people decided to consult his own verses—they were divided up into couplets and one was drawn at random. The selection proved to be most appropriate, even tongue-in-cheek: *"Qadam-e darigh madār az jenāzeh-ye Hāfez / Ke gar che gharq-e gonāh ast miravad be behesht"* [Do not walk with regret from the corpse of Hafez / For though he may be drowning in sin, he is going to heaven]. Thus Hafez earned his burial in the mausoleum that is visited by thousands of Iranians to this day. Although Katouzian writes that the cult of Hafez as we know it today is only about fifty years old (2006: 6), Bell described a long history of *fālgiri* already in 1897 (1928 [1897]: 49).

24. Caron 2013, for example, discusses the political and social critiques of Pashtun poets in Afghanistan and Pakistan.

25. No further details could be found on this incident, so it is unclear what exactly upset the governor, particularly since he is an important ally of President Karzai, who is openly critical of Pakistani interference in Afghanistan. He is, however, a former *mojāhed* and owes his personal fortune to commerce during seven years of exile in Pakistan. Perhaps there were insinuations of this, or allegations of direct Pakistani involvement in this border province, which the governor took as a personal insult.

26. See Bowen 1991: 142 on the right to repress speech and how it relates to political values; also Bourdieu 1977.

27. Compare this to the correspondence between poets in the *qasidah* form in highland Yemen, as described, for example, by Miller, which is called "initiation and response" (*bid' wa jiwāb*) poetry, in which a second poet responds to a poem, matching its rhyme, meter, and theme (2005: 85).

5. Modern Love

The epigraph is based on my field notes, 6 November 2005.

1. Giddens (1992: 38) makes a useful distinction between *amour passion* or passionate love, which he sees as a universal phenomenon, and romantic love, which is the culturally specific elaboration that varies from society to society; I adopt this usage here.

2. I borrow the term *culture of love* from Andrews and Kalpaklı (2005), who describe a similar situation in Ottoman Turkey.

3. See Brookshaw 2009 and the other contributors to the December 2009 issue of *Iranian Studies* (vol. 42, no. 5) on depictions of love in premodern Persian poetry and prose.

4. Commenting on the example of British Bengalis described by Gavron (1996), Gell notes that while for Bengali elders it is entirely rational to maximize the life chances of their offspring by arranging their unions with families whose character and background are known to the elders, the British Bengali youth are increasingly embracing alternative rationalities of love marriage, which he calls the "whims of media-besotted young adults" (Gell 2011). This criticism was very much shared both by Hoodfar's Egyptian informants and her own Iranian grandmother (1997: 62–63).

5. Iranians are not alone in this: people in Turkey are also taught to "revere love," also drawing on a related history of courtly and mystical traditions, with love now supplying the tropes and emotions for reflecting on anxieties of national importance (Stokes 2010: 25–34). Stokes sees this "culture of love" as stretching from Spain to India.

6. Indeed, when Seyyed Abu Taleb Mozaffari was looking for a possible title for his new book, a compendium of a century of Afghan verse, he crowd sourced it on Facebook. Many of his friends suggested some variation on *Sad sāl-e 'āsheqi* (*One Hundred Years of Loving*) as a suitable title.

7. See Tourage (2007) for a fascinating discussion of the bawdy tales and explicitly sexual imagery used to communicate esoteric knowledge in Rumi's thirteenth-century masterpiece, *The Spiritual Masnavi*; see also de Bruijn 1997, Keshavarz 1998.

8. Note, for example, the intertwining of these various registers of love in the *ghazal*s of Sa'di, in which apparent descriptions of carnal passion may alternatively be read as containing petitions to the ruling prince or minister (Arberry 1958: 207).

9. In this chapter I am indebted to Afary 2009 for her rich history of the politics of sex, love, and marriage in Iran, including explanations of the distinctions among the legal categories of *'aqdi* (formal permanent marriage), *sigheh* (temporary marriage), and slave concubinage. Afary writes that in premodern times, while a man could legally have up to four *'aqdi* wives and unlimited slave concubines and (in Shi'i but not Sunni law) temporary marriages, in practice the extent of polygyny varied among different socioeconomic strata in the country, ranging from the populous harems of monarchs and high officials (disbanded in the early twentieth century) to monogamous marriages for the vast majority of their subjects, with middle-class men perhaps taking a second wife or indulging in affairs or de facto prostitution in the guise of temporary marriage. The latter two practices continue to this day. In a context of extensive gender segregation, covert bisexuality has also been common among both sexes.

10. Mousavi also notes that intermarriage has been promoted between Hazaras and Uzbeks in Afghanistan to ensure peaceful relations. Where interethnic marriages occur, hypergamy is a general rule. See Mousavi 1998: 45–61 on the role of family and patriline in Hazara social structure.

11. Translated by Sayd Bahodine Majrouh and Marjolijn de Jager.

12. Translated by Sayed Askar Mousavi.

13. It may also vary by ethnic group or locality. Grima, based on her experience with Pashtun women in Pakistan, argues that Pashtun women do *not* compose love poems, which simply "represent women in men's folklore and fantasy" (1992: 154). Instead, they are more likely to recount narratives of the sorrows they have experienced in their lives.

14. The lyrics here are transcribed to reflect the colloquial Dari pronunciation of Afghan recordings. Hayedeh's recording rather incongruously retains the Dari grammatical structure while altering the pronunciation to colloquial Tehrani (e.g., she sings "*gofteh natuni*" where the Dari is "*gofta natāni*").

15. The traditional status-unequal form of homosexuality persists in some parts of Afghanistan in the practice of young male dancers who dress as girls and become the concubines of wealthy male patrons, although it is coming under increasingly heavy criticism from educated urban Afghans and internationals: see the PBS *Frontline* documentary, *The Dancing Boys of Afghanistan* (Najibullah Quraishi, 2010). One Afghan friend recounted to me a minibus journey she took from Kabul to Badakhshan a few years ago. The driver, out of respect for her as a young woman, swapped the cassette of popular music he was playing—a collection of bawdy songs about female sweethearts—for one about (men's) boy sweethearts that he assumed would be less offensive to her.

16. Giddens has argued that the similar evolution of romantic relationships associated with Western modernity has also been initiated by women (1992).

17. In 2005, close to 70 percent of respondents preferred personal choice in choosing a life partner, and half of those considered love to be more important than parental approval, though parental approval was still sought by most (Moaddel 2008: 9, summarized in Afary 2009: 326).

18. The poem satirized and inverted various well-known sayings of Ahmadinejad: he had called the protesters *"khas o khāshāk"* (lit. dirt and rubbish, meaning scum or riffraff), and they immediately claimed this as a badge of pride or turned it back on him, as in the poem. The "lightless halo" is a reference to Ahmadinejad's claim that when he gave his first speech to the UN General Assembly in 2005, he was aware of a halo of light surrounding his head. He was widely mocked for claiming to be divinely inspired, or perhaps even to be the Hidden Imam, both at the time and four years later in his opponents' presidential campaigns.

19. I asked my research assistant to record all marriages in her wider social circle in the five years up to 2013. Six of the nineteen couples had been involved in self-initiated relationships before marriage, but there was just one elopement—the rest had had to get their families' approval and go through the *khāstegāri* process. The remaining thirteen couples had had the opportunity to get to know each other during the *khāstegāri* process and had had the right to refuse. Of these, in six couples families on both sides had known each other before the *khāstegāri*, two couples were introduced to each other by friends, and two were complete strangers. In the remaining two couples, the marriages were between close relatives; ironically, one of these was the only marriage to end in divorce so far, when the husband and his family, residents of Canada, sent the wife back to Iran and informed her that she had been divorced because her behavior had been insufficiently modest.

20. See Hoodfar (2004: 144–148) for a brief history of marriage customs and attempts at family law reform under the modern Afghan state. See also her detailed work on marriage negotiations in urban Egypt (1997: 66–74).

21. *Shirbahā*, a Persian word, is sometimes also referred to in Islamic terminology as *mahr-e hāzer*, while *mahr* is *mahr-e ghāyeb*, the "present" and "absent" *mahr*, respectively.

22. Compare this to Omidian's findings among Afghans in Northern California (1996). Although an overarching Afghan identity as one among many ethnic communities in the United States was emerging, internal ethnic divisions, families, and patrilines remained an important structuring principle of life there, particularly among the older generations. While ethnic divisions were largely "put on hold" during the Soviet occupation, they reemerged during the civil war of 1992–1996. But, as in Iran, the community is held together to some extent by a common experience of adversity and exile from Afghanistan (1996: 24).

6. "When Your *Darun* Speaks to You"

The epigraph is based on my field notes from January 2006.

1. Cf. Doostdar's (2004) description of unequal distributions of cultural capital in the field of Iranian blogging, which leads some bloggers to denounce the writings of others as "vulgar."

2. Manoukian defines *editing* as a "resilient modality of intervention on objects, images and texts" (2011: 62) and discusses its application in the cultural politics of the Islamic Republic of Iran. While akin to censorship, the term *editing* highlights the process of modifying

a cultural product that is simultaneously repressive and expressive or productive, in that it actually allows the circulation of certain items that would otherwise be forbidden, subject to certain alterations that display it in the way that it "should be" (Manoukian 2011: 105). While Manoukian dwells on external editing applied to existing objects, I discuss a more reflexive process of self-editing, albeit often in response to the demands of others.

3. To name just a few examples, see Fox 2005: 97 on English hypocritical politeness designed to paper over class differences; Mines 1994 on the disjuncture between private and public selves in South India; and Wikan's (1990) contestation of Geertz's claim (1973a) that the Balinese have no emotion except stage fright, arguing instead that their culture puts a premium on the mastery of powerful and disruptive inner emotions to maintain an outward equanimity. For more examples, see Lindholm 2005. Writ on a more collective level, the notion of cultural intimacy indexes the tensions between the mutual recognition of insiders versus representation fit for the consumption of outsiders (Herzfeld 1997; Shryock 2004).

4. These binaries are based on the division between a male public and a female private sphere, and analogous oppositions between veiled/unveiled, inside/outside, and related/unrelated, which structure all aspects of daily life (Graham and Khosravi 2002: 224). Studies of similar dualities and their negotiation in other parts of the Muslim world suggest that these are by no means unique to Iran (e.g., Bourdieu 1990, Abu-Lughod 1986, Booth 2011).

5. Milani writes, for example, on the characters in the novels and short stories of the first great female Iranian fiction writer, Simin Daneshvar, whose "inner voice" is rarely discernible in her work (Milani 1985: 337).

6. Here again, echoes of this critique may be found in other parts of the world, for example in English psychoanalyst Winnicott's theory of the vital, authentic "true self" and the defensive, deadened "false self" (1965).

7. See Zaborowska 2014 for a discussion of the origins and significance of the term *āberu*, literally "the water of one's face."

8. Wealthier families often have more furniture, separate bedrooms, and formal sitting rooms, but dining tables are a rarity; meals are eaten while sitting cross-legged on the floor around a *sofreh* (dining cloth) in almost all the Afghan and many of the Iranian homes I visited.

9. *Qalyān*-smoking is frowned upon by the more socially conservative. The government has periodically cracked down on this activity in public, particularly by women—when I first visited in 2003, some teahouses in Tehran had signs stating that women under the age of twenty-six would not be permitted to smoke, although the reasons for this age limit, as well as its enforcement, seemed rather arbitrary.

10. When I visited Herat in 2007, I heard that it was good form to conceal one's wife's name even from one's close friends; it was nonetheless a common sport among the men of the city to try to discover the names of their friends' wives by various underhanded means.

11. Rejali follows Foucault in arguing that new modes of exercising power in Iran now attempt to fix "a particular type of subjectivity on individuals" rather than gaining access to their interior (Rejali 1994: 137), but it seems that the two forms of control can coexist.

12. For an evocative description of this state of *do shakhsiat* (dual personality) among (mostly) upper-class Iranian youth, who often lead secular, Westernized lifestyles at home, yet are compelled to appear Islamic outside the home, see Varzi 2006.

13. My translation; original in Ayati 1382/2003: 15. Nezami goes on to say that his son will never match him as a poet anyway, so he might as well learn a useful trade, such as medicine!

14. The tenor of this view of poetry seems rather more subtly layered than the earnest European version espoused, for example, by Rainer Maria Rilke, who urges a young poet to "describe your sorrows and desires, the thoughts that pass through your mind and your be-

lief in some kind of beauty—describe all these with heartfelt, silent, humble *sincerity*" (1986 [1934]: 7, emphasis added). In any case, the problem may be tautological since, as Beeman reminds us, sincerity itself is culturally mediated; it must be "performed" by the addresser and assessed as such by the addressee (2001).

15. Finnegan stresses that it is simplistic to see any kind of communication, including the oral, as natural. All communication is based on social and cultural conventions, including human speech (1988: 4).

16. See also the rich ethnographic studies of women's poetry in the Middle East, and the problems particular to it, by Abu-Lughod 1986, Boesen 1983, and Miller 2002. For thorough discussions of women's poetry in Iran, see Milani 1992 and Talatoff 1997. For an anthology of Afghan women's poetry in Persian, see Mirshahi 1383/2004.

17. The colorful lives and works of these women are described in a unique sixteenth-century biographical work on female poets by Fakhri Heravi, a Herati who migrated to India, titled *Javāher al-'Ajāyeb/Jewels of Wonder* (Arbabzadah 2002).

18. Noble women in Afghanistan have also become renowned for their poetry, even in relatively recent times. They were all well-educated daughters or sisters of notable officials and men of culture, encouraged in their work by their families. They are known by their poetic noms de plume: Mastureh of Kabul (1846–1872), Makhfi of Badakhshan (1879–1963), and Mahjubeh of Herat (1906–1966).

19. Milani 1992 offers a thorough treatment of the contributions and challenges made to Persian literature by these female writers.

20. *Ru dar bāyesti* (or, in colloquial usage, *ru dar vāsi*) essentially means "tact" or "restraint," in which one refrains from saying something to someone one does not know well because it might embarrass them or cause one to lose face (*ru*). It is the opposite of *samimiat*: close friends do not have *ru dar bāyesti* between them, and will often state this as an invitation to more open communication, or as an assurance of their sincerity.

21. In Persian, she said *har che az del bar āyad lājaram bar del neshinad*, which is a common saying paraphrased from the last line of a classical poem by Sa'di, *Ke harch az jān berun āyad neshinad lājaram bar del* (Whatever emerges from the soul will naturally sit [well] in the heart).

22. See also a journal entry by one of Varzi's informants from 2000: "Psychologists have started telling us on the radio that it is better to speak than to hold things in, when they know we are in a place that speaking the truth has worse repercussions than social stigma—it could mean imprisonment, lashes" (2006: 159).

23. Several others of my Afghan friends had more than one name, and they used their religious or other connotations to reflect on different strands of their identities.

24. Prostitution is an increasingly common theme in Afghan refugee poetry of both men and women, and in fiction writing, such as in the short stories of Afghan author Mohammad Hossein Mohammadi, as a social reality that is often swept under the carpet by the state but that intellectuals feel the need to address. Ahmadzadeh notes that in the social realist Iranian novels of the reign of Reza Shah (the time between the two world wars), it was a common preoccupation of authors to show sympathy for female prostitutes, even if they were largely blamed for their own destinies (Ahmadzadeh 2003: 119). It was also a theme in the poetry of Simin Behbahani. It must also be noted that prostitution is reportedly common in Mashhad and is often morally spruced up as "temporary marriage" (*sigheh*), with men far more likely to admit to each other that they have been with a *zan-e sigheh'i* (a *sigheh* woman) than with a *ruspi* (prostitute). The niceties spoken by the man in the poem may be an attempt to give this veneer to the relation.

25. The word *pestān* is nonetheless apparently not seen as appropriate for publication in Iran, where another Afghan poet reported that it had been censored from the poetry collection she had submitted for a permit from the Ministry of Culture and Islamic Guidance.

Conclusion

1. Seen at the Kafka Museum in Prague, May 2006.

References

Abbasi-Shavazi, Mohammad Jalal, Diana Glazebrook, Gholamreza Jamshidiha, Hossein Mahmoudian, and Rasoul Sadeghi. 2005. *Return to Afghanistan? A Study of Afghans Living in Mashhad, Islamic Republic of Iran.* Kabul: Afghanistan Research and Evaluation Unit (October).
Abrahamian, Ervand. 2009. "Why the Islamic Republic Has Survived." *Middle East Report,* no. 250 (Spring): 10–16.
Abu-Lughod, Lila. 1986. *Veiled Sentiments: Honor and Poetry in a Bedouin Society.* Berkeley and Los Angeles: University of California Press.
Abu-Sahlieh, S. A. A. 1996. "The Islamic Conception of Migration." *International Migration Review* 30 (1): 37–57.
Adelkhah, Fariba. 1999. *Being Modern in Iran.* London: Hurst and Company, Centre d'Études et de Recherches Internationales.
———. 2009. "Islamophobia and Malaise in Anthropology." In *Conceptualizing Iranian Anthropology: Past and Present Perspectives,* edited by Shahnaz R. Nadjmabadi, 207–224. New York: Routledge.
Adelkhah, Fariba, and Zuzanna Olszewska. 2007. "The Iranian Afghans." *Iranian Studies* 40 (2): 137–165.
Afary, Janet. 2009. *Sexual Politics in Modern Iran.* Cambridge: Cambridge University Press.
Afghanistan Parliamentary Assistance Program (APAP). 2011. "WJ Investigates Censorship of Two Afghan Movies." *Legislative Newsletter* 6 (12): 1, http://www.cid.suny.edu/APAP_Newsletter/2011/APAP_Newsletter_October.21.11.pdf, 21 October.
Ahearn, Laura M. 2001. *Invitations to Love: Literacy, Love Letters and Social Change in Nepal.* Ann Arbor: University of Michigan Press.
Ahmadi, Arash. 2012. "Web Users Angry at Iranian Bid to Expel Afghans." BBC Monitoring, 4 May 2012, http://www.bbc.co.uk/news/world-middle-east-17954943.
Ahmadi, Wali. 2004a. "Exclusionary Poetics: Approaches to the Afghan 'Other' in Contemporary Iranian Literary Discourse." *Iranian Studies* 37 (3): 407–429.
———. 2004b. "The Institution of Persian Literature and the Genealogy of Bahar's *Stylistics.*" *British Journal of Middle Eastern Studies* 31 (2): 141–152.
———. 2008. *Modern Persian Literature in Afghanistan: Anomalous Visions of History and Form.* London: Routledge.
Ahmadzadeh, Hashem. 2003. *Nation and Novel: A Study of Persian and Kurdish Narrative Discourse.* Studia Iranica Upsaliensia 6. Uppsala, Sweden: Uppsala University.
Ajami, Fouad. 1998. *The Dream Palace of the Arabs: A Generation's Odyssey.* New York: Pantheon.
Akhavan, Niki. 2013. *Electronic Iran: The Cultural Politics of an Online Evolution.* New Brunswick, N.J.: Rutgers University Press.

Alexanian, Janet A. 2006. "Publicly Intimate Online: Iranian Weblogs in Southern California." *Comparative Studies of South Asia, Africa and the Middle East* 26 (1): 134–146.
Anderson, Ewan, and Nancy Hatch Dupree, eds. 1990. *The Cultural Basis of Afghan Nationalism.* London: Pinter.
Andrews, Walter, and Mehmet Kalpaklı. 2005. *The Age of Beloveds: Love and the Beloved in Early Modern Ottoman and European Culture and Society.* Durham, N.C.: Duke University Press.
Ansari, Z. I. 1990. "Hijrah in the Islamic Tradition." In Anderson and Dupree, *Cultural Basis of Afghan Nationalism,* 3–20.
Anushiravani, Alireza, and Kavoos Hassanli. 2007. "Trends in Contemporary Persian Poetry." In *Media, Culture and Society in Iran: Living with Globalization and the Islamic State,* edited by Mehdi Semati, 152–166. London: Routledge.
Appadurai, Arjun. 1996. *Modernity at Large: Cultural Dimensions of Globalization.* Minneapolis: University of Minnesota Press.
Appadurai, Arjun, Frank Korom, and Margaret Mills, eds. 1991. *Gender, Genre and Power in South Asian Expressive Traditions.* Philadelphia: Pennsylvania University Press.
Arbabzadah, Nushin. 2002. *Women and Cultural Patronage in the Timurid World.* MPhil thesis, Cambridge University.
Arberry, A. J. 1958. *Classical Persian Literature.* London: George Allen & Unwin.
Arnoldy, Ben. 2005. "Afghan Girls Kick Down Old Barriers." *Christian Science Monitor Online,* http://www.csmonitor.com/2005/0504/p01s03-wosc.html, 4 May 2005.
Atabaki, Touraj. 2008. "Constitutionalism in Iran and its Asian Dependencies." *Comparative Studies of Africa, South Asia and the Middle East* 28 (1): 142–153.
Azoy, Whitney. 2004. Introduction. In Khalilullah Khalili, *An Assembly of Moths,* translated by Whitney Azoy and Masood Khalili, 6–22. New Delhi: Jayyad Press.
Baily, John. 1988. *Music of Afghanistan: Professional Musicians in the City of Herat.* Cambridge: Cambridge University Press.
Baily, John, and Michael Collyer. 2006. "Introduction: Music and Migration." *Journal of Ethnic and Migration Studies* 32 (2): 167–182.
Bakhtin, Mikhail. 1981. *The Dialogic Imagination.* Austin: University of Texas Press.
———. 1986. "The Problem of Speech Genres." In *Speech Genres and Other Essays,* edited by Caryl Emerson and Michael Holquist, 60–102. Austin: University of Texas Press.
Balaghi, Shiva. 2009. "Cultural Policy in the Islamic Republic of Iran." *Middle East Report,* no. 250, 15.
Balland, Daniel. 1978. "La diaspora des Turcs de Basse-Asie centrale soviétique au XXe siècle." *Bulletin de la section de géographie* (Paris), no. 82, 23–38.
Barber, Karin. 1997. "Audiences in Africa." *Africa* 67 (3): 347–362.
———. ed. 2006a. *Africa's Hidden Histories: Everyday Literacy and Making the Self.* Bloomington: Indiana University Press.
———. 2006b. "Introduction: Hidden Innovators in Africa." In Barber, *Africa's Hidden Histories,* 1–24.
———. 2007. *The Anthropology of Texts, Persons and Publics: Oral and Written Culture in Africa and Beyond.* Cambridge: Cambridge University Press.

Barkan, Elazar, and Marie-Denise Shelton, eds. 1998. *Borders, Exiles, Diasporas.* Stanford, Calif.: Stanford University Press.
Bayat, Asef. 2010. "Tehran: Paradox City." *New Left Review* 2 (66): 99–122.
Beck, Lois, and Julia Huang. 2006. "Manipulating Private Lives and Public Spaces in Qashqa'i Society in Iran." *Comparative Studies of South Asia, Africa and the Middle East* 26 (2): 303–325.
Bečka, Jiří. 1968. "Tajik Literature from the 16th Century to the Present." In *History of Iranian Literature,* edited by Jan Rypka, 483–605. Dordrecht, Netherlands: D. Reidel.
Beeman, William O. 1986. *Language, Status, and Power in Iran.* Bloomington: Indiana University Press.
——. 2001. "Emotion and Sincerity in Persian Discourse: Accomplishing the Representation of Inner States." *International Journal of the Sociology of Linguistics,* no. 148, 31–57.
Behrouzan, Orkideh. 2010. *Prozàk Diaries: Post-Rupture Subjectivities and Psychiatric Futures.* PhD diss., Massachusetts Institute of Technology.
——. 2015. "Writing *Prozàk* Diaries in Tehran: Generational Anomie and Psychiatric Subjectivities." *Culture, Medicine, and Psychiatry* 39 (3).
Bell, Gertrude Lowthian. 1928 [1897]. Introduction. In *Poems from the Divan of Hafiz,* translated by Gertrude Lowthian Bell, 25–81. London: William Heinemann.
Betteridge, Anne H. 1985. "Gift Exchange in Iran: The Locus of Self-Identity in Social Interaction." *Anthropological Quarterly* 58 (4): 190–202.
Bhabha, Homi. 1990. "The Third Space." In *Identity: Community, Culture, Difference,* edited by Jonathan Rutherford, 207–221. London: Lawrence and Wishart.
Biehl, João, Byron Good, and Arthur Kleinman. 2007. "Introduction: Rethinking Subjectivity." In Biehl, Good, and Kleinman, *Subjectivity: Ethnographic Investigations,* 1–23.
Bill, James A. 1973. "The Plasticity of Informal Politics: The Case of Iran." *Middle East Journal* 27 (2): 131–151.
Boesen, Inger W. 1983. "Conflicts of Solidarity in Pakhtun Women's Lives." In *Women and Islamic Societies: Social Attitudes and Historical Perspectives,* edited by Bo Utas, 104–127. London: Curzon Press.
Booth, Marilyn, ed. 2011. *Harem Histories: Envisioning Places and Living Spaces.* Durham, N.C.: Duke University Press.
Boroujerdi, Mehrzad. 1996. *Iranian Intellectuals and the West: The Tormented Triumph of Nativism.* Syracuse, N.Y.: Syracuse University Press.
Bosniak, Linda. 2006. *The Citizen and the Alien: Dilemmas of Contemporary Membership.* Princeton, N.J.: Princeton University Press.
Bourdieu, Pierre. 1977. *Outline of a Theory of Practice.* Cambridge: Cambridge University Press.
——. 1984. *Distinction: A Social Critique of the Judgment of Taste.* Cambridge, Mass.: Harvard University Press.
——. 1990. "The Kabyle House or the World Reversed." In *The Logic of Practice,* 271–283. Cambridge, U.K.: Polity Press.
——. 1993. *The Field of Cultural Production: Essays on Art and Literature.* Cambridge, U.K.: Polity Press.

———. 1993 [1983]. "The Field of Cultural Production, or: The Economic World Reversed." In *The Field of Cultural Production: Essays on Art and Literature*, 29–73. Cambridge, U.K.: Polity Press.

———. 1996. *The Rules of Art: Genesis and Structure of the Literary Field*. Cambridge, U.K.: Polity Press.

Bowen, John R. 1991. *Sumatran Politics and Poetics: Gayo History, 1900–1989*. New Haven, Conn.: Yale University Press.

Bowman, Glenn. 1994. "'A Country of Words': Conceiving the Palestinian Nation from the Position of Exile." In *The Making of Political Identities*, edited by Ernesto Laclau, 138–170. London: Verso.

Bromberger, Christian. 2008. "Hair: From the West to the Middle East through the Mediterranean." *Journal of American Folklore* 121 (482): 379–399.

Brookshaw, Dominic P. 2003. "Palaces, Pavilions and Pleasure-Gardens: The Context and Setting of the Medieval Majlis." *Middle Eastern Literatures* 6 (2): 199–223.

———. 2005. "Odes of a Poet-Princess: The Ghazals of Jahan-Malik Khatun." *Iran: Journal of the British Institute of Persian Studies* 43: 173–195.

———. 2008. "Revivification of an Ossified Genre? Simin Behbahani and the Persian Ghazal." *Iranian Studies* 44 (1): 75–90.

———. 2009. "Love and Desire in Pre-Modern Persian Poetry and Prose." *Iranian Studies* 42 (5): 673–675.

———. 2013. "Women in Praise of Women: Female Poets and Female Patrons in Qajar Iran." *Iranian Studies* 46 (1): 17–48.

Brookshaw, Dominic P., and Nasrin Rahimieh, eds. 2010. *Forugh Farrokhzad, Poet of Modern Iran: Iconic Woman and Feminine Pioneer of New Persian Poetry*. London: I. B. Tauris.

Browne, Edward G. 1906. *A Literary History of Persia from Firdawsi to Saʻdi*. London: T. Fisher Unwin.

———. 1914. *The Press and Poetry of Modern Persia*. Cambridge: Cambridge University Press.

———. 1924. *A History of Persian Literature in Modern Times (^{ad} 1500–1924)*. Cambridge: Cambridge University Press.

de Bruijn, J. T. P. 1997. *Persian Sufi Poetry: An Introduction to the Mystical Use of Classical Persian Poems*. Richmond, U.K.: Curzon Press.

Buchta, Wilfried. 2002. "The Failed Pan-Islamic Program of the Islamic Republic: Views of the Liberal Reformers of the Religious 'Semi-Opposition.'" In Keddie and Mathee, *Iran and the Surrounding World*, 281–304.

Busby, Cecilia. 1997. "Permeable and Partible Persons: A Comparative Analysis of Gender and Body in South India and Melanesia." *Journal of the Royal Anthropological Institute* 3 (2): 261–278.

Butler, Judith. 1990. *Gender Trouble: Feminism and the Subversion of Identity*. London: Routledge.

Canfield, Robert. 2004. "New Trends among the Hazaras: From 'The Amity of Wolves' to 'The Practice of Brotherhood.'" *Iranian Studies* 37 (2): 241–262.

Cannell, Fenella. 1999. *Power and Intimacy in the Christian Philippines*. Cambridge: Cambridge University Press.

Caron, James. 2013. "Ambiguities of Orality and Literacy, Territory and Border Crossings: Public Activism and Pashto Literature in Afghanistan, 1930–2010." In Green and Arbabzadah, *Afghanistan in Ink*, 113–139.
Carrithers, Michael, Steven Collins, and Steven Lukes, eds. 1985. *The Category of the Person: Anthropology, Philosophy, History.* Cambridge: Cambridge University Press.
Caton, Steven C. 1990. *"Peaks of Yemen I Summon": Poetry as Cultural Practice in a North Yememi Tribe.* Berkeley and Los Angeles: University of California Press.
Centlivres, Pierre, and Micheline Centlivres-Demont. 1988 [1983]. "Frontières et phénomènes migratoires de 1880 à nos jours." In *Et si on parlait de l'Afghanistan? Terrains et textes, 1964–1980,* 247–274. Paris: Maison des Sciences de l'Homme. Neuchâtel: Editions de l'Institut d'Ethnologie.
———. 2000. "Exil et diaspora afghane en Suisse et en Europe." *Cahiers d'Etudes sur la Méditerranée Orientale et le Monde Turco-Iranien* 30, *Les Diasporas*: 151–172.
Chatty, Dawn, and Gina Crivello, eds. 2005. *Lessons Learned Report—Children and Adolescents in Sahrawi and Afghan Refugee Households: Living with the Effects of Prolonged Armed Conflict and Forced Migration.* Oxford, U.K.: Refugee Studies Centre.
Chatty, Dawn, and Bill Finlayson, eds. 2010. *Dispossession and Displacement: Forced Migration in the Middle East and North Africa.* Oxford: Oxford University Press/British Academy.
Cole, Jennifer, and Lynn M. Thomas. 2009. *Love in Africa.* Chicago: University of Chicago Press.
Colville, Rupert. 1997. "The Biggest Caseload in the World." *Refugees* (Geneva: UNHCR) 108 (2): 3–9.
Coutin, Susan Bibler. 2011. "Prohibited Realities and Fractured Persons: Remaking Lives in Transnational Spaces." *Issues in Legal Scholarship* 9 (1).
Dabashi, Hamid. 1985. "The Poetics of Politics: Commitment in Modern Persian Literature." *Iranian Studies* 18 (2–4): 147–188.
———. 2001. *Close Up: Iranian Cinema, Past, Present, and Future.* New York: Verso.
———. 2004. "Blindness and Insight: The Predicament of a Muslim Intellectual." In *Iran: Between Tradition and Modernity,* edited by Ramin Jahanbegloo, 95–116. Lanham, Md.: Lexington Books.
———. 2007. *Masters and Masterpieces of Iranian Cinema.* Washington, D.C.: Mage Publishers.
Daniel, E. Valentine, and J. C. Knudsen, eds. 1995. *Mistrusting Refugees.* Berkeley: University of California Press.
Das, Veena, and Deborah Poole. 2004. "State and Its Margins: Comparative Ethnographies." In *Anthropology in the Margins of the State,* edited by Veena Das and Deborah Poole, 3–33. Santa Fe, N.M.: School of American Research Press/Oxford: James Currey.
Deeb, Lara. 2006. *An Enchanted Modern: Gender and Public Piety in Shi'i Lebanon.* Princeton, N.J.: Princeton University Press.
De Genova, Nicholas. 2002. "Migrant 'Illegality' and Deportability in Everyday Life." *Annual Review of Anthropology* 31: 419–447.
———. 2004. "The Legal Production of Mexican/Migrant 'Illegality.'" *Latino Studies,* no. 2, 160–185.

———. 2010. "The Deportation Regime: Sovereignty, Space, and the Freedom of Movement." In De Genova and Peutz, *Deportation Regime*, 33–65.
De Genova, Nicholas, and Nathalie Peutz, eds. 2010. *The Deportation Regime: Sovereignty, Space, and the Freedom of Movement*. Durham, N.C.: Duke University Press.
Derrida, Jacques. 2001. "Hostipitality." In *Acts of Religion*, edited by Jacques Derrida and Gil Anidjar, 356–420. London: Routledge.
Donnan, Hastings, and Thomas M. Wilson. 1999. *Borders: Frontiers of Identity, Nation and State*. Oxford, U.K.: Berg.
Doostdar, Alireza. 2004. "'The Vulgar Spirit of Blogging': On Language, Culture, and Power in Persian Weblogestan." *American Anthropologist* 106 (4): 651–662.
Dorronsoro, Gilles. 2000. *La révolution afghane. Des communistes aux taleban*. Paris: Karthala.
Doubleday, Veronica. 2006. *Three Women of Herat*. London: Tauris Parke Paperbacks
Dresch, Paul. 2000. "Wilderness of Mirrors: Truth and Vulnerability in Middle Eastern Fieldwork." In *Anthropologists in a Wider World: Essays on Field Research*, edited by Paul Dresch, Wendy James, and David Parkin, 109–127. New York: Berghahn.
Dumont, Louis. 1970. *Homo Hierarchicus: The Caste System and Its Implications*. Chicago: University of Chicago Press.
Dupree, Louis. 1980. *Afghanistan*. Princeton, N.J.: Princeton University Press.
Eagleton, Terry. 1985. "The Subject of Literature." *Cultural Critique*, no. 2, 95–104.
———. 1990. *The Ideology of the Aesthetic*. Oxford, U.K.: Blackwell.
Ebadi, Shirin. 2008. *Refugee Rights in Iran*. London: UNHCR/Saqi.
Edwards, David B. 1986a. "Marginality and Migration: Cultural Dimensions of the Afghan Refugee Problem." *International Migration Review* 20 (2): 313–325.
———. 1986b. *Pretexts of Rebellion: The Cultural Origins of Pakhtun Resistance to the Afghan State*. PhD diss., University of Michigan.
———. 1996. *Heroes of the Age: Moral Fault Lines on the Afghan Frontier*. Berkeley and Los Angeles: University of California Press.
Eickelman, Dale. 1978. "The Art of Memory: Islamic Education and its Social Reproduction." *Comparative Studies in Society and History* 20 (4): 485–516.
———. 1992. "Mass Higher Education and the Religious Imagination in Contemporary Arab Societies." *American Ethnologist* 19 (4): 643–655.
———. 2002. *The Middle East and Central Asia: An Anthropological Approach*. 4th ed. Upper Saddle River, N.J.: Prentice Hall.
Eickelman, Dale, and James Piscatori. 2004. *Muslim Politics*. 2nd ed. Princeton, N.J.: Princeton University Press.
Elphinstone, Mountstuart. 1839. *An Account of the Kingdom of Caubul*. 2nd ed. London: Richard Bentley.
Emadi, Hafizullah. 1997. "The Hazaras and Their Role in the Process of Political Transformation of Afghanistan." *Central Asian Survey* 16 (3): 363–387.
Fabian, Johannes. 2002. *Time and the Other*. New York: Columbia University Press.
Faiz, Faiz Ahmed. 1995. *The Rebel's Silhouette: Selected Poems*. Translated by Agha Shahid Ali. Amherst: University of Massachusetts Press.
Fakhry, Majid. 2002. *Al-Farabi: Founder of Islamic Neoplatonism: His Life, Works and Influence*. Oxford, U.K.: Oneworld.
Fanger, Donald. 1965. *Dostoevsky and Romantic Realism: A Study of Dostoevsky in Relation to Balzac, Dickens and Gogol*. Cambridge, Mass.: Harvard University Press.

Fanon, Frantz. 1967. *Black Skin, White Masks.* Translated by Charles Lam Markmann. New York: Grove Press.
Farhi, Farideh. 2005. "Crafting a National Identity Amidst Contentious Politics in Contemporary Iran." *Iranian Studies* 38 (1): 7–22.
Finnegan, Ruth. 1988. *Literacy and Orality: Studies in the Technology of Communication.* Oxford, U.K.: Basil Blackwell.
Fischer, Michael M. J. 1980. *Iran: From Religious Dispute to Revolution.* Cambridge, Mass.: Harvard University Press.
———. 2004. *Mute Dreams, Blind Owls, and Dispersed Knowledges: Persian Poesis in the Transnational Circuitry.* Durham, N.C.: Duke University Press.
Fischer, Michael M. J., and Mehdi Abedi. 1990. *Debating Muslims: Cultural Dialogues in Postmodernity and Tradition.* Madison: University of Wisconsin Press.
Fish, Stanley. 1976. "Interpreting the *Variorum.*" *Critical Inquiry* 2 (3): 465–485.
Fisk, Robert. 2008. "Making Movies the Afghan Way." *Independent,* http://www.independent.co.uk/voices/commentators/fisk/robert-fisk-making-movies-the-afghan-way-1027758.html, 20 November 2008.
Foucault, Michel. 1982. "Afterword: The Subject and Power." In *Michel Foucault: Beyond Structuralism and Hermeneutics,* edited by Hubert L. Dreyfus and Paul Rabinow, 208–226. Chicago: University of Chicago Press.
———. 1984. "The Ethics of the Concern of the Self as a Practice of Freedom." *Philosophy and Social Criticism* 12 (2/3): 112–131.
———. 1986. "Of Other Spaces." *Diacritics* 16 (1): 22–27.
———. 1988. *Technologies of the Self: A Seminar with Michel Foucault.* Edited by Luther H. Martin, Huck Gutman, and Patrick H. Hutton, 16–49. Amherst: University of Massachusetts Press.
Fox, Kate. 2005. *Watching the English: The Hidden Rules of English Behaviour.* London: Hodder & Stoughton.
Foyouzat, Forugh. 1996. "Report on Visit to Mashhad." Tehran: ICRI, 18 August 1996.
Fragner, Bert G. 1999. *Die "Persophonie": Regionalität, Identität und Sprachkontakt in der Geschichte.* Berlin-Charlottenburg: Das Arabische Buch.
Friedl, Erika. 2009. "New Friends: Gender Relations within the Family." *Iranian Studies* 42 (1): 27–43.
Fussell, Paul. 1975. *The Great War and Modern Memory.* London: Oxford University Press.
Gardner, Katy. 1995. *Global Migrants, Local Lives: Travel and Transformation in Rural Bangladesh.* Oxford: Oxford University Press.
Gavron, Kate. 1996. "Du mariage arrangé au mariage d'amour." *Terrain* 27 (September): 15–26.
Gawęcki, Marek. 1983. *Wieś środkowego i północnego Afganistanu: Tradycja i próby modernizacji* [The Village in Central and Northern Afghanistan: Tradition and Modernisation Efforts]. Wrocław, Poland: Polskie Towarzystwo Ludoznawcze.
Geertz, Clifford. 1973a. "Person, Time and Conduct in Bali." In *The Interpretation of Cultures,* 360–411. New York: Basic Books.
———. 1973b. "Religion as a Cultural System." In *The Interpretation of Cultures,* 87–125. New York: Basic Books.
———. 1980. *Negara.* Cambridge: Cambridge University Press.

———. 1984 [1974]. "'From the Natives' Point of View': On the Nature of Anthropological Understanding." In *Culture Theory,* edited by Richard A. Shweder and Robert A. LeVine, 123–136. Cambridge: Cambridge University Press.
Gell, Alfred. 1998. *Art and Agency: An Anthropological Theory.* Oxford: Oxford University Press.
———. 2011. "On Love." *Anthropology of This Century,* no. 2, http://aotcpress.com/articles/love/.
van Gennep, Arnold. 1960. *The Rites of Passage.* London: Routledge & Kegan Paul.
Ghani, Ashraf. 1988. "The Persian Literature of Afghanistan, 1911–78, in the Context of Its Political and Intellectual History." In *Persian Literature,* edited by Ehsan Yarshater, 428–543. Albany, N.J.: Persian Heritage Foundation/SUNY Press.
Gheissari, Ali. 1997. *Iranian Intellectuals in the Twentieth Century.* Austin: University of Texas Press.
Giddens, Anthony. 1991. *Modernity and Self-Identity: Self and Society in the Late Modern Age.* Stanford, Calif.: Stanford University Press.
———. 1992. *The Transformation of Intimacy: Sexuality, Love and Eroticism in Modern Societies.* Cambridge, U.K.: Polity.
Glazebrook, Diana, and Mohammad Jalal Abbasi-Shavazi. 2007. "Being Neighbors to Imam Reza: Pilgrimage Practices and Return Intentions of Hazara Afghans Living in Mashhad, Iran." *Iranian Studies* 40 (2): 187–201.
Goffman, Irving. 1956. *The Presentation of Self in Everyday Life.* Edinburgh: University of Edinburgh.
Good, Byron J. 1977. "The Heart of What's the Matter: The Semantics of Illness in Iran." *Culture, Medicine and Psychiatry* 1 (1): 25–58.
Good, Mary-Jo DelVecchio, and Byron J. Good. 1988. "Ritual, the State, and the Transformation of Emotional Discourse in Iranian Society." *Culture, Medicine and Psychiatry* 12: 43–63.
Gow, Greg. 2002. *The Oromo in Exile: From the Horn of Africa to the Suburbs of Australia.* Melbourne: Melbourne University Press.
Graham, Mark, and Shahram Khosravi. 2002. "Reordering Public and Private in Iranian Cyberspace: Identity, Politics, and Mobilization." *Identities* 9 (2): 219–246.
Gramsci, Antonio. 1971. *Selections from the Prison Notebooks.* Translated and edited by Quintin Hoare and Geoffrey Nowell. New York: International Publishers.
———. 1985. *Selections from Cultural Writings.* Translated by William Boelhower. Cambridge, Mass.: Harvard University Press.
Green, Nile. 2013. "Introduction: Afghan Literature between Diaspora and Nation." In Green and Arbabzadah, *Afghanistan in Ink,* 1–30.
Green, Nile, and Nushin Arbabzadah, eds. 2013. *Afghanistan in Ink: Literature between Diaspora and Nation.* London: Hurst.
Grima, Benedicte. 1992. *The Performance of Emotion among Paxtun Women: "The Misfortunes Which Have Befallen Me."* Austin: University of Texas Press.
Hanifi, M. J. 2000. "Anthropology and the Representation of Recent Migrations from Afghanistan." In *Rethinking Refuge and Displacement: Selected Papers on Refugees and Immigrants,* edited by E. M. Gozdziak and D. J. Shandy, 8:291–321. Arlington, Va.: American Anthropological Association.
Harpviken, Kristian Berg. 1995. *Political Mobilization among the Hazaras of Afghanistan: 1978–1992.* Cand. polit. thesis, University of Oslo.

Harris, Clare. 1999. *In the Image of Tibet: Tibetan Painting after 1959.* London: Reaktion Books.
Harris, Kevan. 2012. "The Brokered Exuberance of the Middle Class: An Ethnographic Analysis of Iran's 2009 Green Movement." *Mobilization: An International Journal* 17 (4): 435–455.
Harrison, Frances. 2004. "Iran's Afghan Refugees Feel Pressure to Leave." BBC News World Edition, http://news.bbc.co.uk/2/hi/middle_east/3971711.stm, 1 November 2004.
Hashemi, Sayed Wahed. 2011. "Afghan Children Deported Alone from Iran." *Institute of War and Peace Reporting,* ARR issue 393, http://iwpr.net/report-news/afghan-children-deported-alone-iran, 17 March.
Hegland, Mary E. 2009. "Educating Young Women: Culture, Conflict and New Identities in an Iranian Village." *Iranian Studies* 42 (1): 45–79.
Herzfeld, Michael. 1997. *Cultural Intimacy: Social Poetics in the Nation-State.* New York: Routledge.
Heston, Wilma. 1991. "Footpath Poets of Peshawar." In Appadurai, Korom, and Mills, *Gender, Genre and Power in South Asian Expressive Traditions,* 305–343.
Higgins, Patricia, and Pirouz Shoar-Ghaffari. 1994. "Women's Education in the Islamic Republic of Iran." In *In the Eye of the Storm: Women in Post-Revolutionary Iran,* edited by Mahnaz Afkhami and Erika Friedl, 19–43. London: I. B. Tauris.
Hirsch, Jennifer S., and Holly Wardlow, eds. 2006. *Modern Loves: The Anthropology of Romantic Courtship and Companionate Marriage.* Ann Arbor: University of Michigan Press.
Hoodfar, Homa. 1996. "Bargaining with Fundamentalism: Women and the Politics of Population Control in Iran." *Reproductive Health Matters,* no. 8 (November): 30–40.
———. 1997. *Between Marriage and the Market: Intimate Politics and Survival in Cairo.* Berkeley: University of California Press.
———. 2004. "Families on the Move: The Changing Role of Afghan Refugee Women in Iran." *Hawwa* 2 (2): 141–171.
———. 2009. "Activism under the Radar: Volunteer Women Health Workers in Iran." *Middle East Report,* no. 250, 56–60.
———. 2010. "Refusing the Margins: Afghan Refugee Youth in Iran." In *Deterritorialized Youth: Sahrawi and Afghan Refugees at the Margins of the Middle East,* edited by Dawn Chatty, 145–182. Oxford: Berghahn.
Hooglund, Eric. 2009. "Thirty Years of Islamic Revolution in Rural Iran." *Middle East Report,* no. 250, 34–39.
Houshmand, Zara. 2007. "Bijan Mofid from *The Moon and the Leopard.*" *Words without Borders: The Online Magazine for International Literature,* http://wordswithout borders.org/article/from-the-moon-and-the-leopard, accessed 27 February 2015.
Huang, Julia. 2009. *Tribeswomen of Iran: Weaving Memories Among Qashqa'i Nomads.* London: I. B. Tauris.
Human Rights Watch (HRW). 2002. *Closed Door Policy: Afghan Refugees in Pakistan and Iran* (New York: Human Rights Watch) 14 (2).
Hunsberger, Alice C. 2000. *Nasir Khusraw, The Ruby of Badakhshan: A Portrait of the Persian Poet, Traveller and Philosopher.* London: I. B. Tauris/Institute of Ismaili Studies.

Ibrahimi, Nematullah. 2006. *The Failure of a Clerical Proto-State: Hazarajat, 1979–1984.* Crisis States Research Centre Working Paper No. 6. London: London School of Economics.

International Consortium for Refugees in Iran (ICRI). 1998. "Afghan Women and Children in Iran: A Study of Hard Work and Hope." Report prepared for UNICEF. Tehran: ICRI.

———. 1999. *Report on Developments in the Refugee Situation in Iran.* Tehran: ICRI.

Integrated Regional Information Network (IRIN). 2004. "Iran: Interview with UNHCR Head to Mark the Return of One Million Afghan Refugees," UNOCHA, http://www.irinnews.org/report.asp?ReportID=42985&SelectRegion=Central_Asia, 2 September 2004.

———. 2005. "Afghanistan-Iran: UNHCR Concerned Over Wave of Refugee Arrests." UNOCHA, http://www.irinnews.org/report.asp?ReportID=45021&SelectRegion=Central_Asia&SelectCountry=AFGHANISTAN-IRAN, 12 January 2005.

———. 2007a. "Afghanistan-Iran: Afghan refugees given repatriation extension." UNOCHA, http://www.irinnews.org/report.aspx?ReportId=70450, 28 February 2007.

———. 2007b. "Afghanistan-Iran: Iran Deports Thousands of Illegal Afghan Workers." UNOCHA, http://www.irinnews.org/Report.aspx?ReportId=71865, 30 April 2007.

———. 2007c. "Zahraa, 'I Was Told to Leave My Home for Good within One Hour.'" UNOCHA, http://www.irinnews.org/HOVReport.aspx?ReportId=72149, May 2007.

———. 2007d. "Afghanistan-Iran: UN, Afghan Government Call for Humane Deportations from Iran." UNOCHA, http://www.irinnews.org/Report.aspx?ReportId=72127, 14 May.

———. 2007e. "Afghanistan-Iran: Afghan Deportees Complain of Lack of Aid." UNOCHA, http://www.irinnews.org/Report.aspx?ReportId=73721, 14 August.

———. 2008. "Afghanistan: Stream of Deportees from Iran Continues." UNOCHA, http://www.irinnews.org/report.aspx?ReportId=78881, 23 June.

Jahanbegloo, Ramin. 2000. "Is Iran Democratizing? The Role of the Intellectuals." *Journal of Democracy* 11 (4): 135–138.

———. 2004. "Introduction." In *Iran: Between Tradition and Modernity*, edited by Ramin Jahanbegloo, ix–xxiii. Lanham, Md.: Lexington Books.

Jakobson, Roman. 1960. "Concluding Statement: Linguistics and Poetics." In *Style in Language*, edited by T. Sebeok, 350–377. Cambridge, Mass.: MIT Press.

Jankowiak, William, and Edward Fischer. 1992. "A Cross-Cultural Perspective on Romantic Love." *Ethnology* 31 (2): 149–155.

Johnson, Randal. 1993. "Editor's Introduction: Pierre Bourdieu on Art, Literature and Culture." In Pierre Bourdieu, *The Field of Cultural Production*, 1–25. Cambridge, U.K.: Polity Press.

Kakar, M. Hassan. 1995. *Afghanistan: The Soviet Invasion and the Afghan Response, 1979–82.* Berkeley and Los Angeles: University of California Press.

Kalinock, Sabine. 2003. "Between Party and Devotion: *Mowludi* of Tehran Women." *Critique: Critical Middle Eastern Studies* 12 (2): 173–187.

———. 2004. "Touching a Sensitive Topic: Research on Shiite Rituals of Women in Tehran." *Iranian Studies* 37 (4): 665–674.

Kamal, Sarah. 2010. "Repatriation and Reconstruction: Afghan Youth as a 'Burnt Generation' in Post-Conflict Return." In Chatty and Finlayson, *Dispossession and Displacement*, 147–167.
Kamalkhani, Zahra. 1993. "Women's Everyday Religious Discourse in Iran." In *Women in the Middle East: Perceptions, Realities and Struggles for Liberation*, edited by Haleh Afshar, 85–95. Basingstoke, London: Macmillan.
Kamrava, Mehran. 2008. *Iran's Intellectual Revolution*. Cambridge: Cambridge University Press.
Kantor, Paula, and Mamiko Saito. 2010. "From Mohajer to Hamwatan: The Reintegration Experiences of Second Generation Afghans Returning from Neighboring Countries." In Chatty and Finlayson, *Dispossession and Displacement*, 123–145.
Karami, Arash, and Negar Mortazavi. 2012. "Afghans to be Expelled from Iranian Tourism Province." *PBS Frontline Tehran Bureau*, http://www.pbs.org/wgbh/pages/frontline/tehranbureau/2012/04/behind-the-curtain-afghans-to-be-expelled-from-iranian-tourism-province.html, 26 April 2012.
Karimi-Hakkak, Ahmad. 1985. "Of Hail and Hounds: The Image of the Iranian Revolution in Recent Persian Literature." *State, Culture and Society* 1 (3): 148–180.
———. 1986. "Poetry against Piety: The Literary Response to the Iranian Revolution." *World Literature Today* 60 (2): 251–256.
———. 1991. "Revolutionary Posturing: Iranian Writers and the Iranian Revolution of 1979." *International Journal of Middle East Studies* 23 (4): 507–531.
———. 1992. "Censorship." *Encyclopedia Iranica*, 5:135–142. Costa Mesa, Calif.: Mazda Publishers.
———. 1994. "Authors and Authorities: Censorship and Literary Communication in Post-Revolution Iran." In *Persian Studies in North America: Studies in Honor of Mohammad Ali Jazayery*, edited by Mehdi Marashi, 307–338. Bethesda, Md.: Iranbooks.
———. 1995. *Recasting Persian Poetry: Scenarios of Poetic Modernity in Iran*. Salt Lake City: University of Utah Press.
———. 1997. "Introduction: Iran's Literature 1977–1997." *Iranian Studies* 30 (3): 193–213.
Kashani-Sabet, Firoozeh. 1999. *Frontier Fictions: Shaping the Iranian Nation, 1804–1946*. London: I. B. Tauris.
———. 2002. "Cultures of Iranianness: The Evolving Polemic of Iranian Nationalism." In Keddie and Mathee, *Iran and the Surrounding World*, 162–181.
Katouzian, Homa. 2006. *Sa'di: The Poet of Life, Love and Compassion*. Oxford, U.K.: Oneworld.
Keddie, Nikkie R. 2006. *Modern Iran: Roots and Results of Revolution*. New Haven, Conn.: Yale University Press.
Keddie, Nikki R., and Rudi Mathee, eds. 2002. *Iran and the Surrounding World: Interactions in Culture and Cultural Politics*. Seattle: University of Washington Press.
Keshavarz, Fatemeh. 1998. *Reading Mystical Lyric: The Case of Jalal al-Din Rumi*. Columbia: University of South Carolina Press.
———. 2007. *Jasmine and Stars: Reading More than Lolita in Tehran*. Chapel Hill: University of North Carolina Press.
Khosravi, Shahram. 2008. *Young and Defiant in Tehran*. Philadelphia: University of Pennsylvania Press.

Khosronejad, Pedram, ed. 2012. *Iranian Sacred Defence Cinema: Religion, Martyrdom and National Identity*. Canon Pyon, U.K.: Sean Kingston Publishing.

———. 2013. *Unburied Bodies: The Politics of Bodies of Sacred Defense Martyrs in Iran*. London: Routledge.

Labdaoui, Abdellah. 1993. *Les nouveaux intellectuels arabes*. Paris: L'Harmattan.

Laidlaw, James. 2002. "For an Anthropology of Ethics and Freedom." *Journal of the Royal Anthropological Institute* 8 (2): 311–332.

Lambek, Michael, and Andrew Strathern, eds. 1998. *Bodies and Persons: Comparative Perspectives from Africa and Indonesia*. Cambridge: Cambridge University Press.

Lave, Jean, and Etienne Wenger. 1991. *Situated Learning: Legitimate Peripheral Participation*. Cambridge: Cambridge University Press.

Lavie, Smadar. 1991. *The Poetics of Military Occupation: Mzeina Allegories of Bedouin Identity under Israeli and Egyptian Rule*. Berkeley: University of California Press.

Leach, Edmund. 1976. *Culture and Communication: The Logic by Which Symbols are Connected*. Cambridge: Cambridge University Press.

Lewis, Franklin D. 1994. "The Rise and Fall of a Persian Refrain." In Stetkevych, *Reorientations*, 199–226.

Lewisohn, Leonard. 2010. *Hafiz and the Religion of Love in Classical Persian Poetry*. London: I. B. Tauris.

Lindholm, Charles. 2005. "An Anthropology of Emotion." In *A Companion to Psychological Anthropology: Modernity and Psychocultural Change*, edited by C. Casey and R. Edgerton, 30–47. Oxford, U.K.: Blackwell.

LiPuma, Edward. 1998. "Modernity and Forms of Personhood in Melanesia." In Lambek and Strathern, *Bodies and Persons*, 53–79.

Loescher, Gil. 2001. *The UNHCR and World Politics: A Perilous Path*. Oxford: Oxford University Press.

Losensky, Paul. 1994. "'The Allusive Field of Drunkenness': Three Safavid-Moghul Responses to a Lyric by Baba Fighani." In Stetkevych, *Reorientations*, 227–262.

———. 1997. Translator's Note to "Elegies for a Lost Leader: Six Poems on the Death of Khomeini." *Iranian Studies* 30 (3/4): 277–279.

Mahdavi, Pardis. 2009. *Passionate Uprisings: Iran's Sexual Revolution*. Stanford, Calif.: Stanford University Press.

Mahmood, Saba. 2005. *The Politics of Piety: The Islamic Revival and the Feminist Subject*. Princeton, N.J.: Princeton University Press.

Majrouh, Sayd Bahodine. 2003. *Songs of Love and War: Afghan Women's Poetry*. New York: Other Press.

Makhmalbaf Film House. 2003. "An Interview with Samira Makhmalbaf for the Movie 5 in the Afternoon in the Cannes Film Festival 2003." http://www.makhmalbaf.com/articles.php?a=379.

Malkki, Liisa. 1995a. *Purity and Exile: Violence, Memory, and National Cosmology among Hutu Refugees in Tanzania*. Chicago: University of Chicago Press.

———. 1995b. "Refugees and Exile: From 'Refugee Studies' to the National Order of Things." *Annual Review of Anthropology* 24: 495–523.

———. 1996. "Speechless Emissaries: Refugees, Humanitarianism, and Dehistoricization." *Cultural Anthropology* 11 (3): 377–404.

Manoukian, Setrag. 2004. "Culture, Power and Poetry in Shiraz." *International Institute for the Study of Islam in the Modern World ISIM. Newsletter* 14 (June): 40–41.

———. 2011. *City of Knowledge in Twentieth Century Iran: Shiraz, History and Poetry*. London: Routledge.
Marriott, McKim. 1976. "Hindu Transactions: Diversity without Dualism." In *Transaction and Meaning: Directions in the Anthropology of Exchange and Symbolic Behavior*, edited by Bruce Kapferer, 109–142. Philadelphia, Pa.: Ishi Press.
Matin-Asgari, Afshin. 2004. "Iranian Postmodernity: The Rhetoric of Irrationality?" *Critical Middle Eastern Studies* 13 (1): 113–123.
Mauss, Marcel. 1985 [1938]. "A Category of the Human Mind: The Notion of Person; the Notion of Self." In Carrithers, Collins, and Lukes, *Category of the Person*, 1–25.
Media Watch Afghanistan. 2006. *Journalism Freedom Report, March and April 2006*. Kabul: Nai Supporting Afghanistan Open Media, vol. 11 (24 May).
Mehran, Golnar. 2002. "The Presentation of the 'Self' and the 'Other' in Postrevolutionary Iranian School Textbooks." In Keddie and Mathee, *Iran and the Surrounding World*, 232–253.
———. 2007. "Iran: A Shi'ite Curriculum to Serve the Islamic State." In *Teaching Islam: Textbooks and Religion in the Middle East*, edited by Eleanor Abdella Doumato and Gregory Starrett, 53–70. Boulder, Colo.: Lynne Rienner.
Mehryar, Amir H., Shahla Kazemipour, Hassan Eini-Zinab, and Bahram Delavar. 2004. *Migration and Reproductive Health in Iran*. Working Papers in English No. 11. Tehran: Regional Centre for Population Studies and Research in Asia and the Pacific.
Meisami, Julie Scott. 1987. *Medieval Persian Court Poetry*. Princeton, N.J.: Princeton University Press.
Messick, Brinkley. 1993. *The Calligraphic State: Textual Domination and History in a Muslim Society*. Berkeley: University of California Press.
Milani, Farzaneh. 1985. "Power, Prudence, and Print: Censorship and Simin Danashvar." *Iranian Studies* 18 (2–4): 325–346.
———. 1992. *Veils and Words: The Emerging Voices of Iranian Women Writers*. Syracuse, N.Y.: Syracuse University Press.
Miller, W. Flagg. 2002. "Public Words and Body Politics: Reflections on the Strategies of Women Poets in Rural Yemen." *Journal of Women's History* 14 (1): 94–122.
———. 2005. "Of Songs and Signs: Audiocassette Poetry, Moral Character, and the Culture of Circulation in Yemen." *American Ethnologist* 32 (1): 82–99.
———. 2007. *The Moral Resonance of Arab Media: Audiocassette Poetry and Culture in Yemen*. Cambridge, Mass.: Harvard University Press.
Mills, Margaret A. 1991a. "Gender and Verbal Performance Style in Afghanistan." In Appadurai, Korom, and Mills, *Gender, Genre and Power in South Asian Expressive Traditions*, 56–77.
———. 1991b. *Rhetorics and Politics in Afghan Traditional Storytelling*. Philadelphia: University of Pennsylvania Press.
———. 2013. "Gnomics: Proverbs, Aphorisms, Metaphors, Key Words and Epithets in Afghan Discourses of War and Instability." In Green and Arbabzadah, *Afghanistan in Ink*, 229–251.
Mines, Mattison. 1988. "Conceptualizing the Person: Hierarchical Society and Individual Autonomy in India." *American Anthropologist* 90 (3): 568–579.
———. 1994. *Public Faces, Private Voices: Community and Individuality in South India*. Berkeley: University of California Press.

Mir-Hosseini, Ziba. 1999. *Islam and Gender: The Religious Debate in Contemporary Iran.* Princeton, N.J.: Princeton University Press.

Mirsepassi, Ali. 2000. *Intellectual Discourse and the Politics of Modernization: Negotiating Modernity in Iran.* Cambridge: Cambridge University Press.

Moaddel, Mansoor. 2008. "Religious Regimes and Prospects for Liberal Politics: Futures of Iran, Iraq, and Saudi Arabia." In *Population Studies Center Research Report,* 1–23. Ann Arbor: Population Studies Center, University of Michigan Institute for Social Research.

Moallem, Minoo. 2005. *Between Warrior Brother and Veiled Sister: Islamic Fundamentalism and the Politics of Patriarchy in Iran.* Berkeley and Los Angeles: University of California Press.

Monsutti, Alessandro. 2004. "Cooperation, Remittances and Kinship among the Hazaras." *Iranian Studies* 37 (2): 219–240.

———. 2005a. "La migration comme rite de passage: La construction de la masculinité parmi les jeunes Afghan en Iran." In *Genre, nouvelle division internationale du travail et migrations,* edited by C. Verschuur and F. Reusoo, 179–186. Paris: L'Harmattan.

———. 2005b. *War and Migration: Social Networks and Economic Strategies of the Hazaras of Afghanistan.* New York: Routledge.

———. 2010. "The Transnational Turn in Migration Studies and the Afghan Social Networks." In Chatty and Finlayson, *Dispossession and Displacement,* 45–67.

Morawski, Stefan. 1970. "The Basic Functions of Quotation." In *Sign, Language, Culture,* edited by Algirdas Julien Greimas, 690–705. The Hague: Mouton.

Moretti, Franco. 2005. *Graphs, Maps, Trees: Abstract Models for a Literary Theory.* London: Verso.

Mottahedeh, Roy. 1985. *The Mantle of the Prophet: Religion and Politics in Iran.* Harmondsworth, U.K.: Penguin.

Mousavi, Sayed Askar. 1998. *The Hazaras of Afghanistan: An Historical, Cultural, Economic and Political Study.* Richmond, U.K.: Curzon Press.

Naficy, Hamid. 1991. "The Poetics and Practice of Iranian Nostalgia in Exile." *Diaspora: A Journal of Transnational Studies* 1 (3): 285–302.

———. 2002. "Islamizing Film Culture in Iran: A Post-Khatami Update." In R. Tapper, *New Iranian Cinema,* 26–65.

Najibullah, Farangis. 2013. "Afghan Guys and Gals Meet Facebook to Facebook." Radio Free Europe/Radio Liberty, http://www.rferl.mobi/a/24955148.html, 11 April 2013.

Najmabadi, Afsaneh. 2005. *Women with Mustaches and Men without Beards: Gender and Sexual Anxieties of Iranian Modernity.* Berkeley: University of California Press.

Nandy, Ashis. 1983. *The Intimate Enemy: Loss and Recovery of Self under Colonialism.* New Delhi, India: Oxford University Press.

Nasar, M. Ibrahim. 2000. "Muhammad Gul Khan Momand." http://www.hewad.com/mohammadgul, accessed March 2005.

Navaro-Yashin, Yael. 2012. *The Make-Believe Space: Affective Geography in a Postwar Polity.* Durham, N.C.: Duke University Press.

Nomani, Farhand, and Sohrab Behdad. 2006. *Class and Labor in Iran: Did the Revolution Matter?* Syracuse, N.Y.: Syracuse University Press.

Nooshin, Laudan. 2005. "Underground, Overground: Rock Music and Youth Discourses in Iran." *Iranian Studies* 38 (3): 463–494.

———. 2007. "The Language of Rock: Iranian Youth, Popular Music, and National Identity." In *Media, Culture and Society in Iran: Living with Globalization and the Islamic State*, edited by Mehdi Semati, 69–93. London: Routledge.

———. 2009. "'Tomorrow Is Ours': Re-imagining Nation, Performing Youth in the New Iranian Pop Music." In *Music and the Play of Power in the Middle East, North Africa and Central Asia*, edited by Laudan Nooshin, 245–268. Farnham, U.K.: Ashgate.

———. 2011. "Hip-Hop Tehran: Migrating Styles, Musical Meanings, Marginalised Voices." In *Migrating Music*, edited by Jason Toynbee and Byron Dueck, 92–111. London: Routledge.

Olszewska, Zuzanna. 2005. "Stealing the Show: Women Writers at an Afghan Literary Festival in Tehran." *Bad Jens: Iranian Feminist Newsletter*, http://www.badjens.com/afghan.lit.html.

———. 2007. "'A Desolate Voice': Poetry and Identity among Young Afghan Refugees in Iran." *Iranian Studies* 40 (2): 203–224.

———. 2008. "Afghanistan. XIV, Afghan Refugees in Iran." In *Encyclopedia Iranica Online*, http://www.iranicaonline.org/articles/afghanistan-xiv-afghan-refugees-in-iran-2.

———. 2010. "'Hey Afghani!' Identity Contentions among Iranians and Afghan Refugees." In Chatty and Finlayson, *Dispossession and Displacement*, 197–214.

———. 2013a. "Classy Kids and Down-at-Heel Intellectuals: Status Aspiration and Blind Spots in the Contemporary Ethnography of Iran." *Iranian Studies* 46 (6): 841–862.

———. 2013b. "Lyric Realism: Poetic Reflections of Refugee Life in Iran." In Green and Arbabzadah, *Afghanistan in Ink*, 185–207.

Omidian, Patricia A. 1996. *Aging and Family in an Afghan Refugee Community: Transitions and Transformations*. New York: Garland.

Ortner, Sherry. 2013. *Not Hollywood: Independent Film at the Twilight of the American Dream*. Durham, N.C.: Duke University Press.

———. 2005. "Subjectivity and Cultural Critique." *Anthropological Theory* 5 (1): 31–52.

Osanloo, Arzoo. 2009. *The Politics of Women's Rights in Iran*. Princeton, N.J.: Princeton University Press.

Padilla, Mark B., Jennifer S. Hirsch, Miguel Muñoz-Laboy, Robert E. Sember, and Richard G. Parker, 2007. *Love and Globalization: Transformations of Intimacy in the Contemporary World*. Nashville, Tenn.: Vanderbilt University Press.

Papan-Matin, Firoozeh. 2005. *The Love Poems of Ahmad Shamlu*. Translated by Firoozeh Papan-Matin and Arthur Lane. Bethesda, Md.: Ibex.

Parsinejad, Iraj. 2003. *A History of Literary Criticism in Iran (1866–1951)*. Bethesda, Md.: Ibex.

Pedersen, Gorm. 1990. "Afghan Nomads in Exile: Patterns of Organization and Reorganization in Pakistan." In Anderson and Dupree, *Cultural Basis of Afghan Nationalism*, 154–159.

Piran, Parviz. 2004. "Effects of Social Interaction between Afghan Refugees and Iranians on Reproductive Health Attitudes." *Disasters* 28 (3): 283–293.

Powles, Julia. 2000. *Road 65: A Narrative Ethnography of a Refugee Settlement in Zambia*. DPhil diss., University of Oxford.

———. 2004. "Life History and Personal Narrative: Theoretical and Methodological Issues Relevant to Research and Evaluation in Refugee Contexts." Paper presented at ALNAP workshop "Evaluating the Use of Research Methods in Humanitarian Contexts: Promoting Good Practice." Geneva, April.

———. 2005. "Embodied Memories: Displacements in Time and Space." In *The Qualities of Time: Anthropological Approaches*, edited by Wendy James and David Mills, 331–348. Oxford: Berg.

Raffel, Burton. 1988. *The Art of Translating Poetry*. University Park: Pennsylvania State University Press.

Rancière, Jacques. 2012. *Proletarian Nights: The Workers' Dream in Nineteenth-Century France*. New York: Verso.

Rejali, Darius M. 1994. *Torture and Modernity: Self, Society, and State in Modern Iran*. Boulder, Colo.: Westview Press.

Rilke, Rainer Maria. 1986 [1934]. *Letters to a Young Poet*. Translated by Stephen Mitchell. New York: Vintage.

Rorty, Amelie Oksenberg. 2007. "The Vanishing Subject: The Many Faces of Subjectivity." In Biehl, Good, and Kleinman, *Subjectivity*, 34–51.

Rosen, Lawrence. 1999. "Justice in Islamic Culture and Law." In *Perspectives on Islamic Law, Justice and Society*, edited by R. S. Khare, 33–52. Lanham, Md.: Rowman & Littlefield.

Rostami-Povey, Elaheh. 2003. "Women in Afghanistan: Passive Victims of the Borga or Active Social Participants?" *Development in Practice* 13 (2–3): 266–277.

Roy, Olivier. 1990. *Islam and Resistance in Afghanistan*. Cambridge: Cambridge University Press.

Ruiz, Hiram A. 1992. "U.S. Committee for Refugees Returns to Iran, Finds: Iran Ready to Open Doors to Western NGOs; Afghan Repatriation Off to a Slow Start." Washington, D.C.: United States Committee for Refugees.

Rushdie, Salman. 1992. "In Good Faith." In *Imaginary Homelands*, 393–414. Harmondsworth, U.K.: Granta/Penguin.

Ryle, Gilbert. 1949. *The Concept of Mind*. London: Hutchinson.

Rypka, Jan. 1968. "Persian Literature to the Beginning of the Twentieth Century." In *History of Iranian Literature*, edited by Jan Rypka, 69–352. Dordrecht, Netherlands: D. Reidel.

Sadeghi, Fatemeh. 2009. "Foot Soldiers of the Islamic Republic's 'Culture of Modesty.'" *Middle East Report*, no. 250, 50–55.

Sadr, Hamid Reza. 2006. *Iranian Cinema: A Political History*. London: I. B. Tauris.

Said, Edward. 1993. *Culture and Imperialism*. London: Chatto & Windus.

———. 2002 [1984]. "Reflections on Exile." In *Reflections on Exile and Other Essays*, 171–186. Cambridge, Mass.: Harvard University Press.

Sarhaddi-Nelson, Soraya. 2001. "Afghan Refugees in Iran Learn to Keep School a Secret." *Los Angeles Times*, 25 December 2001.

Sax, William. 2002. *Dancing the Self: Personhood and Performance in the Pāṇḍav Līlā of Garhwal*. New York: Oxford University Press.

Schimmel, Annemarie. 1992. *A Two-Colored Brocade: The Imagery of Persian Poetry*. Chapel Hill: University of North Carolina Press.

Shahrani, M. Nazif. 1995. "Afghanistan's Muhajirin (Muslim 'Refugee-Warriors'): Politics of Mistrust and Distrust of Politics." In Daniel and Knudsen, *Mistrusting Refugees*, 187–206.
Shalinsky, Audrey. 1979. *Central Asian Emigres in Afghanistan: Problems of Religious and Ethnic Identity*. Occasional Paper 19. New York: Afghanistan Council/Asia Society.
Shams, Fatemeh. 2015a. "The Dialectic of Poetry and Power in Iran." *Dirasat* 42 (1): 1–40.
———. 2015b. "Literature, Art, and Ideology under the Islamic Republic: An Extended History of the Center for Islamic Art and Thoughts." In *Persian Language, Literature and Culture: New Leaves, Fresh Looks*, edited by Kamran Talattof. London: Routledge.
Sharlet, Jocelyn. 2011. *Patronage and Poetry in the Islamic World: Social Mobility and Status in the Medieval Middle East and Central Asia*. London: I. B. Tauris.
Shryock, Andrew. 2004. *Off Stage/On Display: Intimacy and Ethnography in the Age of Public Culture*. Stanford, Calif.: Stanford University Press
Siddiqi, Muhammad. 1995. "On Ropes of Memory: Narrating the Palestinian Refugees." In Daniel and Knudsen, *Mistrusting Refugees*, 89–101.
Spiro, Melford E. (1993) "Is the Western Conception of the Self Peculiar within the Context of the World Cultures?" *Ethos* 21 (2): 107–153.
Squire, Catherine. 2000. *Education of Afghan Refugees in the Islamic Republic of Iran*. Tehran: UNESCO/UNICEF/UNHCR, December 2002.
Sreberny, Annabelle, and Gholam Khiabany. 2010. *Blogistan: The Internet and Politics in Iran*. London: I. B. Tauris.
Sreberny-Mohammadi, Annabelle, and Ali Mohammadi. 1994. *Small Media, Big Revolution: Communication, Culture, and the Iranian Revolution*. Minneapolis: University of Minnesota Press.
Stetkevych, Suzanne P., ed. 1994. *Reorientations: Arabic and Persian Poetry*. Bloomington: Indiana University Press.
Stigter, Elca. 2005a. *Transnational Networks and Migration from Faryab to Iran*. Kabul: Afghanistan Research and Evaluation Unit. February 2005.
———. 2005b. *Transnational Networks and Migration from Herat to Iran*. Kabul: Afghanistan Research and Evaluation Unit. January 2005.
Stokes, Martin. 1998. "Imagining 'the South': Hybridity, Heterotopias and Arabesk on the Turkish-Syrian Border." In *Border Identities: Nation and State at International Frontiers*, edited by Thomas M. Wilson and Hastings Donnan, 263–288. Cambridge: Cambridge University Press.
———. 2010. *The Republic of Love: Cultural Intimacy in Turkish Popular Culture*. Chicago: Chicago University Press.
Strathern, Marilyn. 1988. *The Gender of the Gift: Problems with Women and Problems with Society in Melanesia*. Berkeley: University of California Press.
Subtelny, Maria E. 1984. "Scenes from the Literary Life of Timurid Herat." In *Logos Islamikos: Studia Islamica in Honorem Georgii Michaelis Wickens*, edited by Roger M. Savory and Dionisius A. Agius, 137–155. Toronto: Pontifical Institute of Mediaeval Studies.
Talattof, Kamran. 1997. "Iranian Women's Literature: From Pre-Revolutionary Social Discourse to Post-Revolutionary Feminism." *International Journal of Middle East Studies* 29 (4): 531–58.

———. 2000. *The Politics of Writing in Iran: A History of Modern Persian Literature*. Syracuse, N.Y.: Syracuse University Press.
Tapper, Nancy. 1991. *Bartered Brides: Politics, Gender and Marriage in an Afghan Tribal Society*. Cambridge: Cambridge University Press.
Tapper, Richard. 1983. "Introduction." In *The Conflict of Tribe and State in Iran and Afghanistan*, edited by Richard Tapper, 1–82. London: Croom Helm.
———, ed. 2002. *The New Iranian Cinema: Politics, Representation and Identity*. London: I. B. Tauris.
Tavakoli-Targhi, Mohamad. 2001. *Refashioning Iran: Orientalism, Occidentalism and Historiography*. Hampshire, U.K.: Palgrave Macmillan.
Tober, Diane. 2007. "'My Body Is Broken Like My Country': Identity, Nation, and Repatriation among Afghan Refugees in Iran." *Iranian Studies* 40 (2): 263–285.
Tohidi, Nayereh. 2002. "International Connections of the Iranian Women's Movement." In Keddie and Mathee, *Iran and the Surrounding World*, 205–231.
Tourage, Mahdi. 2007. *Rumi and the Hermeneutics of Eroticism*. Leiden, Germany: Brill.
Turner, Victor. 1969. *The Ritual Process: Structure and Anti-Structure*. Chicago: Aldine Transaction.
Turton, David and Peter Marsden. 2002. *Taking Refugees for a Ride? The Politics of Refugee Return to Afghanistan*. Issues Paper Series. Kabul: Afghan Research and Evaluation Unit, December.
United Nations High Commissioner for Refugees (UNHCR). 2001. "Afghan Refugee Statistics 6 May 2001." http://www.un.org.pk/unhcr/Afstats-stat.htm.
———. 2004a. "Afghanistan: Challenges to Return." Geneva: UNHCR, March, http://www.unhcr.org/cgi-bin/texis/vtx/home/opendoc.pdf?tbl=SUBSITES&page=SUBSITES&id=4208f30c4.
———. 2004b. "Briefing Note: UNHCR Sub-Office in Mashhad, Khorassan Province, the Islamic Republic of Iran." Mashhad: UNHCR, 3 October.
———. 2007. "Resettlement Unit Briefing Note." Tehran, UNHCR, May.
———. 2013. "2013 UNHCR Country Operations Profile—Islamic Republic of Iran." http://www.unhcr.org/pages/49e486f96.html.
UNHCR/BAFIA. 2005. *Amayesh* Statistical Database on Afghan Refugees in Iran [consulted in 2005, 2006].
Vahdat, Farzin. 2002. *God and Juggernaut: Iran's Intellectual Encounter with Modernity*. Syracuse, N.Y.: Syracuse University Press.
Varzi, Roxanne. 2006. *Warring Souls: Youth, Media, and Martyrdom in Post-Revolutionary Iran*. Durham, N.C.: Duke University Press.
Wikan, Unni. 1990. *Managing Turbulent Hearts: A Balinese Formula for Living*. Chicago: University of Chicago Press.
Williams, Raymond. 1977. *Marxism and Literature*. Oxford: Oxford University Press.
———. 1988. *Keywords: A Vocabulary of Culture and Society*. London: Fontana Press.
Winegar, Jessica. 2006. *Creative Reckonings: The Politics of Art and Culture in Contemporary Egypt*. Stanford, Calif.: Stanford University.
Winnicott, Donald W. 1965. "Ego Distortion in Terms of True and False Self." In *The Maturational Process and the Facilitating Environment: Studies in the Theory of Emotional Development*, 139–152. New York: International Universities Press.
Witte, Griff. 2005. "Post-Taliban Free Speech Blocked by Courts, Clerics; Jailed Afghan Publisher Faces Possible Execution." *Washington Post*, http://www.washington

post.com/wp-dyn/content/article/2005/12/10/AR2005121001138.html?nav=rss_world, 11 December.
Yarshater, Ehsan. 1960. "The Theme of Wine-Drinking and the Concept of the Beloved in Early Persian Poetry." *Studia Islamica* 13: 43–53.
———. 1978. "Preface." In *An Anthology of Modern Persian Poetry*, edited by Ahmad Karimi-Hakkak, xiii–xiv. Boulder, Colo.: Westview Press.
Zabeth, Hyder Reza. 1999. *Landmarks of Mashhad*. Mashhad: Islamic Research Foundation, Astan Quds Razavi.
Zaborowska, Magdalena. 2014. "A Contribution to the Study of the Persian Concept of Aberu." *Hemispheres* 29 (1): 113–125.
Zarkar, Rustin, Beeta Baghoolizadeh, and Alex Shams. 2013. "Constructing Sacred Space: An Architectural History of Mashhad's Imam Reza Shrine." *Ajam Media Collective*, http://ajammc.com/2013/12/27/constructing-sacred-space-an-architectural-history-of-mashhads-imam-reza-shrine/, 27 December.
Zimbler, Jarad. 2009. "For Neither Love Nor Money: The Place of Political Art in Pierre Bourdieu's Literary Field." *Textual Practice* 23 (4): 599–620.

Persian

Abazari, Yusof. 1386/2007. "Taqdim be Afghān-hā [Dedicated to the Afghans]." *Ham-mihan*, 20 khordād 1386/10 June 2007, 10.
Ahmadi-Aryan, Amir. 1386/2007. "Marz-hā-ye darun o birun: Chand nokteh dar bāreh-ye ekhrāj-e Afghān-hā az Irān [Inner and outer borders: Some remarks on the expulsion of Afghans from Iran]." *Ham-mihan*, 20 khordād 1386/10 June 2007, 10.
Alavi, Elyas. 1386/2008. *Man gorg-e khiālbāfi hastam: Majmu'eh-ye she'r [I Am a Daydreamer Wolf: A Poetry Collection]*. Tehran: Āhang-e Digar.
Ayati, Abdolmohammad, ed. 1382/2003. *Gozideh-ye Leyli o Majnun [A Selection from Leyli and Majnoun by Nezāmi Ganjavi]*. Tehran: Sherkat-e Enteshārāt-e 'Elmi o Farhangi.
BBC Farsi. 1392/2013. "Mokhālefat-e polis-e Iran bā ekhrāj-e Afghān-hā [Iranian Police Opposes Deportation of Afghans]." http://www.bbc.co.uk/persian/iran/2013/09/130915_l01_afghan_refugees_ahmadimoghadam_police.shtml, 15 September 2013.
Baqeri, Leila. 1386/2007. "Vaqti hameh shā'er mishavand: Goft-o-gu bā 'Ali Mo'allem Dāmghāni [When Everyone Becomes a Poet: A Conversation with 'Ali Mo'allem Dāmghāni]." http://www.ketabnews.com/detail-5251-fa-1.html, 7 mehr 1386/29 September 2007.
Behbahani, Simin. 1377/1998. *Az sāl-hā-ye āb va sarāb: montakhab-e haft daftar-e she'r, 1325–1376 [From the Years of Water and Mirages: A Selection from Seven Books of Poetry, 1945–1997]*. Tehran: Enteshārāt-e Sokhan.
Clinton, Jerome. 1372/1994. "Nokteh-ye chand dar bāreh-ye vaz'-e konuni-ye tārikh-e adabi dar Irān [Some remarks on the current state of literary history in Iran]." *Irān Nāmeh* 12: 35–50.
Dorr-e Dari. n.d. *Khatt-e Sevvom [The Third Script]* promotional pamphlet. Mashhad: Dorr-e Dari.
Ebrahimi, Gholamreza. 1384/2006. "Az entehā-ye khotut rahā shodeh: Kārnāmeh-ye zanān dar she'r-e javān-e mohājerat [Released from the end of the lines: An ap-

praisal of the work of women in refugee youth poetry]." *Khatt-e Sevvom*, no. 7 (Spring 1384/2006): 113–116.

Ebrahimi, Mahbubeh. 1386/2007. *Bād-hā khāharān-e man* and [*The Winds Are My Sisters*]. Tehran: Sureh-ye Mehr.

Ekrami, Mahmud ("Khazān"). 1380/2001. "*Inak hamnamak hastim* [Now we break bread together]." *Qods*, 17 ordibehesht 1380/7 May 2001.

Farhang, Omid. 1375/1996. "Kāregarān-e Afghāni, sāzandegān-e bināmva neshān-e Irān." *Goft-o-gu*, 43–49.

Hasanzadeh, Mas'ud. 1383/2004. "Adabiyāt-e Badi [Bad Literature]." In *Majmu'eh-ye Maqālāt: Hamāyeshi dar gostareh-ye adabiyāt dar zamineh-ye adabiyāt-e mo'āser-e Afghānestān*. [*Collection of Papers: Conference on the Contemporary Literature of Afghanistan*], edited by Mohammad Davud Monir, 103–111. Herat: Anjoman-e Adabi-ye Herāt.

Heidarbeigi, Hossein. 1386/2008. *Āhu-ye hamisheh davideh dar man* [*The Deer Always Running in Me*]. Tehran: Entesharāt-e 'Erfān.

Hojjati, Hamideh. 1378/1999. "Adabiyāt-e moqāvemat dar Afghānestān [Resistance Literature in Afghanistan]." In *Dāneshnāmeh-ye adab-e fārsi* [*Encyclopedia of Persian Literature*], 3:64–68. Tehran: Mo'asseseh-ye Farhangi-ye Entesharāti-ye Dāneshnāmeh, Ministry of Culture and Islamic Guidance.

Hosseini, Seyyed Asef. 1385/2006. "Untitled post." *Satl-e āshghāl* [*Wastebasket*] blog, http://asef.blogfa.com/8508.aspx, 8 ābān 1385/30 October 2006.

———. 1386/2007. *Ruz-hā-ye ākhar-e pā'iz: Yāddāsht-hā bar entekhābāt-e pārlāmāni-ye 1384* [*The Last Days of Autumn: Notes on the Parliamentary Elections of 2005*]. Kabul: Friedrich Ebert Stiftung, Afghanistan Office.

———. 1391/2012. *Chahār sayyāreh dar otāqam* [*Four Planets in My Room*]. Czech Republic: Self-Published.

Hosseinzadeh, Zahra. 1382/2003. "Ruzi zan-e Afghānestāni fekr kard [One Day, the Woman from Afghanistan Thought]." *Khatt-e Sevvom*, nos. 3/4 (Spring/Summer 1382/2003): 102–106.

———. 1390/2011. *Palang dar parāntez* [*The Panther in Parentheses*]. Mashhad: Sepidehbāvarān/Dorr-e Dari.

Kazemi, Mohammad Kazem. 1379/2000. *She'r-e pārsi* [*Persian Poetry*]. Mashhad: Mo'asseseh-ye Farhangi, Honari va Entesharāti-ye Zarih-e Āftāb.

———. 1382/2003. *Hamzabāni va bizabāni* [*On Sharing a Tongue and Being without a Tongue*]. Tehran: Entesharāt-e 'Erfān.

———. 1384/2005a. "'Abd al-Qāder Bidel va jāyegāh-ash dar se pāreh az yek peikar [Abd al-Qader Bidel and His Place in Three Fragments of One Body]." BBC Persian service, http://www.bbc.co.uk/persian/afghanistan/story/2005/08/050811_s-bidel-afg-iran-kazemi.shtml, 21 mordād 1384/12 August 2005.

———. 1384/2005b. *Qesseh-ye sang o khesht: Gozineh-ye she'r* [*A Tale of Stone and Brick: A Selection of Poems*]. Tehran: Ketāb-e Neyestān.

———. 1385/2006. "Kongreh-ye bein al-mellali-ye Bidel dar Tehrān [International Bidel Congress in Tehran]." BBC Persian service, http://www.bbc.co.uk/persian/arts/story/2006/12/061202_s-ors-e-bidel.shtml, 11 āzar 1385/2 December 2006.

———. 1386/2007. *Gozideh-ye ghazaliāt-e Bidel* [*A Selection of Bidel's Ghazals*]. Tehran: Entesharāt-e 'Erfān.

———. 1390/2011. "Shamshir o Joghrāfiyā [The Sword and Geography]." *Mohammad Kazem Kazemi*, http://mkkazemi.persianblog.ir/post/704, 6 āzar 1390/27 November 2011.
Kazemi, Mohammad Kazem, ed. 1383/2005. *Bāgh-e besiār derakht [A Garden of Many Trees]*. Tehran: Ministry of Culture and Islamic Guidance.
Kazemi, Mohammad Kazem, and Mohammad Asef Rahmani, eds. 1370/1991. *She'r-e moqāvemat-e Afghānestān [The Resistance Poetry of Afghanistan]*. Tehran: Entesharāt-e Howzeh-ye Honari-ye Sāzmān-e Tablighāt-e Eslāmi.
———. 1380/2001. *Amsāl va hekam-e mardom-e Hazāreh [Proverbs and Maxims of the Hazara People]*. Tehran: Entesharāt-e 'Erfān.
———. 1382/2003. *Dobeiti-hā-ye 'āmiāneh-ye Hazāregī [Hazaregi Folk Quatrains]*. Tehran: Entesharāt-e 'Erfān.
Mirshahi, Mas'ud (ed.) 1383/2004. *She'r-e zanān-e Afghānestān [Afghan Women's Poetry]*. Tehran: Shahāb Publications.
Mirza'i, Amanollah. 1385/2007. *Giāh-e sukhteh [The Burnt Plant]*. Mashhad: Hamyārān-e Javān.
Mirza'i, Rahimeh. 1384/2006. "Soqrāt showkarān khord ammā namord: She'r-e emruz dar neshasti bā shā'erān-e javān [Socrates drank the hemlock but didn't die: Today's poetry in a meeting with young poets]." *Khatt-e Sevvom* no. 7 (Spring 1384/2006): 91–98.
———. 1386/2008. *'Aks-e māh-e to bar divār-hā-ye shab leili-tar and [Your Moonlike Image Is More Leili on the Walls of the Night]*. Tehran: Entesharāt-e 'Erfān.
Mo'allem, Ali. 1370/1991. "Pishgoftār [Foreword]." In *She'r-e moqāvemat-e Afghānestān [The Resistance Poetry of Afghanistan]*, edited by Mohammad Kazem Kazemi and Mohammad Asef Rahmani, 7–10. Tehran: Entesharāt-e Howzeh-ye Honari-ye Sāzmān-e Tablighāt-e Eslāmi.
Mozaffari, Seyyed Abu Taleb. 1384/2005. "Pishgoftār [Foreword]." In *Gisuān-e gij: Daftari az she'r-hā-ye nasl-e javān-e mohājer [Tangled Locks: A Book of Poems from the Young Generation of Refugees]*, edited by Fatemeh Sajjadi, 9–16. Mashhad: Nedā-ye Sokhan.
Navisa, Khaled. 1387/2008. "Dānesh-Ton." *Kabul Nath*, no. 73, http://www.kabulnath.de/Salae_Charom/Shoumare_73/KhaledNawisa.html, jowzā 1387/May-June 2008.
Nurza'i, Mohammad Shafi'i. 1385/2006. "Nadia Anjoman Biography." Exil-Archiv, Else-Lasker-Schüler-Stiftung, http://exil-archiv.de/html/biografien/anjoman.html, accessed 19 November 2006.
Pahlavan, Changiz. 1379/2000. *Afghāni-hā dar Irān [Afghans in Iran]*. Tehran: Entesharāt-e Hirmand.
Parsinezhad, Iraj. 1380/2001. *Roshangarān-e Irān va naqd-e adabi [Intellectuals of Iran and Literary Criticism]*. Tehran: Entesharāt-e Sokhan.
Qasemi, Seyyed Zia'. 1386/2007. *Bāgh-hā-ye mo'allaq-e angur [Suspended Vineyards]*. Tehran: Sureh-ye Mehr.
Raja'i, Mohammad Sarvar. 1386/2008. "Adabiyāt-e 'ajib dar tanz-e *Chahār Khuneh* [Strange manners in the satirical program *Chahār Khuneh*]." Blog *Farkhār*, House of Afghan Literature, www.farkhar.blogfa.com, 11 dey 1386/1 January 2008.
Ravankhah, Ali. 1383/2005. "Vizhegi-ye asli-ye adabiyāt-e mohājerat jur-e digar-e didan ast [The main characteristic of refugee poetry is another way of seeing]." *Qods Daily*, 11 esfand 1383/1 March 2005.

Sadr, Keshavarz. 1335/1956. *Az Rābe'eh tā Parvin* [*From Rabe'eh to Parvin*]. Tehran: Kāviān.
Saheb al-Zamani, Naser al-Din. 1351/1972. *Khatt-e Sevvom: Dar bāreh-ye shakhsiat, sokhanān, va andisheh-ye Shams-e Tabrizi* [*The Third Script: On the Person, Sayings, and Thought of Shams of Tabriz*]. Tehran: 'Atā'i.
Sajjadi, Fatemeh (ed.) 1384/2005. *Gisuān-e gij: Daftari az she'r-hā-ye nasl-e javān-e mohājer* [*Tangled Locks: A Book of Poems from the Young Generation of Refugees*]. Mashhad: Nedā-ye Sokhan.
———. 1385/2006. "Man be dam-e nāmeh-hā-yat zendeh-am [I Am Alive in the Breath of Your Letters]." Untitled blog, http://hesar62.persianblog.ir/pages/5/, 22 āzar 1385/13 December 2006.
———. 1386/2007. "Bayad . . ." Untitled blog, http://hesar62.persianblog.ir/1386/8/, 11 ābān 1386/2 November 2007.
Sarem, Ali. 1390/2012. "Qatl-e 'ām-e ordugāh-e Sefid Sang-e Farimān-e Mashhad! [Massacre at the Sefid Sang camp at Fariman near Mashhad!]." Blog *Mohājer*, http://mahajerchest.mihanblog.com/post/9, 11 dey 1390/1 January 2012.
Shafi'i Kadkani, Mohammad Reza. 1366/1988. *Shā'er-e āyeneh-hā: Barresi-ye sabk-e hendi va she'r-e Bidel* [*The Poet of Mirrors: A Study of the Indian Style and the Poetry of Bidel*]. Tehran: Āgāh.
Zarkub, Fazlollah. 1371/1992. *Barresi-ye she'r-e moqāvemat-e Afghānestān* [*A Study of the Resistance Poetry of Afghanistan*]. Master's thesis, Ferdowsi University, Mashhad.

Index

Page numbers in *italics* refer to illustrations.

Abu-Lughod, Lila, 11–12, 161, 211
Adelkhah, Fariba, 18–19, 64, 75–77, 187; ethic of *javanmārdi*, 19, 209
Afghan refugees: cultural changes in Iran, 72–82, 91–92, 165–172, 191, 199; education of, 65–72, *71*, 215–216, 224n14; ethnic origins of, 22, 218n18; and illegality, 20, 42–44; intellectuals, 2, 31, 63, 65, 84, 91–92, 158, 178, 186; in Iranian discourse, 47–52, 222n21; legal status in Iran, 20, 39–46, 210; literary and cultural institutions of, 2, 23, 101–102, 105–108; literature of, 5, 9, 13, 26, 32–33, 60, 100–112, 114–122, 207; in Mashhad, 23, 26; models of personhood of, 20–21, 33, 210, 213; political and resistance organizations of, 13–14, 23, 37, 94, 100–102, 105; sense of exclusion in Iran of, 37, 47, 62, 65, 91, 210–211; socioeconomic conditions in Iran of, 1, 6, 22, 41, 115–116, 215, 220n3, 221n12; subjectivity of, 19–20, 33, 62, 91, 210–211
Afghanistan, *xii*, 23, 31; cultural politics of, 32, 55, 63, 84, 87, 97, 120, 202, 223n30; customs and culture of, 76, 80, 135, 149, 160–162, 166–169, 171–172, 177, 207, 225n18, 225n24, 232n15; deportation to, 42–43, 45, 221n14; ethnicity in, 20, 171–172, 219n19, 160, 232n10; Iranian views on, 47, 49–51, 222nn20–21; literature of, 9, 27, 48, 52–55, 59, 64, 97–98, 102, 125, 133, 134, 151–153, 161, 217n8, 222n22, 228n10, 229n1, 231n24, 235n18; migration in/from, 37–39, 42, 66, 72, 220n2, 233n22; political history of, 31–32, 37, 52, 55, 40–41, 101, 104, 147–148, 220n1, 221n9, 225n22, 227n4, 228n17, 231n25; refugee ties with, 6, 12, 22, 35, 55–57, 61–62, 70, 84, 87–88, 101, 105, 110, 123, 130, 147, 172–173, 175, 210–211, 213, 215; relations with Iran, 20, 37–38, 40, 67, 97, 101, 218n17; repatriation to, 42, 45, 71, 81, 109, 123, 132, 147, 215, 221n10, 223n31, 224n12; Soviet invasion of, 11, 21, 37, 39–41, 94, 100; war in, 13, 20, 41, 51, 84, 87–88, 94–95, 100–101, 103, 105, 115, 146

Ahmadi, Ma'sumeh, *4*, 65, 108; "The Bench Opposite" (poem), 93–94, 98
Ahmadinejad, Mahmud, 51, 164, 233n18
Akhavan-Sales, Mehdi, 25, 84, 148
Alavi, Elyas, 2, 5, 26, 46, 112, 117, 126, 129–130, 132, 150, 229n6; "A Desolate Voice" (poem), 46; "Oh, My Poem" (poem), 117, 119
Al-e Ahmad, Jalal, 87, 219n25
Anjoman, Nadia, 151–152
Arts Center of the OIP (Howzeh-ye Honari-ye Sazman-e Tablighat-e Eslami), 100–101, 105, 110–111, 227n8
Attar, Farid al-Din Neishaburi, 60, 228n9
audiences, 5–7, 9, 13–15, 30, 32, 50, 95–96, 98, 100, 102, 104–105, 111–114, 121–122, 124, 132, 137–138, 139–140, 144, 146, 152, 159, 185, 187, 196, 200, 208, 217n8, 228n16; crisis of, 112. *See also* publics

Bad Literature (movement), 119–120, 202
Bakhtin, Mikhail, 12, 95, 146
Barber, Karin, 7, 14, 95, 228n16
bāten (inner self), 187–190, 193, 197. See also *darun* (inner self)
Beeman, William O., 12. 145, 188, 192–194, 235n14
Behbahani, Simin, 147, 229n21, 235n24; "I Will Rebuild You, My Homeland" (poem), 147–148
Betteridge, Anne H., 188, 190
Bidel, Abu al-Ma'ani Abd al-Qader Dehlavi, 27, 56, 66, 143–144, 147; commemoration of, 54–55; life of, 54
blank verse, xi, 94, 97, 99–100, 102, 111–112, 115, 119, 139–140, 144, 185, 194, 196, 202, 230n15
Boesen, Inger, 11, 161, 211
Bourdieu, Pierre, 7, 17, 111, 124; field of cultural production, 7, 13, 95, 112–114; position taking, 7, 13–14, 95, 114–115
Bowen, John, 12–13, 230n17, 231n26
Brookshaw, Dominic P., 136, 159, 190, 198–199, 231n3
Browne, Edward Granville, 9, 151
Bureau for Aliens and Foreign Immigrants' Affairs (BAFIA), 41–42

259

Caton, Steven, 11, 128
censorship, 75, 99–100, 113–115, 189–190, 200; self-, 189, 199, 201, 233n2
Committed Literature (*adabiyāt-e mota'ahhed*), 7, 99, 103, 115–119, 206; authors of, 64, 86, 113
communism, 40–41, 66, 68, 87, 105–106, 221n10
Constitutional Revolution, 9, 97, 226n33, 227n5

Dabashi, Hamid, 49, 98–99
Dadaism, 120
Damghani, Ali Mo'allem, 103, 105, 117, 120
Dari, ix, 55
darun (inner self), 109, 129, 142, 185, 187, 189, 195–196, 201. See also *bāten* (inner self)
De Genova, Nicholas, 42, 44
divination. See Hafez, Khwaja Shams al-Din Mohammad Hafez-e Shirazi: divination using poems of
divorce, 116–117, 160, 169–170, 184, 233n19
dobeiti (folk quatrain), 34, 46, 123, 125, 196
Dorr-e Dari (Mo'asseseh-ye Farhangi-ye Dorr-e Dari, Pearl of Dari Cultural Institute), ix, 2, 3, 6, 26, 64, *83*, 111, 119, *124*, 134–135, 145, 146, 192–193; history of, 105–108, 215; members of, *4*, 22, 63, 66, 71, 78, 84, 87, 91, 120, *135*, 155, 172, 184, 196, 199–200, 215; poetry criticism sessions, 2–5, 27, 32, 122, 123–125, 133, 136–144, *138*, *139*, 185, 208. See also *Third Script* (magazine)
Doubleday, Veronica, 80, 120, 160, 166, 225n17, 225n24, 229n5
Dumont, Louis, 16

Ebrahimi, Gholamreza, *4*, 89–91, 199, 213; "The End of the World" (poem), 89–91; "Identity Card" (poem), 46
Ebrahimi, Mahbubeh, 61, 78, 129, 146; "Border" (poem), 61–62
Edwards, David B., 11, 103–104, 211, 228nn13–14
esteqbāl (response poetry), 132, 152
E'tesami, Parvin, 199, 227n3

Farrokhzad, Forugh, 126, 180–181, 199, 229n3
Ferdowsi, Hakim Abu al-Qasem, 25, 27, 126, 227n9
festivals, literary, 26–27, 32, 43, 54, *79*, 111, 115–117, 121, 127–129, 132, 134, 144–145, 147, 152–153, 229n6, 230n16
Foucault, Michel, 15, 17, 182, 211, 218n11, 234n11

Geertz, Clifford, 12, 16, 234n3
Gell, Alfred, 14, 157, 231n4
ghazal, 54–55, 58, 61, 115–117, 147–148, 149–150, 182–183, 194, 206–207, 229n21, 230n21, 232n8; classical, 148, 183; formal properties of, 102–103; neoclassical, 90, 139
Ghaznavid Dynasty, 27, 53, 60
Giddens, Anthony, 18, 156, 168, 183–184, 231n1, 233n16
Gramsci, Antonio, 20, 91

Hafez, Khwaja Shams al-Din Mohammad Hafez-e Shirazi, 66, 104, 120, 126–127, 142, 149, 159, 190, 195; divination using poems of, 32, 149–151, 231n23
Haram. See Shrine of Imam Reza
Hasanzadeh, Mas'ud, 119, 120
Hazarajat, 1, 35, 38–39, 66–67, 101, 103, 108, 123, 125–126, 150; civil war in, 23, 37, 67, 100–101, 150, 224n8; social change in, 67
Hazaras, 20, 22, 35–39, *36*, 42, 66–67, 81, 88, 100, 105, 108, 115, 125–126, 160, 166–167, 208, 218n18, 219n19, 224n8; folk poetry of, 34, 46, 123, 125, 161–162, 196; and hypergamy, 171, 173–174, 232n10; women, 80, 161, 208, 225n24
Hedayat, Sadeq, 84
Heidarbeigi, Hossein, *4*, 35, 37, 132, *138*; "Gol-shahr" (poem), 34–35
Herat, 22, 37–38, 47, 49, 70, 77, 125–126, 148, 151, 167, 234n10; literary history of, 133–134, 198, 235n17; poets from, 52, 54, 56, 119–120, 235n18; prewar customs of, 80, 160, 225n17, 225n24, 229n5
Heratis, 22, 37, 76; *hosseiniyeh* of, 76–77; poets, 105, 108, 208
Hidden Imam. See Twelfth Imam
hijab. See veiling
Hoodfar, Homa, 41, 47, 66, 68, 79–80, 166, 168, 170, 218n14, 231n4, 233n20
Hosseini, Asef, 132, 147–148, 164, 182, 195–196, 210; "It's No Longer Necessary for You to Stay with Me, My Dear" (poem), 182–183; "Nobody Knows the Length and Breadth of the World" (poem), 204–205, 208
Hosseinzadeh, Zahra, 63–64, 78, 109–111, *118*, 206–208; life of, 115–116; "The Pit-Dwelling Pigeon" (poem), 116–117; "Take a Number on Saturdays" (poem), 206–207
Howzeh. See *howzeh-ye 'elmiyeh* (religious seminary)

howzeh-ye 'elmiyeh (religious seminary), 24–26, 35, 67, 77, 84, 101, 105, 219n20, 224n7, 224n9

Imam Ali, 126, 202
Imam Reza, 23, 72
India, 39, 220n1, 223n28, 232n5; Persian literature in, 10, 27, 52–54, 60, 235n17; personhood in, 16, 20–21, 189, 218n9, 218n12, 234n3
Indian style, 53–55, 143, 222n25
individualism, 16, 78, 91, 183, 213
individuality, 20–21, 129, 187–188, 209
intellectuals, 112, 121, 211, 213; Afghan, 2, 6, 10, 14, 19, 22, 25, 31–33, 37, 55–56, 58, 60, 63–65, 67, 78, 82–87, 91–92, 97–98, 104–105, 108, 111, 147, 158, 172, 177–178, 212, 235n24; Arab, 84; French, 112, 213; Iranian, 48–49, 60, 83, 86, 99, 104, 112, 134, 163, 178, 217n2, 219n21, 222n18, 226n27; Islamic, 228n17; Third World, 226n30. See also *rowshanfekr*
Islamic Republic of Iran, *xii*; cultural politics of, 10, 12–13, 26, 189, 233n2; education in, 66, 68–72; ethnography of, 6–8, 16–19, 218n13; ideology of, 23, 31, 49, 65, 91, 194, 208, 211; literary patronage in, 100–102, 121, 132, 144–145; refugee policy of, 6, 21–23, 39–46; religion in, 72–78; social change in, 18–20, 163
Islamic Revolution, 25, 75, 84, 109; literature of, 99, 102

Jami, Abd al-Rahman, 52, 66, 198
Javan, Rambod, *No Men Allowed* (film), 165

Kabul, 21–23, 27, 38–39, 49, 51, 54, 67, 102, 136, 147–148, 183, 208, 213, 221n15, 223n4, 225n23, 226n26, 232n15, 235n18; Dorr-e Dari branch in, 215
Kafka, Franz, 211
Karbala, 39, 74; battle of, 65, 69, 75; ideological use of, 103, 228n11
Karimi-Hakkak, Ahmad, 53, 96, 97–99, 104, 139, 189, 212, 222n25
Kazemi, Mohammad Kazem, 27, 56–60, 56, 100–101, 105–106, 108, 121, 125, 147, 223n31; "Return" (poem), 57–58, 62, 72, 152–153; role in Dorr-e Dari, 127–128, 134, *139*; "The Sword and Geography" (poem), 58–60
Khamenei, Ayatollah Ali, 60, 82, 115–116
khāstegāri (marriage suit), 165–168, 171, 174, 233n19

Khatami, Mohammad, 26, 51, 82, 110
Khatt-e Sevvom. See *Third Script* (magazine)
Khomeini, Ayatollah Ruhollah, 8, 40, 47, 67, 75–76, 82, 132
Khorasan, 23–26, 39; Greater Khorasan, *xii*, 23–24, 37; Khorasan-e Razavi (province), 23
Khosravi, Shahram, 17, 218n13

landay, 11, 161, 228n12
Lewis, Franklin D., 127–128, 131–132, 152
LiPuma, Edward, 16
literacy, 9, 19, 40, 64, 66, 68, 70, 96, 98, 111, 156, 198, 219n21, 223n4, 224n10
Lorca, Federico García, 2
Losensky, Paul, 131–132, 152
love, 21, 28, 32, 51, 136, 155–156, 158, 193, 197–200, 205; culture of, 157–158, 231n2, 232n5; extra-structural, 32, 157, 161, 163; as Persianate poetic trope, 32, 74, 88, 89–90, 96, 102–104, 117, 119, 132, 146, 148, 150, 157, 164, 178–180, 182–183, 228n12, 230n21, 232n8; in popular culture, 158, 161–165, 229n1; romantic, 11–12, 32, 127, 156–158, 163, 172–175, 178, 182, 184, 211, 213, 231n1, 233n16
lyric realism, 89, 206

Mahdavi, Pardis, 17, 191, 218n13
Mahmood, Saba, 17
Mahmud of Ghazni, 24, 53
Majidi, Majid, *Baran* (film), 51
majles (poetic gathering), 133–134
Makhmalbaf, Mohsen, 50; *Kandahar* (film), 222n21
Makhmalbaf, Samira, 50; *At Five in the Afternoon* (film), 51–52
Manoukian, Setrag, 10, 25, 186–187, 190, 204, 233n2
Marquez, Gabriel García, 190
marriage, 32, 79, 82, 116, 135, 149, 158–164, 172, 232n9, 233n19, 233n20; arranged, 78, 155, 157, 160, 163, 165–168, 172; companionate, 32, 156–158, 168, 177–178, 183–184, 213, 231n4; contract (*'aqdnāmeh*), 167; costs and payments, 169–170; cousin, 160, 163, 165–167; elopement, 28, 161, 165, 170–171, 233n19; endogamous, 160, 166, 176, 233n19; hypergamous, 161, 171, 174, 176, 232n10; rituals and parties, 168, *169*; temporary (*sigheh*), 160, 232n9, 235n24. See also divorce; *khāstegāri* (marriage suit)
Marxism, 17, 21, 72, 99, 103

Index

Mashhad, 1, 2, 29–30, 235n24; Afghan community of, 22–23, 26, 218n18, 224n10, 224n11, 225n23; Afghan neighborhoods of, 1, 22, 29, 35, 36, 194; cultural history of, 23–26, 219n22
masnavi, 54, 57, 87, 94, 100, 103, 227n9, 230n14, 232n7; formal properties of, 102–103
Mauss, Marcel, 16
Milani, Farzaneh, 30, 189–191, 194, 197–199, 234n5
Miller, W. Flagg, 13
Mills, Margaret A., 145–146, 152, 217n8
Mines, Mattison, 16, 20
Ministry of Culture and Islamic Guidance (MCIG), 99–100, 145, 227n8, 236n25
Mirza'i, Amanollah, 4, 74, 120–121; "Cut to the Next Sequence" (poem), 74–75
Mirza'i, Rahimeh, 2–6, 4, 129; "Mona Lisa" (poem), 4–6, 156
modernism: in Iran, 163, 219n21; Islamic, 13; Persian literary, 55, 84, 95–100, 125, 187, 195
modernity, 14, 21, 64, 156, 175, 187, 233n16; in Afghanistan, 86, 227n4; Iranian, 49, 64, 75, 78, 99, 108, 163, 187, 197; Islamic, 20, 22, 56, 62, 66, 75, 91, 116
Mohammad, Prophet, 22, 74, 76, 138, 171, 202, 220n4
Moharram, 25, 73, 89–90, 138
Monsutti, Alessandro, 37–39, 44, 160
Mozaffari, Seyyed Abu Taleb, 4, 5, 27, 32, 48, 85, 100–106, 106, 125, 130, 132, 149, 208, 226n30, 232n6; life of, 84–86; "Mother" (poem), 87–88; role in Dorr-e Dari, 108, 123, 127–128, 134, 137, 141–147
music, 9, 25–26, 27, 30, 54, 120, 126, 133, 144, 162–163, 165, 192, 198, 212, 217n3, 219n22, 227n8, 232n15; poetry set to, 147, 158, 165

Nabizadeh, Lina, 138; "When You're a Refugee" (poem), 69
Naser Khosrow Qobadiyani, ix, 222n26
nationalism, 13, 59, 61; Afghan, 57, 228n14; Arab, 226n34; Iranian, 10, 31, 37, 47, 52, 55, 96, 101, 163
Nezami Aruzi Samarqandi, 127–128, 151, 195–196
Nezami Ganjavi, 66, 103, 162, 195–196, 227n9, 234n13
1979 Revolution. *See* Islamic Revolution

'*olamā*, 24
Omid, M. *See* Akhavan-Sales, Mehdi

orality, 10–15, 102, 125–126, 131, 145, 161–162, 217n8, 228n12, 235n15
Organization of Islamic Propaganda (OIP, Sazman-e Tablighat-e Eslami), 100, 105, 111, 145, 227n8
originality, 111, 121–122, 124, 130–132, 154
Ortner, Sherry, 15, 113

Pahlavi Dynasty, 18, 24, 98, 163
Pakistan, 38, 55, 60, 67, 152, 160, 174, 228n16, 231nn24–25, 232n13; Afghan refugees in, 218n16, 220n7, 228n14
Pashtu, 53, 55, 70, 161, 223nn29–30, 224n13, 228n12, 228n14, 229n19
Pashtuns, 11, 39, 103, 108, 160, 218n16, 218n18, 223n30, 228n13, 231n24, 232n13
patronage: in Hazara-Seyyed relations, 219n19; literary and artistic, 23–24, 95–96, 98–102, 105, 113, 121, 128, 132–134, 144, 153, 198, 212, 229n20
Persian poetry: circulation of, 6, 145, 213; classical, 9–10, 26–27, 52–55, 59–60, 90, 94, 98, 100, 102–104, 108, 110, 112, 122, 124–126, 131–132, 138, 140, 144, 146, 148–151, 154, 157–159, 162, 164, 183, 186, 222n24, 228n10, 229n2, 230n12, 235n21; composition of, 6, 9, 11, 14, 26, 46, 54, 123–124, 127, 129, 131–133, 151, 161, 200; court, 10, 54, 60, 119, 121, 132–133, 157–159, 198, 229n20; inspiration for, 32, 130–132, 200; interpretation of, 54, 94, 98, 124, 141–142, 146, 148–150, 159, 205, 217n8; meta-poetics of, 27, 194–197; meters of, 90, 94, 97, 100, 102–103, 125, 129, 131–132, 138, 196, 230n12; modern, 60, 95–114, 124, 140, 144, 196, 227n1; neoclassical, 102, 115, 139, 196; postmodern, 26, 33, 115, 119–122, 186, 196; rhyme in, xi, 66, 88, 90, 94, 96–97, 100, 102–103, 125, 129, 131, 139; sociality of, 133–136; training in, 32, 111, 124–129, 140. *See also* audiences; blank verse; *dobeiti* (folk quatrain); *esteqbāl* (response poetry); *ghazal*; *majles* (poetic gathering); *masnavi*; orality; originality; patronage; polysemy; *qasideh*; quotation, poetic; Sufism; *talmih* (allusion)
personhood, 6, 14, 32–33, 64–65, 186–187, 210, 213, 218n12; anthropology of, 15–21; dividual, 16; individual, 16, 18–20. *See also* individualism; individuality
pilgrimage, 24, 39, 54
polysemy, 146, 148, 158, 164, 230n21
postmodernism, 226n35; in Iran, 86, 221n17; in Persian poetry, 26, 33, 115, 119–122, 186, 196, 212

prostitution, 203, 232n9, 235n24
publics, 60, 97–98, 110

Qajar Dynasty, 24, 39, 47, 230n10
Qand-e Parsi (literary festival), 27, 111, 116, 129, 147
Qasemi, Seyyed Zia', 35, 61
qasideh, 102–103, 225n19, 231n27
quotation, poetic, 145–149, 151–152, 154, 230n19
Qur'an, 18, 66, 76–77, 88, 101, 134, 195, 207, 220n4, 228n18, 231n22; schools, 25, 223n5, 224n9

Rahmani, Mohammad Asef, 105, 228n10; "The Arena of Death" (poem), 93–95, 100, 102–104
Rejali, Darius, 45, 64, 194, 234n11
rend (libertine), 190, 212
resistance poetry, 101–105, 112, 228n10, 228n14
Reza Shah, 24, 235n24
riyā (hypocrisy), 190, 194
Rostam (mythical hero), 59, 94, 200
Rowhani, Hassan, 33, 215
rowshanfekr, 31–32, 63–64, 86–87, 96, 98, 186, 212
Rumi, Mowlana Jalal al-Din Balkhi, 27, 59, 61, 66, 142, 147, 148, 159, 222n27, 228n9, 230n14, 232n7; life of, 52, 54; "The Third Script" (poem), 149
Rushdie, Salman, 212

Sabk-e hendi: See Indian style
Sacred Defense, The (Iran-Iraq war), cinema of, 211; literature of, 99, 102, 105, 110, 164, 196
Sa'di, Abu Mohammad Mosleh al-Din ben Abdallah Shirazi, 66, 104, 126, 159, 222n26, 232n8, 235n21
Safavid dynasty, 24, 53–54, 74
Said, Edward, 8, 211
Sajjadi, Fatemeh, 107, 124, 172–182; "I Have to Pretend I'm Fine" (poem), 180–182; "Your Letters" (poem), 178–179
Sepehri, Sohrab, 142, 227n1, 230n15
sexuality, 119, 163, 185, 198, 202, 206, 211, 232n9, 232n15
Seyyeds (*Sādāt*), 22, 29, 37, 66–67, 101, 108, 125, 219n19; challenges to hypergamy, 171, 173–174, 176; hypergamous marriage practices of, 161, 171–172
Shāhnāmeh (*The Book of Kings*), 27, 59, 94, 103, 126, 227n5, 227n9
Shamlu, Ahmad, 2, 84, 97, 179
Shari'ati, Ali, 25, 75, 84, 219n21, 226n30

she'r-e sepid. See blank verse
Shi'ism, 22, 74, 121, 146, 160; as revolutionary ideology, 22, 31, 76, 84, 91; as state religion of Iran, 24, 31, 53, 72, 76; tenets and jurisprudence of, 187, 224n9, 232n9
Shrine of Imam Reza, 1, 22, 24, 72, 193, 225n19; history of, 23–24; importance to Afghans, 72
Sorush, Abdolkarim, 49, 84, 86
subjectivity, 5–6, 8–9, 13; of Afghan refugees, 22, 44, 64, 91, 104, 122, 212; anthropology of, 15–16; in Iran, 16–21, 33, 75–76, 121–122, 234n11
Sufism, 10, 128, 159, 187, 190, 198, 225n19

Taheri, Maral, 126, 131, 200–202, 207–208; "And When the Man Stood on Top of the Woman" (poem), 202–204
Tajikistan, 53–54, 57, 59, 230n18
Tajiks (ethnic group), 22, 37, 208, 218n18
Talattof, Kamran, 98, 99, 196, 217n2
talmih (allusion), 103
Tarzi, Mahmud, 55, 97, 217n7, 227nn4–5
Tavakoli-Targhi, Mohamad, 48, 52–53, 104, 222n19, 222n23, 226n33, 228n15
Third Script (magazine), 63–64, 84, 98, 106, 107, 108, 110–111, 116, 134, 140, 148, 199
Timurid Dynasty, 24, 49, 54, 133–134, 198
Torkamani, Maryam, 200–201; "I Come from the World of Freedom" (poem), 81–82
Twelfth Imam, 26, 56, 146, 233n18

United Nations High Commissioner for Refugees (UNHCR), 40, 42, 66, 68–69, 80, 215, 220n3, 220n5, 220n7, 221nn10–11

Varzi, Roxanne, 17, 82, 109, 150–151, 211, 218n13
vatan (homeland), 97, 104, 147–148, 226n33, 228n15
veiling, 29, 51, 77, 82, 172, 188–189, 191–192, 194, 198, 225n24, 234n4; unveiling, 24, 197

Winegar, Jessica, 14–15, 28, 114
women, 104, 159, 233n16; of Dorr-e Dari, 78, 134, 136, 137, 155, 185, 193, 200, 208, 215; education of, 67–68, 71, 78, 156; and inside/outside dichotomy, 188–189, 191–194, 202, 204, 225n24; in Islamic Republic, 63–64, 78–80, 91, 208, 218n14, 223n1, 224n9; and marriage, 160–184, 169, 215; as poets, 129, 133, 155, 177, 182, 185, 200; and Persian literature, 133, 187, 198–199, 235nn16–18; poetry of, 81–82, 116–117, 126, 129, 161, 180, 204, 232n13; religious practices of,

72, 225n17, 225n22; rights of, 92, 116, 163, 167, 173, 178; rise in status of refugee, 63, 78–81, 91, 109, 225n25; sexuality and, 185, 198, 202, 208, 211, 213. *See also* veiling

Yushij, Nima, 60, 96–98, 100
zāher (outer self), 187, 190, 196–197, 201; of artistic works, 197, 208
Zimbler, Jarad, 13, 113–114

ZUZANNA OLSZEWSKA is Associate Professor in Social Anthropology of the Middle East at the University of Oxford and fellow of St. John's College, Oxford. She holds a DPhil in Social Anthropology and an MSt in Forced Migration from the University of Oxford. She has taught anthropology at the University of Oxford and the London School of Economics and Political Science. She is the author of numerous articles on the ethnography of Iran and Afghanistan, as well as a translator of Persian-language Afghan poetry.

www.ingramcontent.com/pod-product-compliance
Lightning Source LLC
Chambersburg PA
CBHW050433240426
43661CB00055B/2370